MEMORY AND AMNESIA

Dear Seb,

I really hope
you enjoy this book,
which is written by
one of my favourite
professors from
University.

It explains and
will let you under-
stand the Spanish
political culture
and also me!

Big hugh

Michelle

Madrid, Febreo 2012

MEMORY AND AMNESIA

The Role of the Spanish Civil War in the Transition to Democracy

PALOMA AGUILAR

TRANSLATED BY
MARK OAKLEY

Berghahn Books
New York • Oxford

Published in 2002 by

Berghahn Books
www.berghahnbooks.com

Reprinted in 2004, 2006, 2008

© 2002, 2004, 2006, 2008 English-language edition, Berghahn Books

© 1996 Paloma Aguilar Fernández

© 1996 of the Spanish-language edition, Alianza Editorial, S.A.
Originally published as *Memoria y olvido de la Guerra Civil española*

This publication has been translated with a grant from the General
Department for Books, Archives and Libraries of the Spanish
Ministry of Education, Culture and Sports

Library of Congress Cataloging-in-Publication Data
Aguilar Fernández, Paloma, 1965–
    [Memoria y olvido de la guerra civil española, English]
    Memory and amnesia : the role of the Spanish Civil War in the transition
to democracy / Paloma Aguilar : translation by Mark Oakley.
        p. cm.
    Includes bibliographical references.
    ISBN 1-57181-757-3 (cloth : alk. paper) -- ISBN 1-57181-496-5 (pbk. : alk.
paper)
        1. Spain--History--Civil war, 1936–1939--Psychological aspects.
    2. Spain--History--Civil War, 1936–1939--Historiography.
    3. Spain--History--Civil War, 1936–1939--Influence.
    4. Memory--Social aspects--Spain.   5. Spain--History--1975–   I. Title

    DP269.8.P75 A38 13 2002
    946081--dc21   2002018428

British Library Cataloguing in Publication Data
A catalogue record for this book is available
from the British Library.

Printed in the United States on acid-free paper.
ISBN 1-57181-757-3 (hardback)
ISBN 1-57181-496-5 (paperback)

This book is for Jesús, Susa, Ángel,
Susana, Sonia and Óscar.

Dear Seb,

CONTENTS

ACRONYMS

AGA   Archivo General de la Administración
General Government Archive

AP   Alianza Popular
Right-wing coalition party

BOC.C   Boletín Oficial de las Cortes. Congreso
Official Bulletin of the Cortes. Chamber of Deputies

BOC.S   Boletín Oficial de las Cortes. Senado
Official Bulletin of the Cortes. Senate

BOCE   Boletín Oficial de las Cortes Españolas
Official Bulletin of the Spanish Cortes

BOE   Boletín Oficial del Estado
Official Bulletin of the Spanish State

CCOO   Comisiones Obreras
Workers' Commissions. Communist trade union

CEDA   Confederación Española de Derechas Autónomas
Right-wing confederation of parties

CGT   Confederación General del Trabajo
Trade union formed in 1989 by former members of the CNT

CIS   Centro de Investigaciones Sociológicas (anterior IOP)
Centre for Sociological Research (former IOP)

CNT   Confederación Nacional del Trabajo
Radical anarcho-syndicalist trade union

DSC	Diario de Sesiones del Congreso *Record of Sessions in the Chamber of Deputies*
DSS	Diario de Sesiones del Senado *Record of Sessions in the Senate*
FET	Falange Española Tradicionalista *Spanish Falange and Carlists*
IOP	Instituto de Opinión Pública *Institute of Public Opinion*
JONS	Juntas de Ofensira Nacional Sindicalistas *Fascist Trade Union*
PCE	Partido Comunista de España *Spanish communist party*
PCOE	Partido Comunista Obrero Español *Radical communist party*
PSOE	Partido Socialista Obrero Español *Spanish socialist party*
UCD	Unión de Centro Democrático *Reformist centre coalition party*
UGT	Unión General de Trabajadores *Socialist trade union*

GLOSSARY

Alzamiento: uprising or revolt. *Glorioso Alzamiento:* Glorious Uprising.

Aperturismo: policy of openness

Aperturista: said of politicians in favour of reform and openness; reformist.

Cara al sol: Falangist hymn. Literally, 'Face to the Sun'.

Caudillo: literally 'The Leader'; similar to Der Führer or Il Duce.

Congreso (de los Diputados): the lower house of the Cortes or Spanish parliament under democracy; the Chamber of Deputies.

Cortes: the Spanish bicameral parliament under democracy; also the Francoist pseudo-parliament.

Foral: adjective which refers to the *fueros,* the special privileges enshrined in a code of laws that historically were granted to certain regions in Spain (e.g., Navarre).

Inmovilista: staunchest and most reactionary member of the Franco régime; opposite of *aperturista.*

Joseantoniano: adjective describing the supporters of José Antonio de Primo de Rivera within the Falange.

Juancarlismo: enthusiastic popular support for the figure of the King himself, Juan Carlos I, although not necessarily for the Monarchy as such.

Juanista: monarchist supporter of the pretender to the throne Don Juan, Juan Carlos' father.

Largocaballerista: extreme-left branch of the PSOE, headed by Largo Caballero.

Movimiento: the Movement, institutional framework of Francoism.

Patria: Homeland, 'Fatherland'.

Ponencia: drafting committee for the Constitution featuring representatives of the main parliamentary groups.

Ponente: member of the *Ponencia*.

Procurador: member of the Francoist pseudo-parliament, the Cortes.

Procurador familiar: member of a section which made up one-third of the Francoist pseudo-parliament and was elected by male heads of the family and married women.

PSOE-Histórico: returned exiles and old militants who had not recognized the fact that Felipe González had replaced the Toulouse-based émigré leaders.

Ruptura democrática: a movement based on the opposition's desire to bring about a total break with the Francoist régime and set up a democratic system.

Rupturista: a supporter of the *ruptura democrática*.

Senado: the upper house of the Cortes or Spanish Parliament under democracy; the Senate.

Tácito: the Tácitos were a group of conservative Christian Democrats committed to peaceful reform of the system from within. Many members later joined UCD, led by Adolfo Suárez.

Tercio familiar: family-based corporativist section of the Francoist pseudo-parliament consisting of *procuradores familiares*, which made up one-third of the Cortes as a whole.

Trágala: an imposed constitution; literally 'swallow it', derived from the song that the most radical supporters of the Liberal Constitution of Cádiz chanted at their defeated adversaries who favoured an absolute monarchy.

Valle de los Caídos: the huge mausoleum built by Franco to pay homage to the Nationalist soldiers who died in the Civil War. Franco himself is buried there. Literally: 'The Valley of the Fallen'.

ACKNOWLEDGEMENTS

This book is the result of the revision and updating of a doctoral thesis which I initially presented in March 1995. It is only fair that the individuals who helped me to complete that research, whose names appear in the corresponding acknowledgements, should be cited again here. However, in order to avoid repeating the endless list of names which I included in that work, I hope that none of the individuals concerned will be offended if I refer the reader to the corresponding pages in the thesis itself.

Having said that, I cannot help but repeat some of the names and institutions that I mentioned somewhat more than a year ago. For example, how can I not thank my parents, Ángel and Susa, my sister Susana and Jesús once again for their support, generosity and patience? Throughout the year that I have spent revising the original text, not only have they made light of the considerable burden which I placed upon them during the last years of my thesis, but they have even offered to re-read the text and make a considerable number of observations. As always, Jesús has played a leading role in this respect.

I would also like to express my sincere gratitude once again to the Centro de Estudios Avanzados en Ciencias Sociales at the Instituto Juan March and to all those who work there. The considerable generosity of this institution has been decisive in enabling me to carry out my research over the last eight years.

I would like, once again, to thank the Department of Political Science and Administration at the Faculty of Political Science and Sociology at UNED, where I currently teach. It was this department that provided me with a grant so that I could complete my thesis, and subsequently awarded me a Special Prize for it. It was the Head of the Department himself, Andrés de Blas, who proposed the idea that I should send the text to

Alianza Editorial and who suggested a large number of changes that needed to be made.

The observations made by the Viva Panel for my thesis were both highly accurate and extremely useful, and many of the comments were taken on board for the new text. My thanks also go, therefore, to Santos Juliá, José Álvarez Junco, José María Maravall, Andrés de Blas and Javier Roiz.

Along with the many colleagues, teachers and friends who, at various times, read through the rough drafts I produced, other figures (although sometimes the same individuals) became involved in helping me with the new version. María Fernández Mellizo-Soto read the preface and first chapter; Luis Ragel did the same, later sending me a tape with the observations that had occurred to him while listening to my text in the solarium at the swimming-pool 'Stella'; my good friend María Jesús Díaz Pérez went to work on the last chapter and dictated a number of corrections over the telephone; José María Maravall and José Ramón Montero made various suggestions concerning the publication of the text; José Álvarez Junco made a number of bibliographic recommendations; I enjoyed a series of meaty telephone conversations with Xavier Casals, some of which were even connected to the book, and he also suggested some possible titles; Elisa Chuliá and I held a number of interminable chats about our respective research, during which I never failed to learn something new thanks to her enormous professionalism; I also discussed various matters, between mouthfuls, with Begoña Calvo and Luis Miguel Turégano; finally, Jacqueline de la Fuente helped me, once again, with the tables and graphs.

The following researchers were also kind enough to send me their observations regarding my work, all of which were of great use: Stanley Payne, Edward Malefakis, Paul Preston, Juan J. Linz and Michael Mann.

It only remains for me to acknowledge the debt I owe to my most esteemed teachers, Víctor Pérez Díaz and José Álvarez Junco. Their influence will fortunately accompany me throughout my entire professional career.

ACKNOWLEDGEMENTS FOR THE ENGLISH EDITION

It was only possible to publish this book in English thanks to the help of a series of individuals to whom I would like to express my most sincere gratitude. First of all, Douglas J. Forsyth suggested that the book be translated into English and, in this respect, placed me in contact with Marion Berghahn who, from the very beginning, was extremely enthusiastic about the idea and willing to publish it. Laura Malefakis served as a liaison between the Spanish publisher (Alianza Editorial) and the British publisher (Berghahn Books) and made all the contract arrangements. Nigel Townson found a meticulous translator for the book, Mark Oakley, with whom it was a pleasure to work. I would also like to express my gratitude to Martha Peach for the excellent index she created specially for the English edition.

This edition was translated with the help of a grant from the Book, Archives and Libraries Department at the Spanish Ministry of Education, Culture and Sports. In turn, Teresa Atienza, working at the Department, provided me with rigorous professional guidance so that I could prepare the material required to make the grant application.

Last, but not least, Jesús Cuéllar has played a crucial role both in the writing of this book and in the author's life as a whole, for which I would like to express my fondest thanks.

FOREWORD FOR THE ENGLISH EDITION

This book was published in Spanish in 1996. When I began my research in 1990, hardly any works existed concerning the role played by historical evocation in political decision-making processes. Neither had much attention been paid to the symbolic meaning of political monuments and ceremonies or to their socialising effects on the population. Finally, the moderating effect that certain traumatic collective memories of past conflicts can exercise had hardly been addressed in the vast literature produced on political transitions. This obliged me to construct my own methodology in order to analyse a series of sometimes traditional sources – such as the press, speeches given by the political élites or party manifestos – and other much less conventional sources, such as film documentaries, Francoist political ceremonies and the commemorative monuments of the Civil War that were erected during the dictatorship.

Subsequently, a large number of studies have been produced on these matters. The challenges that have forced the former communist countries to address the question of how to tackle their past have made such studies on the influence of history in processes of political change quite fashionable, along with the investigation of purges, trials on human rights violations and the establishment of truth commissions. In addition to the countries of Central and Eastern Europe, the importance that the developments in South Africa, Argentina and Chile have had on this literature is difficult to measure. Finally, the creation of the International Criminal Court in the Hague has also helped to raise awareness of a political problem of considerable significance and scope. This book obviously does not include this literature on the legacies of authoritarian régimes and retrospective justice, as it is just a translation of the 1996 work. Nevertheless, the conclusions reached in this book stand as they are, as the work directly addresses the presence of the historical memory of the Civil War on the Spanish Transition, as well as the development of official Francoist discourse on the war. I have addressed the specific role played by the legacies of Francoism in the Transition in another book published jointly with Alexandra Barahona de Brito and Carmen González (*The Politics of Memory and Democratisation*, Oxford University Press, 2001).

PREFACE

Memory and learning are closely linked terms, given that without a retentive capacity it is not possible to apply the lessons of the past, and that without the light which learning sheds on the present memory is of little use to us. Until very recently the study of both these concepts was limited to the field of psychology, which has produced a great deal of research regarding the workings of memory and different forms of learning, although these relate only to the individual.

In the last few years a new approach has emerged, especially in the United States and France, in which an analysis of collective memory and learning has been undertaken from the perspective of sociology, political science and history. In Spain, however, virtually no study has been carried out of these two phenomena within the three disciplines. References have often been made either to the presence or the absence of the Spanish collective memory, although these allusions are not based on any kind of reflection regarding the theoretical or methodological implications which are derived from using such a concept.

My interest was initially aroused by the contradictory impressions that I formed from reading the abundant literature which exists regarding the Transition as well as numerous pieces from the daily press. From my reading of the former I sensed the existence of a deliberate silence regarding the recent past, which, nevertheless, seemed to underlie the most important decision-making processes of that period. The obsession with peace and stability, the particular caution regarding issues relating to public order, the systematic avoidance of conflictual issues and the constant search for consensus among all parties as the only way – we might almost say the only legitimate way – of taking decisions, all led me to focus my attention on the collective memory of the Spanish people and their historical learning over the last few decades.

Conversely, when reading the newspapers I was struck by the large number of references to the alleged *amnesic ailment* suffered by the Spanish, a recurring theme even up to the present day, although it is never properly elucidated. I was also able to observe the considerable interest aroused by the most recent of the civil wars which have taken place in our country, not so much as a free and open topic for debate, but as a literary, cinematographic and, subsequently, even as an historical subject. What struck me as somewhat paradoxical was that, whilst numerous voices in the daily press repeatedly denounced the collective amnesia of the Spanish regarding the Civil War, the public were veritably inundated with literary and film works about the war.

All of this proved to me that I was dealing with a crucial and dramatic memory for all Spaniards, whose repercussions had not yet been investigated. What I proposed, therefore, was to present an in-depth analysis of the particular features which shaped the process of political change known as the Transition by addressing an aspect which, although frequently forgotten, was nevertheless decisive: the existence of a traumatic collective memory of the Civil War (1936–1939).

The importance of that memory during the Transition, a period governed by profound transformations and plagued with uncertainty, is undeniable. It is, however, essential to go back to the handling of the memory of the war under the Franco régime, from the heart of whose institutions the transition towards democracy was, in the last analysis, born, and under whose auspices the collective memory of the Civil War crystallized. We cannot ignore the dictatorship's multiple attempts at socialisation, nor the means of ideological dissemination at its disposal, nor the pre-eminence of the Francoist discourse during these attempts when it comes to analysing the political culture of the Spanish during the 1970s. This is true to the extent that a section of society existed that refused to accept the values propounded by the régime, in the same way as another section of society assimilated a significant part of the Francoist view, although this may not have always been a conscious process.

This is not, therefore, a book about the Spanish Civil War, but an analysis of the political discourse relating to that war, of the transmission of this memory through multiple sources and of the significant effect which this memory had on the incipient democratic political process, a memory which still exists today. Fundamentally, it is a study of the political learning propitiated by the existence of a certain historical memory.

A knowledge of the historical memory of a country is essential in understanding its institutional make-up. However, it is equally true that the institutions of a society constitute a fundamental resource which can be analysed in order to trace the development of that memory. This memory is especially important when studying institutions which manage to adapt to processes of political change, such as the Spanish Transition, when the uncertainties surrounding the future of the country are greatest and when, as was the case in Spain, the trauma of war remains, a war which society wishes to avoid at any cost.

Nevertheless, collective memory does not only play a crucial role in processes of political change, as it impregnates the entire institutional fabric which is created during such periods, leaving a mark on daily political practices once the new régime has become established. However, a study of the memory of the Civil War today exceeds the limits of this research, which concludes at the end of 1978 with the passing of the Constitution.

Throughout the Spanish Transition a tacit pact was formed among the most visible élites in order to silence the bitter voices of the past which caused such unease within society. A part of this anxiety seemed to be based on a fear of the imminent resurrection of the old resentments of the war which were, perhaps, not quite as much a thing of the past as the political leaders and some sections of the media tried to make the population believe. This was probably due to the fact that no formal and explicit reconciliation had ever taken place within Spanish society. The defeated elements of society had been gradually, and almost always silently, reincorporated into the life of the country, and only the most famous cases had been publicly addressed, with the individuals in question thus being partially rehabilitated. Any reading of the literature regarding the Transition reveals the leading role played by the war and how it constituted a problem which was still unresolved and which presented no easy or obvious solution.

Although no systematic study exists which traces the handling of the Civil War from the Franco period to the present day and which attempts to demonstrate the importance that the historical memory of the war had for the Spanish Transition, certain studies have been produced which, in one way or another, deal with the existence of the collective memory of the war. Before the Transition, although to a greater extent after that change took place, various studies considered the effects of the trauma produced by the memory of the Civil War among the Spanish. Many have claimed, not without a certain pessimism, that this war has left an indelible mark on the nation, which, at critical moments, could once again undermine the peaceful fabric of Spanish society.[1]

The truth is that the majority of the authors who have revealed concern about the possible repercussions of this legacy of violence and destruction were only half right in their assertions. It is correct to state that the Civil War, as a memory, is still present forty years after its end and has left an indelible mark on Spanish society. Nevertheless, far from representing an obstacle to the creation of a harmonious society, it became the necessary spur which facilitated the multiple negotiations which were required during the Transition. To a certain extent it is natural that, on occasions,

---

1. See, among others, Nicolás Ramiro Rico (1977); Jorge de Esteban and Luis López Guerra (1977); Manuel Ramírez (1978) and Carlos Moya (1983).

pessimism should flourish when reflecting on the war. Unfortunately, it would not be the first time that the memory of a conflict has been used to fan the flames of discord. Our own experience and that of others not only demonstrates that, very often, lessons from the past fail to be learned, but also that a period of civil war can be used as a weapon by political adversaries, as has been the case in the former Yugoslavia. Why this did not happen in Spain – in fact the very opposite occurred – is one of the questions which I shall attempt to address in this study.

Other authors have established a more direct relationship between the memory of war and the politics of transition.[2] "Aversion to risk", for example, is one of the most important variables in explaining the strategies employed by politicians during a change of régime, in accordance with gambling theory. According to this theory, the references of the main actors during the Spanish Transition were readjusted in order to meet the priority objective of avoiding any repetition of a civil war, the obsessive memory of which led them to fear a similar conflict.[3] Using similar arguments we might explain the quick suppression of destructive and conflictual opinions and the subsequent strengthening of a conciliatory and peaceful rhetoric. The confrontation of 1936 was interpreted by all of the important political forces as a catastrophe which must never be allowed to occur again.[4]

Finally, many authors over the last two decades have elaborated theories about transitional processes towards democracy. The opposition between the practically discredited functionalist current of thought, which focuses on the structural prerequisites for the establishment of democracy,[5] and what is known as the genetic current of thought, which places priority on the strategies of the various actors, both social and political, in transitional processes, is well known.[6] Nevertheless, neither of these two currents of thought have conceded, in general terms, sufficient importance to the collective learning of a country, in spite of the fact that this is a fundamental variable when it comes to analysing a change in régime. In this book I shall show how the strategic options of the actors are conditioned by their perception of the political process, and how that perception, in turn, is strongly influenced by the lessons which those actors have been able to learn from the memory of situations which are more or less similar (Bermeo, 1992; Jervis, 1976).

It is the collective memory which provides us with a framework and a metaphor for understanding and interpreting the present. The collective memory of a country is essential, given that national identities are built on the foundations of tradition and memory, both of which are more or

2. See Víctor Pérez Díaz (1993).
3. Josep María Colomer (1990: 31-32).
4. Del Águilar and Montoro (1984: 192).
5. See Lipset (1959).
6. See O'Donnell and Schmitter (1986).

less invented, as well as other aspects which are forgotten and which are more or less genuine. On the other hand, the traditions and memories which are needed to construct or reconstruct these identities are not always freely available. In processes of change, memory and historical traditions play a fundamental role, either as positive reference-points (evoking glorious events, or institutions which worked well in the past) that provide examples worthy of being followed, or as negative reference-points (evoking shameful episodes, spectres of destruction, or institutions which failed disastrously) which indicate courses of action that must be avoided.

With this book I aim to promote a new way of approaching both the study of authoritarian régimes and processes of political transition. Both fields of research have by-passed the study of collective memory and learning since these are considered to be practically inaccessible aspects of social research. An analysis of these variables, in effect, requires the researcher to seek out various unusual sources of documentation, and also apply a new methodology to those sources. All of this implies a clear reliance on an interdisciplinary approach. Indeed, this kind of approach is essential when it comes to analysing subjects as unusual as societal memory and learning.

CHAPTER 1

REGARDING MEMORY, LEARNING
AND AMNESIA

The concept of collective memory involves numerous complexities. Below, with the help of the theoretical contributions of various authors and diverse currents of thought, I shall attempt to explain what is understood by this concept and observe its usefulness within the field of social science. As I stated in the introduction, in this research I aim to complement, and in some sense enrich, existing theories on transitional processes towards democracy by including a new element that I consider to be a key factor, especially in these processes of change. This element is the collective memory, which consists of the memory that a community possesses of its own history, as well as the lessons and learning which it more or less consciously extracts from that memory. This variable includes both the substance of that memory (recall of specific historical events) as well as values associated with their evocation (historical lessons and learning), which are modified, very often, by the vicissitudes of the present.

In studying the memory of the Civil War, the guardian of that memory is, effectively, collective, which does not mean that all of the persons who make up the same group have an equal factual memory of a particular historical episode. It is even quite common to come across individuals who have an autobiographical memory of the event in question, whilst others would only have an inherited or transmitted memory of that event. It is necessary, therefore, to tackle the added difficulty of the fact that individual memory and collective memory coexist in time, interrelate and mutually influence each other. We must also take into account the fact that different generational memories exist. Further-

1

more, it is not only age groups that share certain memories; we could also talk about the existence of specific memories based on religion, social class, gender, profession and other variables. Conversely, although autobiographical and factual memory – this being a record of an event which has been experienced by a particular person – is individual, the learning process, both of the person and of those who have not actually lived through the historical period in question, is more susceptible to being shared by the community.

Certainly, individual and collective memory coexist, and, although they do not always coincide, the most important aspect for the stability of a régime is that they should not seriously contradict each other. The differences between a personal experience and the official record, which tends to be the one which predominates in the media, in speeches, and also sometimes in literature, the cinema, and even in architecture (art is also a guardian of memory) must not differ to the extent that they are unable to coexist, if a certain degree of political stability is sought.

On occasions, when numerous kinds of memory openly contradict one another during a critical period in which there is a particular need for consensus and equilibrium (such as the Spanish Transition) what may happen is that, in view of a possible confrontation of memories, either a search is carried out within history itself (sometimes *inventing* an adequate memory, should one not exist) for an official memory which satisfies everyone (this memory tends to be evaluative, as in 'we were all to blame', and not factual, given that it is more difficult to achieve a consensus about specific episodes) or all references to the event in question are silenced in order to avoid controversy as far as possible.

Over time, those who had lived through the Civil War found an opportunity to compare and complement their personal experience of the war, using not only the versions of other individuals, but also the official version released by the régime, as well as that portrayed by the novels and films which addressed this subject. Furthermore, the passing of time enables the memory of an historical event to be associated with its results, and this is essentially where the evaluative aspect of memory enters the equation: that aspect which relates to the lessons of history. Finally, although it may seem obvious, we must remember that the effects of amnesia are necessarily heightened over time.

In turn, that section of society which had not personally experienced the Civil War possessed a memory that was conveyed by multiple sources, having been socialised by a variety of media. If the results of family-based and official socialisation are very different, it is necessary to determine which of them prevailed in the crucial process of passing these values on to the new generations. This is a very complex matter, which depends on many other factors, such as the profusion and quality of official propaganda, the willingness of families to convey certain values, the existence or nonexistence of certain conditions of cultural plurality and freedom of choice. Whatever the case may be, socialisation always takes place through a variety of sources, and, although one source may finally prevail over the others, it is quite probable that more than one source will influence the behaviour of individuals.[1]

The Generational Question

Before I present the various theories on collective memory, it is worth reflecting upon what is known as the 'generational effect', as this is a factor that is intimately related to the study of collective memory. Groups of individuals of the same age or generation have been studied from various perspectives by a diverse range of authors. The influence that certain decisive events have had on different generations within a country has recently been studied in the United States in order to comprehend the variety of attitudes that have been adopted regarding the Vietnam War, depending on whether that war was personally experienced or not.[2] Schuman and Scott (1989) carried out an exciting study on the various effects that the same historical events produce in different generations of the same country. In order to do this they studied the repercussions that the most important events of the last fifty years have had on different generations of Americans. The conclusion was that the Second World War meant something very different to those who had experienced it during a key period of their lives, which the authors considered to be between the ages of seventeen and twenty-five, than to those who lived through the Vietnam War at the same age. The shame of defeat in Vietnam meant that its participants glorified and justified the Second World War without any hesitation, revealing a mythicised and heroic view of this conflict which was not shared at all by those who were obliged to participate in it.

Karl Mannheim (1952) has produced one of the most important contributions to the study of generations. He criticised positivist and historicist approaches, the two currents of thought which had tackled the question of generation up until that time, for not having incorporated the social dimension of the phenomenon into their analyses, a task that he attempted to undertake. He claimed that generation, rather than being a purely biological or mental factor, was an eminently social phenomenon, which entailed a common location in historical time and space, creating a predisposition towards 'a certain characteristic mode of thought and experience, and a characteristic type of historically relevant action' (Mannheim, 1952: 291). Mannheim also highlighted the existence

---

1. Regarding the process of political socialisation in Spain throughout the Franco period, see José María Maravall (1975, 1978).
2. See, among others, Howard Schuman and Jacqueline Scott (1989); Robin Wagner-Pacifici and Barry Schwartz (1991); Ole R. Holsti and James N. Rosenau (1980).

of 'generational units' within the same generations, these being specific groups which draw a particular set of conclusions from their shared experiences and which, for this reason, share a 'common destiny'. These generational units can be formed after having experienced a particular event which, as a result of education or the social, economic or professional status of the group, has affected them in a particular way, subsequently serving as a unifying element. In Spain, for example, the generations of 1898 and 1927 are famous for being specific groups within wider groups of individuals which correspond to them, for historical and geographical reasons.

The study of generation is intimately linked to that of historical memory, given that it helps us to understand how the collective memory of a country develops as new generations progressively take charge of it. It is not only true that different generations live through different historical events, but that, even when living through the same events, they interpret them and are affected by them in a specific and unique way. As Ortega y Gasset, one of the few Spanish thinkers who has addressed this question, has stated 'an identical event which has occurred to two different generations is a living, and therefore historical, experience which has two completely distinct meanings. Thus, the event of war has the most varied range of meanings according to the date on which it occurs, because Man draws the most contrary conclusions from it' (Ortega, 1967; 1976: 79). Later on, Paulino Garagorri, Ortega's student who carried on his work, stated that the fact of 'being ten, forty or sixty years of age on the day on which the Hiroshima bomb exploded – or of being in Spain on 18 July 1936 – endows this event with a value and personal significance which are absolutely diverse... A generation is, therefore, the group of men for whom the present, the past and the future, as far as these shape the horizons of their lives, have similar scope' (Garagorri, 1970: 164–166).

According to this line of thought, it was not only the survivors of the winning side who feared a return to democracy. They believed that a return to party politics, the granting of political amnesty and the return of exiles, could, on the one hand, revive the 'chaos', 'violence' and 'anarchy' of before and, on the other, fan the flames of former resentments and open the wounds of the defeated who might return to Spain with a desire to seek revenge or satisfy former demands for justice. Some of those who had experienced the war from the other side of the trenches also feared renewed conflict, given that they did not consider part of the Francoist political class to be prepared to cede power peacefully. In particular, they were obsessed by the idea that the largely stalwart army which supported the Franco régime might carry out a coup d'état and, thus, drag the country back to a situation similar to that of 18 July 1936.

The psychological repercussions of the Civil War were such that they also affected generations of those who had not been alive during the war.[3] They were the children of the victors or the defeated and they grew up under a régime that inculcated them with certain values that had a lot to do with the legacy of the Civil War. Within these generations it is possible to distinguish between at least two groups: one in which the members lived through the war during childhood and adolescence (not being sufficiently old to participate actively in the war) and another in which the members were born in the midst of war and grew up amid the ruins, hunger, misery and fear of the postwar period. A large part of our current political class belong to this second group, given that they were born either during the war or in the years immediately following it (at the beginning of the 1940s). It is no coincidence that it was this group, and not another more mature and more politically experienced generation, which assumed the reins of power in Spain from the very first years of democracy.[4]

Along with an inherited and transmitted trauma of war, this generation also had the trauma of the postwar period etched in its memory. In this sense, memories from childhood (of divided families, of a country in ruins) were fused with those of repression, silence, distorted historical facts and fears perceived within a family setting, to the extent that the terrible war became associated with the no less terrible postwar period.

The result of all this is that, irrespective of who was most responsible for the events that occurred, or why passions were unleashed in such a way or of how these historical events might be assimilated, the choice was made to hold back the tide of history and silence it, to pursue a sole objective: to *never again* endorse civil war. This went beyond the Republican sentiments of the majority of the opposition, beyond their declared wish to bring about a break with the past, beyond extremist rhetoric, social conflict and desires for reform. In this sense, Eduardo de Guzmán has stated that the Civil War, 'the cruelest and most merciless of fratricidal conflicts' has had such a profound and long-lasting effect that, 'far from losing its interest over time, it has become progressively more important as a wider perspective has

3. In Mannheim's incisive words: 'in estimating the biographical significance of a particular experience, it is important to know whether it is undergone by an individual as a decisive childhood experience, or later in life, superimposed upon other basic and early impressions. Early impressions tend to coalesce into a *natural view* of the world. All later experiences then tend to receive their meaning from this original set' (Mannheim, 1952: 298). In this sense, the generation which lives through war at an adult age will have already formed other previous impressions during the key stages which shape its identity; nevertheless, the generation which lives through war and a postwar period during childhood, forms the deepest impression of this experience and finds it difficult to conceive anything different, given that the first experience known consists of the ruins and all of the psychological scars of violence.
4. The role played by this postwar generation was crucial to the Franco period. As Maravall has pointed out, the university conflicts of the mid-1950s, which were so important, took place, among other reasons, because 'they were the years in which the first age-group born after the Civil War reached university' (Maravall, 1978: 164)

enabled us to measure, in all their magnitude, the various phenomena which continue to have such a direct repercussion on the lives of all Spaniards; *even – and fundamentally – on the lives of those who had not even been born yet*' (De Guzmán, 1982: 323. The italics are mine).

In short, generational change is not only inevitable, but also essential, given that 'it serves the necessary social purpose of enabling us to forget. If society is to continue, social remembering is just as important as forgetting' (Mannheim, 1952: 294). The fact is that the postwar generation did not draw the same conclusions regarding the conflict as those who actually fought in it.

Theoretical and Conceptual Framework

When undertaking a study of collective memory, it is not only necessary to tackle a number of methodological difficulties (the existence or nonexistence of sources and interpretation of these sources), but also previously address the theoretical and analytical problems that this concept entails. First of all, as we might expect, no single universally accepted definition of the concept of 'collective memory' exists. Some authors do actually use this term. Others, however, talk about 'historical memory', 'social memory', 'public memory', 'dominant memory', etc. In this research, the expressions 'collective memory', 'historical memory' and 'social memory' shall be used interchangeably, given that we presuppose the global nature of this memory (social or collective) and its historical content (it is the memory which a community has of its own history). On the other hand, there are authors who distinguish between historical memory and memory based on experience or autobiographical memory, and although they are certainly different, many authors consider the latter to be an addition to the former, to the extent that, both he who has experienced the historical event in question and he who only has a transmitted or inherited memory of that event, are able to share the same collective memory. This is true of the person who has experienced the event, because the passing of time has enabled him to complement his interpretation of the facts with other versions and to learn the lessons that are derived from them in the medium or long-term. He who has not experienced the event personally is able to share this collective memory because the version that he has received may, in some way, have become predominantly accepted within the community as a whole.

In effect, we are dealing with a collective concept – 'historical memory' – which is an abstraction and simplification of the plurality of memories that exists within any given society. In this respect, it is worth wrestling first with the old problem of universal phenomena and, consequently, making some reference to the traditional debate between 'holists' and 'individualists' or 'nominalists'. For followers of the former approach, transpersonal realities do, in fact, exist, and the most radical advocates state that the properties of a society explain the characteristics of the individual, given that the society precedes the individuals who constitute it. However, for followers of the latter approach, the universal lacks real content, this being simply a term that has no substance. Society is nothing more than a group of individuals and there is no characteristic of society that cannot be entirely explained by describing the characteristics of the individuals who constitute it.

This philosophical debate has recently been raised in the discussions between the followers of Durkheim, who defend universal concepts, and methodological individualists, who explain social phenomena in exclusively individual terms. For Durkheim (1973), society is a group of individuals who possess a 'collective conscience' that is reflected in societal institutions. He understood universal concepts in an attributive way, which is to say that what may be predicated of the whole is not applicable to each of the individuals who make up that whole. According to the individualists, however, what may be stated of the whole must apply to each of the parts, given that the whole is made up of these parts. This controversy may also be applied to this study, where the followers of Durkheim would defend the existence of a collective memory which may be distinguished from various individual memories but which is made up of the latter, whilst the individualists would state that collective memory is nothing more than the sum of various individual memories.

Although it is true that only individual memories exist initially, it is also true that with the passing of time, as societies become increasingly complex, memories are deposited in institutions of a very diverse nature and in this way the collective memory of a society becomes a kind of common patrimony, which the individual experiences from the moment he is born. Memories, due to the very passing of time, cannot always be maintained by individuals as personal experiences, which is why they end up being stored in social deposits (archives, monuments, museums), in numerous 'sites of memory', thus shaping a tradition prior to the existence of individuals of subsequent historical periods (Nora, 1984). These collective memories become associated with individual memories, exercising a kind of mutual influence. Furthermore, collective memories are periodically revived by means of ceremonies or public rituals which aim to legitimise a present rooted in a specific tradition, whilst also familiarising new citizens with community traditions by evoking a shared past.

In every historical period, therefore, a plurality of autobiographical memories exists of the same fact or event, and these memories are as varied as the individuals who possess them. At the same time, a more uniform inherited collective memory exists, which, although it need not be unique nor entirely homogenous, does offer a general and, in some sense, hegemonic view of the past. With collective memory we find that individuals not only recall the same fact or event, but also share the values and lessons associated with it. In this respect, although the substance of the memory varies from one individual to another (the narration of the facts is never the same) it is nevertheless possible to find some kind of consensus regarding the lessons that should be drawn from the memory in question. When this kind of agreement within a community regarding the lessons of the past does not exist, we are faced with a conflictual historical memory, based on which it is almost impossible to build a common future, or achieve social harmony and political stability.[5]

These cases of conflictual memory are especially delicate during periods of political transition. This was evident in the case of Spain, given that the protagonists were attempting to reconstruct a political reality – democracy – that had previously ended in bloody conflict, and it was necessary to bring a number of former enemies together around the negotiating table. Although the élite classes during the Transition were, in large part, young enough not to have lived through the war, they did nevertheless partially represent the parties, tendencies and ideologies, which had fought so savagely against one another in the past. Fortunately, in Spain, even before the death of Franco, an historical memory based on a sufficiently wide consensus had been formed regarding the lessons that needed to be drawn from the Civil War. At least the élite classes were aware that the idea of 'never again' should constitute the absolute priority of all Spaniards, which meant that renunciations, concessions and compromises would be required of all.

In relation to this matter we must also address a different problem, namely, how to distinguish between historical memory and history itself. To do this, we must first differentiate the past from what constitutes history. Some authors offer us a quite radical distinction between the history

---

5. This is what happened in the case of Yugoslavia, where memories of the Second World War were so contradictory that it proved extremely difficult to reach any agreement regarding their interpretation, one which would enable the country's citizens to move on whilst maintaining the unity of the Federation. It was not only that different versions existed about the events that took place, but also no agreement was achieved regarding the lessons that were to be drawn from such an inopportune past. It is difficult to compare the case of Spain with that of Yugoslavia, since they are so very different. In the pioneering research which Archie Brown and Jack Gray carried out on the political culture of the European communist régimes, David Dyker emphasised the considerable degree of social and cultural fragmentation that existed in Yugoslavia, which meant the country had a considerable potential for instability and polarisation, given that it did not even seem to have a common future project (in Brown and Gray, 1977; 1979). In addition, researchers who have studied the topic of civil war have reached the conclusion that it is more probable that conflicts will be repeated based on issues relating to identity and religion, rather than those based on fundamental ideological differences, as was the case in Spain (Licklider, 1995). Finally, one study regarding Yugoslav economic policy has stated that the failure of the political régime to combat the existing high levels of unemployment (full employment being one of the priority objectives of communism), caused the main political institutions to suffer a substantial loss of legitimacy, which explains, rather better than pre-existing ethnic conflicts, the subsequent civil war (Woodward, 1995).

and the past, according to which the past is defined as having always been used for specific ends (as a legitimising instrument which serves a particular authority or ideology), whilst history may be defined as an approximation to the objective truth established by means of a scientific method (Plumb, 1969; 1990). Other scholars distinguish the past from historical fact, claiming that 'not all facts about the past are historical facts' (Carr, 1987: 10). According to this view, until the historian begins to compile data, these are not considered to be history.

History is that part of the past that has, in some way, been recorded and stored in the memory's various deposits. Thus, history is a section of the past that is susceptible to being recorded through documentation and testimony. The past is obviously something much wider, much vaster and harder to pin down. So what distinguishes historical memory from history? Could we say that it is history recalled, or institutionalised memory? What is it that makes it so important, at any given moment, to collective memory?

The collective memory of a country does not contain each and every one of the past episodes that the country has lived through. During each period of the life of a state, nation or nationality there are certain historical moments which, due to their special relevance to the present, acquire greater importance and are more likely to influence the train of events witnessed during that specific period of time. Sometimes a kind of natural selection process takes place in the memory whereby only that which has some suasive relevance to the present reemerges. We could say that the historical memory of a nation is that part of the past which, as a result of a certain situation or context, has the ability to influence the present, either in a positive sense (an example to be followed) or in a negative sense (a counter-example, a disagreeable situation which must be avoided). In the majority of cases, the revival of this memory is due to the existence of a certain analogy, real or imagined, between the present situation and the past as experienced. Occasionally, the most important aspect is not that two historical situations should actually be similar, but that they should be perceived to be similar by political and social protagonists.

A kind of mutual influence is established between the past and the present: in the present, that part of the past which is relevant to each moment is selected, and, in turn, that selected past influences the present. In the case of the memory of the Civil War, although it may continue to be an important theme today, its significance is much lower than it was during the Transition, a time when, precisely because of the analogies that could be drawn with that time, it played a warning role which favoured consensus. The similarity in this case was perceived as being greater than it actually was due to the obsessive and ongoing memory of the war. Nevertheless, although it may have been exaggerated, a similarity did exist between the Spanish situation in the 1930s and that of the 1970s when Franco died, this being precisely what produced the fear of repetition.

What was important was not whether things really had changed since the Second Republic, but people's subjective perception of the situation and the intensity with which the present was able to evoke the past.

'Dominant memory' is understood to mean the public memory as represented in the media.[6] This memory influences, to a varying extent, the way in which people recall their own past by shaping personal memory. Social memory and personal memory are linked, and although the former may not be understood in the same way by all and may not coincide precisely with the latter, what must not happen, for social harmony to be maintained, is that they should substantially contradict one another. Social memories must include both public representations of the past as well as the memories of individuals. In spite of the differences that may exist among the multiple social memories, a certain kind of consensus-based collective memory may be achieved.

Conversely, any social memory represents a simplification of events in the sense that 'an overemphasis is placed on drama in narratives – wars are very apt; one-dimensional characterizations are favored – heroes and villains; and memories of social pasts tend to be romantic or demonic' (Nerone, 1989: 95). The moral dimension of social memory is important, given that such memories always contain lessons and meanings and attempt to provide a coherent image of society. They are the product of both consensus and conflict, and historians play an especially prominent role during periods of revision and controversy, which is when the history professionals, whose job it is to institutionalise memory, have the greatest capacity to influence social memory.

No clearly defined and independent theoretical corpus exists regarding the subject of collective memory, but in its place various authors have approached the matter from different perspectives. It seems that the first social scientist to be concerned about the collective dimension of memory (psychologists had already been dealing with the purely individual dimension for some time) was Maurice Halbwachs (1877–1945). This French sociologist was first a disciple of Henri Bergson and, later, of Emile Durkheim, and his contact with them left a deep impression on his work. Under Bergson he became interested in how time is conceived and how the collective memory is articulated (Bergson, 1939; 1990), although their respective theses regarding the latter would finally disagree.[7] Under

6. 'Dominant memory' is that which has the most important and best means of dissemination at its disposal, in contrast to 'hegemonic memory', which is that memory which predominates throughout most of society irrespective of the opportunities for dissemination that it may have. In democratic régimes it is very probable that the two will coincide, whilst in authoritarian régimes it is usual for them to differ quite drastically.

7. Among other points of disagreement, Bergson emphasised the continuing existence of the past within the present, whilst Halbwachs insisted that the memory of the past is constantly reconstructed from the present. This difference became, from that moment on, a classic controversy, first among historians, and later on among sociologists. See the works of Carr (1961), Schwartz (1982; 1991) and Lowenthal (1985).

Durkheim, with whom he would write a large part of his work, he was exposed to multiple influences. Halbwachs bases his theory on Durkheim's concept of 'collective consciousness' and states that the memory is always a social construction. He argues that the memory cannot always be considered exclusively as an individual faculty, given that individuals are able to recall the past precisely because they belong to a social group. The interests and experiences of the group shape the memories of its members and the very fact that they belong to the group helps them to remember (by means of referral) and to recreate their own experiences collectively. Not only are memories acquired through society, but they are also recalled, acknowledged and located socially. In this sense, remembering involves being linked to a collective framework and sharing social reference points which enable memories to be positioned within space and time: within time, because the memory lives on as long as their attachment to the group persists, and in space, because the memory is linked to certain spatial images.

These two elements, space and time, are what make the trauma of the exile doubly intense; on the one hand, he loses his group of reference, which is split and dissolved; on the other hand, he loses his familiar spatial images, the graphical reference points of daily life. Furthermore, when he returns, not having been inculcated with the values which have socialised the rest of society over so many years, being unaware of the historical memory which has been transmitted and having only his personal experience to fall back on, the subsequent break with his generation, with members of the former groups he belonged to and with his geographical area, is much greater. The function that his memory of the war serves is very different to that of those who remained, and the lack of understanding and the barriers that emerge between the exile and his generation are great, because, among other reasons, the political learning process has been very different. Similarly, the geographical element has changed so much that the exile is hardly able to recognise himself in the images that surround him upon his return. He thus feels that his memory has betrayed him and feels he has been distanced from an environment which he has idealised for so long.[8]

---

8. José-Carlos Mainer, when researching the culture of transition, refers to the trauma of the exile by quoting Max Aub who exemplifies 'the inevitable limits of reunion', the bitter, confused and ill-adjusted behaviour of the political émigré. The quotation, taken from the book *La gallina ciega*, runs as follows:

    I returned and now I depart. At no time have I had the feeling that I formed part of this new country which has usurped the place of the one which was here before: that place was not inherited. I am talking about petty theft, not robbery. These Spaniards of today took what existed here before, but they are different. Understand me! Of course they are different, because of the times, but not only because of that: it's that and something else: I notice it in the different way they speak and face up to life. (Quoted by Mainer, 1992: 318)

Memory fulfils a very important social function in helping to structure experience and ensure the continuity and the traditions of groups. The collective memory not only consists of traditions, but also of ideas and images which are generated by the present and rooted in the present; it is not only made up of memories, but also of reconstructions. Remembering is an activity that depends largely on the memories of the rest of the group, which helps us to reconstruct our own memory. Memory, in short, cannot be detached from the circumstances in which it is produced, given that memory always includes elements of the present. Moreover, given that memory is something widespread, constantly developing and in a permanent state of flux, it is obvious that every time a memory is evoked it must pass through the filters of the present. In this respect, every time the past is called upon, slight modifications are made and new nuances are derived from the present.

Halbwachs recognises, of course, that a person can recall moments which no other person has experienced (such as a solitary walk, for example) but what he is saying is that, in order to gain access to this memory, the mind needs to know and employ other media which go beyond the individual, such as time, space and the names of the objects which surround us. Memory, on the other hand, can never be detached from the circumstances in which it is generated; in some way, the past filters through the present in order to reach us. According to this view, if we wished to gain a profound insight into a distant historical period, we would have to follow the advice of Anatole France in the preface to his life of *Joan of Arc* when he says:

> To feel the spirit of a past era... the difficulty is not so much in what one must know but in what one must not know anymore. If we really want to live in the 15th century we have so much to forget: sciences, methods, all the acquisitions which make us modern. We must forget that the earth is round and that the stars are suns, and not lamps suspended from a crystal ceiling, forget the system of the world of Laplace to believe only in the science of St. Thomas, of Dante, of the cosmographers of the Middle Ages who teach us the Creation in seven days. (quoted by Vromen, 1986: 59)

In short, other memories provide us with the information required in order to complete our own memories and fill in the gaps concerning our past caused by amnesia.

The sociological research carried out by Halbwachs links society to the individual precisely through the memory. For him, recalling the past reinforces social ties, by which amnesia is explained as a split away from the reference group. Whilst contact and identification with the group is maintained, featuring shared experiences and contexts, each member's past has common reference points, which survive simply due to the continuing existence of the group. The duration of our memory within a certain period of our lives depends either on the duration of the group itself or on our links to that group; when one of these two factors ceases to exist, when the group disappears, or when contact with the group is lost and a former member joins another group, the memory of the experiences throughout that period begins to deteriorate. The ease with which we are able to recall the past depends, therefore, on the current proximity of people from different groups with whom we live, sometimes quite closely. Although memory is collective, the act of remembering is individual, each memory represents a particular point of view with respect to the collective memory, which changes when the position of the subject within society changes and his relationships are altered.

Other authors also recognise this eminently collective and social dimension of memory. Michael Schudson, for example, states that the memory is essentially found in institutions, both in the form of norms, laws and procedures, as well as in the form of monuments, books, public holidays, statues, etc. Wherever the memory may be found within individuals, it usually happens that that memory is characteristic of either generational or occupational groups (Schudson, 1992: 51). Serge Gagnon also believes that memory is a collective phenomenon when he states that it must simplify and dignify the past, given that it is a powerful agent of social solidarity which explains the present and offers lessons for the future, at the same time as it guides individual and collective action and encourages the participation of men within the community (Gagnon, 1982).

Halbwachs distinguishes between two kinds of memory:; one would be 'autobiographical memory', this being the memory of each individual, an internal and personal memory in the sense that it emerges from that person's life, even though it always contains, as we have explained above, a collective dimension. The other is 'historical memory', which is the 'loaned memory' of past events that the subject has not experienced personally. This memory may be augmented and modified by reading, as well as by other means, but it depends entirely on the memory of others. This is what historical narration is. According to Halbwachs, narratives of historical events, 'have deeply influenced national thought, not only because they have altered institutions, but also because their tradition endures, very much alive, in region, province, political party, occupation, class, even certain families or persons who experienced them firsthand' (1950: 51). These narrations, these traditions, are symbols; they can be imagined but not recalled. It is obvious that although historical memory can encompass longer periods of time than autobiographical memory, the former is more schematic and impoverished than the latter.

Among the most recent scholars who have studied the memory, one of the most interesting is Barry Schwartz, who does not simply limit himself to expounding theoretically upon what should or should not be understood by 'collective memory', but also applies his analytical framework to specific historical examples. This author talks about the existence of two theoretical currents of thought within the study of collective memory. On the one hand, he describes the point of view that he calls 'presentism',[9] by which the past is constantly modified by the beliefs, aspirations and fears of the present. On the other hand, he describes the 'conservative'[10] approach, which holds the past to be something sacred and unchangeable that determines the present; traditions persist throughout time and are taken up again in unaltered form by each new generation. Other authors, frequently locating their arguments within one of these two perspectives, have emphasised the importance of amnesia, political learning processes and, finally, ceremonies and rituals that publicly evoke and recall the past.

Presentism

Among those who state that the past is constantly modified depending on the interests of the present, we might mention in addition to Halbwachs: David Lowenthal (1985), Trevor Lummis (1987), Eric Hobsbawm (1987) and John Nerone (1989). These authors stress the capacity of the present to shape the past and impose various versions of it depending on the changing circumstances of the present moment. According to Lummis, 'popular memory' is the collective and generalised memory of the past, which, in spite of being sustained by society, does not originate from it. This common memory is very strongly influenced and shaped by insti-tutions which have economic, political and social power in the present, and it is through these powerful social media that these institutions help to popularise certain images of the past at the expense of others. The memory does not recall things as they happened, but represents a recon-struction of the past from the present, which modulates, recreates, forgets and interprets the past in various ways. According to this view, it is essential to consider how history in the life of a nation is officially pre-sented in order to observe how – with a greater or lesser degree of success – an attempt is made to shape the overall perception of the past.

Therefore, a hegemonic memory exists, of a general nature, which must be articulated in accordance with a country's various traditions and memories (according to regions, cultures, generations) with a varying degree of influence being exercised on these, in turn, by the multiple 'popular memories' that may contradict it. In some cases, a conflict may emerge regarding the common past, given that the dominant memory, which is the 'official' version of the past, is never passively accepted, since it bears a dialectical relationship with other versions based on the experiences of those who perceive it.

9. This group emerges within historiography under the famous precept coined by Benedetto Croce: 'all history is contemporary history' (quoted by Carr, 1987: 19).
10. The author calls this current of thought 'conservative'. However, given that the ideo-logical connotations of this term could obscure rather than clarify this concept, we have opted for the term 'historical taxidermism', which we consider to be clearer and less pejorative.

According to this view, the élite classes are more prone to rationalise and revise their memories in the light of their present ideology; their political pragmatism enables them to be more flexible when interpreting their own past.[11] Nevertheless, for the rest of society personal memories are somewhat more difficult to forget and even to adapt in accordance with the passing of time and the changing circumstances that take place.

Amnesia is just as important as memory. For Lummis, what is not recalled always presents a greater danger than what is. Silences latently express a collective form of self-censorship, the existence of open political wounds and of live underlying problems within the life of a country. However, amnesia can also be as important as memory in cementing the peaceful bonding of a nation.

Lowenthal is another of the theorists included in this first group, who has devoted a large part of his work to demonstrating that the past is a strange place when viewed from the present, given that it presents an ever-changing image which is constantly being reinterpreted according to the needs of the moment: 'The past *is* to some extent, our own creation' (Lowenthal, 1985: 410). The past loses, in this case, its autonomy and even its very substance. Recollections of the past are filtered through our own memories and through those that others convey to us, in which sense, each new evocation of the past takes on a specific guise. Not only is the past modified, in effect, by the present, to which it remains inextricably linked, but according to Lowenthal this is both desirable and good for Mankind.[12]

Taxidermism

This current of thought is difficult to find nowadays in its purest form. For this reason, in this section we shall present the contributions made by those theorists of collective memory, such as Schudson (1989; 1992) and Schwartz (1982; 1991) who have placed emphasis in recent years on the limits that exist regarding the manipulation of the past. Furthermore, we shall present the ideas of a second group of writers who, without belonging to the wide-ranging group of 'collective memory theorists', have revealed considerable interest in the historical learning of political

---

11. It was also the élite classes who created, in large part, the nationalist ideologies which emerged during the nineteenth century. It was these classes who searched for and invented their own national past, who revived and compiled popular folklore, who composed hymns, orchestrated national ceremonies and established the dates on which these were to be celebrated.

12. Lowenthal states:

> It is far better to realize the past has always been altered than to pretend it has always been the same... We can use the past fruitfully only when we realize that to inherit is also to transform. What out predecessors have left us deserves respect, but a patrimony simply preserved becomes an intolerable burden; the past is best used by being domesticated – and by our accepting and rejoicing that we do so. (Lowenthal, 1985: 412)

protagonists and in the weight which the past brings to bear on public decision-making processes, such as Robert Jervis (1976), Peter Hall (1990) and Nancy Bermeo (1992). None of them deny the possibility of manipulating the past, but their main preoccupation resides in demonstrating the firm constitution of the past and the difficulties that exist regarding any attempt to distort or freely reconstruct that past.

One of the writers who focuses on the capacity of the past to resist multiple attempts at being used for particular ends is Michael Schudson, who, in his most recent book, studies the impact which the Watergate case had on the American psyche, as well as on existing political institutions. In order to do this, he analysed the various versions of the scandal that emerged at the time in order to examine how they were constructed, revised and transmitted, and to determine what specific weight they have retained to this day. In studying the collective memory of this event he uses a wide variety of sources (newspapers, television programmes, films, literature, text books), as he is not so much interested in what people remember about the event in question, but, 'under what circumstances their memories of Watergate affect their views and actions on contemporary issues' (Schudson, 1992: 4). In accordance with this, Schudson defines social and collective memory as, 'the ways in which group, institutional and cultural recollections of the past shape people's actions in the present' (Schudson, 1992: 3).

This emphasis on contemporaneity and the importance that collective memory has for the present, which defines it as such, is the most decisive contribution that we shall make in our analysis. 'Historical memory' is not understood to be just any event in the past which, in some way or other, has been stored in the multiple deposits of the memory, but only those events that have immediate relevance to the present and exert some kind of influence on it.

Schudson recognises that society, as well as organisations and countries, construct their own past. Nevertheless, as he himself states, 'they do not do so in conditions of their own choosing, with materials of their own making, or even with their memories acting entirely under their own volition' (Schudson, 1989: 87). The resistance of the past is a considerable obstacle to be taken into consideration. The fact that it cannot be constructed simply according to the will of one person does not mean that there are not those who try to do exactly that, given that a capacity to influence social memory is a political resource of vital importance, and this is why régimes, through the building of monuments, the creation of national holidays or the staging of military parades, attempt to establish a certain memory within society.

Some of the main obstacles highlighted by Schudson that prevent the past from being freely reconstructed include the following: first of all, the existence of a living memory of the events which are sought to be manipulated, provided that some generation exists which actually witnessed the events directly.[13] Second, we must take into account the fact that multiple versions of the past tend to coexist during the same historical period, especially in pluralistic and democratic societies, and that these versions also tend to be recorded and protected in archives and documental sources from any attempt to conceal or distort them. Third, we must mention the professional constraints which historians encounter when it comes to manipulating history, given that they must subject their research to the judgement of an academic universe governed by certain objective and rigorous criteria, which, although flexible and imperfect, impose certain limits on the free interpretation of the facts. Anyone who fails to use the sources which have been sanctioned by the academic community or who fails to comply with the criteria of accuracy and rigour established by that community, will not be considered to be a 'professional' of history, but shall be relegated to a lower and more speculative rank, one which barely does justice to the essayist. Finally, it may be argued that the past can be sufficiently traumatic and painful to leave scars of such a magnitude that they cannot be easily concealed by politicians or historians.

Amnesia

The relationship that exists between amnesia,[14] forgiveness and reconciliation is extremely complex.[15] On the one hand, we could say that the ideal example of reconciliation is that which is based on mutual and explicit forgiveness, as well as an acknowledgement of responsibility for the error committed. If this were to be based on sincere intentions, it would not be necessary to forget the past in order to live in peace, given that the problem would have been solved and any possibility of conflict surmounted. In this case, it would be possible to bring the main perpetrators of the crime in question to justice and memory would be able to play a highly positive role by preventing the events from ever occurring again.

On the other hand, certain kinds of reconciliation become impossible without recourse to amnesia, to the extent that amnesia is able to function in a similar way to forgiveness (amnesty and amnesia have the same origin). This tends to occur when the offences which must be pardoned

---

13. As the author himself points out 'As people who lived through Watergate pass from the scene, conflict over its memory will decline' (Schudson, 1992: 210).
14. Collective amnesia and social amnesia are extremely complex phenomena, which have only begun to be studied quite recently. The recent waves of democratisation that have swept over Latin America and Eastern Europe have been a fundamental source of inspiration for many authors concerned about subjects relating to justice, revenge, memory, reconciliation and amnesia. Among many other works we might highlight those of Clara Eugenia Rodríguez (coord.) (1986), Lawrence Weschler (1990), Alain Brossat et al., (1990; 1992), Carina Perelli (1992), Georges Mink and Jean-Charles Szurek (1995), Jonathan Boyarin (1994), David Pion-Berlin (1994) and Cathy L. Schneider (1995).
15. See the article by Anne Sa'adah (1992). The journal *Politique Étrangère* also published a monograph entitled 'La Réconciliation' in 1994.

are so unpalatable that reconciliation is only possible through amnesia, as was the case with the Civil War during the Spanish Transition, and only after those who committed the offence have acknowledged their guilt; in the case of Spain, it was the two sides who took part in the conflict who requested a general pardon for their aggressions and who acknowledged that they were equally guilty for the events which occurred. In such cases, the problem is temporarily and provisionally settled, although it is essential that the desire for reconciliation should remain active over time so that resentment and ill feeling should not reemerge. It is most frequently the case that the individuals responsible for the crisis escape judgement, given that since this kind of reconciliation is somewhat fictitious in the sense that it is based on amnesia and not directly on forgiveness, anything which involves an evocation of past events could lead once again to controversy, which is precisely what is sought to be avoided (especially in the case of civil war, where a fear of repetition tends to determine the attitudes of the protagonists). Here, memory plays an ambiguous role. Although certain lessons have been drawn from history that enable the past to be forgotten – or more precisely, establish the pretence that it has been forgotten – because of its especially traumatic nature the recollection may not have really disappeared and, thus, could reemerge unexpectedly with unforeseeable results. In this respect, it is worth creating the institutions that are required in order to contain, as far as possible, the unpredictable consequences of latent memory.[16]

Finally, there are cases in which reconciliation appears to be impossible, given that no desire to resort to amnesia even exists to settle former disputes. This tends to be so in cases where the perpetrated deeds are too serious, or too recent, providing no easy way out and sometimes not even a temporary remedy, as has been the case in Yugoslavia. These are countries in which history repeats itself because the lessons drawn from the past are not based on the idea of *never again*. Collective memory plays a clearly inflammatory role here, legitimising conflict precisely as a result of the existence of a plurality of conflicting memories and the nonexistence of a shared memory of past events.

In line with these observations, there are various writers who theorise about the virtues of amnesia and, on the contrary, others who insist on the perpetual need to recall the past and the dangers of amnesia.[17] Both groups concede fundamental importance to the weight that the past brings to bear on the present, in the first case with a view to removing the sometimes unbearable burden of the past, and in the second case with a view to ensuring that the errors of the past are not repeated.

16. There are cases, as Sa'adah points out, where stability and memory become mutually exclusive goals given that 'at the most dramatic moments in the life of a political community, good history can be bad politics' (Sa'adah, 1992: 104).
17. Regarding the distortions of amnesia, see the book by Javier Roiz (1993).

The essential need to forget is fervently propounded by Friedrich Nietzsche, who considers it to be the only recourse available to Mankind that
enables him to endure the heavy burden of the past, one which inex-
orably conditions his behaviour, projecting its influence over life in the
form of a sombre shadow. Happiness, according to Nietzsche, means being
able to forget, to the extent that it would be possible to live happily without almost any memory, although it would be impossible to live without
being able to forget. The past must never be allowed to bury the present
and, in this sense, the curative virtues of amnesia must be applied.[18]

The predominant view in Jewish literature concerning the Holocaust
could not be more contrary to this idea. The avalanche of memories
experienced and narrated regarding this terrifying period serve the purpose of recalling the past in order, on the one hand, to restore the
memory of the murdered and humiliated Jewish people, in perpetual
homage to its long-suffering memory, and on the other hand, to prevent
the precious lessons of the past from being forgotten in the future, thus
ensuring that the tragedy is never repeated. This is a symbolic way of
exercising justice. It is not so much a question of simulating the obsessive
and tenacious hunt of the most famous 'Nazi-hunter', Simon Wiesenthal,
but of narrating a series of personal experiences as a form of therapy and
denunciation, in an attempt to come to terms with the past.[19]

Learning

The concept of 'political learning', which has recently gained considerable importance in political sociology, perfectly complies with the
theoretical contributions which we have described above regarding memory.[20] Political learning represents a process of cognitive change, which
is key to democratic reconstruction (Bermeo, 1992: 273). The experience

18. The troubled German philosopher also talked about the danger of judging the past, the
   inappropriateness of weighing history on the scales of justice:

   > For since we happen to be the products of earlier generations, we are also the products of
   > their blunders, passions and misunderstandings, indeed, of their crimes; it is impossible to
   > free ourselves completely from this chain. If we condemn those blunders and exempt our-
   > selves of guilt for them, we cannot ignore the fact that our existence is rooted in
   > them...knowledge of the past in every age is desirable only insofar as it serves the future
   > and the present, and does not weaken the present or eradicate a vital future (Nietzsche,
   > 1990: 103).

19. The literature on the memory of the Holocaust is very extensive. Some of the most
   recent and original contributions in this respect can be found in various issues of the
   journal *History and Memory*, published by the University of Tel Aviv.
20. This term will be of greater use in the chapter regarding the Transition than in the one
   that deals with Francoism, given that it involves analysing the lessons drawn in Spain
   from the Civil War and from the Franco experience. In turn, it could link up with the
   various theories regarding democratic transition processes, enriching them with this
   analytical contribution that is fundamental to any analysis of the always uncertain
   processes that govern the change of a régime.

of a dictatorship can provide some profound lessons, whilst also obliging the protagonists to reevaluate the nature of régimes in general, the nature of our former enemies, our own objectives and our behaviour.

According to Nancy Bermeo, the process of redemocratisation features three stages: first, the fall of the dictatorship; second, the creation or reconstruction of democracy; and, finally, the consolidation of the new régime, with political learning playing an especially important role in the second stage. Bermeo offers us the following definition:

> political learning is the process through which people modify their political beliefs and tactics as a result of severe crises, frustrations and dramatic changes in environment. All people...are capable of learning from experi-ence... Crises often force people to reevaluate the ideas that they have used as guides to action in the past... The concept of political learning is based on the premise that beliefs are not fixed immutably in childhood and that they can be 'affected by political events'. (Bermeo, 1992: 274)

This process of learning based on critical experiences of the past may force a change not only in the tactics employed in a particular action, but also in the principles on which the actions adopted by political protago-nists are based.

During the second stage of the redemocratisation process, the learning of political leaders plays a crucial role; as Bermeo points out, popular movements can bring down a dictatorship, but do not build a liberal democracy per se. This involves reaching institutional agreements (such as the drafting of a Constitution), which must necessarily be designed by small groups. Bermeo claims that the architects of democratic recon-struction tend to be former enemies, given that any *re*-construction entails the existence of a break with the past, a break that is often violent and traumatic. Thus:

> élites representing groups who are willing to harass and perhaps even kill each other at one time sit down and construct democratic accords at another. The fact that they are willing to construct democratic accords means that they are willing to reconstruct a kind of régime that failed in the past. Ideas about this type of régime and about the various opposing groups that will operate inside it must change in order for the reconstruction to begin. (Bermeo, 1992: 276)

The logic of political learning consists precisely of this; what worked in the past tends to be revived and what failed tends to be avoided, some-times even too frivolously.[21]

---

21. During the Spanish democratic transition, the tendency was to avoid the institutional design of the Second Republic. What is more, constant emphasis was placed on the dif-ferences between the two régimes, highlighting how different the Spain of the 1930s was to that of the 1970s, which was quite true, although it was difficult to see it quite so clearly at that time.

Carr also considers history to be a learning process, which is, in short, the classic conception of history as *magistra vitae*. What people learn from the past (or believe they have learned) is highly revealing when it comes to interpreting their behaviour, and Carr states that, 'One reason why history rarely repeats itself among historically conscious people is that the dramatis personae are aware at the second performance of the denouement of the first, and their action is affected by that knowledge' (Carr, 1987: 70).

Peter Hall employs the concept of learning when it comes to explaining the choice of certain economic policies in Great Britain, reaching the conclusion that 'policy responds less directly to social and economic conditions *per se* than it does to the consequences of past policy' (Hall, 1990: 4). This does not mean that the state takes decisions in an independent and isolated manner, given that what normally happens is that both society and the state compete with different versions based on their own political teachings, which are derived from past experiences.

Finally, among the works produced by writers who are interested in analysing the lessons of history, we find the now classic research carried out by Robert Jervis, who devotes a large part of his book to describing how politicians learn from history when it comes to taking decisions regarding international issues, which could equally be applied to national affairs, given that, 'we cannot make sense out of our environment without assuming that, in some sense, the future will resemble the past' (Jervis, 1976: 217). The lessons of the past, according to Jervis, shape future predispositions when it comes to acting in one way or another.

The learning process is extremely complex; the most important lessons are not always retained and applied, although the most evident lessons and those that affect us most personally, are. When a political decision is successful, the costs of that decision are rarely considered, nor is any consideration given to whether a different decision might have been able to produce better results. This means that, in many cases, few lessons are learned when the outcome is successful, given that nobody ever inquires into whether this outcome has really been achieved as a result of a political decision or whether, on the contrary, it has been achieved in spite of that decision.[22] Conversely, something similar happens in the case of failure; nobody is concerned about whether the result, undesirable as it may be, was the consequence of the measure that was considered to be the best decision among the possible options available at the time. In this respect, the kind of decision that led to failure tends to be avoided, without considering the consequences that would have ensued if a different policy had been implemented. Nevertheless, what is certainly true is that those who take political decisions tend to place excessive emphasis on the lessons which derive from their own personal

22. 'Nothing fails like success' (Jervis, 1976: 278).

experience and undervalue the lessons which derive from the experience of others, in such a way that, 'people who experience a natural disaster are much more affected than those who only see the damage' (Jervis, 1976: 241), a form of reasoning which can be applied perfectly to the Spanish Civil War. Pursuing the same line of argument, the two main consequences that derive from the excessively heartfelt lessons one learns from one's own experiences, especially if these are traumatic, include, on the one hand, the fact that one tends to view one's current adversaries in the light of the adversaries one has encountered in the past and, on the other, that the probability of perceiving current problems incorrectly increases when a protagonist has directly experienced similar situations in the past that those who work alongside him have only learned about indirectly. For example, the perception that the aged and paralysed army had of the Communist Party during the Spanish Transition was very different to the perception that a younger political class which had not lived through the Civil War possessed, in spite of the fact that its ideology, at least in the case of U.C.D., whose leader actually propitiated the legalisation of the party, was conservative. In this respect the generational change proved quite necessary and even essential, especially when we consider that the protagonists were obliged to confront a dramatic and difficult past, one which presented a multitude of badly-healed wounds.[23] On the other hand, the lessons of the past, in the same way as memory itself, tend to be institutionalised through textbooks and regulations and even through language, thus constituting a shared and accessible source of learning for all citizens.

The events from which we normally learn most are those which take place at an early stage of our lives and which, on occasions, create a 'generational effect', as we saw at the beginning of this chapter. Not having definitively formed our own character nor having lived sufficiently long for certain events to no longer surprise us, the experiences we have during the early years of life, in which we are most susceptible to all kinds of influences, are those that have the strongest effect on our way of interpreting life and make up the 'perceptive predispositions' with which we approach events.

With respect to 'generational effects', Jervis states that people also absorb the beliefs and values of their time, especially those that they encounter when they begin to become aware of the political game in which they are immersed. Those who achieve this state of maturity at the same time will be affected by major events witnessed at that time in a similar way (in spite of any existing differences regarding the interpretation of the facts as a result of prior experiences in each case) and the

---

23. Jervis states that 'an actor will learn most fruitfully from events that he knows well enough to analyze in some detail, but that are not so close that they dominate his future perceptions' (Jervis, 1976: 246).

conclusions which are drawn from such events will accompany their generation throughout its entire existence.

As a consequence of all this, we find what Jervis calls 'delayed effects' in political decision-making. This delay in applying the lessons of history is due to the fact that the lessons that had the strongest impact on a young generation take some twenty years to become apparent. This is approximately the period required for this group to come to power, as a result of the inevitable emergence of new generations.

Ceremonies and Monuments

Investigations that have focused on studying sites of memory and ritual celebrations have produced real methodological innovation within the fields of history and sociology, with regard to both the selection of sources and their handling.[24] When it comes to understanding the importance of the collective unconscious, of traditions, of mythical references in speeches, or of the symbols employed in official ceremonies that recreate the past, the conventional tools of the historian and the sociologist are insufficient. It is, therefore, essential to acknowledge the importance of certain alternative sources and documents, on occasions used by other social sciences such as anthropology, whose employment can help us to understand these phenomena better.

The pioneer in this kind of study, which focuses on 'sites of memory', is Pierre Nora (1984), who has compiled various contributions on the various deposits of memory in France. On the one hand he has studied celebrations, emblems, monuments, commemorations, dictionaries and museums as examples of sites of memory. On the other hand, he has placed special emphasis on collective subjects, both private and public, which transmit memory: school, the Church, the family and the state. Barry Schwartz has also carried out some curious research regarding the statues on Capitol Hill in the United States, which consisted in analysing how the context at any given moment influenced the choice of figures to be honoured and how this really represented an attempt at the time to resolve, at least symbolically, the existing problems of integration prior to the American Civil War (Schwartz, 1982). Finally, Schudson has carried out a study on the American memory of the Watergate affair through an analysis of various forms and vehicles of memory, the most important of which include the following: 'career, myth, reform, celebrity, anniversary, reputation, language, metaphor, expectations and pedagogical lessons'. Those which have secondary importance include: 'any parts of the human world with the property of duration...human beings themselves...social

---

24. An increasing number of researchers are devoting time to studying these matters. Among others, we might highlight the following: Gerard Namer (1987), Paul Connerton (1989), Jean Davallon et al. (1993), Michael Kammen (1993), James E. Young (1993), John R. Gillis (ed.) (1994) and Jay Winter (1995).

institutions...culture, symbols or objects people transmit across genera-tions...vehicles...through which time travels' (Schudson, 1992: 5).

In relation to Spain, a study has been carried out in Salamanca regard-ing the sites of memory concerning the Civil War. This study sought to elucidate the legitimising efforts of the New State (Madalena et al., 1988: 489). The authors emphasised the régime's intention to reconstruct memory through its use of a policy of symbolism and its aim to perpetu-ate the memory of the war through an attempt to both eradicate the Republican memory and construct a Nationalist memory, and to dissem-inate the latter throughout the country. In this respect, they studied the names of streets and plazas, a variety of funerals and examples of homage, commemorations, celebrations and architecture.[25]

To recapitulate, we could say that the simultaneous presence of 'inher-ited memories' and 'invented memories' does not constitute an anomaly that requires explanation. It is true that the present is made up of the past, but it is also true that the retention and reconstruction of the past are rooted in the present. What the most radical 'taxidermists' fail to see is that the present itself can sustain various memories, and that various kinds of present can sustain the same memory. The past is neither totally immutable nor entirely unstable, but forms a picture to which new ele-ments are periodically added. Although it is true that the past is reconstructed in order to legitimise the present, that past, in some aspects and under certain conditions, presents firm resistance in the face of any attempts to conceal or change it. Sooner or later it ends up reemerging. Institutions and various forms of commemoration aim to ensure that the past survives, in spite of the passing of time and genera-tional changes. On the other hand, the initial construction of an historical fact limits what can subsequently be said about it.

Although it is necessary to elaborate facts and recognise that no inter-pretation is entirely objective, this does not mean that some interpretations are not truer than others. We must also be wary of the idea that since the historian sees the past in the light of the problems of the present, his interpretation of the facts is purely pragmatic. Carr states that Man:

> is not totally involved in his environment and unconditionally subject to it. On the other hand, he is never totally independent of it and its uncondi-tional master... The historian is neither the humble slave nor the tyrannical master of his facts (Carr, 1987: 29).

Here we shall propose the existence of a third way, which we might call 'relativist' and which would consist of the claim that the pre-emi-

---

25. Other authors who have analysed Francoist ceremonies, symbols and rites from simi-lar perspectives include: Giuliana di Febo (1988), Ángela Cenarro (1992) and Cándida Calvo (1992).

nence of the past over the present (or vice versa) depends, in many cases, on the specific historical context and that, whatever the case may be, past and present exercise mutual influence over each other.

Methodology and Sources

The main hypothesis that this research aims to corroborate or refute could be formulated in the following manner: the existence of a traumatic memory of the Spanish Civil War played a crucial role in the institutional design of the Transition by favouring negotiation and inspiring a conciliatory and tolerant attitude on the part of the main actors. However, what kind of memory existed, exactly, about the war? This is a fundamental question, given that the mere existence of a traumatic memory of a civil war does not in itself necessarily lead to peace and reconciliation.

In order to discover the kind of memory that existed in Spain at the time of Franco's death, it is essential to analyse the official handling of this event, so that we might understand why the collective memory of the Civil War in Spain, unlike Yugoslavia, played a peacemaking role. It is a matter of observing how the war was remembered; not so much what was actually remembered about it (factual memory), but what values and lessons were linked to this memory (memory as a function) and why (process of socialisation). These questions may be resolved by researching the years that preceded the Transition, the historical awareness of the Spanish, the process of Francoist socialisation and its reflection in political culture, and the values associated, either directly or indirectly, with the memory of the war.

From the above we might infer that the key to resolving the main hypothesis regarding the Transition is directly linked to another secondary hypothesis concerning Francoism, which may be formulated as follows: only a memory of the Civil War of the kind which existed in Spain, due, among other factors, to Francoist socialisation, was able to favour consensus during the Transition. The régime deliberately associated the memory of the war, at least from the early 1960s onwards, with political stability, social peace, national unity and harmony and, especially, with economic progress and rising standards of living. Throughout this period the régime strove to legitimise both its founding myth and its own survival; first, through a black-and-white narration of the war in which it sought to justify the 'need' for the Uprising and, second, by associating, over time, this memory of the war with peace and progress, legitimising the régime further by appealing to the results of its administration (performance-based legitimacy) rather than its origins (origin-based legitimacy), although without losing sight of the latter for an instant. Finally, Francoism instilled a ferocious, obsessive and omnipresent fear of any repetition of the Civil War, justifying the survival of the régime by alluding to the alleged dangers that a liberal democracy could hold for Spain, thus taking refuge behind a traumatic memory on which the 'never again' consensus was already built. It is also true that other factors were involved in this process, such as the very passing of time, factors which helped to facilitate both forgiveness and an ability to forget.

The mere presence of the memory of the war is not enough to explain the resulting consensus. We must consider the role that its evocation played in each context, its interrelation with the present and the lessons of the past that were extracted at each moment in order to understand how the present shapes our interpretation of the past and how the past weighs down on the present, fulfilling one function or another depending on the kinds of values and learning processes which it symbolises.

In short, what this research aims to analyse is the way in which the Transition was brought about: why the maintenance of public order and social peace was given priority; why consensus was adopted as a form of political action; why extremist proposals were banished and negotiation was encouraged among the main actors. The answer to all these questions will be based on a study of two factors: first, the existence of a traumatic collective memory of the Civil War, which drove the majority of the protagonists to seek to avoid its repetition at any cost; second, the process of socialisation that was witnessed throughout the Franco period, which will help to explain the attitudes of Spaniards during this period whilst considering what kinds of values the régime wished to instil in the population, what instruments it employed and what degree of success it achieved in its endeavours.

It is obviously no easy task to research the memory of a society, and even less so when no surveys and hardly any studies on oral history exist which would allow the researcher to penetrate the subject. However, although it is undoubtedly difficult to gain a precise understanding of how the memory of the two adversaries – the victors and the defeated – regarding the war actually developed and how it may have changed over time, it is possible to trace its existence through various other indirect sources, in addition to studying the development of the régime itself through its explicit or implicit handling of this matter. By analysing the régime's policy of socialisation, it is also possible to detect the values that were associated with the memory of the war in the policy of permanent recollection that existed concerning the Civil War. Furthermore, as the collective memory of a country is represented in its most important institutions, through the design of these very institutions we can explore the kind of historical evocation that inspired their architects.

In order to confirm the hypothesis outlined above, we shall use various sources on Francoism that we consider to be crucial by virtue of their extremely wide dissemination and the fact that they are clear examples of the régime's attitudes towards the historical and symbolic handling of the Civil War. One source is No-Do, a collection of newsreels and documentaries, which was compulsorily shown in all commercial cinemas between 1943 and 1975 (and voluntarily between 1976 and 1981). Another important source will be provided by the various history and political education textbooks that were used at various teaching levels between the end of the war and the death of Franco.

With regard to the Transition period, we need to discover what kind of historical lessons were derived from the memory of the experience of the Second Republic and the Civil War, to which end we shall use other first-hand sources, such as documentation from the Cortes, parliamentary debates, legislation, the press, history books, memoirs and autobiographies, the works produced by some intellectuals and various official publications.[26]

26. The main archives consulted include the Archivo General de la Administración, that of the Congreso de los Diputados and that of No-Do. The most frequently used databases include those of the Centro de Investigaciones Sociológicos. The most important libraries which were consulted for this research include the following: Library of the Centro de Estudios Avanzados en Ciencias Sociales (Instituto Juan March), the Biblioteca Nacional, Library of the Congreso de los Diputados, Pedagogical Library of CSIC, Library of the Centro de Estudios Constitucionales, Library of the Boletín Oficial del Estado, Library of the Colegio De Croly, and the Libraries of the Political Science and Sociology Faculties of the Universidad Complutense and the Universidad Nacional de Educación a Distancia. I was granted access to the documentation centres of the newspapers *El País* and *ABC*. Finally, I also consulted the documentation centres of the PSOE and the PCE. I did not visit that of the PP, given that access to this documentation centre is extremely difficult to obtain.

CHAPTER 2

FROM THE JUSTIFICATION OF WAR TO THE EXALTATION OF PEACE

THE DEVELOPMENT OF OFFICIAL DISCOURSE DURING THE FRANCO PERIOD

Throughout the thirty-six years between the end of the Civil War and the death of General Francisco Franco, Spain was governed by a heterogeneous and ever-changing élite, made up of the victors in the war, under the permanent authority and leadership of Franco. The power of this political élite depended on the institutions (some of which were designed in the very midst of war) of a régime that was totalitarian in its origins and initial pretensions, but that subsequently adopted authoritarian characteristics.[1] In spite of this development, the régime always paraded its victory and discriminated in favour of the victors in the Civil War in various ways, although with differing degrees of intensity.

In this chapter we shall attempt to analyse how the official Francoist discourse regarding the Civil War evolved, a discourse that came to represent the dominant memory, although not the hegemonic memory, of the war. The study of this discourse includes the arguments that were directly produced by the main institutions of the régime, or that were subject to their control. No-Do, for example, was a public body that produced ideological messages of an official nature, whilst textbooks had an indisputably official character as a result of the fact that they were subject to a kind of censorship that not only prohibited the mention of certain topics and even

---

1. The classic study on the early transition from incipient totalitarianism to authoritarianism is by Juan Linz (1964).

certain terms, but was also prescriptive at times, imposing certain contents and the way in which they should be addressed. Furthermore, all textbooks had to be approved by the Ministry of Education.

An analysis of this official discourse will enable us to study the kind of version of the Civil War that the régime wished to convey to the generations that had not lived through the war, as well as to those that had taken part in it. In the first case, the régime's intention was to shape their perceptions of the war; in the second, it attempted to modify them. Through a study of some of the instruments that the political authorities employed in order to promote their particular view of historical events, we shall observe how it used the past, nearly always with legitimising and propagandist intentions, in relation to both the alleged necessity for a war that had left such a strong impression on the Spanish nation, as well as for the political system that began to emerge during the war and was institutionalised at the end of the conflict.

Our purpose is not to produce an exhaustive analysis of all the aspects that may have helped to shape the collective memory of the war, nor study all of the sites in which the official discourse that emerged finally developed. A large number of sources are valid in tracing the transformations that the memories of a community may undergo and in observing how the versions that emanate from various spheres regarding a specific historical episode may change. However, given that an exploration of a collective memory that does not relate to an immediate event can only be carried out through indirect sources (unless surveys are available concerning the matter or a sufficient number of high-quality autobiographical writings from the period actually exist), the official memory must be studied, since this constitutes the public manifestation of the memory of a particular historical episode, that is projected through a multitude of media, in order to achieve the highest possible levels of influence and dissemination. It is very difficult to determine exactly the capacity that governments (authoritarian or democratic) have to influence the population, but they undoubtedly play a part in the socialisation process. In particular, those that have monopoly control over information-producing bodies are able to shape, at least partially, the views that people possess concerning everyday events, also managing to modify their interpretation of the past. The media, as tightly controlled as they were under the Franco régime, produced a series of values and historical myths which, although they may not have been accepted by all sections of society, did have a considerable influence on the perceptions of many of its members.

All totalitarian régimes, and, to a lesser extent, authoritarian régimes, aspire to meticulously monitor any source of culture (information, art, literature) in order to consolidate their power and legitimise their dominion. Problems arise when, in the case of totalitarian countries, the official memory no longer enjoys a monopoly over the interpretation of history or, as is the case in authoritarian countries,[2] no longer exercises the role of dominant memory. When this occurs, a confrontation of memories takes place as a result of the emergence of one or various widespread versions of the past that contradict the narrative that has been dominant up until that time. During the 1960s, Spain witnessed a progressive replacement of the official discourse on the war with another version that was to gradually gain ground. As control over the cultural means of production was reduced, new versions of the conflict began to emerge, and if these were warmly received by society in spite of the socialising efforts of the régime, this was because they corresponded better to the memory that a large section of the population had acquired through other channels of information that were not subject to state control: clandestine literature, families and some schools (Maravall, 1978). During the Franco period, these alternative narratives concerning the Civil War emerged only gradually, and not solely through private bodies, but also through certain official departments. Nevertheless, in many official bodies no change ever took place, and in those where some change was possible, this was of limited scope. The fact is that the official bodies that produced new versions of the war did everything they could to ensure that it complemented the former version. Within private circles, however, the narratives that emerged were, in many cases, incompatible with the official versions, given that they not only provided alternative interpretations, but also supported views that were actually contrary to the official narrative.

Political stability is endangered when at least two versions of the past exist, based on two general historical memories regarding an important event for a particular country that are mutually exclusive and highly contradictory, both regarding their substance and the lessons that may be derived from it. During the democratic transition, although it was initially thought that a risk of confrontation might exist as a result of the large number of interpretations of history and their apparent incompatibility, a consensus was finally achieved through the acceptance of a shared lesson. However, this was only possible because agreement as to what the war had actually meant and which lessons should be drawn from it had already been reached, somewhat spontaneously, some years earlier.

It is obvious that the Civil War was a fundamental event for the Franco régime, given that it provided its founding myth par excellence. In this respect, it was an overwhelming and obsessive preoccupation throughout almost the entire period. It constituted an important instrument of legitimisation for the régime that was set up at the end of the war, being

2. The absence of a consensus-based version of the past raises more serious problems for totalitarian régimes than for authoritarian régimes, and more serious problems for the latter than for democratic régimes. However, in none of the three cases does it cease to be a disturbing and uncomfortable matter.

presented as both the inevitable and necessary result of a critical situation that offered no possible alternative solutions. This view was imposed on all the various media, whilst any view that was derived from alternative memories and contradicted the official version was subject to rigid censorship, at least during the first two decades of the régime.

Official history can play a legitimising role with regard to the present and, of course, to the future. The historian, considered by many to be a producer of memories, has an influence on collective memory and also on personal memory, at the same time as personal memory also influences the historian. In spite of this mutual influence, during authoritarian periods in which intellectual production is subject to censorship, it is the official historian, faithfully reflecting the dominant discourse, who disseminates the hallowed version whilst other memories are dissipated throughout the private sphere of life. This ceased to be the case as Spanish society began to change through the progressive liberalisation of the régime. The situation is very different in democracies, where the historian is much more aware of the existence of social memories that could be quite different from the official version and are also liable to be explicitly voiced. In such cases it is also more likely that shared memories will exist and that the official version will be both more flexible and plural than in authoritarian régimes.

After the Civil War, Spain was forced to face a panorama of divided memories. A large proportion of the memories of the losing side no longer resided in Spain, but in exile, and those that remained were silenced through repression and censorship. In fact, these memories only existed at a family level, and even then this was not always the case due to the fear of repression and the wish of many families to hide their Republican past from their children in order to protect them from discrimination. The children of the winning side were subjected to a considerable amount of Francoist propaganda, although some of their families had sufficient means to redirect the education of their offspring along very different paths.[3]

Attempts at political socialisation through the imposition of an official discourse are quite obvious. The aim is to impose a black-and-white view of the past and de-legitimise democracy by denigrating both political parties and Parliament, along with any related institutions. There were

3. This matter is analysed by José María Maravall (1978), who shows how the influence of some families, especially Republican families, was made felt through various means, ranging from family conversations to the friendships established by the parents, as well as the schools that were chosen (lay and élite), the attitude of the parents towards the children (tolerant and approachable), the lessons taught by the parents, trips abroad, etc. It appears that a considerable degree of continuity existed between Republican parents and their children, who became the leaders of student unrest in favour of a more democratic university system and political régime. On the other hand, it is also true that there were many cases of children from the winning side also turning against the régime (Sáez, 1988:487; Marsal, 1979).

essentially two important channels of socialisation in shaping the political culture of the Spanish. On the one hand, there were those we might call *official channels* (encompassing everything that the political authorities attempt to convey, with differing degrees of success, through a wide range of media). On the other hand, we have the *private channels* (family, friends, teachers), that might either reinforce, complement or, finally, counter the influence of the official versions.

The official memory of the war became something that was very difficult to avoid and that the régime initially associated with values of national and religious unity and later with peace and economic progress.[4] Nevertheless, certain limits regarding the manipulation of the past exist wherever some vestiges of freedom remain. This is the case even in countries with totalitarian régimes where hardly any limits are encountered; where memory has not only been strongly repressed, but even eliminated[5] as we have been able to witness recently in the former communist countries of Europe.[6]

Alternating Legitimacy

Not only were the legitimising attempts of the Franco régime supported, in good part, by an evocation of the war, but the very legitimacy of the régime turned out to be incompatible with a reconciliation of the two sides that had fought against each other. Contrary to what might be thought, the stability of the régime would have been endangered by a real reconciliation based on forgiveness and an acknowledgement of guilt, given that the legitimising arguments of the régime were inextricably bound up with a policy of marginalising the losing side, a justification of war and the exhibition of victory.

For these reasons two interrelated problems had to be resolved during the democratic transition. The first was the survival of the painful memory of the Civil War and the other was the awareness that no official reconciliation had taken place between the two sides. The traumatic nature of the memory of the Civil War is largely explained precisely by the fact that no explicit reconciliation was ever attempted by the authorities, given that this almost represented a *contradictio in terminis* with regard to the legitimacy of the régime itself.

4. The type of nationalism exhibited during the Franco period was, in the majority of cases, exclusive and discriminatory, a fact that can be clearly observed in the régime's attitude towards members of the losing side. The latter were considered, for many years, to be foreigners, estranged from the *Patria* and anti-Spanish. Over time, more generous and inclusive versions appeared that began, at least, to acknowledge the nationality of the adversary.
5. In this respect, see the contributions made by James C. Scott (1990).
6. In relation to this matter, see the work of Alan Brossat et al. (1992).

   In spite of the emergence of certain conciliatory signs, many other indications were clearly far from conciliatory. These were evident both actively and, when we consider everything that could have been done in favour of reconciliation but was not done, passively. For example, no laws were passed to protect disabled former members of the Republican Army, nor its retired soldiers or the widows and orphaned children who remained. This becomes a harsh comparative reality when we consider that the widows, orphans, disabled former soldiers and former prisoners of the winning side received special treatment under the Franco régime. Neither were many of the civil servants, teachers and members of the liberal professions ever rehabilitated. Furthermore, a considerable number of the former Republicans who did manage to attain social and professional integration did not enjoy the same rights or receive the same treatment. Those who had lost the war – or, according to the most benevolent interpretation, had chosen the 'wrong' side – continued to pay for their errors. It is not surprising, therefore, that no monument was ever built that was unconditionally to 'all' of those who died in the Civil War.[7]

   It is obvious that many levels of reconciliation exist, along with various ways of actually bringing it about. Contradictory policies may also exist that are conciliatory in some respects but not in others. On the other hand, reconciliation is not understood in the same way by a person who has lived through a conflict as it is by one who has not, or in the same way as by a person who has suffered a traumatic loss during a war. The scope of what many people within the régime understood to be reconciliation, even during the mid-1970s, was profoundly different and smaller than the idea that was entertained by those who had fought in the war. Not everybody drew the same lessons, or assimilated the memory in the same way, or possessed, naturally, the same will to forgive or the same capacity to understand the reasons of their adversaries. Some, declaring in the prefaces to their books a determined will to overcome the hate and resentment of the war, did not manage to achieve this in practice, or at least their desire for reconciliation was not sufficiently intense in this respect. In many cases, the contents of their books undermined the initial declaration of intentions.

   Those who believed that there was a possibility of a new civil war occurring, who stated that a danger of this kind existed, did so because they knew that no reconciliation had ever taken place and this worried them. This concern was shared by those inhabiting various ideological sections of society, both left and right-wing, throughout the Transition.

---

7. The country had to wait, as we shall see later on, until King Juan Carlos I inaugurated a monument in the Plaza de la Lealtad in 1985 devoted to all those who had died for Spain, thus avoiding any explicit reference to the thorny issue of the Civil War.

Origin-based Legitimacy and Performance-based Legitimacy

The Franco régime employed a dichotomous concept of legitimacy in order to underpin its political authority. In doing so, it made use of the distinction between the terms 'origin-based legitimacy' and 'performance-based legitimacy' that dates back to the oldest pronouncements of political theory regarding the origin of authority and reasons for consent, which seem to originate in Spanish scholasticism.[8] In its first theoretical expressions, the dichotomy referred to tyranny rather than legitimacy. The key work in this respect is the famous *Vindiciae contra Tyrannos* (see Sabine, 1937; 1988: 282 ff.). Subsequently, we can find references in Molina, Castro, Soto, Mariana and Suárez, among others. Mariana spoke of the 'origin-based tyrant' and the 'régime-based tyrant'. The former is illegitimate as a result of his very origin; that is to say he gains access to power illegitimately, which means that he can be disposed of by any citizen. The latter rises to power legitimately, but, once he has gained it, exercises that power in a tyrannical manner, which is why he can be deposed by the masses.

This idea is also reflected in the work by Francisco Suárez (1612) entitled *Tractatus de legibus ac de Deo Legislatore in X libros distributos*.[9] For Suárez the origin of legitimacy resided both in nature and in society, because both were equally created by God. In this sense, 'the holder of said authority requires just title...this problem constitutes and is known by the name of legitimacy of origin and concerns any who may govern or aspire to govern the political community' (De Asís, 1963: 248). Furthermore, there exists the problem of the purposes of political authority:

> The fulfilment of said purposes and respect for the limits of authority constitute what is known as performance-based legitimacy, that may even provide sufficient entitlement to hold political power, in such a way that, if two opponents should manifest one form of legitimacy or the other, the latter should prevail. (De Asís, 1963: 248)[10]

8. This was the research theme of the doctoral thesis produced by Francisco Tomás y Valiente, entitled: 'La doctrina del tiranicidio en los tratadistas españoles del siglo XVI. Fundamentos del derecho de resistencia al poder arbitrario o injusto' (cited in *Saber Leer*, 1993, No.61, p.1).
9. A bilingual edition by Luciano Pereña (1972–1975) exists in 5 volumes.
10. This analytical distinction was to be taken up by some Spanish constitutionalists between the 1940's and 1960's due to the revival of Thomism and Spanish scholasticism. Manuel Fraga Iribarne (1965), in particular, was to use it to justify both the origin of the Franco régime and the Civil War, as well as to explain and justify the régime's survival. According to this theory, the legitimacy of the régime was based on its origin, since it brought down, through a revolt that led to civil war, a republic that was illegitimate both because of its origin (the confusing results of certain municipal elections, which Fraga branded as a 'coup d'état') and its performance (economic crisis, social disorder, religious intransigence etc.). According to Fraga, after the new régime was established, it obtained an additional performance-based legitimacy which, over time, acquired greater importance than its origin-based legitimacy. This was founded on economic development and social peace, as well as on institutional consolidation.

All of this touches on the rather contemporary concern regarding the extent to which an origin-based tyrant can become legitimate as a result of his performance, a crucial question in any study of Francoism.[11]

The Franco régime seemed to wish to convince the Spanish that, whilst accepting that the Second Republic would have been legitimate based on its origins (that is somewhat doubtful since in the municipal elections the Monarchist candidates had obtained a larger number of votes, although these were concentrated in small provincial capitals and rural areas) it may well have been de-legitimised as a result of its ineffective performance. The Franco régime, on the other hand, in the eyes of the majority of the population, gained power illegitimately, but sought to become legitimate based not only on its military victory, but also on its effective economic and social management.

Performance-based legitimacy is directly related to what Pérez Díaz calls 'substantive legitimacy', which he believes to reside in, 'the capacity of the State to resolve fundamental problems' (Pérez Díaz, 1993: 83). Díaz highlights the possible existence of an 'instrumental consent of authority based on its success in resolving certain basic societal problems' and he claims that, 'in the long term, only if this ability exists, does society consent to the authority of these politicians' (Pérez Díaz, 1993: 225).

The circumstances that give rise to a new régime provide, without any doubt, the crucial point of reference during the early stages of its administration. As time passes, this origin-based legitimacy must be progressively strengthened through the exercise of power itself. Nevertheless, the origin will not disappear as a collective point of reference, as the régime, owing its very existence to this origin, can never entirely renounce it without being seriously harmed. However, it is quite probable that this founding moment will acquire different meanings depending on the needs of the present.

The Franco régime emerged from a coup d'état that led to civil war. This point of origin was not, as one might expect, immediately accepted by society, even though a large proportion of those who most strongly opposed the régime were in exile. The precarious legitimacy of this initial period led the régime to resort to violence and terror in order to consolidate its political power.[12] The situation, at least during the first two

---

11. In view of Adolph Hitler's rise to power, the political theory of this century would once again raise the question of what should be done in the face of authority that is legitimately acquired based on its origin (democratic elections) but is illegitimate as a result of its performance.

12. According to the entry for 'Legitimacy' in the *International Encyclopedia of the Social Sciences*:

> Revolutions, unlike usurpation or *coups d'état*, are not necessarily illegitimate. If they succeed, they introduce a new principle of legitimacy that supersedes the legitimacy of the former régime. Under such circumstances recognition by the people will often be acquired only as the new government begins governing, and the process of becoming legitimate may include

decades, was certainly difficult, although victory in war always endows the winning side with a kind of residual and somewhat primitive legitimacy that is difficult to transform.

As the years passed, a series of laws were passed that consolidated the régime and its institutions, leading to a certain political stability and social order and, in turn, a less intense form of repression on the part of the political authorities. Furthermore, the régime gradually gained the recognition abroad that it had originally been denied. As a consequence of all this, it slowly built up a kind of legitimacy that was more profound than origin-based legitimacy, and that would otherwise have lost credence with the corresponding generational changes, given that the new individuals incorporated into public life had not experienced the war and possessed weaker emotional ties in this respect. As this origin, in spite of the initial epic and heroic narrative, was to assume an increasingly dramatic and fratricidal significance, it was more susceptible to being questioned by those who had not experienced it at first hand.

By 1959 the first important concession to performance-based legitimacy had already been made at the expense of origin-based legitimacy. The economic maxim of autarky rooted in initial Falangist rhetoric was sacrificed. A new political rhetoric, free of explicit ideological references, was adopted on the advice of the technocrats in order to undertake a new course towards economic liberalisation through the Stabilisation Plan. This Plan, combined with economic growth witnessed on a worldwide scale, led to a soaring Spanish economy and a general rise in the standard of living. These were key factors in legitimising the administration of the reigning authority.

In the following years, both forms of legitimacy would appear alternately in official discourse, demonstrating, once again, the disconcerting functional flexibility of the Franco régime and its ability to adapt to changing circumstances. Depending on the demands of the domestic and foreign situation, the régime either emphasised its origin-based legitimacy or its performance-based legitimacy (especially outside Spain), employing a shrewd strategy that enabled it both to call on the past and use it as an extremely powerful weapon (especially when it came to repressing opposition or refusing to make concessions) and boast of the present and its economic achievements, especially when it sought acquiescence at home or acceptance abroad.

However, the Franco régime did not always have the ability to play both cards skilfully, given that the authoritarian leanings that it always retained meant that it lost its poise on more than one occasion. The fact is, however, that in general it was able to alternate these options in order

---

violence and terror. Foreign diplomatic recognition, while not essential, may help internal consolidation and therefore speed acceptance of the new pattern of legitimacy (Sills, 1968: 244).

to hold on to power with little difficulty, right up to the death of its main architect and anchor, Francisco Franco.[13]

The two kinds of legitimacy described above can be combined with the three ideal types of legitimacy outlined by Max Weber (Weber, 1968; 1978: 31–38; 212–301; 941–1372). Weber defines domination as 'the probability that certain specific commands (or all commands) will be obeyed by a given group of persons' (Weber, 1968; 1978: 212). All domination requires an 'administrative staff' that may be linked to authority for various reasons, whose nature will determine the type of domination. These reasons tend to be augmented by a 'belief in legitimacy'.

As Weber says:

the 'legitimacy' of a system of domination may be treated sociologically only as a *probability*...It is by no means true that every case of submissiveness to persons in positions of power is primarily (or even at all) oriented to this belief. Loyalty may be hypocritically simulated...on purely opportunistic grounds...for reasons of material self-interest. Or people may submit from individual weakness and helplessness because there is no acceptable alternative. (Weber, 1968; 1978: 214)

This may have occurred during the early period of the Franco régime, when the authorities felt that their situation was somewhat precarious and were overcome by what Guglielmo Ferrero calls 'the fear of power', which consists of a violent attitude produced by the fear of losing authority (Ferrero, 1988; 1992).

The three pure types of legitimate domination, according to Weber, are the rational, the traditional and the charismatic. The first is based on the existence of a bureaucratic régime, where obedience does not rest on the figure of the sovereign, but on an impersonal order. This is 'the most rational known means of exercising authority...in precision, in stability, in the stringency of its discipline, and in its reliability' (Weber, 1968; 1978: 223). This is the kind of administration that we encountered, in good part, when Franco died, and which began to emerge in the 1950s and 1960s. It was the same bureaucratic framework that the new democratic government would leave almost intact, due to the reigning confidence in its form of recruitment and in its ability to manage policy matters effectively. Proof of this is provided by the fact that no purges took place within the administration and a large propor-

---

13. It is true that legitimacy may not only be based on consent, since it is very often based on the brutal repression of society, as was the case with early Francoism. When the régime became more liberal we find, however, a much more significant degree of acceptance, given that opposing the régime, or at least expressing dissent, was no longer as costly as it had been initially, and certain forms of participation even emerged that were not entirely manipulated.

tion of the civil servants openly declared themselves to be in favour of democracy (CIS, 1983).[14]

In traditional domination, 'Obedience is owed not to enacted rules but to the *person* who occupies a position of authority by tradition' (Weber, 1968; 1978: 227). In this sense, we might say that Franco devised the idea that his government, although essentially new, had re-established the tradition of other supposedly glorious periods in the history of Spain. He also claimed to link up with eras in which order, unity and Catholic values had reigned throughout the country, in which respect he resuscitated the myth of El Cid and the memory of the reign of the Catholic Monarchs.[15] The aim was to obtain traditional legitimacy in addition to the charismatic type, by presenting Francoism both as something new and revolutionary, based on charismatic legitimacy,[16] and as the executor of the Catholic and Spanish imperial tradition in accordance with traditional legitimacy.

For his part, Franco (in the same way as various theorists on charismatic leadership, such as Francisco Javier Conde) attempted to strengthen both his personal legitimacy and that of the régime by resorting to the most archaic source of power, that based on the divine origin of political authority. To this end he ordered coins to be minted with his name and image that claimed that he was the 'Caudillo', or Leader of Spain, 'by the grace of God', a formula that is believed to have been originally adopted by Charlemagne. He also claimed that he was only obliged to answer 'before God and before history', which exempted him from any responsibility regarding his government or those who were governed.

However, since charismatic leadership demands certain exceptional qualities, it tends to be ephemeral. It tends to emerge, at least in Western

14. In 1983 the CIS carried out a survey among civil servants inquiring, among other matters, into their opinion regarding the legitimacy of democracy. The vast majority of the respondents had obtained their employment during the Franco period and yet 89 percent believed that democracy was preferable to any other form of government. This percentage fell depending on age (only 80 percent among the over-1960s), the lower their level of education and among the practising Catholics. When they were asked about whether they agreed with the assertion that 'parties only serve to divide people', a question which, furthermore, evoked memories of the Civil War, 70 percent disagreed with this statement, a figure that varied according to age (35 percent of the over-sixties agreed with this assertion). Curiously, greater consensus was achieved regarding the issue that referred to the moderate and responsible attitude of the parties under Spanish democracy. 71 percent of the respondents agreed with this form of behaviour and the same percentage was recorded among the over- sixties. A partial working of this survey appears in No.23 of the *Revista Española de Investigaciones Sociológicos* and a more in-depth work on the same survey may be found in the book by Miguel Beltrán (1985).
15. Both El Cid – battling against the Moors – as well as the Catholic Monarchs, appeared on the covers of many primary-school textbooks throughout the entire period.
16. Charismatic legitimacy, according to Weber, 'repudiates the past, and is in this sense a specifically revolutionary force' (Weber: 1968; 1978: 244).

societies, in the aftermath of exceptional situations, such as civil war, and continues to function as long as references to the origin that led to this new form of domination remain fresh and active in the minds of citizens. Sooner or later, certain doses of rational legitimacy are required in order to prevent this form of domination from collapsing, either through failed administration, through the natural erosion of charisma, or through a progressive distancing from the founding moment.

Conversely, a very common process consists of what Weber calls 'the routinisation of charisma', which tends to culminate in one of the two other forms of legitimacy, and that takes place when the charismatic form of domination attempts to prolong its hold. The progressive remoteness in time of the Civil War helped to normalise political authority at the same time as the supposedly charismatic qualities of the leader became weaker as he grew older and began to appear vulnerable. A crucial moment in charismatic domination is when the decision is made regarding the succession procedure, a development that finally took place in 1967 with the passing of the Law of Succession, which required the successor to swear loyalty to the spirit of 18 July, that is to say, to the origin-based legitimacy of the régime.

It would also be interesting, in the Spanish case, to establish certain distinctions between the legitimacy of the régime and that of the leader himself. The latter was rather more charismatic and traditional and the former more legal and rational. Nevertheless, both joined together in a kind of alternating preeminence, although the latter tended to prevail during the last two decades of the régime. The mere presence of Franco immediately evoked the origin of the régime, whilst the régime itself was able to evoke both its origin and its performance.

The Francoist theorists of the 1940s, such as Conde, made every effort to consolidate the charismatic aspect of leadership, linking it inextricably to origin. They also attempted to link Franco's personality with the Spanish ultraconservative and nationalistic historical tradition. Later on, in the 1960s, other theorists, supported by a climate of economic development, attempted to portray the régime from a more rational perspective based on the effective management of resources, and on a more legal perspective by means of the progressive institutionalisation of the régime. They did this without ever ceasing to rejoice in its origin, given that their aim was not to undermine but to strengthen the authority of a régime founded on both the past and the present.

Champions of Francoist Legitimacy

One of the theorists who provided the earliest assertion of the origin-based legitimacy of the régime was Conde, the author of a theory of leadership that attempted to strengthen acceptance of Franco's personal leadership, whose value, according to Conde, had been amply demonstrated during the war. In the end, an image of Franco was created in which a series of martial characteristics predominated, such as austerity, courage and self-denial, whilst also emphasising the idea of the skilful strategist who had managed to become 'the youngest general in Europe'. According to Conde, *'to lead is, above all, to govern legitimately'*. Furthermore, 'what defines leadership is the predominance of charismatic legitimacy over the other two kinds. The rational and the traditional elements, especially when leadership is born, are reduced to a minimum' (Conde, 1941: 374; 378–379).

Conde was to base his argument on both charismatic legitimacy and traditional legitimacy, and it was not until the 1970s that a new attempt at theoretical legitimisation took place, this time based on a rational/legal perspective. This approach was adopted by Rodrigo Fernández Carvajal, Jesús Fueyo and Gonzalo Fernández de la Mora, among others, in various of their writings, although especially by the latter in his works *El crepúsculo de las ideologías* ('The Twilight of Ideology') and *El Estado de obras* ('The State of Public Works'). All of them joined the attempt to bring about a definitive institutionalisation of the régime, witnessed particularly through the passing of the Organic Law of State during the latter half of the 1970s.

The famous piece by Fernández de la Mora about the decline of ideology represented the most conscious and explicit attempt to legitimise the Franco régime based on the perspective of its performance. However, at the same time it advocated the de-ideologisation of the Franco régime, albeit indirectly, as Fernández de la Mora intended his work to have overall validity and provide an objective description of a number of symptoms that he claimed to perceive throughout the developed western world, which is why he hardly made any reference to Spain. It is obvious, however, that he wrote the work with Spain in mind and that he attempted to consolidate the foundations of the régime by promoting a style that had already begun to appear in Spain following the technocrats' rise to power in 1957. The latter opened an era of relatively aseptic rhetoric, placing emphasis on development, on effective management and on the purely technical and professional dimension of politics. Fernández de la Mora contributed a more theoretical substance to the practice that was initiated by the technocrats, by writing an intelligent and controversial essay that was to be widely distributed.

The technocrats perceived the decline of the régime's origin-based legitimacy in the same way as Fernández de la Mora, who was very closely connected to them. As time passed, the obsolescence of both ultra-conservative and Falangist political rhetoric became undeniable. One of the main objectives of the new team of administrators was to bring Spain up to the same economic level as the rest of Europe, whilst maintaining the basic tenets of the Francoist project. The liberalisation that they advocated in economic affairs did not apply to the political sphere, where they proved to be rather reluctant to entertain any attempt at introducing a more open régime.[17] Nevertheless, they were sufficiently shrewd to see that it was necessary to present a different kind of régime to Europe. In this respect, they attempted to disguise Francoism by changing their traditional political discourse and replacing it with one that placed emphasis on development and efficiency, objective principles that could be compared with those of any Western democracy.[18]

It is curious that Manuel Fraga Iribarne, having written a book entitled *Horizonte Español* ('Spanish Horizon') in 1965, the purpose of which was to address various issues relating to legitimacy whilst also aspiring to place emphasis on administration, should adopt a stance of direct confrontation with Fernández de la Mora. The main difference between them resided in the fact that Fraga believed that political development was also necessary and that it should coincide with economic development. This would consist in the progressive liberalisation of the régime's institutions and thus lead to its legitimisation both at home and abroad. In his opinion, it was impossible to develop economically without bringing about political liberalisation, given that the new economic climate would lead to changes in the social structure of the country, changes which, although unforeseen, were no less obvious for that reason.

It is true that Fraga was in favour of placing greater emphasis on the legitimacy of performance, although he did not discard the origin-based form, mentioning on various occasions the importance of the war as an essential and indisputable foundation for the régime. He also believed, unlike Fernández de la Mora, that politics was something more than just effective management, given that decisions taken when exercising power

17. Always protected by Luis Carrero Blanco, many of them opposed the passing of a law to liberalise the press. At first sight, it might seem paradoxical that they should have such a staunch ally who was such an open defender of loyalty to the spirit of 18 July. However, they formed a perfect alliance between origin-based legitimacy, represented by Carrero, and performance-based legitimacy, represented by the technocrats, who never sought to forget the war, but rather to relegate it to the background in order to implement their economic projects more efficiently.

18. This idea is very similar to the phenomenon that Manuel García-Pelayo addressed in his book *Burocracia y Tecnocracia*, where he studied 'the effects of technological civilization on the political system and especially on the birth and expansion of technocracy' (García-Pelayo, 1974: 11). According to García-Pelayo, one of the consequences of the technological era has been the emergence of a new kind of legitimacy which, although initially complemented by the other forms, ends up dominating the others and becoming the hegemonic form of legitimacy. According to this new principle, 'legitimacy is efficiency, and efficiency is that which promotes and ensures techno-economic development in certain given environmental and contextual conditions'. It is a kind of rational-functional legitimacy, 'in whose name partial phenomena may be justified that are illegitimate from the perspective of other principles of legitimacy'. All this, 'creates the possibility of concealing interests...under the cloak of technical efficiency and of justifying the exclusion or repression of problems that are inconvenient for the system, under the pretext of their dysfunctional nature' (García-Pelayo, 1974: 52–53).

are not only based on their economic consequences, in cases where these are foreseeable, but, in many cases, on the choice of certain objectives at the expense of others, of certain means and not others, this being an eminently political matter in which economic experts have little to contribute that is more rational and sensible than politicians.

According to the view held by Fernández de la Mora, the Civil War was a consequence of the ideological explosion of the time, which in turn was a result of the slight degree of political development and the general absence of effective political management that had existed; the politicians of the Second Republic were considered to be neither experts nor technocrats, but merely rhetorical figures who believed that they could govern the country with the spoken word. According to Fernández de la Mora, another kind of politician emerged during the Franco period, basing his management on economic efficiency and discarding questions of an ideological nature. The economic development that this new kind of politician propitiated meant that the population came to progressively dismiss ideological issues, being content with their rising standards of living. According to this version, 'in the reordered scale of values, security takes precedence over freedom, and finance over representation' (Fernández de la Mora, 1965; 1986: 117).

This was, in short, a novel apolitical sermon that sought to overcome the ideological and rhetorical anachronisms of Francoism. It was an attempt to maintain the essence of the régime by simply altering its appearance, except in the field of economics, where it was advocated that no authoritarian principle should interfere with the task of achieving greater profits, although state intervention in the economy was fully guaranteed. The ideal climate for economic development was created by a stable political situation, and where else could such a climate be guaranteed as effectively as under an authoritarian régime?[19]

The Civil War was always present in Fraga's thought, as a necessary (although occasionally inconvenient) reference-point that marked the founding of the régime. In 1958, as a result of the passing of the Law on the Principles of the National Movement, Fraga wrote an article in which he described the unalterable and perpetual nature of these principles based on questions of legitimacy that were impossible to renounce. The preamble to the law also stated that these principles reflected the 'communion of the Spanish with the ideals that inspired the Crusades' (Servicio Informativo Español, 1967: 21). The reference to origin-based legitimacy could hardly have been any clearer. Fraga, however, in a supreme effort to free the régime from its discriminatory image regarding the losing side, instead of referring to this preamble, claimed that:

---

19. This line of argument has been questioned by José María Maravall. Regarding the links that exist between economic performance and the type of political régime, see his book (Maravall: 1995).

the Principles are not the *ideology* of the victors in a civil war that they brandish as a canon of political orthodoxy and use as a means of setting apart or oppressing the defeated. Far from it, the Principles are proclaimed based on nearly a quarter of a century's perspective, in view of the inevitable generational changes that must take place. Questions are no longer asked about *membership* of the Movement in 1936; the question relates to *loyalty now* to its principles. Nobody is forced to assume public responsibilities, but we are all obliged to take them on in a legitimate manner.

He continues:

If a State brings a civil war to an end, legitimacy can only become established when that war enters the realms of the distant past, and everyone knows that their only interest is to look ahead. And if 'in the beginning it was action', heroic and almost desperate action, that was required to save the *Patria*, now the time has come for the Word. The difficult task of giving *form* to the community, of establishing its foundations of coexistence. (Fraga, 1958: 521)

He also stated that the legitimacy of the Principles was unalterable given that any modification would lead to the destruction of social peace, the most valuable of all goods.[20]

Another text that undertook a theoretical analysis of legitimacy was provided by the conference that Jesús Fueyo gave in 1964 at the Instituto de Estudios Jurídicos (Institute for Legal Studies). After claiming the need to justify all kinds of power, Fueyo stated that this was only achieved when that power was capable of achieving a certain level of technological development and 'in accordance with its functional capacity to transform reality' (Fueyo, 1964: 19), to the extent that it conceived this transforming myth, and no other, as the real 'permanent revolution', attempting to combine origin (the old Falangist aspiration of 'permanent revolution') with the exercise of power (the technological revolution).

In the same way as Fernández de la Mora, Fueyo believed that the factors that made this technological development possible were, on the one hand, the considerable changes witnessed in the social strata and, on the other hand, the exhaustion of the ideological conception of the world. Both factors were extremely positive and would lead to the institutionalisation of the régime, a stage that was previously undesirable given that the degree of development required had not yet been achieved. Both the faded protagonism of ideology, as well as the disappearance of deep social divisions, had led to three consequences of considerable importance. First, they had made national coexistence easier; second, they had

20. Fraga wrote numerous essays on the Spanish situation, but it was following his incorporation into government in 1962 that he began to base his political administration on an exhibition of the economic, social and cultural achievements of the régime, as could be observed in the commemoration of the '25 Years of Peace'.

brought former adversaries together; third, they had removed the danger of civil war. As Fueyo himself claimed, 'This development...allows us to harbour the well-founded hope that the last civil war has taken place in the history of Spain' (Fueyo, 1964: 46). And he continued:

> There are reasons to believe that Spain has reached that level at which a return to insanity is simply the delirious wish of a minority of fanatics, who will never find their wish echoed by society, a society which is conscious of the fact that, although ultimate happiness has not been achieved, both Spain and every individual have their own interests and possessions to pre-serve. (Fueyo, 1964: 47)

The logical conclusion of this argument was that economic experts should be the ones who form the political class, since, as Fueyo stated, 'If we compare the messages conveyed by outstanding political leaders today with the rhetoric of the great men of the 1930s, we can clearly observe the radical transformation of the emotional climate: some arouse emotions, others present balance-sheets!' (Fueyo, 1964: 17–18). Fueyo proposed, at least partially, to support the Development Plan designed by the technocrats to consolidate the growth of the Spanish economy. It was in that same year (1964) that a part of this political class, under the umbrella of the '25 Years of Peace', attempted to tailor the régime to fit a new kind of legitimacy and achieve its definitive consolidation based on foundations other than origin, although these foundations were comple-mentary. It is understandable that this led to a fundamental split between the traditional Francoist supporters, seeking refuge behind a form of legitimacy based on origin, the modern Francoist supporters, who espoused a form of legitimacy based on performance, and an intermedi-ate group that tried to combine both forms of legitimacy, whilst placing greater emphasis on the latter and supporting the partial political liber-alisation of the régime.

From War to Peace

The development from origin-based legitimacy to performance-based legitimacy may also be studied from the perspective of the changing meaning of the two most important ritual commemorations of Franco-ism: 18 July and 1 April. 18 July, which marked the anniversary of the military rebellion or, as the protagonists would call it, the 'glorious upris-ing', or the beginning of the 'crusade',[21] was to have different connotations to 1 April when it came to commemoration. Nevertheless, both events were to form a coherent part of the legitimising discourse of

---

21. Some sections of the régime never came to acknowledge that a 'civil war' had taken place among Spaniards and devoted a large part of their energies to demonstrating the opposite. See the articles by Colonel Juan Priego López (1963), General José Díaz de Villegas (1966) and that of Javier María Pascual (1961).

the régime. The former date, which evoked the beginning of the war, was gradually transformed from being simply an heroic event to one that possessed overtones of a dramatic nightmare. The other anniversary, however, in spite of marking the victory of one side over another, would retain, after numerous official propaganda efforts, somewhat more positive connotations, marking the end of a tragedy and the advent of peace. As the war itself began to be regarded as a sad and cruel episode, peace was to be progressively reevaluated.

The political discourse of the time made use of both dates, and although 18 July lost its initial preeminence to 1 April in the 1970s, it partially recovered its importance later on. Even when peace emerged as the principal basis of legitimacy, it was not possible to discard the war. To this end, the paradoxical reasoning that claimed that the war had been necessary in order to achieve the long-desired and idealised peace was proffered. The official propaganda texts stated that Franco had been forced to wage war in order to impose a definitive peace on the Spanish nation and, in this respect, to be able to build the foundations of a stable and prosperous future. In the early years, given that the main source of legitimacy was derived from the outcome of the war itself, it was necessary to present a convincing case to justify the need for the coup d'état and the conflict that followed. That which alters the stability of a legitimately constituted régime, however precarious that stability may be, cannot go unexplained.

The New State would invest a large part of its initial efforts in disseminating the idea that the régime it had brought down – the Second Republic – was not legitimate, given that it proposed to abandon national sovereignty by placing it in foreign hands, more specifically, Soviet hands (many claimed that this infiltration had already taken place). It was illegitimate, they claimed, because it was unable to maintain public order, unable to contain street violence, unable to prevent the invasion of national territory, to defend Spanish interests, to preserve the legacy of Catholic tradition and protect the sacred unity of the *Patria*. This need to delegitimise the political adversary had been felt even before the war began, although it became stronger during the course of the war itself and even more intense during the postwar period.

Prior to the *coup d'état*, arguments such as those we have just mentioned were proposed. However, during the war and in its aftermath, other delegitimising arguments were added to the previous ones that referred to the actions of the Republicans during the three-year war and even in exile. In this respect, all those who fought against the Nationalist side were portrayed as being cruel and inhumane in battle; they murdered ruthlessly, destroyed the national heritage (especially religious heritage) and they committed all kinds of outrages wherever they retained political control. Therefore, no desire to forget and no indulgence existed with regard to the defeated. The victory was not shared, although it was rhetorically claimed that both the victory and the peace constituted a legacy to be enjoyed by all Spaniards. In order to justify the continuing vigilance and repression when the war ended, the régime would resort to arguments based on an alleged conspiracy of exiles, one that was kept alive by those outside the country and from within by those who had infiltrated the country. On some occasions it was even claimed that the only desire of the victors was to ensure that the country be free of enemies, so that the régime might progress towards liberalisation as soon as possible.

These arguments were repeated time and again, not only to justify the Uprising, but also the Civil War itself. The crucial part of this explanation claimed that the war had not only been inevitable, but also, and above all, necessary.[22] According to this version, a practically unanimous belief among the victors, the situation in the 1930s had become so shameful that it was necessary to resort to the purifying fire of battle, to the healthy destruction of a series of corrupt structures, to the elimination and expulsion of those who, according to this view, could hinder the future peace of the Spanish nation.

In a somewhat apocalyptic tone, rather in keeping with the new Nationalist–Catholic era, the purifying potential of the destruction and suffering that was proposed was infinite, and essential for the commencement of a new era. Following an unfortunate precedent in Spanish history, national unity was reestablished through the elimination and/or expulsion of the enemy, as had occurred in 1492 with the Jews and in 1502 with the Moors. From this time on, a shameful practice seemed to set in that consisted of dispensing with the adversary, or even eliminating him once he had been defeated, as also occurred partly after the Carlist Wars. No effort in favour of real unity based on tolerance and respect was made. It is not surprising, then, that fictitious and temporary periods of peace were established that never addressed the real problem of harmonious coexistence, nor encouraged any kind of reflection on the matter, which meant that no adequate conflict-solving tradition ever emerged.

In spite of certain shared characteristics with other periods of intolerance within the history of Spain, the Franco era represented a huge qualitative leap regarding the practice of elimination, persecution or sim-

---

22. It was only inevitable, but not necessary, for those, like José María Gil-Robles, who had supported the revolt against the Republic and fought against it in the war, but who subsequently came to adopt a stance of semi-opposition to the Francoist régime. Thus we find that the title of the most famous book by Gil-Robles is *No fue posible la paz* ('Peace was Not Possible'), which is tantamount to saying that the war was inevitable. For those who had fought on the side of the Republic, the war was always something that would never have occurred if the coup d'état had not obliged them to take up arms to defend themselves. The hispanist Edward Malefakis stated in the collection on the Civil War (1936–1939) published by *El País* on the 50th anniversary of the war, that it could well have been avoided.

ple marginalisation of the losing side.[23] The defeated, as we shall see, were eventually invited to rejoin the nation provided that they accepted the rules of the winning side, recognised the legitimacy of the Francoist victory and régime, acknowledged their own errors and performed visible acts of contrition and repentance.[24] They were required, in short, to subject themselves, quite unconditionally, to the political monopoly of the victors. In many cases they were not even able to claim back their former jobs. In the beginning, the reincorporation of the defeated depended, in the most favourable cases, on the good will of the victors and, more specifically, on the guarantees that families of proven loyalty to the régime wished to give them. Initially, these guarantees were indispensable in enabling them to return to the country and find work, although they did not necessarily spare them from judgement or sentencing. They were designed for those who, whilst being emotionally linked to the Second Republic, had not assumed any direct political responsibilities nor committed any crimes that were pending judgement.

Little by little the official discourse was to reveal and exploit the many possibilities of 'peace', until this became the element that endowed the Francoist political régime with the greatest dose of legitimacy. During the 1960s, the press, official publications, Franco himself and the governments appointed by him, repeated with dauntless insistence that the years of peace – or at least, absence of openly-declared war[25] – that Spanish society had witnessed since 1939, constituted such an exceptional period in the history of the country that it had no precedent throughout the previous two centuries. Over and again they recounted the litany of conflicts that had taken place in the past, civil wars and ancestral battles, which, they claimed, had contributed to the dismemberment of the Spanish nation and had been on the point of extinguishing the very essence of the nation during the first third of the twentieth century. Since Spain was in danger of

23. The thoroughness with which this was carried out was made possible by the rigorous confiscation and subsequent classification of documents belonging to the opposing side throughout the war. This was in direct contrast to what occurred, especially at the beginning of the war, in the irregular and sometimes chaotic Republican seizures which, in many cases, destroyed rather than preserved the documents relating to individuals closely involved with the military coup, as was the case with Ramiro de Maeztu. The Francoist side was so scrupulous in its preservation of all documentation because it knew that, if were to win the war, it would be obliged to proceed to a rigorous form of repression in order to survive without suffering setbacks, a task for which it required a considerable amount of information to be able to monitor those who were hostile (or potentially hostile) to the régime.
24. As in the case of the Jews and the Moors, who were allowed to stay after the expulsions of 1492 and 1502 in exchange for their conversion, Francoism was to accept 'the converted'. These admissions were always precarious since, as highlighted by the comparison with the Jews and Moors, the converts were also eventually expelled in the seventeenth century.
25. We must not forget that the years of fighting against the 'maquis' were interpreted by many as a continuation of the Civil War.

being eliminated by the imminent rise to power of the 'Reds', the Uprising was fully justified and with it everything that subsequently occurred.

Once the country began to develop economically, peace became the main legitimising factor for the régime. Peace was necessary, indispensable, for economic prosperity, for the political stability of the régime and for the maintenance of Spanish unity.

Sources of Political Socialisation

Among the sources of socialisation employed by the Franco régime to disseminate its ideology, we might highlight two, given their importance and considerable scope: No-Do and textbooks, although we shall also briefly examine part of the academic historical literature that supported the régime. In this sense, we aim to highlight the Francoist intention of perpetuating a partisan memory of the war.

No-Do

The Historical Archive of Radio Televisión Española contains the collections of what formerly constituted the state-owned body known as No-Do (Noticiarios y Documentales Cinematográficos) founded on 29 September 1942 by agreement of the Vicesecretaría de Educación Popular (Vice-Secretariat for Popular Education) which began to operate in January 1943. In December of that same year this body was granted a monopoly on cinematic news and documentaries and the exhibition of its productions in all commercial cinemas was made compulsory (BOE 22/12/42). This meant that the régime was able to gain exclusive control over both news and documentary productions, using them, at the same time, as a form of propaganda and political socialisation.

Initially, No-Do existed under the auspices of the Vice-Secretariat for Popular Education, subject to the authority of the General Secretary of the Movement. After 1945 this Vice-Secretariat for Popular Education would become the Sub-Department for Popular Education (Sub-secretaría de Educación Popular) attached to the Ministry of National Education. In 1951, No-Do was placed under the authority of the Ministry of Information and Tourism (Ministerio de Información y Turismo) initially attached to the Cinema and Theatre Department (Dirección General de Cinematografía y Teatro) and then, as of 18 January 1968, to the Radio and Television Department (Dirección General de Radiodifusión y Televisión). When this Ministry was dismantled, No-Do was placed under the auspices of the Ministry of Culture. In 1975, a ministerial directive removed the compulsory exhibition clause, becoming effective as of 1 January of the following year, thus coinciding with the decline of No-Do upon Franco's death.[26]

26. BOE No.225, 19/9/75.

This documentary source is of considerable importance in analysing the Franco period and the political culture that existed under the régime. Its dissemination was extensive given that the productions were shown obligatorily and, in particular, as a result of the fact that Spaniards, especially during the early decades of the régime, did not have any other means of gaining access to cheap and attractive culture or entertainment.[27]

The cinema became the most important form of escapism of the Spanish,[28] especially up until the mid-1970s, which is when television began to appear in most Spanish homes.[29] Up until that time, cinema had provided a cheap and accessible source of entertainment and in this respect the extremely wide dissemination of No-Do productions was guaranteed. It was not surprising that No-Do prided itself on placing 'the entire world within the reach of all Spaniards'.

It was precisely in the 1960s when No-Do, having to compete for the first time in its history with another information medium which, in turn, presented much more up-to-date news and documentaries as well as a more varied production, was obliged to change its traditional format and introduce a 'Colour Page', in order to strengthen its appeal. Furthermore, in 1968 it no longer called itself the 'Noticiario Cinematográfico' ('Cinema Newsreel'), becoming the 'Revista Cinematográfica' ('Cinema Magazine'). This signified a new role for No-Do that was 'not to offer news, but to comment upon events that are considered to be common knowledge, to recreate them...to reveal incidents or curiosities that are not known to the public, but that are not linked to current events'. In this respect, according to No-Do itself, it was able 'to carry out an estimable campaign of popular education' (No-Do, 1970: paragraph 4).

According to an article published in the magazine *Primer Plano* of 27 December 1942, the creation of No-Do represented 'a new triumph' for Spanish cinema.[30] The article also stated that this body 'must reflect all of the noble aspects of the life of our nation... It must, in short, inform, instruct and recreate' at the same time as it must 'ridicule the cretins who slander us'. The aim was, 'to produce general propaganda documentaries for our *Patria*' (Cabero, 1949: 518) and 'to disseminate the Work of the

---

27. According to the body's own statement that appeared in an internal publication, 'the only information in moving-pictures that the Spanish public received was that which was provided by NO-DO' (No-Do, 1970: paragraph 4), at least until the arrival of television.

28. Various authors have highlighted the importance of cinema during the period due to the existence of 'an entertainment industry that was not very diversified, where only the Church, bull-fighting, cafés and football offered alternative shows or spectacles'. This, according to the same testimony, made the cinema 'the most effective propaganda instrument for the State' (Hernández, 1976: 161–162).

29. The body Televisión Española was created in 1956, but it was not until the following decade that it began to play a leading role and reached a widespread audience.

30. The expressions 'triumph' or 'triumphal' were widely used in these early years since they directly evoked the recent war victory.

State within the wide-ranging context of national reconstruction', as well as broadcasting documentaries that 'effectively and honourably promote the industrial, aesthetic and folkloric values of our *Patria*' (Cuevas Puente, 1950: 121).

The first No-Do newsreel was shown on Spanish cinema screens on 4 January 1943 and one or two weekly editions of each newsreel were produced intermittently up until 1946, the year in which the two weekly versions became the norm ('A' and 'B'), and continued up until 1960. During this last year, coinciding with the incipient growth of the Spanish economy, three weekly versions of the newsreels began to be produced ('A', 'B' and 'C'), a trend that continued until 1967 when two versions were broadcast again. These two weekly versions continued up until 1977, the year in which only one weekly newsreel was broadcast. Only in 1980 and 1981, the last two years of the existence of No-Do, did the two weekly versions return. Running from number 1,830 up to number 1,935 (corresponding to the years 1978–1980) a version was even produced in Catalan.

The total number of newsreels produced between 1943 and 1981 came to 4,016, not including the documentaries. The documentaries began to be produced in 1945 and came to a total of 498 colour documentaries and 216 black-and-white documentaries. Furthermore, within the No-Do organisation, the cinema magazine programme 'Imágenes' ('Pictures') was produced, which, in turn, featured some 1,219 black-and-white documentaries.[31]

Various testimonies confirm that, during the early postwar years when No-Do newsreels began to be shown, the public gave the productions standing ovations and saluted in the fascist manner. During this period certain members of the audience even sang the *Cara al Sol* ('Face to the Sun') which, according to Sheelagh Ellwood, demonstrated how the régime used the cinema 'for the construction and transmission of its particular system of socio-political values and for the circulation of its own mythology' (Ellwood, 1987: 229).

What is certain is that these newsreels and documentaries constitute an essential source for the study of the régime's discourse regarding numerous aspects of the Civil War; for example: victory marches, the inauguration of monuments to the fallen, the commemoration of diverse war events in various provinces, the setting-up of fraternities of war-veterans, the reconstruction of towns and cities devastated by the war, the celebration of 18 July, the 25 Years of Peace etc. Very few sources offer such an excellent opportunity to analyse the propaganda of the Franco régime, and they could hardly have guaranteed such high audience figures. No-Do was, furthermore, an important organisation in itself, given that it was an institution created by Francoism in order to legitimise its régime.

31. See the No-Do General Numerical Tables.

The considerable complexity of this source calls for some prior methodological clarifications in order to explain how the information that is subsequently commented upon has been extracted. The summaries of all the versions of each newsreel contain an outline which includes the general title of each item of news and a brief résumé of that news.[32] Each version of the newsreel has a summary containing various items of news. The average number of news items varies between five and ten depending on the period, and the average duration of a news item is approximately ten minutes. Finally, the newsreels can also be consulted in original format or on video.

This research is primarily based on the newsreel scripts. Those news items were chosen from among all the summaries (4,016) that revealed some kind of connection to the Civil War. Then, a sample of all the news scripts was extracted, based on two criteria. First, certain key years regarding the commemoration of the Civil War were chosen, such as 1961 and 1964, along with other important years for the régime, such as the first three years of No-Do broadcasting, 1943 to 1945, these being the final years of the Second World War, as well as all of the years between 1975 and 1981. Second, samples were taken every five years, with the following years being chosen: 1943–1945, 1950, 1955, 1960, 1961, 1964, 1965, 1970, 1975–1981.

Having established from the summaries those scripts which, either directly or indirectly, evoked the Civil War at that time, both a quantitative and qualitative study was carried out using the script texts.[33] Through an analysis of these texts, we attempted to observe whether any development existed regarding the régime's handling of the history of the Civil War, and to discover what kind of memory of the war the régime tried to create during the various stages that the country witnessed over these years. Having completed an initial study of the contents of the news items selected, the following analytical categories were established in order to classify them both qualitatively and quantitatively:

(1) Direct and explicit evocation of the Civil War.
(2) Implicit evocation of the Civil War.
  (2[a]) The Victory Parade.
  (2[b]) Twenty Five Years of Peace.
(3) Monuments, buildings and commemorative plaques relating to the Civil War.
  (3[a]) The Alcázar of Toledo.
  (3[b]) The Valley of the Fallen.
(4) Indirect references to the Civil War in speeches.

---

32. See the summary on the cover of Newsreel No.1, page 427.
33. The information contained in the news items selected appears in summarised form in my doctoral thesis, published in a non-commercial edition by the Instituto Juan March in 1995 under the title *La memoria histórica de la Guerra Civil española (1936–1939): un proceso de aprendizaje político*.

In addition to the news contents, the duration of the news was also taken into account, as well as the order in which it appeared within the newsreel, in order to analyse the development of No-Do's treatment of the war. In the No-Do Numerical Tables relating to the Civil War a number of totals appear that enabled us to create the No-Do Graphs. The first table refers to overall results, whilst the rest refer to the various analytical categories separately.

TOTAL 1: Time devoted during that year to the remembrance of the Civil War (28 metres of film is approximately equivalent to one minute).

TOTAL 2: Percentage of newsreels that include some kind of reference to the Civil War out of the total number of newsreels for the year.

TOTAL 3: References to the war according to analytical category.

TOTAL 4: Percentage of news items relating to the war that occupy the first or last place within the newsreel (reserved for the most important news) out of the total number of news items recorded.

TOTAL 5: Number of news items a year that make reference to the Republicans.

TOTAL 6: Number of minutes a year devoted to the Victory Parade.

A brief description of the graphs enables us to trace the development of Francoist discourse on the Civil War quite precisely. Graph 2.1 shows the overall total for the number of minutes devoted to the remembrance of the Civil War. If we remove the years 1961 and 1964 from this first graph, we can see that, following the considerable importance attached to the war in 1943 – the first year of No-Do broadcasting – a sharp decline took place, followed by a levelling-off to between twenty and thirty minutes a year, an output that was only altered in 1975, the year of Franco's death. That was again followed by a sharp decline and even the complete disappearance of such references in the years 1978 and 1981.

The first decline, after 1943, may well have been due to developments relating to the Second World War. Up until that year many believed that a victory of the Axis Powers was possible, and it was not until 1944 that the course of the war changed and the scales began to weigh in favour of the Allies. The Franco régime, which had declared its sympathy for, and affinity with, the fascist countries on so many occasions, began to sense the negative consequences that Spain might have to face if the Axis lost the war. The insistently heroic and black-and-white version of the Civil War, the only view espoused by the régime during the early years, was appropriate as long as expectations were maintained that Germany and Italy would triumph. It was thought that if the political model that was imposed on Europe were similar to that of Spain, then the situation would stabilise until it was definitively consolidated. Nevertheless, if Germany and Italy lost the war, the Spanish model would fall into disgrace among the democratic countries that would now predominate, and if the losing side in the Spanish Civil War were capable of effectively mobilising the winners of the Second World War, the Spanish political régime might well begin to be marginalised, or even openly attacked from abroad at a time of extreme economic difficulty. It could be said that the rhetoric of the régime, both with regard to the quantity and quality of the Francoist references to the war, constitutes an interesting yardstick which enables us to gain an insight into the pretensions of the régime and the backtracking it was prepared to undertake in order to remain in power, both at home and abroad.

Finally, the years 1961 and 1964, marking the twenty-fifth anniversary of the beginning of the civil war and its end, respectively, and thus being especially important years regarding the memory of the war, correspond to a pronounced rise in the curve that represents the official memory of the Civil War. Nevertheless, as we shall see in our study of the analytical categories, the kinds of issues focused on were different to those of before. The tone was now more technical, less political, and, of course, much less anachronistic. The last increase in the amount of time devoted to the war took place in 1975, which may well have signified a last warning from the régime to the Spanish nation in view of the changes that were envisaged upon Franco's death.

In Graph 2.2 we can observe the percentage of newsreels in which references were made to the Civil War out of the total number of newsreels that were produced each year. The pattern up until 1961 is very similar to that of the previous graph. Nevertheless, 1961 not only fails to witness any sharp rise, but even falls, although only slightly. Neither can we observe any sharp rise in 1975, although the rest of the years are very similar. Therefore, in spite of the fact that more minutes were devoted to recalling the war in 1961 and 1975, fewer, rather than more, newsreels actually touched on the subject during these years. The allusions to the war were not, therefore, as dispersed as in other years, but were concentrated within fewer newsreels, featuring longer news items.

The percentage-based comparison of the references to the four wide-ranging analytical categories is represented in Graph 2.3. The variables 2T and 3T group together the remaining references that have the same number (2, 2^a, 2^b and 3, 3^a, 3^b, respectively). Out of the news items that refer to the war, the percentage of those that refer to each analytical category out of the total has been calculated.[34]

The first category, (1), which represents explicit references to the war, rises slightly until 1945, only to fall again, and even disappear at the beginning of the 1960s. After 1961 it was to disappear again and reemerge

---

34. Due to the possible confusion that the four intercrossing lines in this graph might produce, other graphs have been included separately for each analytical category. Graph 2.3.1. contains the first (1); Graph 2.3.2. contains the second (2T); Graph 2.3.3., the third (3T); and Graph 2.3.4., the fourth (4).

in 1970, being the only category that rose spectacularly after 1978, the year in which the other categories disappeared. In 1978 no news items were produced in which we were able to find even indirect references to the war, despite such references occurring frequently just a year before. As we shall see when studying the Transition, 1978, the year in which the Spanish Constitution was put to referendum, was quite possibly the year that the greatest need for consensus was required and the year that the greatest effort was made to bring about a reconciliation among the Spanish.

The second category, (2), which refers to the celebrations and com-memorations of the war that were frequently organised to mark an anniversary of the conflict, began by being the most important and then declined up until the mid-1950s only to reemerge strongly during the 1960s. It was during this decade that the régime implemented its greatest legitimisation drive through the staging of ceremonies, blending origin-based legitimacy with performance-based legitimacy, as in the '25 Years of Peace'. As of 1975, this category would progressively decline until it finally disappeared in 1977.

The third category, (3), which refers to the most graphic and perennial aspects of memory (monuments etc.) began at a low level, probably as a result of the precarious economic situation, but became more prominent during the 1950s, when the Valley of the Fallen was inaugurated. After the supreme financial effort entailed by the construction of this monu-ment in 1959, this category was to follow a downward course, except for a few brief and rather mild exceptions, disappearing entirely in 1977.

Finally, category (4), the widest of them all, which refers to indirect references to the war, began from the lowest possible starting-point, given that references to the war were initially almost exclusively direct and graphic. It maintained this level until 1964, when a considerable change took place in the régime's rhetoric. From then on, the régime continued to refer to the war, but the mentions were less frequent and more dis-creet. The direct and indirect references, as we can observe in the graphs, generally follow opposing directions until 1964 (when one rises and the other falls), and then rise together slightly as the other two categories fall significantly, eventually settling at an equal level in 1975. Subsequently, whilst the explicit references continue to fall until the year of the Con-stitution, the implicit references increase. In 1979 and 1980 No-Do, clearly under new management and serving different purposes, not only placed itself at the service of democracy, but also set about rehabilitating, as far as possible, various members of the losing side. In this sense, the only references to the war during these years were explicit and they all related to the losing side.

The three remaining graphs hardly require any explanation. Graph 2.4 reflects the quality of the news relating to the war (measured by the number of times this news appears in a prominent position within the newsreel) which, as we shall see, is quite high, given that it only falls below fifty percent in 1975. It is not only a question of the war featuring on No-Do with a certain frequency, but that when this kind of news does appear, it is placed in a position of honour within the newsreel as a whole. Graph 2.5 shows the news items on the war in which some kind of reference is made to the defeated. In the beginning, a greater need existed for the régime to refer to the image of the defeated in order to demonise and condemn them. As time passed, the defeated became a kind of invisible presence that it was better not to refer to if possible, given that any mention of them would evoke the tragedy of the dispersion and the rift that had taken place within Spanish society. The memory of the Civil War was bitter, both for the defeated who remained in Spain as well as for the victors, although for different reasons, and because of this, a relative and imposed amnesia was resorted to. Only after 1975 would such references reemerge, although this time with rare intensity and in a very different form.

Finally, Graph 2.6 presents the total minutes per year devoted to the Victory Parade ('El Desfile de la Victoria'). The year that greatest importance was accorded to this ceremony was 1961, the year which marked the twenty-fifth anniversary of the beginning of the war. Considerable attention continued to be paid to this event in 1964, when it was commemorated under the name of the Peace Parade ('El Desfile de la Paz'). Then a sharp fall took place, although a slight recovery was witnessed in 1975. The prominence of news items on the Victory Parade within the newsreels as a whole is overwhelming. Only on three occasions do these news items fail to occupy first or last place in the newsreel. Even the last parade, which took place in 1977, continues to play a prominent role within the newsreel.[35]

In addition to the newsreels that this study has been based on, there are three documentaries on the war deposited in the No-Do archives. Two of them, one British-made and the other American, were produced using footage from the war itself. The first was made in 1965 under the title 'The Spanish Turmoil' and the second, in 1968, under the title 'Only the Brave Are Free'. Finally, a Spanish documentary on the war can be found in the archive which was also made with footage from the war in 1959, the year that marked the twentieth anniversary of the end of the conflict and the inauguration of the Valley of the Fallen. Its title is a faithful reflection of the change that had begun to be implemented in the remembrance of the war: 'El Camino de la Paz' ('The Path of Peace').[36] The Civil War began to be presented as the only and obligatory course

35. The documentary department at the No-Do Archive produced its own list of newsreels on the War, entitled 'Guerra Civil Española en el Noticiario No-Do', based on footage that appeared in the newsreels regarding the Civil War (See the No-Do Appendices).
36. Topographical catalogue number: 149 (No-Do Archive); 7 rolls; duration approximately 64 minutes.

towards peace. This documentary promotes an extremely black-and-white viewpoint, but one in which we can already make out certain conciliatory overtones. It talks about the 'Reds' and the 'Nationalists', but also about the 'Civil War' as such, in place of the War of Liberation or the Crusade. The picture it depicts of the war is more tragic than heroic, although the heroism is associated primarily with the Nationalist side. The narrative is also quite conventional: it talks about churches having been set alight and destroyed and about the outrages committed by the 'Reds', never those of the other side; although certain virtues are granted to the defeated, at no point does the documentary establish an equal share of guilt. This initial mood deliberately creates a climate of violence that seeks to lead the viewer towards the conclusion that the war was inevitable, necessary and indispensable, both in establishing peace and in banishing the fratricidal instinct of the Spanish.

One of the clearest aims of this documentary was to ensure that nobody should forget the events that took place. All of the footage used in making the documentary was taken during the conflict itself. This was not an attempt, as in 1964, to commemorate 20 years of peace by exhibiting the achievements of the régime. 1959 was the year that the country began to emerge from crisis, thanks to the Stabilisation Plan, even though its effects would take some years to appear. In 'El Camino de la Paz' the Civil War was the only protagonist, as the documentary emphasised the idea that the conflict was undertaken in order to achieve the peace that was now being enjoyed. Five years later, as we can see, the idea of peace was associated with progress and development and the claim was made that these social goods were only made possible by the peace, which, in turn, only existed because of the war. In this way, all the loose ends were tied up in the reasoning that official sources employed to establish the legitimacy of the régime. It was the victory of the Nationalists that 'cleared away such nightmares from the face of Spain forever'.

The documentary ends with the following words:

> This was the path towards peace. A painful course that left thousands of dead in its wake. This was Total Victory, a victory for all; nobody was left by the wayside, excluded or abandoned... The blood shed by all those who fell does not abide the possibility of forgetfulness, futility or betrayal. It fell to some to fight for Spain, that was losing it way, making the ultimate sacrifice in order to achieve it. Today it is a matter of preserving what has been achieved and working to achieve what is required, with the no less heroic effort of the quiet labour of each day, so that that generous sacrifice may ever yield an era of peace for our *Patria*. And so, together, we pray to God that blood should never more be shed in Spain in civil wars and 'that our victory should be an entire verse in Spain's glorious and universal song.[37]

37.   'El Camino de la Paz', roll 7. Topographical catalogue number: 149 (No-Do Archive).

No-Do also produced the film magazine programme 'Imágenes' ('Pictures'), and this programme, throughout a good part of 1964, devoted eight episodes to commemorating the '25 Years of Peace'.[38] In order to mark this anniversary, No-Do also covered, among other events, the meetings of veterans that were held in various Spanish provinces to celebrate the 'liberation'. The reports were to talk about peace, but also about the crusade and victory, never about civil war; monuments were raised to the heroes of the war and homage was paid to the martyrs to the cause and the fallen.

For a long time, the only film footage of what was happening both abroad and in Spain was produced by No-Do, featuring the especially high impact and credibility typical of graphic reports. It would have been difficult during the years of the Transition to find anybody who had not seen various newsreels in their life, even among the youngest members of society (let us not forget that the broadcasting of these newsreels was compulsory until 1975 and that, between 1976 and 1981, various cinemas continued to hire the reports). The decline of No-Do coincided exactly with Franco's death, and it was then that a drastic reduction in the number of newsreels a year was witnessed. We can also observe a clear shift in the ideological premises of the productions. At this point, as we mentioned above, No-Do's documentaries began to play a supporting role for democracy and its institutions, and No-Do even seemed to set itself the task of undertaking the rehabilitation of the defeated, devoting the few news items that referred to the war (either directly or indirectly) to certain Spanish figures from exile.

Historical Narrative

Our objective is not to carry out an exhaustive analysis of Francoist textbooks, a task that has already been carried out, at least for the first half of the 1950s.[39] We simply aim to provide a brief presentation of the development of the narrative relating to the Civil War in the history and politics textbooks (such as those on the 'Training of the National Spirit') that were used at various teaching levels.[40]

38. This great event was to be more widely commented upon later on. The titles of these eight episodes included the following:
   - No. 1017: 'Veinticinco Años de Arte'.
   - No. 1022: 'Veinticinco Años de Agricultura'.
   - No. 1025: 'Veinticinco Años de Desarrollo Industrial'.
   - No. 1028: 'España y el Mundo (XXV Años de Paz)'.
   - No. 1031: 'Veinticinco Años de Espectáculos'.
   - No. 1034: 'España Edifica'.
   - No. 1037: 'España Edifica'.
   - No. 1040: 'Cultura Española'.
39. See the works of Rafael Valls (1983; 1984; 1986; 1988; 1990; 1991), Gregorio Cámara (1984) and Luis Martínez-Risco (1991), among others.
40. The bibliography includes both the textbooks themselves that were consulted for this section, as well as the secondary bibliography of studies that were produced based on textbooks.

The most important texts for this study include those that represented a change of course regarding the narrative on the war, which coincide with the texts that had the largest print runs and the most numerous reprints. These textbooks were produced by the publishing company Doncel for the National Youth Delegation (Delegación Nacional de Juventudes). As one scholar on the Youth Front (Frente de Juventudes) has stated when talking about the publishing change that was witnessed under the management of Jesús López-Cancio, Doncel was created at the end of the 1950s 'as a commercial body which included the Political Education texts among its star-collections, whose purchase was compulsory for secondary school students' (Sáez, 1988: 405). This was the publishing company that influenced a large part of the political, economic and cultural élite of the Transition, broadly the same élite that survives to the present day.[41]

During the Spanish postwar period a number of textbooks were adopted which, in many cases, originated from previous periods and were rapidly revised and updated in order to include both the Civil War and the New State. They also had to offer a version of the Republic that was consistent with the justification of the Uprising and subsequent Civil War, as well as a general version of Spanish history that coincided with that espoused by the supporters of the Franco régime.

In 1940 a book by Agustín Serrano de Haro was published entitled *España es así* ('Spain is Like That'), a work that was reprinted several times and that even received an award from the Manuel Llorente Foundation.[42] This text is typical of the period, given that it follows the classic schema which consisted in first recounting what we might call 'the

41. The books published by Doncel were obligatory throughout the period that has been studied least by pedagogues and historians who have analysed textbooks: the late 1950s and 1960s. All of the *Doncel* texts consulted, except for two, the book by Fernández Carvajal and the one by Hellmuth Günther Dahms, belong to the collection 'Educación Política'.

42. In the 1940s the same author published a book entitled *Yo soy español* ('I am Spanish') which was reprinted several times. This text was aimed at first-year school-children studying history and sought to instil a xenophobic black-and-white image of the most famous Spanish legends. It might almost be said that the books encouraged children, through a series of extremely violent illustrations, to give up their lives for God and for the Patria, suffering terrible physical torture and even death in the process, should this be required. The story is told of the alleged murder of the children Justo and Pastor by the Romans, and the crucifixion of Dominguito by the Jews, upon which the author writes: 'Even the children gave their lives gladly for Jesus' and 'the children died so happily because they were giving their lives for Jesus' (Serrano de Haro, 1962: 29; 31). After relating the episode of the defence of the Alcázar in Toledo by General Moscardó, the children were recommended to repeat the following prayer: 'Moscardó allowed his son to be killed in order not to surrender the Alcázar in Toledo. I am prepared to sacrifice everything for God and for Spain' (Serrano de Haro, 1962: 87). The book ends by stating that 'if Spain needs my life, my life I must give' (Serrano de Haro, 1962: 92).

disasters of the Republic' in order to demonstrate the illegitimate nature of a régime overwhelmed by political chaos and disorder on the streets. It then goes on to describe the 'assassination of José Antonio', the 'Glorious Uprising', 'the Red terror', 'the religious persecution', and finally reserves a special section for the figure of 'the Caudillo' in an attempt to strengthen his leadership by attributing certain extraordinary character traits to him, as well as powerful charismatic qualities.[43] It ends, however, with what was at the time an atypical recommendation, 'Let us forever forget the rancour and discord that troubled our peace and shed blood on our soil and let us strengthen our ties of mutual understanding and trust' (Serrano de Haro, 1940: 323).

The same thematic outline is shared, with very few differences, by the texts written by Antonio Ballesteros Beretta (1942), Ernesto Giménez Caballero (1943), Ricardo Ruiz Carnero (1943), the *Manual de Historia de España y Lecturas Históricas* (1944), *Lecturas* (1949), those that formed part of *Historia de España* produced by the publishing company Bruño (1948 and 1949), *Historia de España* by the publishing company Luis Vives (1951), the book by Manuel Álvarez Lastra (1955), José L. Asián Peña (1955), Alejandro Manzanares Beriain (1957) and many others.[44] It is true that after the Second World War the texts tended to tone down the fascist symbols, and references to the Axis Powers, as well as to the Second World War itself, were dealt with more prudently and distantly. Nevertheless, the treatment afforded to the Second Republic, the Civil War and the early years of the Franco régime hardly varied.

An heroic depiction of events predominated, more so in the books aimed at a young readership (the younger the readers, the more distorted the image conveyed to them) whose unconditional loyalty to the Francoist cause was sought through a sense of patriotic exaltation. The tragic element in these early versions formed part of the heroic narrative. This sense of tragedy was not unmitigated, but it was precisely this tragic dimension that led to the exaltation of the epic tale and the heroic sense of the narrative. The evaluation of the leading historical protagonists

43. The children's comic entitled *Caudillo invicto* ('Unbeaten Leader') was published at the end of the 1960s and, in spite of this late date, emphasises the super-human characteristics of the 'Caudillo'.

44. This uniformity is logical if we take into account the recommendations that Eladio García Martínez made to the rest of the primary school teachers in 1941 in his book *La Enseñanza de la Historia en la Escuela Primaria*. Not only does he not hide the War from children, but he even praises it by emphasising, 'those armed events that produced a clear and strong desire to live in a more dignified way, guaranteeing the independence of peoples... And in ours, more than in others, the Nation and the Army together have ensured the continuation of our historical being more than once' (García Martínez, 1941: 15).

accorded absolute priority to militaristic virtues such as bravery, heroism and self-denial.

Generally, the Civil War was not referred to as such, but was nearly always called the 'Crusade' or the 'War of Liberation' or the 'Glorious Uprising', deceiving the youngest readers about the fratricidal nature of the war. An attempt was made to convey the image that the battle was not fought against an internal enemy, against a Spanish opponent, but that the 'Nationalists' were forced to confront foreign invading forces (thus the expression 'War of Liberation' and the parallels that were very often drawn with the War of Independence against the French). At best, the enemy was anti-Spanish, a traitor to the *Patria* who had conspired with the greatest communist power, the USSR, to set up a proletarian dictatorship in Spain. It was a matter of good against evil, of Spanishness against anti-Spanishness, of believers against atheists (thus the expression 'the Crusade', which was coined by the Spanish Church), of law-abiding people against anarchists, of reason against barbarism.

These early textbooks do not present any significant variations that allow us to observe any differences in the treatment afforded to the defeated, in their view of the war or in their interpretation of the history of Spain. However, as time passed and the roar of battle died down the narratives began to adopt a more serene approach, new alternative versions began to appear.

In the mid-1950s certain changes took place that made it possible to modify the initial atmosphere in the classroom. According to Manuel de Puelles, who has analysed the question of ideology in Spanish school education, 'when the Civil War broke out, education began to be employed entirely as an ideological instrument' (De Puelles, 1986: 348). Later on, when the Civil War ended, 'all of the teachers who were able to prove their hostility to the Republic nevertheless had to undergo various examinations and follow a series of professional orientation courses in order to imbue them with the religious and patriotic meaning that underlay our Crusade' (De Puelles, 1986: 368–369). With the appointment of Joaquín Ruíz-Giménez as Minister of Education in 1951, a certain flexibility was introduced into the education system. Thus, although 'ideological values persisted...exalted nationalism tended to decrease'; 'the new law of 26 February 1953 – Ley de Ordenación de la Enseñanza Media / Law on the Planning of Secondary Education – not only represented the repeal of the law of 1938, but also managed to go beyond the belligerent context in which the latter was created' (De Puelles: 1986, 387).

Later on, towards the end of the 1950s, some texts attempted to present the Civil War as the result of an unfortunate autochthonous historical tradition according to which, due to the decadent state that the country had fallen into, especially since the end of the nineteenth century, the Spanish had become embroiled in various fratricidal disputes for any reason whatsoever.[45] This seems to have been an attempt to eliminate the unusual nature of the latest, longest and most painful of wars by interpreting it in the light of a long process of national disorders which inevitably led to the last and definitive confrontation, one that would put an end to all the rest and to the causes that made them possible. By linking the war of 1936 with previous civil wars, it not only became a necessary result of the disorder witnessed under the Republic, but it also became quite irremediable, as it had been brewing for decades and nothing can stand against the tide of history. This interpretation also served to legitimise Francoism as the maker and executor of peace, and delegitimise liberal and democratic régimes for being eternal harbingers of discord, chaos and, consequently, war.

When Spain began to be accepted into international circles, this aggressive rhetoric was progressively modified. At the same time, members of society had the opportunity to observe that traditional democracies such as the democratic system in England existed, that did not undergo civil wars or especially virulent disturbances. That was when these initial versions began to be qualified by the modification that it was not simply a matter of inorganic democracies being perverse in themselves, but that the Spanish nation, due to its intrinsic characteristics and its historical development, was not capable of living under régimes of this kind, as demonstrated by the failure of the two Republican experiments. Therefore, although establishing relations with democratic countries was perfectly compatible with the objective of maintaining 'national essences', Spain had to defend the unique features of its organic democracy, which seemed to be tailor-made for it, with the sole purpose of maintaining peace at home. Any other democratic experiment would lead, once again, to war. This ended the possibility of any development of the régime taking place, without any further justification being required. As one of the books at the time claimed: 'peace would not have been possible for us under the systems and régimes which preceded us' (Various Authors, 1945: 181).

Curiously, in 1959 a somewhat critical version of the situation at that time appeared. It is no coincidence that this text was produced by the Sección Femenina ('Women's Section') of FET and of the JONS given that the 'camisas viejas' or 'old shirts' of the Falange, the staunchest defenders of the creed according to José Antonio Primo de Rivera, were the ones

---

45. The text by Fernández-Miranda states the following: 'The sad history of Spain from the time of Fernando VII to the present day is the history of a nation which fails to achieve Statehood and which sheds blood in constant civil war, which is repeated time and again. The historical significance of the Spanish crusade of '18 July' and the field of political organization which it made possible, is precisely based on the tense and sustained effort to achieve a *definitive victory*, that is to say, an *unavoidable* order and an *indestructible* peace' (Fernández-Miranda, 1960: 117).

who had felt most intensely disappointed, and even deceived, by the course that the régime had taken. These purist Falangists were able to act with greatest freedom and impunity within the Falange youth organisations (Frente de Juventudes and Sindicato Español Universitario, as well as in the Falangist publications aimed at a youth readership[46]) and in the Sección Femenina. The Sección Femenina, headed by José Antonio's sister, Pilar Primo de Rivera, was considered by the régime to be a somewhat stubborn women's organisation that posed little threat to its integrity. Thus, members of this organisation spoke about 'the Spanish Civil War' and stated that 'the revolution still remains to be waged; the problems, more or less attenuated and evolved, still exist which gave rise to the birth of a revolutionary conscience among Spaniards...since this has not coincided with the dismantling of capitalism, rather the latter has considerably increased its dimensions. Historical pessimism, on the other hand, has very often been replaced with an easy and pompous jingoism' (Sección Femenina, 1959: 116).

The degree to which all of these versions from the early Franco period (up until the mid-1950s) may have influenced the historical memory of the schoolchildren of the time is difficult to measure. Nevertheless, it appears that those who were subjected to the most black-and-white versions, in the 1940s and early 1950s, having subsequently gained access to other interpretations or received different versions at home, may have been able to reject what they were taught as children.

When alternative and supposedly different memories to the official version exist, it is difficult to impose the truth of the official version, in spite of repression and the uniformity of the messages conveyed.

The versions produced during the second stage, basically those offered by Doncel, did appear, however, to have made a deeper impression, at least with regard to the lessons that were to be extracted from the experience of the Civil War, which now began to be referred to as such in the majority of texts produced by this publishing company. Furthermore, in general, derogatory labels such as 'Reds', 'Marxist hordes' and others of a similar nature were abandoned. The virtues that these texts attempted to foster in young people related to the ideas of tolerance, dialogue and peace, in contrast to the martial values of the early years. In short, these virtues included any that favoured a sense of 'national harmony', which appears to have been the priority of the generation that played the leading role during the Transition.

At the end of the 1950s and during the early 1960s, the first editions of the 'Political Education' texts by Doncel began to appear.[47] In 1959,

---

46. In relation to this matter, see the book by Juan F. Marsal (1979).
47. The texts by Enrique Fuentes Quintana and Javier Velarde Fuertes (1968), and that of Efrén Borrajo Dacruz (1965) are not analysed as they do not contain any references of interest to this study.

Eugenio Frutos wrote *La Convivencia Humana* ('Harmonious Human Coexistence') whose title is already quite revealing. The régime began to show a certain concern for the problems of coexistence that had afflicted the Spanish of recent decades. This word would begin to appear in great abundance within the press and in political essays, also providing a point of reference for the books that appear below.[48] In the preface, Frutos stated that with this book he aimed to facilitate 'necessary social coexistence' (Frutos, 1959: 9). Furthermore, the book was an attempt to legitimise the Franco régime, given that 'authority' was presented as an essential and inalienable factor in obtaining national unity, social order and peace, all essential elements of successful coexistence. The performance-based legitimacy espoused in the textbooks produced during this period was based on its capacity to maintain order and peace within the Spanish nation, rather than on the economic achievements of the régime. Frutos claimed that the Delegación Nacional de Juventudes (National Youth Delegation) was created at the end of the war because 'the Spanish State, keen to avoid further civil unrest, realised the need to provide young people with an adequate political education in order to achieve the unity and historical continuity of our *Patria*' (Frutos, 1959: 153). The main objective of the Delegación, therefore, consisted, 'in civil training for a better and happier coexistence among Spaniards' (Frutos, 1959: 154). It was at this time that the question of Spanish regional plurality and diversity and its rich benefits began to be discussed, as well as the respect, understanding and even encouragement that these unique aspects deserved to receive, issues that had been completely overlooked in many school textbooks up until that time.

The following year, 1960, Torcuato Fernández-Miranda published *El Hombre y la Sociedad* ('Man and Society') featuring a first print run of 50,000 copies. In the introduction, the author declared that the book had been written 'based on a healthy desire for a stable and definitive coexistence, founded on justice and peace, for our nation' (Fernández-Miranda, 1960: 10). The aim of all these texts was, evidently, to socialise young people by inculcating them with the values of peace, coexistence, order, tolerance and harmony, in order to avoid, in this way, any future repetition of the Civil War, an obsessive aim pursued by a large majority of the authors of these handbooks.[49] The aim was to inculcate the new generations with their own historical learning in order to prevent them from repeating the same mistakes as their elders.

In 1961 Gaspar Gómez de la Serna published a highly revealing text entitled *Cartas a mi hijo* ('Letters to My Son'). The first edition, which had

48. Fraga, for example, wrote a book in 1961 entitled *Organización de la Convivencia* in which he dealt with the Civil War, origin-based legitimacy and the need for peaceful national coexistence.

49. Fernández-Miranda refers on various occasions to Thomas Hobbes, possibly the most ardent of political theorists in the cause of avoiding civil war.

a print run of 75,000 copies, was reprinted at least eight times, in addition to winning the *Premio Nacional '18 de Julio'* (18 July National Prize) in the year that it came out. This was one of the first texts that employed the metaphor for the Civil War that would later become so popular, referring to it as 'collective insanity'. Here, the Civil War finally took on completely tragic overtones, unmitigated by heroic references of any kind. It was:

the worst kind of monologue capable of shattering national harmony...that which rises up like a deadly spectre on each side of the trenches of a civil war. This is the worst of all afflictions that can befall a country; that which, at any cost, must be avoided forever.

He continues by means of an entirely original line of thought:

I am not going to speak of the last Civil War, precisely because it was your father's generation that was called to play the leading role in it and this war is so close that I would not wish my words, tainted as they still are by blood and suffering, to seem to you to be the passionate echo of one of those dramatic monologues that sustained it. On the other hand, unfortunately Spain has, with depressing frequency, since the second half of the nineteenth century, insisted on destroying itself in civil wars, so that now we have ample testimony of these conflicts in the form of past and objective history.

For the first time, the Civil War was concealed on the excuse that it was impossible to maintain a sense of impartiality. Even the acknowledgement of this was new, as if it were a shameful episode. This was a war that a father, having participated in it, would not relate to his son with all the epic pride of the great battles, but that he would prefer to conceal from the child, protecting him from such a painful, although instructive, memory. In order not to lose the didactic nature of the experience and the lessons relating to dialogue, tolerance and the concept of 'never again', the author referred to other Spanish civil wars, not simply with the intention of narrating them to his son (for he states that he will find 'blood and destruction' all around him), but in order to observe that in all of these wars beats 'an awareness of the enormous disgrace that befalls the country'. In this respect he ends by quoting a text taken from the draft of the Vergara Accord which brought the Carlist Wars to an end. The choice of this text was no coincidence; as is well known, the last civil war did not end with any kind of accord.

The message of historical learning is explicit and self-evident and reads:

what I now need to emphasise to you...is that, in the same way in which you must employ your will in order to participate in national unity through dialogue, you must also employ all your strength to prevent your *Patria* from splitting itself in two in a civil war. (all of the quotations are from Goméz de la Serna, 1961: 157–167)

Gonzalo Torrente Ballester wrote *Aprendiz de Hombre* ('Apprentice of Man') in 1965, and, after just two years, nine editions had already been published of this work. This book emphasised the idea of solidarity and highlighted the virtue that consists of 'knowing how to win and knowing how to lose'. It reads as follows:

> Victory can offend the dignity of the loser and this reduces the dignity of the victor. The loser can offend the dignity of the victor and sour his triumph. What a difficult game it is, this game of victory and defeat! (Torrente Ballester, 1965: 222)

It seems obvious that this is nothing if not a metaphor for the war.

The narrative style of Gómez de la Serna's work is shared by Eugenio de Bustos in his book *Vela y Ancla* ('Sail and Anchor') where a father also explains various matters to his son by means of literary or historical illustrations. However, this author drifts away slightly from the general tone of the books published by Doncel, imposing a more heroic value on the war than the rest by reproducing the words uttered by José Antonio before the tomb of Matías Montero and by highlighting the sense of loyalty that derives from an inheritance of 'pain and glory mixed with blood' (De Bustos, 1966: 174).

The books by José M. Poveda Ariño, *Formación Social* ('Social Training') and *Convivencia Social* ('Social Harmony') resume the course set by the publishing company. Both books begin with a paragraph that relates the first successful ascent of Mount Everest, which runs as follows:

> for the first time a victory of a group of men did not imply the defeat of any opposing side. There was not, nor had there been, any opposing side...they turned their victory into a victory for us all...an enterprise that did not pursue material goals...let alone partisan objectives. (Poveda, 1966)

The historical parallel that is intended by this example is obvious. According to Poveda, the Franco régime intended to distribute the fruits of victory among all Spaniards – at least, this was the aspiration to be pursued. The first of these books places special emphasis on strengthening 'peaceful coexistence' and on the defects that Spaniards were obliged to fight against if they were to achieve it. This line of thought is followed in the second book, although this work is seasoned with a slightly more heroic description of the war.

In spite of their similarities with other textbooks of the period, it is clear that the books produced by Doncel afforded a unique and innovative treatment of the Civil War and of the lessons that were to be derived from it, which, quite possibly, would have made an impression on those who read them. It is impossible to be sure whether these texts exercised a definitive influence on their age, or whether the publishers at Doncel limited themselves to simply reflecting the collective memory that began to emerge at that time, reproducing it in their books. The fact is that the lessons regarding the Civil War that formed the majority consensus and that were applied during the Transition coincide, in large part, with those that were espoused in the books produced by this publisher.

In addition to school texts, we must also analyse the role played by professional historians. Some authors claim that it is the historian who lays down the guidelines regarding what must or must not be recollected and who popularises the memories that are to be retained based on the interests of the present. Nevertheless, as Schwartz has stated, the construction of social memory is a process of mutual influence between the 'producers' and the 'consumers' of memory. In fact, according to Schwartz, the producers do nothing but follow the consumers in the reconstruction of history.

The truth is that historical production played an important role in legitimising the régime throughout this entire period, especially what we might call 'official history', which includes both the history produced by the régime's institutions (for instance, the 'Department for Studies On the War of Spain' within the Ministry of Information and Tourism, which was headed by Ricardo de la Cierva) as well as that history generated by historians who openly defended Francoism.[50]

Ricardo de la Cierva joined the Ministry of Information and Tourism in 1964[51] through the public entrance examinations system. His university training had nothing to do with history, but, upon being placed in charge of the Documentation Department at the Ministry, replete, it seems, with books on the Civil War, his vocation changed. In 1965 a 'Special Department' was created within the Ministry for the study of the Civil War, with De la Cierva in charge. The purpose of this Department was to counterbalance the influence of the foreign publications on the Spanish Civil War that slipped across the borders so easily, by launching, with official backing, a more objective view of the conflict than that which had been propounded up until that time, whilst maintaining a favourable and apologetic tone with regard to the Nationalist side and the régime.[52]

50. We shall not carry out an exhaustive analysis of the historiography of the period, but shall only briefly study those cases that we consider to be most representative of the part of governmental historiographic production that possessed the greatest pretensions of rigorousness and objectivity, aspects which lend it a certain weight.

51. A good part of the information that appears here regarding Ricardo de la Cierva is based on a personal interview that I held with him on 26 November 1991.

52. The story that Ricardo de la Cierva tells in order to explain the creation of this Department is really quite curious. It seems that Fernando Castiella, the Minister for Foreign Affairs at the time, arrived at a Cabinet meeting in May 1965 in a considerable state of indignation, having read the English edition of a book by Gabriel Jackson on the Civil War. Castiella showed the book to Franco and asked him why the régime allowed itself to be insulted in this way without offering a categorical response. The Minister of Information and Tourism, Manuel Fraga Iribarne, suggested that Ricardo de la Cierva, through the creation of a special department at the Ministry, should be the

The Department published three books: *Cien libros básicos sobre la Guerra Civil* (1966) ('One Hundred Basic Books on the Civil War'), *Los documentos de la primavera trágica* (1967) ('Documents Concerning the Tragic Spring'), and a bibliography on the 'War of Spain' and its background[53] (1968). De la Cierva was possibly one of the first government historians who made use of an extensive number of Republican sources in his research.[54] The author claimed that the first of these texts contained, 'definitive praise for books produced in the Republican Zone and in the Nationalist Zone; here there are condemnations directed at books produced in the Nationalist Zone and the Republican Zone'. Towards the end, De la Cierva stated that:

> it is a book made in peace and in favour of peace. In favour of the peace that now reigns over our countryside, although our recent historiography may consider it to be a peace that has never begun. (De la Cierva, 1966: 9 and 13)

It is interesting to note the acknowledgment that 'the War of Spain has continued in the printing presses' (De la Cierva, 1966: 13), providing official recognition of the existence of a considerable degree of polarisation regarding the historiography relating to the Civil War, a conflict that both De la Cierva and Palacio Atard, along with historians of similar affiliations, referred to as 'the War of Spain'. This was the expression that was to become common currency among those who did not wish to use the terms 'Crusade' or 'War of Liberation' and who did not want to get involved in an argument with the régime regarding the civil nature of the war. They referred to the War of Spain as if there had only been one in the country's history, although it seems that the vagueness of the

---

one responsible for offering an assessment of what was published, both within Spain and abroad, concerning the Civil War, whilst also launching an official version of the war that was more aseptic and exportable than those that had been offered up until that time. Thus it was that in May 1965 this Department was created, and would continue its work until the year De la Cierva joined the UCD Government as Minister of Culture in 1980. According to his testimony, if the Department wanted to ensure that its publications had widespread influence and effect, the only criteria to be applied clearly had to be those of objectivity and rigorousness. His task, he has claimed, was not to convince the reader by offering him a unilateral perspective, but to begin the process of reconciliation of the Spanish by incorporating some of the points of view of the defeated into official history.

53. De la Cierva boasts that it was he who ensured that the sleeve of this work featured the famous photograph of the dying militiaman by Robert Capa.

54. He claims that he was the first to show a certain understanding towards the defeated. According to his testimony, the Department carried out extremely important reconciliatory work by making a new climate of openness possible that put an end to the black-and-white perspective of good and bad. According to De la Cierva, the Department was the first government institution to acknowledge that crimes had been committed on both sides.

expression did not prevent anyone from knowing which war was being referred to, not only due to its traumatic nature but also because it was the most recent. In the 'Preface' to the following publication produced by the Special Department about the 'tragic spring', the 'War of Spain' or the 'Spanish War' was mentioned on various occasions, but the term 'Civil War' was not mentioned once.

Another important experiment regarding the narration of the Civil War from the perspective of a kind of Francoism that was relatively *aperturista* was headed by Vicente Palacio Atard at the Universidad Complutense in Madrid, along with various other historians. These publications were the famous *Cuadernos bibliográficos de la guerra de España (1936–1939)* ('Bibliographic Booklets on the War of Spain:1936–1939).[55] It is curious that both De la Cierva's and Palacio's initiatives should be based on an aspect of research as apparently neutral and free of polemic as that of the task of bibliographic compilation. Palacio Atard, along with De la Cierva and Ramón Salas Larrazábal, published three series of these Booklets and two Supplements. The first series consists of two volumes and brings together bibliographic information regarding pamphlets published during the war. The second series, consisting of just one volume, features the periodical publications of the time. The third, featuring three volumes, brings together an extensive bibliography of memoirs relating to the war. The second Supplement was written by María José Montes and deals with literary works produced on the war. The first is entitled *Aproximación histórica a la guerra española (1936–1939)* ('Historical Approach to the War of Spain') and it features possibly the most important list of historians allied to the régime who specialised in the Civil War.

According to its authors, this book aimed to evaluate the state of existing research on the Civil War, as well as contribute knowledge of a 'scientific' nature to the research carried out on the war. The tone of the authors contrasted with the former unhistorical black-and-white approach of the régime, although all of them reflected a clear bias in favour of the winning side in the war. In addition, they cited and criticised various texts published abroad, including some written by Spanish exiles.

In one of the chapters, entitled 'La Literatura Histórica sobre la Guerra de España' ('Historical Literature on the War of Spain') Palacio Atard considered the question of why the war was still able to arouse considerable interest among the Spanish in 1970. He divided the population into two parts, depending on their age; the first group, made up of those who lived through the war:

feel attracted now by accounts which constitute, above all, for them, an evocation with which to revive their personal memories... These are the

55. In this case, at least, the date of the conflict is mentioned in order to clarify the reference to the 'War of Spain'.

readers whom we might consider to be interested in 'what' occurred, given that they aim, above all, to recall or learn about incidents and details relating to the events, their formal and anecdotal aspects mainly; they are the ones who seek to relive past years with nostalgia...or with the emotional charge of passions which the passing years have never lain to rest.

However, there are other readers:

for whom the war is no longer a memory or an evocation...who are interested mainly in 'why' it happened, the rational explanation. (Palacio Atard et al., 1970: 12–13)

Palacio was not convinced of the possibility of writing about the war objectively, given that it was so recent and so fresh in the minds of both those who had lived through it and the new generations. For him, the historiography relating to the war was:

at a pre-scientific stage. Any attempt to surmount it falters on the obstacles inherent in the limitations of information and the passion which the subject arouses. Writing has been produced and is produced on the war based on subjective perspectives full of passion. (Palacio Atard et al., 1970: 31)

A tragic view of the war appeared in these writings, although the heroic view persisted at times in comments such as 'our war, prodigious in its number of outrages, was also generous in examples of human heroism, which constitutes a moral corrective' (Palacio Atard et al., 1970: 54). Salas Larrazábal also wrote for this first Supplement, contributing various fragments of military history and examples of foreign interventionism, as did De La Cierva, who blamed the Civil War on everyone, without any exceptions, and denied that the war was a crusade.

Obviously, other historians and other books also studied the Civil War from similar or opposing perspectives. However, those mentioned were probably the most important scholars of this historical event as a result of the wide repercussions of their work, as well as their pretensions of rigour, albeit within their sense of loyalty to the régime. Both De la Cierva and Palacio Atard allowed Francoism to reach the end of its days with versions of the war which, although not always popular or warmly received, nevertheless offered a more tolerant and integrative view than before. They never denied the inevitability of the war, but they did deny the need for it. Furthermore, the overall acknowledgement of guilt was radically new and facilitated a certain rapprochement between the Republicans and the Nationalists under the banners of 'we were all to blame' and 'never again'; slogans on which the consensus-based memory of the Transition would finally be built.

The victors do not construct all history all of the time; what they attempt to do is to use the past as a legitimising instrument and a means of training new citizens, whilst also using historical narration as an instrument of political education and socialisation. 'History' is always something much wider and more complex than what is set down in writing by the victors, who, furthermore, always have something of the defeated in themselves.

Commemorations of the Civil War

18 July and 1 April

The celebration of 18 July and 1 April were evident exhibitions of the outward signs of victory. They became (especially the second date) complex rituals which, year after year, were repeated with considerable ostentation and publicity. These historical commemorations not only sought to establish what were purported to be the most significant facts of the country's history in the collective memory, but also to impose a specific lesson to be derived from their evocation.

Nevertheless, not every crucial date in the life of a nation is considered to be worthy of commemoration or is liable to be celebrated. Political régimes tend to choose the events in a nation's history that create the greatest degree of social consensus, those that best serve common objectives of integration, harmony and equilibrium. The dates that signify division, tension and violence tend to be either relegated or omitted from the official calendar, or recalled prudently, but not celebrated as such. Francoism, however, considered both 18 July – the date that the longest Spanish civil war began – as well as 1 April – the date that one of the two sides achieved total victory – as occasions that were not only worthy of evocation, but also of celebration, without any pact ever having been reached between the two sides or the victors ever having made concessions to the defeated.

Both dates are of considerable importance in Spanish history and that is how they are recorded in current textbooks and in historical treatises of an academic nature. Nevertheless, although the events that took place then have not been forgotten, neither of the two dates is considered to be worthy of celebration today as they evoke sad events which, moreover, do not command the degree of consensus that might be desired. It is true that some agreement exists regarding the teachings that should be extracted from the event of war, but not from the specific events that took place during the war itself.[56]

The end of a civil war could well be an appropriate date for a large and joyful celebration, but a war that ends with the absolute victory of one

56. With regard to the substance of the memory itself, that is to say, a meticulous description of what actually occurred, no consensus even exists today. This is true both within left-wing and right-wing circles, although especially so in the former case. Films such as *Tierra y Libertad* ('Land and Freedom') by Ken Loach (1995) have revived the old conflict between the communists on the one hand, and the 'poumistas' and anarchists on the other, regarding the effect that the attempt at social revolution witnessed in part of the Republican-controlled zone had on their final defeat in the war. (A commentary that compares Loach's film with *Libertarias* by Vicente Aranda, appears in Aguilar, 1996).

side over another and that produces a high number of exiles and victims of reprisals is not something that should be celebrated. If the Civil War had ended with a pact of tolerance, with a commitment to peaceful coexistence, the meaning of the evocation would have been much more agreeable, in spite of the acts of violence and the deaths that occurred.

Franco trusted that nobody would forget that he had managed to rise to power through the force of arms and that his victory conferred on him the legitimate enjoyment of that power. Nevertheless, celebrating a victory over an adversary/brother is an extremely delicate matter. One of the aspects of the trauma that tends to be produced by a civil war is the difficulty of combining a sense of jubilation as a result of victory with the drama of a fratricidal conflict, or a sense of delight at the end of hostilities with the fact that a victory of one group of compatriots has taken place over another. The only really memorable event would have to be the end of the war, and this is what the Victory Parade would end up signifying for many, in spite of its name. At one point, as we shall see later on, it even seemed that this parade was going to be definitively turned into a Peace Parade, although this never actually happened. The régime continued to need the legitimacy that it derived from its origin, from its victory, in order to justify its power. Peace was certainly commemorated, but, for Franco, it never stopped being an 'armed' and 'vigilant' peace, as stated in official documents. It is not surprising, therefore, that peace was celebrated with the exhibition of arms in a military parade. This is where another of the ambiguities of Francoism lay. Peace was celebrated, that is true, but it was a peace lying in wait, a vigilant calm, one that did not overlook the enemy within; it was a peace that warned the opposition of the defensive and offensive capacity of the régime. It was an almost aggressive peace, incapable of producing either social integration or creating a valid collective identity for all.

The date of 18 July was of considerable symbolic importance throughout the Franco period. Many of the régime's most important inaugurations took place on this date. During the 1940s and 1950s it was used to evoke the régime's origin-based legitimacy. Nevertheless, with the economic development of the 1960s and 1970s, many inaugurations would have a more economic and social character, which meant that 18 July also ended up being used to confirm the régime's performance-based legitimacy.[57]

57. In the Official State Bulletins of the Spanish Cortes, from now on referred to as the BOCE, we can find various examples of exaltation regarding the anniversaries of 18 July. Nevertheless, as of 1958 no further record of these events was made, at least according to the contents lists of the Bulletins:
BOCE No. 265; pp.4825–6; 14/7/1948.
BOCE No. 402; pp.7416–8; 15/7/1952.
BOCE No. 434; pp.8140–2; 13/7/1953.
BOCE No. 538; pp.10768–9; 14/7/1956.
BOCE No. 563; pp.11461–2; 15/7/1957.
BOCE No. 601; pp.12438–41; 15/7/1958.

There were other dates of considerable importance to Francoism that were periodically evoked, but with much less ostentation. Significantly, these dates tended to refer to events directly relating to the Civil War, such as the capture of the Alcázar in Toledo, the Battle of Belchite, the Battle of Santa María de la Cabeza, the Battle of El Alto de los Leones; dates that either recalled battles and moments of victory for the winning side, or symbolised the heroic resistance of the Nationalists, duly mythicised by the régime, that occasionally ended in partial defeat. Nevertheless, all of these dates provided anchorage for the origin-based legitimacy of the régime.

Monuments of the Victors

Francoism was systematically prodigious in its construction of the outward signs of victory, given that these also played a key role in the process of political socialisation. In addition to the numerous commemorative rites of victory, it also created various 'sites of memory' (or 'lieux de mémoires' in the words of Nora) such as the monuments, crosses and plaques it erected that recalled the war.[58]

Although victory and peace constituted a source of legitimisation for the supporters of the régime, it was necessary to somehow calm the passions of the relatives of victims of the winning side, to somehow silence the voices of so many deaths which, after the clamour of battle, might have seemed unnecessary. One of the ways of achieving this was through the explicit, public and visible acknowledgement of the fallen on the Nationalist side. A subtle way of 'compensating' relatives and friends for their loss was to portray the victims as 'heroes and martyrs' within the history books and, in sight of all, on the multiple plaques that evoked the local deaths of only one side,[59]

58. According to Sueiro:

> Crucifixes and stone crosses began to appear everywhere in homage to and remembrance of the heroes, of the martyrs, of the fallen in the Crusade. On the secular stones of Romanesque hermitages, on walls, on the façades of haughty Gothic cathedrals, alongside church doors, under the colonnades and the eaves of Renaissance buildings, in large towns and cities, in small provincial capitals and in remote villages, the names of those who died on the winning side were inscribed around the arms of the cross. (Sueiro, 1976: 15)

59. These lists of dead were headed by the most important Nationalist victim of the war, José Antonio Primo de Rivera. These inscriptions, incidentally, remain on an infinite number of churches, without any political measures ever having been passed to end such discrimination and make all the victims of the war equal. In order to illustrate this point I shall mention a recent case, reported in *El País* on 31 January and 1 February 1994. The members of the Free Association of Lawyers of Madrid requested that the Governing Council of the Bar Association of Madrid either remove the commemorative tablet featuring the lawyers who had 'fallen for God and for Spain' or replace it with another stone paying homage to all of the victims of the war, free of discrimination. The petition had been repeatedly made in recent years without any result, since those who opposed it claimed that 'it would provoke a conflict among the Bar Association members' (*El País*, 31/1/1994). However, 'according to official sources, a series of works are planned for the functions room, which could provide an opportunity to remove the tablet' (*El País*, 1/2/1994).

and in the crosses and monuments that sprang up throughout the whole of Spain. These were the outward signs of victory, which provided a justification for the Nationalist deaths. No memorials were raised for the Republican deaths; their family members were not even conceded this symbolic compensation.

The Valley of the Fallen

It is essential to analyse the symbols employed in the most important Francoist monuments that were raised to commemorate the Civil War, with a view to understanding both the socialising attempts of the régime as well as the collective memory of the Civil War that persists to this day. Below we shall consider a specific place, a monument, and the intentions of the collective body that promoted its construction, the state, although the peculiarities of the Spanish authoritarian régime that emerged from the war oblige us to pay special attention to its most prominent figure, Francisco Franco, in order to understand what was intended by building such a striking architectural work.

The Valley of the Fallen, described by many as being a 'Pharaonic' monument, must be understood through an examination, above all, of the declarations that Franco, or others speaking on his behalf, made regarding the monument. It appears that this gigantic mausoleum was the result of the endeavour of just one man and that it was based on an idea that had dominated his thoughts since the beginning of the war. It was Franco who, without being the actual architect, initially designed its basic outline, personally supervised the whole process, accepted or rejected the changes that were proposed and who even decided upon every one of the minute details that were to make up the Cuelgamuros monument.

Nevertheless, according to Daniel Sueiro, the widely-believed story that the idea to build this monument originated with Franco himself during the war forms part of the mythology that surrounds the site. Sueiro tells us in his exhaustive study on the Valley of the Fallen, that it was three individuals on the Nationalist side in the Republican-run Madrid of the end of 1936 who, 'rolling their three professions into one' (sculptor, architect and soldier), planned the construction of 'a triumphal arch and a huge pyramid in order to proclaim victory and honour the dead' (Sueiro, 1976: 9). However, irrespective of the question as to who actually conceived the original idea, Franco made this project his own, actively sponsoring it at the end of the war and devoting a considerable amount of his own time to it right up to the very day of its inauguration. His interest even extended beyond this date as, according to his wishes, the site also provided the setting for the most important ceremonies staged by the régime and became a compulsory visit for all foreign leaders who came to Spain.

According to Diego Méndez, the architect of the huge cross that presides over the monument:

Franco felt the moral need, we might almost say the physical need, to hon-our the dead in the same way they honoured us. The idea matured as the campaign progressed, based on a search for an achievement befitting the intention. Thus arrived 1 April 1939. The war had ended. One million dead awaited, including those from jails, military prisons, the funeral pyres of the murdered, those executed under fallacious 'Republican legality', from attacks on enemy trenches, from bombardments, from the last-ditch defence of a house, from the battle for a town.[60]

According to Tomás Borrás, it was a question of raising a monument to bring about a 'posthumous reunion of the best', of the 'fallen in the Cru-sade', of the 'heroes and martyrs' who sacrificed themselves in order to save the country, the victims of the 'red patrols' that found 'in every good Spaniard an enemy to be exterminated' (Borrás, 1957). In short, it seems that it was only a question of paying homage to the Nationalists who died, the victims of the insanity of the other side.

The decree that ordered the building of the monument dated from very early on in the régime's existence, 1 April 1940, the first anniversary of the Francoist victory. In the preamble it stated that an anniversary as glorious and significant as that of the war could not be evoked by small and simple monuments, but only by grandiose sites that 'challenge the passing of time and fading memory' in homage to 'our dead...the heroes and martyrs of the Crusade'. That very day, Franco and his closest advi-sors, along with the German and Italian ambassadors, left for Cuelgamuros after attending the second Victory Parade in Spain, so that they could hear the plans for the mausoleum *in situ*.

Franco was always in a rush to complete the monument and many witnessed his impatience and irritation at the various delays that the works experienced. The fact is that it was quite impossible to carry out a building project of such magnitude in just a few years, due to the eco-nomic circumstances of the time.

Nevertheless, in order to facilitate the building process and also make it less costly, the builders resorted, in large part, to the use of a work-force consisting of political prisoners who were able to partially redeem their sentences in this way. This was, and still is, a highly controversial issue. According to Sueiro, Francoist supporters tend to minimise the number of convicts who laboured at the Valley of the Fallen; the architect, Diego Méndez, claims that only eighty prisoners worked there, without whom, as he is prepared to acknowledge, it would not have been possible to complete the excavation works on the mountain:

60. Quoted in an article by Tomás Borrás in *ABC* (21/7/1957) entitled: 'Novena Mar-avilla: el Valle de los Caídos'. Diego Méndez repeated the legendary but inaccurate figure of 'one million dead', attributing, furthermore, the 'ownership' of these victims exclusively to the Nationalist side. It seems as if the only deaths had been those of the winning side; as if no Republicans had died on the fronts and in the rearguard, or had been shot in the subsequent period of repression.

These men, mostly convicted for bloodcurdling crimes, were quite fearless by nature and did not worry about running the greatest risks. They tunnelled through the granite, climbed up implausible scaffolding, handled dynamite... Day after day they played with death...without them, the work would have taken many more years to complete, requiring a larger number of machines and greater squandering of resources. (Borrás, 1957)

This reveals that it was the convicts, including both normal criminals and political prisoners, who ran the greatest risks in building the mausoleum of the winning side, although many accepted the danger gladly in view of the prospect both of reducing their sentences and of escaping, at least temporarily, into the open air and leaving the oppressive atmosphere of prison behind.[61]

The testimonies gathered together by Daniel Sueiro mention many more political prisoners working there, including both prisoners-of-war and persons subsequently imprisoned for political reasons. The majority of the work-force, according to direct witnesses interviewed by Sueiro, was of this kind; in fact, the majority of the prison population during the early years of the régime consisted of political prisoners.[62] The system whereby sentences could be reduced through work programmes, that the régime was so proud of, aimed to ensure, according to the claims made by its promoters, that those who had contributed to destroying the country should now work to rebuild it. However, the idea was also founded on a Catholic-style doctrine that consisted of 'the spiritual and political improvement of the prisoners' families and the prisoners themselves' while aiming, at the same time, 'to purge the prisoners and their families of poisonous anti-patriotic ideas and hatred'. All this was based on the

61. There were many who also believed that it would be easier to escape from there, as witnessed by the spectacular escapes that took place from the construction site. One of the most famous attempts was undertaken jointly by Manuel Lamana and Nicolás Sánchez Albornoz, with the aid of Barbara Probst Solomon. Each of the three participants has written a book about this event. On 3 February 1993 a conference was held at the Students' Residence entitled 'Del Valle de los Caídos al Mar de Plata', which dealt with the life and work of Lamana, to which the three escape participants were invited. Curiously, none of them made any reference to the Valley, nor to the escape, and it was not until the question-and-answer session that the issue had to be faced. Significantly, Sánchez Albornoz refused to call the monument 'The Valley of the Fallen' and stated that he preferred to refer to it as 'Cuelgamuros', the name of the site on which it was built. By stating this he was saying that, like many other Spaniards, he did not consider it to be a monument built in homage to the victims of the war, as the régime vaguely intended, but as a disproportionate tribute to the victims of the Nationalist side and to Franco himself.

62. We must bear in mind that, at the end of the war, a pardon was published that offered amnesty to all those who, after the establishment of the Republic, had committed crimes 'against the Constitution, against public order, breach of laws regarding the possession of arms and explosives, homicides, injuries', provided that they could prove that they agreed ideologically with the Franco régime (Decree-Law of 23 September, 1939).

view that it was not possible to release back into society any 'damaged or perverted elements, poisoned politically and morally'.[63]

This system of redeeming sentences became quite widespread and a large part of the prison population was employed by the Department for Devastated Regions in order to rebuild towns, build dams, roads and complete various other tasks. In some cases, the convicts were forced to work in extremely precarious and dangerous conditions, similar to those typical of concentration camps. Many died in the work camps, although global figures regarding accidents at work for all of the labour projects undertaken by the prison population do not appear to exist. Those who carried out the most dangerous tasks received a higher wage, but many workers, such as the tunnellers at the Valley of the Fallen, ended up dying young as a result of silicosis.

In the case of the Valley of the Fallen, some prisoners were finally allowed to bring their families with them; their children – some of whom ended up working on the project themselves – were even born in the poor barrack huts that were provided for the prisoners. Some prisoners stayed on at the Valley once they had completed their sentences in view of the difficulties they encountered in finding work, sometimes because of their age and always because of the added problem of their past. One of them claimed, 'They say that it is essential to forgive, although not to forget. But there are two places there I cannot visit, because of the bad memories they bring me, and because of how badly they treated me' (Sueiro, 1976: 45–46).

When references were made to 'the fallen', especially during the first two decades of the régime, the Republicans were ignored; their existence was forgotten or they were explicitly denied any kind of recognition. We are free to infer who enters under the heading of 'those who fell for Spain and for God' and who does not. This is not because the Republicans did not fight 'for Spain' or because some of them did not believe in God, but because the war was considered to be a crusade, or a war of liberation and not a civil war. The mere existence of this unquestionable starting-point automatically deprived the Republicans of their status as Catholics (in the case of the believers, as the Nationalists claimed that it had been a religious crusade, based on the religious crimes that various groups on the Republican side had committed) as well as their status as Spaniards; according to the dominant view of the winning side, the enemy was an anti-Spaniard, a foreigner. As the Under-Secretary of the President, Luis Carrero Blanco, claimed at the time (at the Valley of the Fallen itself):

the war that we Spaniards were obliged to fight between 1936 and 1939 was not a civil war in any sense, but a War of Liberation fought to free our

---

63. José A. Pérez del Pulgar: 'La solución que España da al problema de sus presos políticos', in *Redención*, No.1, Valladolid, 1939. Quoted by Sueiro (1976: 49).

homeland from the dominion of a foreign power and, at the same time, to wage a crusade in defence of the Catholic Faith, which that power sought to banish as a result of its atheist doctrine. (Carrero Blanco, 1974: 102)

This quote by Carrero Blanco is taken from a speech that he gave on 28 January 1964 during the visit of Cardinal Cicognani to the Valley of the Fallen. There is no doubt that this testimony faithfully reflects the thoughts of Franco and his own intentions regarding the monument. Given that Carrero belonged to the staunchest section of the régime, we can observe how, even though Spain was in the midst of celebrating the 25 Years of Peace and the victors were supposed to be behaving magnanimously towards the losing side, the régime's discourse had failed to develop at all, continuing as it did to deny the civil nature of the war. First, it aimed to perpetuate, 'the most important event in our History, not in the passive sense of simply recalling it, but in the permanent and much more effective and constructive form of prayer and study'. According to this version, the monument commemorated:

a victory, but not a victory over a political adversary, as twisted and false interpretations have tried to make us believe, but the victory of Spain over the enemies of its independence and its faith, the only ideals whose defence justifies the ultimate sacrifice of life. (Carrero, 1974: 101 and 102)

Second, the monument was meant 'to perpetuate the memory of the Fallen; honouring those who gave their lives for God and for the *Patria* so that it should serve as an example for future generations'. (Carrero, 1974: 104).

A somewhat dubious dose of magnanimity was later revealed when, in open contradiction with the rest of the speech, it was claimed that:

the Caudillo wanted a huge Cross, the largest that could be built, to crown, as a symbol of our Faith, the burial place of all those who fell during the war, without making any distinction between the two sides...he [Franco] also wanted a Centre for Studies to be set up on the same site in order to promote men's knowledge and enjoyment of peace. (Carrero, 1974: 104)

The rhetoric of peace was preponderant at that time, accompanied by the warning that it was a 'vigilant peace'. Nevertheless, the inclusion of the defeated under the heading of 'all of the fallen' was a completely new development and it is worth considering it in a little more detail.

Lieutenant-General Francisco Franco Salgado-Araujo, a cousin and close supporter of Franco, makes a few observations regarding the meaning of the funeral monument in his memoirs. Although he criticised the Americans in 1954 for not being capable of understanding the reasons for investing huge sums of money in the Valley, 'a romantic and spiritual work that reveals a considerable religious sense and a wish to pay homage to the fallen in the war of liberation' (Franco Salgado-Araujo, 1976: 46), by the following year he had already changed his opinion, stating:

> I respect what the Generalísimo did by spending millions on the Valley of the Fallen in order to commemorate the Crusade, but I think it would have been more affirmative and practical to have set up a large foundation in order to bring together all of the children of the war victims; in the case of the Whites, as a reward for the sacrifice made by the parents; in the case of the Reds, in order to demonstrate our lack of ill-feeling towards the blameless children of those who, in our opinion, were mistaken. This foundation could have been endowed with sufficient resources to last for many years and, thus, remind future generations that those who stood up to fight for a better Spain bear no resentment and that we would not wish hate and intransigence to forever come between those who are children of the same *Patria* and that we only wish to endow the country with greatness. (Franco Salgado-Araujo, 1976: 118)

Subsequently, in July 1957, he would be obliged to reiterate, in fear, what he had written in 1955:

> The sufficient climate does not exist in Spain for this monument, since although the fear of another civil war persists, a large part of the population have tended to forgive and forget. I do not believe that the families of the Whites or the Reds would wish their relatives to be placed in the crypt, for if it is meant only for the Whites, it will establish an eternal disunity among Spaniards. (Franco Salgado-Araujo, 1976: 215)

Franco's personal secretary was right in suspecting that the monument, initially designed exclusively for the victors, was rather inopportune in the way it perpetuated the hatred and divisions that existed among Spaniards. This was a cause for concern among some sections of the régime that did not approve of the hatred and resentment that might be aroused. Franco Salgado-Araujo's view was coherent in proposing, as a real conciliatory gesture – at least with regard to the children if not their parents – that a charitable foundation should be created in order to accord equal treatment to the descendants of those who died on both sides. He did not believe that the Valley of the Fallen was the most appropriate means of reconciling the Spanish and much less a means of encouraging a willingness to forgive and forget, which, in his opinion, existed among most of the Spanish population.

In 1958 Franco Salgado-Araujo noted down a conversation that he had with Franco about the Valley of the Fallen in which the Head of State claimed that, 'in some sections it had gone down badly that those who had died for the Crusade could have been buried alongside the Reds in the same crypt', pointing out that, 'in that respect they are alright where they are'. However, Franco 'had also heard of instances of praise which claimed that he had been inspired by the Catholic Church' (Franco Salgado-Araujo,

1976: 239). Franco went on to state that 'it is true that there have been some quite correct inferences regarding our intention to forget the sides on which the Catholic dead fought', in which respect he acknowledged, however, that this had not formed part of the original idea and that this initiative had not been his own, but that of the Church.[64] He continued:

> It seems fine to me, since there were many on the side of the Reds who fought because they believed they were fulfilling their duty to the Republic, and others who were drafted by force. The monument was not built to continue dividing Spaniards into two irreconcilable sides. It was built, and this was always my intention, as a commemoration of a victory over communism, which tried to take over Spain. Thus, my wish that the Catholic victims of both sides should be buried there. (Franco Salgado-Araujo, 1976: 239)

Obviously, for Franco, the Valley of the Fallen was another monument devoted to perpetuating his victory, and the scope for encompassing the losing side, a possibility that was only considered at the very last moment, was rather limited. It only included a few Catholic Republicans, considerably restricting the range of victims incorporated from the losing side, and confirming yet again the arbitrary nature of the choice – even this small concession encountered a certain degree of opposition on the part of the staunchest section of the régime, in spite of the fact that the year was 1958, and almost twenty years had passed since the end of the war and the situation in Spain had undergone a profound change. The much longed-for international recognition of the régime had finally been achieved and the end of the régime's isolation meant that it ceased to be permanently on the defensive.

Developments in the foreign context were reflected within the domestic sphere, including, for example, the public handling of the collective

64. The role of the Church in this matter was highly ambiguous, (not for the first time in the history of Francoism). On the one hand, we have the testimony of Friar Justo Pérez de Urbel, the first Abbot of the monastery at the Valley of the Fallen, who, while serving as Prior at the Church of Monserrat in Madrid before accepting the position, acknowledged that in 1956 he received a letter from Father Escarré, the Abbot of Monserrat, in which Escarré wrote, 'under no circumstances accept the Valley of the Fallen; it is something that we must not commit ourselves to' (quoted by Sueiro, 1976: 208). We can see from this that a section of the Church existed that wanted nothing to do with what was, for many, a quite inopportune monument. On the other hand, however, another part of the Church (probably the majority) accepted the monument with its mausoleum, basilica and monastery, and its centre for studies devoted to promoting the Social Catholic doctrine. In reality, it seems unlikely that the monument would have been rejected, plastered as it was with religious symbolism. In the end, the Church was to make another commitment to the régime by allowing the monastery to be inaugurated on 1 April. Even in 1960, during the Papacy of John XXIII, it was declared a minor Basilica. In spite of everything, it appears that it was the Church that suggested that the dead from both sides should be buried there, thus leading to a conciliatory spirit that was to become much more explicit in subsequent years. With regard to the attitude of the Church under Francoism, see Víctor Pérez Díaz (1991b).

memory of the war, which led to the partial inclusion of the defeated in the victors' mausoleum. This significantly changed the initial intention of the project, perhaps not so much as a result of a coinciding shift in the spirit that inspired it, but as a result of the need to adapt to a new context of friendly coexistence with the democratic countries, which demanded certain changes in the régime's behaviour up until that time.

In this respect, it is interesting to observe the differences between the text of the 'Dedication' that was included in the Guide for the Valley of the Fallen that the Patrimonio Nacional (National Heritage Organisation) published in English in 1959 and that of the Spanish version of 1969. The two guides are practically identical in format, text, photographs, etc. However, certain differences exist that might be overlooked in a quick reading, but are crucial in allowing us to discover the intentions of the régime in its foreign affairs. These alterations reveal a deliberate attempt to soften the harshest expressions in order to make the régime appear to be more tolerant and conciliatory abroad than it actually was at home. The Spanish guide reads thus: 'The Monument to *those who fell for Spain*, an idea conceived during the *Crusade* and decided upon when it ended, should be regarded by all Spaniards as a just tribute to the memory of all those who, in defending such a pure ideal, sacrificed the greatest and purest gift of any man: life'. The English guide reads: 'The Monument to *all who fell in the Spanish Civil War*, the erection of which was considered while the *war* was still in progress, and decided upon when it ended, should be regarded by all Spaniards as a just tribute to the memory of *all those who gave their lives for their ideals*. No man can give more.' As we can see, the term 'Crusade' disappears in the English text, whilst those killed during the war are no longer 'those who fell for Spain' but 'all those who fell in the Spanish Civil War' and 'all those who gave their lives for their ideals', whomever they might be.[65]

The ambiguity of the monument and the ongoing doubts regarding what it is supposed to symbolise are reflected very clearly in an anecdote

---

65. Going beyond the 'Dedication', this comparison of the two guides continues to be relevant. When the Spanish text says: 'It would not be fair if the survivors of the struggle were to forget the effort and actions of *all those who joined us* in the struggle for victory', the English text reads: 'It would not be fair if the survivors of the struggle were to forget those who sacrificed their lives in the struggle for victory', eliminating the limitation 'all those who joined us' and extending the idea to all those who sacrificed their lives in the struggle for victory. When, once again, the English text emphasises that: 'The geographical centre of Spain was chosen as the most appropriate site, in order to emphasize the fact that it is a monument *to all Spaniards*', the Spanish text restricts itself to the following: 'It is no surprise that, given its national character and its dedication to Spain, the centre of the country should be chosen as the site for its erection'. Finally, when the guide published in Spanish refers to a monument dedicated to 'the best', the English version states that it was built 'in the memory of *all* those who lived up to their ideals in the name of Spain' (The italics in the text and in the commentary are mine).

told by its architect, Diego Méndez, regarding the polemical decoration of the crypt, the only matter that he claims to have disagreed about with Franco. Located to the left and right of the crypt, Franco wanted to include some bas-relief work that would depict various episodes of the war by means of a parade of heroes and martyrs. In his own words, Méndez thought this was 'an outrage', given that such motifs would not only fail to withstand, 'the passing of time and fading memory' – which is what Franco always intended the monument to do – but would also serve to increase hatred and hinder reconciliation. Franco refused to relinquish his idea, and so a series of sketches were produced based on his ideas for the proposed bas-reliefs. Another opinion then entered the fray, that of Bishop Eijo Garay, who claimed that Franco's idea would 'embody hatred to too great an extent, manifest a battle within the Church, and a Church should not provide a setting for a battle amongst men, nor a war, and even less a war among brothers'.[66] The idea was then broached that the bas-reliefs could be replaced with paintings, but these also turned out to be too warlike and were also rejected. In the end, various tapestries were hung up depicting the Revelation of St. John, although the 'Hero Saints' and the 'Martyred Saints' ended up being portrayed in the iron-work railings surrounding the crypt. Furthermore, the huge dome also featured forty-two hero saints and thirty-four martyred saints, followed by Spanish heroes and martyrs, although it did not actually depict episodes of war.

Other figures that symbolised the war were also included, for example, the Virgen de África (Virgin of Africa), evoking the beginning of the war and the passage of the Francoist troops though the Straits, as well as the Virgen del Pilar, who 'reminds us that it was at the Battle of the Ebro that the Civil War was decided' (Sueiro, 1976: 184). The figure of the Virgen de la Merced (Virgin of Mercy) also appears, the patroness of all prisoners. All of these figures were chosen by Franco.

In the end, the most famous sculptor at the Valley of the Fallen, Juan de Ávalos, stated that he was glad that:

> nothing had been placed there that might hurt or rub salt in the wounds of others, of the Republicans…because it is good that the themes should all be religious and that all of our dead should be buried under the cross. Let's have no more lectures, shall we, because the hatred has been excessive. (Sueiro, 1976: 180–181)

In contrast, Sueiro points out that there are no references to the Republicans in a text from 1946 regarding the victims of the war who were to be buried there.[67] Nevertheless, although it is true that the official texts made no references to them:

66. This episode is described in Sueiro (1976: 137ff.).
67. The official text refers to 'the remains of the fallen in our War of Liberation, both whether they perished in the ranks of the Nationalist Army or whether they were murdered or executed by the Marxist hordes' (quoted by Sueiro, 1976: 226).

administrative and official language began to reflect the idea that the Valley belonged to everyone and was for everyone, that all of the victims of the war would find peace and fraternity there, without any distinction as to sides, tendencies or ideologies'. (Sueiro, 1976: 226)

This gesture was officially sanctioned in 1958 when it was stated that it was this Christian spirit that had inspired the building of the monument from the very beginning.

However, the families of the Republican victims were obliged to prove that they had been Catholics and, what is more, family approval was required in order to move the remains to the Valley. It is obvious that many were unable to fulfil the first requirement or that, being able to fulfil it, were unable to prove it. In fact, various applicants were denied the right to bury their loved ones there. In the end, many families on both sides refused to allow their dead to be moved there, as was the case with the family of the first martyr of the Civil War, José Calvo-Sotelo, who is still buried in the Cemetery of La Almudena. The martyr who *was* buried at the Valley, with all the honours, was José Antonio, with the full approval of his brother and sister, Miguel and Pilar, although with the silent opposition of the Falange.

By the time the Valley of the Fallen was opened on 1 April 1959 (on the twentieth anniversary of the Victory) some twenty thousand victims had been buried in the crypt; in the end, around seventy thousand were to be buried there, the majority victims from the Nationalist side. On the day of the inauguration, Franco gave a somewhat anachronistic speech in which he claimed that the 'devil' continued to lie in wait while plotting 'new ruses and disguises' more befitting to the times, in a reference to the alleged enemies of Spain, thus justifying the need for an armed and vigilant peace. A large part of his speech was devoted to emphasising the reconstruction work undertaken by the régime, the economic recovery of the country that he himself had brought about and the despicable acts of the Reds, who, in addition to having stolen the gold from the national coffers, still conspired to destroy the country from exile.

In short, it appears that the signs of reconciliation only applied to some of the dead victims on the Republican side and under no circumstances to the surviving members. Sueiro states that the political prisoners of the time 'whose lives were in danger or who faced long sentences...when told that all of the victims of the war would be laid to rest together, asked themselves in desperation whether it wouldn't be more fitting, before a reconciliation were brought about among the dead, for a reconciliation to take place among the living' (Sueiro, 1976: 54). In fact, no reconciliatory texts exist at the Valley. If reconciliation had really been its intention, we might have expected the victors to have included a lavish range of symbolic and conciliatory statements. It is a monument infested with religious symbols, but lacking any evident political message, in that the main tenets of the Movement do not even appear, nor any words penned by Franco or any other written text. The reconciliatory advice that Santiago Alba – according to his biographer – gave the architect Pedro Muguruza, the Director General of Architecture, was not followed. Santiago Alba offered him a text for his 'valley of peace', which is what the site might have been but never became, a kind of neutral monument to the soldiers who fell during the war. The text suggested by Alba consisted of the toast proposed by Simón Bolívar at the meeting in Santa Ana, that reads as follows:

> To the heroic steadfastness of the soldiers of *both armies*; to their unprecedented loyalty, suffering and valour. To the worthy men who, through horrific sufferings, maintain and defend their liberty. To those who have died gloriously in the defence of their homeland or their Government. To the leaders of *both armies*, who have displayed their intrepidity, their dignity and their character. *Everlasting hatred to those who seek blood and wish to spill it unjustly.* (García Venero, 1963: 376; the italics are mine)

This thought, combined with the sensible words of Franco Salgado-Araujo, express very well what might have been done to promote reconciliation and was not. After all is said and done, if the régime had wished to end the bitterness and hatred, it could have been much more explicit about it. As it is, Franco's speeches and the legal discrimination that the defeated and their families continued to suffer in many areas, belie the supposedly conciliatory nature of the monument. These testimonies reflect the reigning opinion in various sections of the governing coalition (the most *aperturista* or reformist, the youngest members, disenchanted Falangists, some Catholics) that were beginning to become concerned by the obsessive emphasis that Franco and the most reactionary elements continued to place on the war, in tones that were excessively black-and-white and vengeful. The most reactionary elements continued in the same vein, using the same expressions as in the postwar period. We believe that a large part of the population felt a profound need to forget the war and encourage a sense of forgiveness, out of a fear that if reconciliation among all Spaniards failed to be achieved, the tragedy might be repeated. This was, very probably, an important point of conflict within the reigning élite, implicit because it was an extremely delicate issue, and moreover, a means of sustaining the origin-based legitimacy of the régime. Some sections of the régime made every effort to move definitively on from origin-based legitimacy to performance-based legitimacy in their speeches, but Franco, along with others, never sought to forget the war nor definitively integrate the defeated.

However, it appears that a large part of the population did not approve of the fact that it was the defeated side and their ideological heirs who were obliged to suffer the indignity of building the tomb of the victors –

which is exactly what people finally considered it to be, as reflected in collective memory. On this occasion, the official version was unable to impose itself on the general consciousness, and the Valley of the Fallen is remembered as an ostentatious and inopportune pantheon, built by Franco for himself and the winning side in the war. Some voices were raised in order to turn the project into a symbol of reconciliation, but, in spite of the fact that some of the Republican victims of the war were buried there, very few were ever convinced of this alleged intention. Many more gestures and many other policies would have been required to make the intended reconciliation of the two sides a reality. Even so, it is important to recognise that this partial inclusion of the defeated in the Valley of the Fallen project was actually considered to be necessary with regard to both home and foreign affairs, because it indicates the existence of a collective consciousness which, in spite of the official discourse, sought reconciliation and, above all, wished to forget the past. It was Franco, along with the staunchest sections of the régime, who insisted on reminding everyone of the war.[68]

The Victory Arch in Madrid

This huge arch was built on one of the most famous battlefields of the Spanish Civil War. The site that formed the Ciudad Universitaria (University City) front was almost entirely destroyed by the end of the war; even the current Air Ministry building was built over the ruins of the Model Prison of Madrid, which was used during the war to imprison and, on occasions, execute the supporters of the Uprising and constituted one of the most widely vilified places under Francoism.

At the end of the war, the Department for Devastated Regions[69] would use part of its budget for reconstruction work in this area, which was shortly to include various monuments commemorating the victory and the martyrs of the Nationalist side. According to Palacio Atard:

> many triumphal arches have probably been built around the world to welcome victorious armies... But perhaps this Madrid monument is the only

---

68. On 26 April 1992, fifty-three years after the end of the war, an article appeared in *El País* entitled: 'The official guides to the Valley of the Fallen cover up its black history'. This report denounced the current silence in tourist guides concerning those who built the monument and the meaning of 'one of the largest displays of Francoist cruelty during the postwar period'. It stated that only certain foreign guides 'revive the memory of what was a huge concentration camp devoted to the building of a fascist monument'. In the current guide produced by the Patrimonio Nacional 'Franco is only mentioned once' and it does not mention the Republican penal workforce, nor those who died or were afflicted with silicosis for the rest of their days. All of this reveals the prevailing trauma of the war, of Francoism, and the problematic nature of dealing with both memories, even today (*El País*, 26/4/1992).
69. Regarding the work carried out by this body, see the book published by the MOPU: Various Authors (1987): *Arquitectura en Regiones Devastadas*.

triumphal arch built on the battlefield itself. In this case, it was raised on the site of the longest battle in our war, that featured some of the most intense fighting at certain times. (Palacio, 1973: 125–126)

The idea of erecting a victory arch on the current site dates back to 1942,[70] although the first architectural drafts were not produced until 1943.[71] According to these designs, a huge victory arch would serve as a gateway to the city and an equestrian statue of Franco on a great pedestal would be built in front of it. This project was shelved, presumably for budgetary reasons, and not resumed until 1946, the year that the régime felt obliged, as a result of the foreign opposition which emerged at the end of the Second World War, to reaffirm its position at home.[72] It is well known that the defeat of the fascist powers in the Second World War revived the hopes of Franco's enemies in exile and at home. The régime appeared to falter at times as various democratic countries withdrew their embassies and other measures were taken at international forums to morally condemn the Spanish dictatorship. In reply, Franco and his supporters spread the rumour that a foreign and domestic conspiracy was seeking to revive the Civil War (let us not forget that the 'maquis' became active during this period) and with this excuse they decided – not for the first time in Spain's history – to close the country off from abroad and surround it with a *cordon sanitaire* to prevent the circulation of foreign news against the régime. At the same time, a cosmetic but nevertheless important transformation was brought about. Some of the Falangist symbols were progressively removed from public ceremonies in an attempt to eliminate the otherwise strong connections with the Axis countries.

Work on the Victory Arch began in 1950 and it took five years to be completed. It was at that time that the inauguration of the monument was scheduled for 18 July 1956, the year that the twentieth anniversary

70. According to another testimony:

> the initial idea to raise a monument to Franco, 'the forge of victory', arose from the Municipal Corporation of Madrid in a session that took place on 27 April 1939. The Chairman of the meeting proposed to the Management Committee 'that an artistic monumental fountain depicting the most glorious events of the Spanish Crusade should be erected in an Imperial urban thoroughfare bearing the General's name, financed by national subscription'. At the session of the Municipal Standing Committee of 3 May 1939, Mr. Lafarga suggested setting up a national subscription scheme in order to build, in 'the very heart of Madrid, a monument to victory, to which would be added a Museum of the Revolution, a Veterans' Centre, a Centre for Former Prisoners and a Centre for the War-Wounded. (Fernández-Delgado, et al., 1982: 405)

None of these ideas was ever implemented, but this text enables us to reconstruct the climate that existed at the time and observe the intentions of the victors with respect to themselves and the defeated.

71. It was precisely in this year that the rest of the monuments that were planned to be raised in the area were presented; these included a 'Monument to José Antonio and to the 'fallen student' (Fernández Delgado et al., 1982: 406).

72. 'In the session of the Committee held on 16 May 1946, the latter ratified its agreement to raise a victory arch, as an act of "national affirmation" in the face of political isolation abroad' (Fernández et al., 1982: 408).

of the Uprising was to be celebrated. However, in the end, the arch was not opened on this date, or on any other date. Palacio Atard wrote that, 'it is difficult to explain why this occasion faded into oblivion' and towards the end of his article he added, 'God Willing that the inevitable evocation of war should not ruin that other main purpose of the university milieu, so that, as stated in the Latin inscription which decorates the monument, it may serve as the mansion in which the arts and sciences may flourish, in harmony and peace' (Palacio, 1973: 141–142).

Palacio, a defender of the Franco régime and open admirer of the 'dignified' and 'sober' monument, could not help but be concerned about the clear 'evocation of war' that it represented. The arch did not aim to commemorate peace, but victory, and this may be observed in the inscriptions of the original project as well as in the current inscriptions.[73] For this very reason and because, over time, the régime became less interested in the graphic display of victory and more interested in exploiting the 'victories of peace', we believe that no official inauguration was ever staged for this monument, which proved to be so inopportune for those who had lost the war and so meaningless to those who had not lived through it. It was probably for this reason that Franco himself chose to change the location of his equestrian statue, which had been designed to stand underneath the arch, finally moving it to the area surrounding the former Ministry of Housing (today the Ministry of Public Works) to be inaugurated by Franco and the appropriate Minister on 18 July 1959.

If the conciliatory will and the desire to integrate the defeated that some members of the winning side attributed to the régime really had existed, the order would never have been given to erect a victory arch on a battlefield where so many soldiers lost their lives and on the ruined site of that mythical front which, at the end of 1936, led to the defeat of the Nationalist attempt to conquer Madrid, a monument to victory built over the spilt blood of the vanquished. It is perhaps for this reason that the régime, conscious of the bitter and rather unsubtle symbolic significance of the monument, chose not to inaugurate such an enormous arch,[74] in order not to fan the flames of discord any further.

73. The Latin inscription of the initial project read thus: 'To the most eminent Caudillo de España, Francisco Franco, who contributed to the greater glory of this city of knowledge, destroyed by warlike passion and most lavishly restored in the year 1943'. The current inscriptions read, on one side: 'The intelligentsia, always victorious, dedicated this monument to the armies that achieved victory here'. On the other side they read thus: 'Founded by the generosity of the King, restored by the Leader of all Spaniards, this centre for studies in Madrid flourishes in the presence of God' (Palacio, 1973: 140).

74. Octavi Martí relates how the work *España otra vez* by the film-maker Jaime Camino was censored in 1967 because, among other reasons, 'it showed the monument raised to Victory and stated that that was what it was, a monument to victory' (*El País*, 12/5/1994). It is obvious, then, that this arch became a liability for the régime, and that it would become more so over time.

It is, indeed, a huge triumphal arch that aimed, through its size and grandiose nature, to perpetuate the memory of a victory of one part of Spain over another in a civil war. The obvious and explicit intention of the régime was to pay lasting homage to the victors, to remind the defeated of this victory, and to leave the sad legacy that any victory in a civil war entails to posterity and subsequent generations.

In addition, the mysterious open and circular monument, flanked by large columns, that stands just behind the Arch and is dedicated to the Fallen of Madrid, was the result of a tender held in 1949 upon the initiative of Madrid City Council. The first stone was laid on 29 October 1954 and surrounded, quite significantly, 'with bricks from the Montaña Barracks and the Model Prison' (Fernández et al., 1982: 388), places that recall the victims of the winning side. The Nationalist 'fallen' from the episode involving the Montaña Barracks have another monument dedicated to their memory (on the steps that lead up to the esplanade where the Templo de Debod is located) that was inaugurated on 20 July 1972, marking the thirty-sixth anniversary of that event.[75] The original project included, in addition to the monument that exists today, a frieze 'featuring a depiction of the battle between the Centaurs and the Lapithae at the wedding of Pirithous'. However, this frieze 'raised various protests since it was not considered to be fitting for a homage to the 'fallen'' (Fernández et al., 1982: 169) which is why it was finally left out. Naturally, by the 1970s, the political socialisation carried out by the régime emphasising the values of peace had taken effect and the public began to notice a contradiction that had not been so evident during the first two decades of Francoism: that between the sad evocation of the victims of war and the exaltation of the epic values of the conflict itself. The monument actually consists of a trench, above which lies a mutilated body symbolising the horrors of battle, while paying homage to the fallen on the winning side.

As far as the Monument to the Fallen of Madrid is concerned, the works for this project first ground to a halt in 1957. Later on, nobody was quite sure what use should be made of the various parts of the building. In 1962 it was suggested that the building could form an extension of the Valley of the Fallen, but the idea never materialised and the uncertainty surrounding its fate continued. Various bodies requested the use of the building for their own purposes, but on 6 July 1972 the City Council decided that it would be used exclusively for worship. However, the building work remained at a standstill and the building fell into disrepair.[76]

---

75. According to the press report, the fascist anthem 'Cara al sol' was sung at the opening ceremony.
76. Fernández Delgado states that, upon completion of his book, the monument still remained unfinished, although it was already known that it would not feature the monumental cross that had been conceived in the original plans. Today it houses the City Council of La Moncloa.

Legendary Sites of the Defeated

The testimonies of those who evoke the Franco period in their writings, especially those who lived through the war as children and recall the experiences of their postwar childhood, are full of allusions to silence and fear.[77] Adults concealed information from the youngest children in order to protect them, whilst school presented numerous taboo subjects and a considerable part of the recent history of Spain was omitted from the history books.

The legendary sites of the defeated were vilified at first and later ignored. The bombing of Guernica was hardly mentioned and when it was, no acknowledgement was given to the fact that it was German planes which, with the permission of the Nationalist government, dropped the incendiary-bombs on the civil population. In the majority of cases, the inhabitants of Guernica themselves were blamed for setting fire to their own town. According to the official version, the defeated did not have any heroic battles to their credit either, not even examples of honourable resistance. Their actions were only highlighted to demonstrate their cruelty or the extent of the destruction that they caused, as was the case in Belchite.

This town in Saragossa was deliberately omitted from the reconstruction process so that it might survive as a living example of the catastrophe that had befallen Spain and of the alleged insanity of the Republicans. The meaning of this site of memory is very different to that which still exists in the centre of the former West Berlin. The ruined spire of a large church, partially charred by flames, rises up on a very prominent site within a city that had to be entirely rebuilt. It is known as the 'Church of Remembrance' and is not the only destroyed religious building in Germany that aims to permanently remind the Germans of the disastrous consequences of a war that they themselves began. Above all, it constitutes a graphic evocation and warning that the Germans have left to remind themselves of the results of their imperialistic, xenophobic and totalitarian past.

In Spain, on the other hand, the tragic dimension of the war took much longer to emerge due to fact that the heroic exaltation of war reigned supreme in the early days. The differences between the German and the Spanish case are easy to understand. Germany was a country which, as a whole nation, lost an international war. The winning side, in this case, was foreign and was able to impose on Germany the sites of memory that would facilitate its political learning. In Spain, on the other hand, one of the two sides defeated the other and the winner did not feel obliged to acknowledge the dreadful consequences of a war which, in the last analysis, that side had initiated itself. In Spain, the task of national

---

77. See, for example, *Memorias de un niño de derechas* by Francisco Umbral (1972).

reconstruction was rapidly undertaken in order to remove the signs of internal strife. Only the old town of Belchite was deliberately left in ruins.

The absence of any monuments dedicated to the defeated is quite blatant.[78] Hardly any plaques exist that recall the victims on the Republican side in the places where the great battles were fought and so many Republicans died. The rehabilitation of intellectuals in exile was long-delayed and incomplete and their valid reasons were never officially acknowledged. The defeated were regarded, at best, as people of good faith who had been wickedly deceived, but always as individuals who had chosen the wrong option.

All kinds of homage were paid, on the other hand, to the Nationalist fallen, and every means was sought to ensure that their memory was periodically honoured and the victims were recalled in very prominent public places. The decision to inscribe the names of the victims of the war from the winning side on the walls of all the churches alongside the name of the 'victim *par excellence*', José Antonio Primo de Rivera, was taken by the Junta Política de la Falange (Political Council of the Falange) in 1939. In this respect, Dionisio Ridruejo states, in the honourable vein that characterises his memoirs: 'The name of the leader was followed by a list of the inhabitants of each town who had died in action. It was an imitation of something that had already been done in France after 1918. But that was an international war and the victims belonged to all the French. Here, sooner or later, the issue was to become a litigious matter

---

78. Very close to Teruel, within the municipal boundaries of Caudé (kilometre 126 of Carretera Nacional 234), a monument exists that is known as 'los pozos de Caudé' or 'the pits of Caudé'. Towards the end of the Civil War, it was into these natural pits that the Nationalists threw hundreds of dead from the Republican side who had apparently been executed. A layer of quicklime was successively thrown over each layer of corpses until the pits were full. These pits were also used during the postwar repression. Alongside the pits, a rather deteriorated monument exists, erected partly by the PSOE-UGT and partly by the PCE. Alongside this monument stands another rather more modest monument erected by the CNT. There are also various Christian gravestones erected by some family members. This might be called a 'living' monument, since every 1 May, participants celebrating Labour Day go up to the monument in order to place flowers there in memory of all those who lost their lives in the Civil War and during the Franco period. This is not a monument to the defeated in general, since not even the political groups who raised it were able to reach agreement and the anarchist dead are buried in a different place to the rest. Furthermore, according to José Manuel Conejero Fernández (telephone interview of April 1994), a CNT militant in Teruel, problems even arose over the inscription. The socialists wanted the inscription to read 'Fallen in defence of democracy' whilst the anarchists preferred 'Murdered by Francoism'. What is more, according to Conejero, there have even been disputes between anarchists and socialists on 1 May when they have visited the monument, something that does not usually occur because they avoid meeting there. Other pits exist in the region that were used for similar purposes. One of them, near Albarracín, features a bronze plaque in memory of fifteen executed Republicans. The town cemetery also displays a plaque dedicated to various women who were executed. Nevertheless, this town also has a monolith dedicated to the Nationalist fallen.

and an example of aggressive remembrance. However, since it is my custom to confess my culpability, I shall not omit to mention that I was the one who signed the order for this measure to be carried out.' (Ridruejo, 1976: 175).

Policies of Reconciliation and Policies of Vengeance

From Punishment to Forgiveness

Purges and Forms of Legal Discrimination

It is well known that the régime developed an extensive and exhaustive range of legislation regarding political responsibilities with which it marginalised the majority of the defeated and, in many cases, even deprived them of their jobs. It is not surprising that a régime which based a large part of its legitimacy on victory in a civil war should create legislation in order to discriminate against the losing side. The winners, according to this logic of the absolute victor, reward the living and the dead on their own side and punish those of the opposing side. Even when the repression abated, the defeated were prevented from acquiring the same rights and prerogatives as the victors. The pardons that were issued ended the punishment, but did not impose equality; in fact, they did not annul the crime at all, an issue that has rather more to do with the idea of amnesty than that of a general pardon. It is matters of this nature that highlight the limited scope of the rehabilitation and reconciliation that the defenders of the régime occasionally boasted about.

The fact is that a real sense of equality between the victors and the defeated would have entailed the loss of certain privileges that the victors enjoyed, and this might have led to serious protests. In many cases, especially during the early years of the régime, it was essential to remove many individuals from their jobs in order to reward those who had loyally served on the Nationalist side. A percentage of the posts in the civil service was reserved for former prisoners, the war-wounded, veterans etc., of the winning side.[79] Furthermore, those who had interrupted their studies as a result of the war were able to enter what were known as 'patriotic exams', in which, according to witness accounts, it was enough to simply turn up in the uniform of the Falange, shout '¡Arriba España!'

---

79. As Ricardo Chueca states,

> it was necessary to improvise in the case of a large number of civil servants… It is easy to imagine where this new staff came from after everything we have mentioned concerning the preference criteria that worked in favour of veterans, former prisoners, militants of the only Party and life-long right-wingers. These civil servants thus felt that they had been vested with extra authority and legitimacy, since their position was not only – and sometimes not at all – the result of free competition, but something similar to a kind of war booty. (Chueca, 1983: 89)

('Long Live Spain!') or prove one's political loyalty in order to pass with-out any further difficulty (Chueca, 1983: 254–257; 329).

A book published in 1976 entitled *Los mutilados del ejército de la República* ('The War-Wounded of the Republican Army') spoke out against this state of affairs. In this case the complaint only originated from within a certain section of the losing side: the Republican war-wounded. Their claims, however, might have been perfectly applied to all members of the losing side. The book featured a transcription of a document produced by the National Commission 'Justicia y Paz' ('Justice and Peace'), in which the following demand was made: 'economic, social and political equality of the war-wounded who served in the Republican Army with respect to those of the Nationalist Army'. (Bravo-Tellado, 1976: 138). The same demands could also have been made by the widows, orphans and former prisoners-of-war on the Republican side.

The problems relating to the war-wounded are extraordinarily wide-ranging and complex. This was a matter that was never actually settled by the Franco régime and was left for subsequent democratic govern-ments to resolve. Whilst concern for the wounded of the Nationalist Army was a constant feature in the Cortes, the Republican war-wounded were left in a state of pitiful abandon. Given that they had no right to draw a pension, the majority did not even have any kind of regular income. Many had lost their jobs either because they were members of the Army who had suffered from reprisals, or civilians who had either been expelled from their jobs for political reasons or who, as a result of their injuries, were unable to find employment. The first denunciation of this unjust treatment of the Republican war-wounded was made by the *procurador familiar* Manuel María Escudero y Rueda[80] by means of a peti-tion presented to the Cortes in 1971.[81] This petition proposed the creation of a 'League of War-Wounded and Invalids from the War of Spain', the 'Liga de Mutilados y Inválidos de la Guerra de España', thus overcoming the division established by the existence of the veterans' brotherhood, the Hermandad de Caballeros Mutilados, which only admitted members of the winning side. He explained that the situation of the Republican war-wounded was untenable and stressed the idea that 'the war ended in 1939'. The response from the Ministry for Army Affairs was swift and brief. It stated that the legislation on the war-wounded 'is based on cer-tain principles and on a budget that does not permit coverage to the extent that is suggested'.

---

80. He was one of the most active *procuradores* in denouncing the legal destitution that the defeated were subjected to. Escudero was only eighteen years old when he fought in the Civil War as a member of the Alféreces Provisionales, a fact that did not prevent him from recognising the need to achieve reconciliation with the Republican side.
81. BOCE No. 1150; pp.28028–30; 7/6/1971.

As highlighted in the book by Bravo-Tellado, the war-wounded of the Republican Army managed to persuade a number of *procuradores* to sign (on 17 March 1973 and 12 January 1974) a document committing them to support their petitions.[82] If we analyse the origin of these forty-seven *procuradores*, who only represented 8.3 percent of the Cortes (561), we can observe that the majority of them (32 percent) originated from the family-based corporativist section of the Francoist parliament, the *tercio familiar*, a percentage that is much higher than the figure that corresponded to the representation of this body in the Cortes (18.5 percent). The *procuradores familiares* were elected by the male heads of the family and married women, which, irrespective of the limited suffrage within the electorate, made them the most representative elected members of society. The rest of the Chamber was made up mainly of *procuradores* who had gained their seat as a result of their posts or who had been appointed directly by Franco. We cannot really draw any decisive conclusions from these facts, but we might at least deduce that those *procuradores* who most faithfully represented popular feeling were the most conciliatory, and from this we might suppose the existence of an equally conciliatory spirit on the part of the majority of society.

Other attempts similar to that of Escudero were made, especially by another *procurador familiar*, Eduardo Tarragona Corbella.[83] This *procurador* also tried on various occasions, although with the same lack of success, to persuade the authorities to extend coverage to the Republican war-wounded.[84] Their situation did progressively improve thanks to the Comisión de Gobernación (Home Affairs Committee) and later the Comisión de Defensa (Defence Committee) with the eventual passing

---

82. The lists of the *procuradores* who signed the document appear on pages 126–129 of *Los mutilados del ejército de la República* (Bravo-Tellado, 1976).

83. This *procurador* was quite unique. He was born in 1927, which meant that he was not old enough to have fought in the war. In 1967 he was elected as a *procurador* in Barcelona with 437,000 votes. His speeches had a wide-ranging impact, due to his support for administrative decentralisation, the democratic election of mayors, amnesty for civil servants penalised as a result of the Civil War etc. In October 1967 he presented his resignation as a *procurador*, the only case of its kind in the Francoist Cortes, in protest at the lack of attention and interest that his proposals received. In 1971 he was elected again with 394,950 votes, making him the *procurador* who had received the largest number of votes in the entire legislature. This fact reveals how the reformist and conciliatory ambitions of Tarragona were shared by a wide spectrum of Spanish society, or at least that part of society that was entitled to a vote and exercised that right.

84. BOCE No. 1268; pp.30839-41; 5/4/1973. BOCE No. 1525; pp.36871-2; 12/8/1976. BOCE No. 1524; pp.37272-4; 9/12/1976. The first petition was supported by the *procurador* José María Adán García (BOCE No. 1275; pp.31079; 10/5/1973).

of the 'Law on the War-Wounded for the *Patria*'[85] (BOE N° 63, 13/3/1976: p.569).

The pardon published in 1966,[86] which ended all political liability of the defeated by means of a Political Liability Settlement Committee, gave false hope to many individuals. On 23 July 1968, Juan Manuel Fanjul proposed, along with other *procuradores*, a bill in which he requested the incorporation of Central Government civil servants who had been 'removed as a result of political reasons originating from our Civil War' (Cortes Españolas, 1971: 987). Fanjul stated at the time that both the law of 1966 as well as some 'subsequent official declarations...created the mistaken image that the entire discriminatory past resulting from the national historical episode between 1936–1939 had disappeared' (Fanjul, 1970: 34). The same situation would be repeated with the pardon published in 1969.

The text of this proposed bill consists of various articles that are highly revealing with regard to the inadequate rehabilitation measures of the time:

Civil staff of the State Administration, no longer pursuing their careers as a result of purges, resignation from their posts, final judgement or any other cause of a social-political nature relating to our Civil War, and who are still of working age in their respective Corps, may request their incorporation by means of application addressed to the Staffing Committee of the Presidency of the Government.

Civil servants who have passed the working age of their respective Corps shall present an application based on the same conditions for pension purposes.

Widows and other beneficiaries of deceased staff who were purged as a result of the socio-political reasons indicated above, may also present the same application, exercising the rights of the deceased relative.

Pensions shall be determined in accordance with the salaries which the subjects earned at the time of their dismissal, with any raises being accorded to them which would have applied to the pension categories had they remained an equal period of time, in accordance with current legislation.

Interested parties who currently reside abroad may also present their applications under the present Law at the Spanish Consulate closest to their place of residence. Once the re-incorporation of the applicant has

85. A motion first presented by Luis Peralta España led this issue to be raised on the Comisión de Gobernación (Home Affairs Committee) (Diario de Sesiones de las Comisiones No. 485; session No. 5; 20 March 1975). Subsequently, the Comisión de Defensa Nacional (National Defence Committee) was to assume responsibility for the discussion of the Law on the War-Wounded, that required six long sessions to finally pass the law: Diario de Sesiones de las Comisiones No. 683; session No. 24; 17 February 1976; Diario de Sesiones de las Comisiones No. 684; session No. 25; 18 February 1976; Diario de Sesiones de las Comisiones No. 685; session No. 26; 19 February 1976; Diario de Sesiones de las Comisiones No. 686; session No. 27; 20 February 1976; Diario de Sesiones de las Comisiones No. 687; session No. 28; 24 February 1976.

86. BOE of 12/11/1966.

been agreed, he must be accepted into the position attributed to him within the non-extendable period of three months (Fanjul: 1970: 35–36).

On 23 December 1968, the Government rejected the bill for budgetary reasons; according to the official version, approval would have represented a considerable increase in public expenditure.

Later on, the Cortes were obliged to respond equally negatively to similar petitions presented by the *procurador* Fanjul, who very sensibly based his plea on both the Decree-Law passed in 1969 by which all crimes committed during the Civil War were prescribed, with 'any penal consequence deriving from what was, in its day, a struggle among brothers, united today in affirming a common Spain, thus being legally inoperative',[87] as well as on the words that the Minister of Information and Tourism had expressed in reference to the pardon, 'the war has ended in all senses and definitively for the good of Spain'.[88]

Fanjul stated that if the Decree-Law of 1969 really sought to remove the penal consequences of the war, it would be necessary to undertake the urgent task of reincorporating the civil servants who were *separados*[89] or 'separated' from the administrative corps for political reasons. He states:

> It would be completely incongruous as well as incomprehensible that whilst the spirit of the Government is clearly reflected in the decision of 28th March and the consequent Decree-Law of the 31st, a proposed bill should be blocked whose sole and exclusive purpose is to achieve precisely the same end: to urgently make amends for a 'consequence deriving from what was, in its day, a struggle among brothers'. (Cortes Españolas, 1971: 988)

This petition, formulated in April 1969, received an answer from the Government in May of the same year. The response stated that, in spite of the fact that the Government agreed, in general terms, with the thrust of Fanjul's text, certain 'financial'[90] and 'legal' considerations existed that prevented the reintegration of the corresponding civil servants. Two months later, another *procurador*, Eduardo Tarragona,[91] stated that he was

---

87. BOE of 1 April 1969.
88. However, in his memoirs, Fraga does not refer to the passing of this law nor to its political consequences.
89. Note the officially sanctioned term for designating the purge of sympathisers on the Republican side.
90. The alleged financial reasons cited by the régime for not reincorporating the purged civil servants appear to be an excuse. Since the régime was unable to contradict itself by refusing to uphold in practice what the text of the 1969 pardon appears to establish, it preferred to claim, in line with its new apolitical and economic-based rhetoric, grave budgetary reasons for not implementing any reincorporation. It was no longer necessary to resort to obsolete historical enmities nor alleged attacks on the origin-based legitimacy of the régime; functional economic claims provided the perfect excuse.
91. It is highly significant that while both Fanjul and Tarragona referred to the 'Civil War', the expression 'War of Liberation' appears in the official Cortes text.

dissatisfied with the answer that the Government had given Fanjul and claimed that no legal considerations existed. With respect to the financial considerations, he requested more specific figures. 'I am unable to understand, therefore, how support can effectively continue to be given to a series of penalties for civil liability that weigh heavily on the working lives of many Spaniards – including the consequent sad effect on their private and family life – when responsibilities of any criminal nature and all their corresponding punishments have been declared ineffective' Tarragona argued in the Cortes (Cortes Españolas, 1971: 1041). Subsequently, the *procurador* Francisco de Asís Gabriel Ponce presented two further texts similar to those of his colleagues[92] with the same lack of fortune.

Although these examples do not exhaust all of the discriminatory measures that survived throughout the Franco period or all of the attempts made by various isolated individuals to end them, they do attest to the existence of this discrimination, the discomfort that this caused among certain sections of the Spanish population and the reaction of the Government to the criticisms that it received as a result. Society was probably prepared to carry out a real reconciliation. However, the 'fear of power', as Guglielmo Ferrero (1991) might term it, prevented the régime from bringing a reconciliation about, believing that such a measure would undermine the foundations of its legitimacy.

The Legislation of Clemency

Wide-ranging legislation was produced consisting of the pardons issued concerning various eventualities relating to the Civil War.[93] The Government seemed to suffer from certain pangs of conscience regarding the numbers that crowded its prisons and it was well aware that pardons were very well received both at home and abroad. Thus, on 9 October 1945, shortly after the end of the Second World War, when the régime was weathering a rather precarious political and economic climate, it decided to issue a decree of pardon[94] for 'crimes of military rebellion, against the security of the State or public order'.

The text of this decree is rather curious given that, in addition to referring to those who remained loyal to the Republic as 'rebels', it states that, 'the Government, conscious of its strength and the support of the Nation, is prepared to undertake another step in the progressive normalisation of Spanish life'. The situation did not exactly favour the permanence of a régime which associated itself with the nations that had lost the Second World War and that was subject to a considerable number of pressures from abroad. The Government set out to convey a more benevolent and tolerant image abroad than it had been projecting up until that time, and

92. BOCE No. 1070; pp.26218-9; 21/10/1969. BOCE No. 1083; pp.26433-4; 26/12/1969.
93. The book by Ramón Tamames on Francoism includes a somewhat incomplete list of these pardons (Tamames, 1983: 371-373).
94. BOE of 19-21/19/1945, p.1569.

that was why it issued this decree of pardon, the scope of which is somewhat arbitrary, given that it excludes those prisoners 'who may have taken part in acts of cruelty, death, rape, desecration, theft or other acts which, by their nature, may disgust all honourable men'.

The following pardon, issued on 17 July 1947,[95] a date that commemorated the passing of the Law of Succession, affected 'prisoners guilty of common and special crimes' and seems to be a result of the previous decree. In this case, it was also stated that the pardon would include 'Spaniards located abroad' (in accordance with a previous decree of 27 December 1946).

Other pardons were passed on the following dates: 9 December 1949,[96] 1 May 1952[97] to mark the Eucharist Congress, 25 July 1954[98] to mark the Year of Our Lady and Xacobeo, 31 July 1958[99] to mark the Enthronement of Pope John XXIII, 11 October 1961[100] to mark the commemoration of the Twenty-fifth Anniversary of Franco's Leadership of the State, 24 June 1963[101] to commemorate the appointment of Paul VI, 1 April 1964[102] to commemorate the '25 Years of Peace', 22 July 1965[103] to mark the celebration of the Jubilee Year of Santiago de Compostela, 10 November 1966[104] to mark thirty years since the beginning of the Civil War, 31 March 1969[105] to mark the thirtieth anniversary of the end of the war and 9 October 1971[106] to mark the thirty-fifth anniversary of the 'Proclamation of the Caudillo of Spain as Head of State'.

The pardon issued in 1969 was one of the most widely publicised and discussed by the press and by political leaders.[107] Fraga, for example, made various declarations that very year in which he stated, 'we have definitively put behind us all remaining former divisions and we have drawn a line under our last civil war' (quoted by López Rodó, 1991: 474). It was obvious that an open wound, a painful memory of the war existed, although it was not usual to refer to the existence of this memory as a

95. BOE of 1–2/8/1947, p.1254.
96. BOE of 19–20/12/1949, p.1377.
97. BOE of 1/5/1952, p.434.
98. BOE of 25/7/1954, p.824.
99. BOE of 6–7/11/1958, p.1497.
100. BOE of 11–12/10/1961, p.1250.
101. BOE of 1–2/7/1963, p.1158.
102. BOE of 7/4/1964, p.688. This decree was complemented by that of 2 May (BOE of 4–5/5/1964, p.863) and that of 22 May of the same year (BOE of 28/5/1964, p.1014).
103. BOE of 24/7/1965, p.1143.
104. BOE of 12/11/1966, p.2121.
105. BOE of 1/4/1969, p.559.
106. BOE of 26/10/1971, p.2355.
107. In fact, as we shall see later on, the Instituto de Opinión Pública (Public Opinion Institute) carried out a survey on current issues in March 1969 which introduced a question regarding Spaniards' opinion of the pardon, proof of the symbolic importance that the régime attributed to such issues (CIS, Study No. 1,038, March 1969).

problem, except when some official initiative (pardons, laws, commemorations) was meant to have provided a solution to it. The preamble to this pardon refers to the 'peaceful coexistence of the Spanish over the last thirty years', which, according to the text, 'has consolidated the legitimacy of our Movement, which has been able to give our generation thirty years of peace, development and legal freedom'. Later on, it refers to the 'War of Liberation' as 'a struggle among brothers, united today in the cause of a shared and more representative Spain and more prepared than ever to work for its future greatness'. Nowadays, it is difficult to reconcile this 'war among brothers' with the 'War of Liberation', but at that time the public discourse was riddled with contradictions and ambiguities of a similar kind.

Such a considerable number of pardons attests to the rather limited scope of each one (many of them applied to only one type of crime).[108] The truth is that, although it is undeniable that many of these pardons reduced the sentences of a considerable number of prisoners, in the last analysis there was always an element of arbitrariness in the application of the law, which limited its scope.

Memory of the Civil War

In relation to the pardons that were issued, one of the most important and widely publicised pieces of legislation was said to be the pardon granted in 1969, thirty years after the end of the war. Under this decree, crimes committed prior to the date of 1 April 1939 or, similarly, those limited to the war period, were declared to have been prescribed.

It is highly significant that the Instituto de Opinión Pública (Public Opinion Institute) (the predecessor of the Centro de Investigaciones Sociológicos – Centre for Sociological Research) should include, in a study it was carrying out on current issues and the very month the decree was passed, the following question:

> The Spanish Government has declared all liability for acts committed before 1 April 1939 to have lapsed. What is your opinion of this decision?:
> – Very good
> – Good
> – Quite good
> – Bad
> – I don't know. No response.[109]

---

108. In this respect, the text of the decree of 11 October 1961 is highly significant in stating that the régime's actions were guided by a spirit of 'generosity', 'although with the constraints required by the inescapable demands of security and social defence'.
109. Study No. 1,038. Title: Current Issues. Scope: National. Universe: Spanish population of both sexes over eighteen years of age. Size: 1,953 interviews. Date of implementation: March 1969. This study can be found at the Centro de Investigaciones Sociológicas.

Seventy-seven percent of the population considered the pardon that had been passed by the Government to be 'very good' or simply 'good'; 6.5 percent thought it was 'quite good' or 'bad' and 14.4 percent did not respond to the question.[110] Therefore, a large majority of society was in favour of pardoning the defeated. A certain consensus existed regarding the reconciliation of the Spanish, given that only a small percentage of the respondents objected to this measure.[111]

Three decades had passed since the end of the war and approximately 63 percent of the population had not actually fought in it (the older respondents included in this percentage were hardly ten years of age at the end of the war) although we must bear in mind that all of the respondents were over eighteen years of age. The percentage mentioned above thus falls from 63 percent to 43 percent if we deduct that section of the population aged under eighteen.[112] Without including that part of the population under eighteen years of age, those who lived through the war and were over ten years of age represented 58.8 percent, although in the sample they are somewhat underrepresented, accounting for only 50 percent.

If we analyse the responses to the question according to age-groups, which is essential in order to establish generational variations, we can observe the following: if we combine the first two age-groups, including the 18 to 29 year-olds and 30 to 39 year-olds, that is the war children (under 10 years of age) and postwar children, and even those who came afterwards (those who were eighteen in 1969 were born in 1951), it turns out that the percentages obtained for the category 'very good' are slightly higher than the average: 46.69 percent in the first case and 49.17 percent in the second case, with the average standing at 45.6 percent. The next age-group up, from 40 to 49 years of age, including those who were between 10 and 19 years of age during the war, achieves a percentage figure within this same category that is practically identical to the average, but much higher in the less conciliatory category ('bad'), where it achieves the figure of 3.16 percent as opposed to an average of 1.9 percent. This group is somewhat more polarised than the rest. Those respondents over 50 years of age, who actually fought in the war (older than twenty years of age) are less in favour of the pardon, especially those respondents over 70 years of age, only 37.1 percent of whom consider it to be 'very good'. Nevertheless, they do not consider it to be 'bad' in numbers that are significantly higher than the average.

110. High abstention figures were a constant feature of the sociological studies of those years, as they are of surveys carried out in various countries that have non-democratic régimes.
111. In fact, only 1.9 percent thought it was really 'bad'.
112. Nevertheless, this segment of the population, represented by those who were between the ages of 18 and 39 when the survey was carried out, is slightly overrepresented in the sample (49.4 percent) with regard to the percentage that corresponded to its actual weight in society at that time (43.1 percent).

The age-group that is most conciliatory, the one that varies most from the average – exceeding it within the 'very good' category and failing to achieve the average within the 'bad' category – is the group aged between 0 and 9 years of age when the war ended, that is to say, children who suffered the shortages and fears of the postwar period, the same individuals who, in 1977, would be between 38 and 47 years of age and who would be so important, along with the first age category of the survey (those born between 1940 and 1951) in the transition towards democracy.[113] In 1977, for example, 73 percent of the parliamentary members elected democratically were under 49 years of age (the oldest members of this group were eleven years old when the war ended). This means that they belonged precisely to the two age-groups that were revealed as being most conciliatory in the survey carried out in 1969.

According to other variables, such as gender, it is not so much a case of women being less conciliatory than men, but that the rate of abstention of women is much higher (23.18 percent compared to an average of 9.79 percent). Whatever the case may be, the male opinion results are more polarised than the female results; the male respondents are more strongly in favour, but also more strongly opposed to the pardon.

If we consider the civil status of the respondents, related in many cases to age, we can observe that the single and married respondents are much more conciliatory than the widowed respondents, who are probably older and who, in addition, may well have lost their spouses in the Civil War, a circumstance that would naturally make them less prepared to forgive and forget.

With regard to the profession of the respondents, we can observe that their desire for reconciliation increases depending on their professional category (except for 'students' or 'learners' who are, logically, very young) with a figure of up to 64.21 percent who considered it to be 'very good' being achieved among the most highly qualified (senior civil servants etc). The lowest levels are represented, once again, by women ('housewives') and old people ('retired persons', 'pensioners'). The same occurs with regard to their level of studies; the higher their training, the more in favour they are of the pardon, although it is true that the rate of abstinence is very high among the lower categories. If we consider income level, something similar occurs. The higher the income, the greater the desire for reconciliation (up to 71.43 percent of those who earned over 50,000 pesetas a month considered it to be 'very good').

If we analyse the respondents' answers according to the size of the municipal areas that they lived in, we can observe a somewhat paradox-

113.   As we stated above, those who suffered directly, not from the war, but from its most immediate consequences, were the ones most inclined to avoid it in the future, the most liable to seek consensus and negotiation in order to avoid a conflict whose ravages they would have to suffer, without having had any responsibility in bringing them about.

ical set of results. The most conciliatory came from municipalities of between 2,000 and 50,000 inhabitants (between 2,000 and 10,000 and 10,000 and 50,000) and the least conciliatory, from those municipalities of under 2,000 inhabitants and those of between 50,000 and 100,000. The respondents who came from municipalities of over 100,000 achieve almost average results.

If we compare, finally, the results obtained with the region of origin of the respondents, we can observe that the Spanish Region most openly in favour of the measure was Asturias-Galicia, followed by the Levant, the Island Regions and the Basque Country-Navarre (in none of whose opinion the decree is considered to be 'bad'). The region most opposed to the pardon was Castile-León, followed by Western Andalusia and Extremadura and Catalonia. The rest, Eastern Andalusia, Aragón and Central Spain, fell below the average when it comes to accepting the pardon, but are, nevertheless, closer to it.

With this brief analysis of the data available to us, we have attempted to demonstrate both the largely conciliatory desire of the Spanish population, as well as its complex variations depending on the different variables taken into account. A large part of society seemed to have considered that the time had come to forgive and, quite possibly, to forget.

From Munich to the Organic Law of State

The conflicts that took place within the Madrid university scene in 1956 are well known and their consequences were to include various sudden dismissals of both critical Falangists and progressive Catholics. However, the most important aspect of these events was that they revealed, as Stanley Payne has indicated, 'a new internal opposition, one that stemmed not from the Republic or the emigrés of the 1940s but from the new generation who had begun to grow up under the régime during the 1950s' (Payne, 1987: 444).

The first internal dissension, therefore, began to emerge in the form of a more-or-less tolerated semi-opposition, based on a broadly liberal perspective. The change of government which, as a consequence of this crisis, took place the following year, consisted of incorporating a new political force that was destined to play an extremely important role in the future of the country. This marked the inclusion of a group known as the 'technocrats' into positions of power. The technocrats were known as such because of their tendency to deal with political issues from the perspective of a technical and economic approach that was apparently free of ideology.

This young group, many of whom were members of Opus Dei (the Roman Catholic organisation of laymen and priests founded in Spain in 1928), had good professional qualifications and espoused a conservative ideology. They presented themselves as a new source of impetus that would enable the régime to consolidate its power through competent economic management. Their political philosophy consisted in achieving far-reaching results within the economic field while avoiding the thorny issue of political rhetoric, thereby endowing the régime with a new and more wide-ranging legitimacy. These are, indeed, the main practical and rhetorical factors on which performance-based legitimacy is founded, although the political theory surrounding these ideas was to be more carefully designed, some time after the first economic achievements, by Gonzalo Fernández de la Mora, the main champion of this new form of legitimacy based on 'public works'.[114]

The 'Conspiracy'

The events that took place at the meeting held in Munich between 5 and 8 June 1962 among members of the moderate opposition to Francoism from both inside Spain and from exile, have been described in considerable detail on various occasions (see, for example, Satrústegui, 1993; La Porte, 1992; Álvarez de Miranda, 1985). We do not intend, therefore, to detail these events once again, but to highlight the most important aspects of the meeting with regard to its evocation of the Civil War and how this influenced the legitimacy of the régime.

Contacts between those who declared themselves to be pro-European and normally belonged to moderate groups that either formed part of the open opposition to the régime abroad or part of the semi-opposition or clandestine opposition within Spain, had already taken place prior to this date.[115] However, it was not until the meeting in Munich of the Movimiento Europeo (European Movement) that these groups debated the future of Spain, agreeing to impose certain political conditions regarding the admission of the country into the European Community, which had recently been requested by the Franco régime.

Prior to the meeting, the semi-opposition groups, led by the former head of CEDA, José María Gil-Robles, had taken certain precautions, which consisted of sending letters to certain important figures within the country explaining the reasons for their participation in the meeting. Some members also revealed some considerable apprehension which, in certain cases, translated into an open reluctance to meet members of the opposition in exile. Due to this reticence, it was initially agreed that the participants from exile (39) and those from within Spain (80), would get together at different forums so that they could reach their own resolutions, independently from each other. The texts that were drafted and debated by the committees on the first day, one chaired by Gil-Robles and the other by Salvador de Madariaga, featured one main point of dis-

---

114. With regard to this author, see the article by Pedro Carlos González Cuevas (1989).
115. The PCE, the Spanish Communist Party, was anti-European at that time. Only later, probably in light of the events that took place in Munich, and the prospect of remaining isolated from the rest of the opposition in exile, did it rectify its attitude when it witnessed the surprising consensus that Europeanism had aroused.

agreement: the choice of political system that was to replace Francoism. For the internal opposition within Spain, the Monarchy, personified by Don Juan, was unquestionably the only institution capable of guaranteeing the peaceful transition of the Spanish nation towards democracy. The representatives from exile, however, contemplated the staging of a referendum in order to decide the form, republican or monarchic, that the new régime should adopt. In spite of this, both groups agreed that an inorganic form of democracy should be adopted, being opposed to the 'organic' democracy of Francoism, and that the restoration of the party system and the recovery of civil liberties were the indispensable prerequisites for Spain's incorporation into Europe.

The organiser of the Congress, Van Schendel, managed to overcome the only obstacle that divided the two groups by avoiding the thorny issue of the political system and proposing a text that would be to the liking of all. This text, in addition to proposing the establishment of democratic institutions, stated that:

> the immense majority of the Spanish people wish this development to take place in accordance with the rules of *political prudence*, as rapidly as circumstances may permit...*with a commitment to renouncing all active and passive violence, before, during and after the process.* (Satrústegui, 1993: 180; the italics are mine)

The two groups may not have agreed about the issue of the referendum, but they did share a clear desire not to confront each other on this matter, not to resume the arguments brandished during the Civil War either for or against each of the political systems. They also shared an obsessive desire to undertake a peaceful and stable course towards democracy. The ghosts of the war were eminently present at the meeting, especially due to the graphic and self-evident fact that the members from outside Spain lived in exile largely because they had lost the war. In this sense, it was essential, some twenty-three years after the end of the conflict, for a reconciliation to take place among Spaniards that would allow them to live together once again in freedom.

Judging by the documents available, once a rapprochement had taken place between the two positions, resulting from the consensus achieved by the text proposed by Robert Van Schendel, the atmosphere became more cordial and a large amount of the tension and suspicion that had existed on the first day dissipated. The following day, open meetings took place and there was a considerable flow of representatives moving to and fro between the two committees. A highly significant consequence of this new climate was the request presented by the émigrés that Joaquín Satrústegui should explain to them the reasons why his group believed the referendum should not take place and why, furthermore, a monarchic form of democracy was the most appropriate for the future. Satrústegui presented his argument in the following manner:

first of all, we Spaniards must resolve two basic issues: it is essential for us to overcome our Civil War; it is necessary for us to form part of Europe... With the Monarchy we can achieve it; with the Republic, we cannot. And I say this because the Republic, having been at the centre of our Civil War, is unable to overcome it. Let us not forget that hundreds of thousands of Spaniards fought and died for the Republic, that is defending it. You can certainly boast about how, for those very Republican ideals, such a great number of compatriots fought and fell; but do not forget that hundreds of thousands of Spaniards also fought against the Republic and died. This simply proves that the Republic was at the heart of a tragic conflict. How could it ever go beyond it?

He also stated, however, that

the Crown remained on the sidelines of that war among brothers... Consequently, the Monarchy is in a unique position to overcome our war.[116]

With respect to the popular referendum he said the following:

We are also opposed to the plebiscite for another reason: as responsible men we are not prepared to participate in any political operation which may provoke once again violence among Spaniards...either I do not know my countrymen at all, or this would represent the reawakening of a machine which would stir up the ashes of our tragic conflict and lead to renewed violence in the streets and in the countryside. (Satrústegui, 1993: 181–188)

Texts of this kind, full of direct allusions to the Civil War and its dramatic and fratricidal nature, the need to overcome it through the reconciliation of all Spaniards, and a wish to avoid any repetition of the tragedy at all costs, were numerous among the papers presented to the Congress and those that were subsequently drafted by the various groups on the meeting. The Congress ended on 8 June after the reading, first of all, of an emotional address by De Madariaga and, then, a more aseptic address by Gil-Robles. The first speech, which met with excited applause, highlighted the fact that:

the Congress of Munich shall be a unique and illustrious day in the history of Spain. The Civil War that began in Spain on 18 July 1936, and that the

---

116. This statement is not entirely true, as the successor to the throne whom they proposed, Don Juan, twice tried to enlist as a voluntary soldier on the Nationalist side and was turned down by Franco on both occasions. The latter knew that, should a hypothetical restoration of the monarchy take place, it would not be appropriate for a future monarch to have inclined so far towards one of the sides in the Civil War. The power of the Crown represented that of the arbiter *par excellence* and it had to be capable of remaining above political divisions. It is worth recalling here the almost systematic amnesia regarding Don Juan's failed attempts to participate in the Civil War, especially after his death, an event that was used to portray him as a tireless champion of democracy.

régime has maintained artificially through censorship, the monopoly of the press and radio and victory parades, ended in Munich the day before yesterday, 6 July 1962. (Satrústegui, 1993: 188)

Why did the participants at the Congress insist so strongly, then and later, that the Civil War had ended? It was probably due to the symbolic dimension that the meeting had acquired in their eyes, having achieved something that they had believed to be still far beyond reach: the recovery of their capacity to debate peacefully with their former enemies. The opposition groups from within Spain and from abroad had brought their prejudices and suspicions with them to Munich, especially, as the documents reveal, the Spanish-based opposition groups, and both groups had found, to their surprise and delight, that the barriers between them had collapsed with hardly any effort at all. It was obvious from the very beginning that agreement existed on the most important issues, and the only matter that appeared irreconcilable was quickly put aside in order to reach a consensus on their willingness to undertake a peaceful process of change towards democracy. Rodolfo Llopis even went so far as to ask Satrústegui in private to inform Don Juan that, 'the Socialists had a commitment to the Republicans that they did not intend to break, but he wanted him to know that, should it be the Monarchy that were to establish democracy, it would have the support of the Spanish Socialist Party' (La Porte, 1992: 406).

The fundamental basis of agreement was clear. In the medium term, they were in favour of inorganic democracy (with political parties and civil liberties) and against Francoism. In the short term, they actually urged Europe – although those in exile considered it to be a much more explicit pressure than those from within Spain – not to admit Spain into its Community until it satisfied the democratic requirements that the rest of the countries fulfilled. They were conscious of the fact that the Franco régime would receive a considerable dose of additional legitimacy if the European Community accepted Spain and that this would make the régime much more difficult to replace. The truth is, had it not been for the excessive response of the Franco régime to the Munich Congress, various small cosmetic changes on the régime's part would probably have been enough for some member countries of the Community to have secured Spain's membership.

The Franco régime reacted with considerable clumsiness and severity, to the extent that some of the Congress participants from inside Spain chose to join the list of exiles, whilst others, upon their return, were punished with exile. Francoism also assessed, in its own manner, the symbolic importance of the meeting. It represented an attempt at partial reconciliation between the winning side and the defeated outside of the régime's sphere of influence or, rather, in spite of it. This angered the Government, given that such a gesture placed it in an embarrassing position both within and outside of Spain, undermining its origin-based legitimacy, on which it had founded the repression and discrimination of the defeated side.[117] It also represented a desire to return to a democratic régime expressed by a group formed by members of the winning side in the war, a system that they had actually fought against, and all this in spite of the propagandist efforts of the régime to definitively banish such a possibility from the collective conscience of the Spanish nation.

The maintenance of a black-and-white image of the Civil War within the collective memory was so vital to the régime that merely questioning it produced a reaction that was so excessive on its part that it ended up being counterproductive by damaging its chances of forming part of the European Community. The repression of the participants at the meeting, as well as the spectacular press campaign aimed at publicly discrediting and condemning them, finally proved right those who had claimed that it was impossible to incorporate a dictatorial régime, such as that which existed in Spain, into Europe.[118]

The Franco régime, in spite of a few errors of political calculation such as this, demonstrated, on various occasions, an extraordinary capacity to react and adapt to new developments. In this case, it ended up by changing the government in order to get rid of the Minister of Information and Tourism, one of the main instigators of the ferocious press campaign that was unleashed. With considerable shrewdness, Franco proposed a new government that was to be more *aperturista* than the former, in order to present a more modernising and exportable image. In replacing Arias Salgado, he appointed the young reformist, Manuel Fraga Iribarne, whose administration was to be of such importance to the country.

As with so many other episodes of supreme importance, Fraga hardly mentions the 'Munich incident' in his memoirs. Perhaps the only

117. The régime was particularly suspicious of any attempt at reconciliation that originated from exile. It had already revealed this distrust upon publication of the document entitled 'Reconciliación Nacional' (National Reconciliation) by the PCE in the mid-1950s. The book produced by the Secretary-General of the Movement entitled *Texto de las orientaciones que se consideran con valor permanente* ('Approaches Considered to Be of Permanent Value') attacks the PCE publication by stating that the only reconciliation was that which 'the social policy of the régime has been progressively bringing about' and that Franco 'is the real artifice of national reconciliation... Anything else, propounded by political groups in exile, merely represents a desire for vengeance and concealed political slogans' (Delegación Nacional de Provincias, 1961: 40).

118. This campaign, directed by the Ministry of Information and Tourism headed by Gabriel Arias Salgado, imposed such rigid slogans that these even aroused the anger of the journalists who supported the régime, who would have voluntarily condemned the Munich events anyway. We do not know whether the Minister himself overstepped the mark in his zeal to condemn these events, or whether the instructions he received were equally harsh. The fact is that, since Arias Salgado was the most visible head of this excessive campaign, he would also be the one to suffer the consequences of its inexpediency.

interesting reference is that of 10 August 1962, a date on which a cabinet meeting was held at which:

> the Minister for Home Affairs attempted to impose a hailstorm of economic sanctions on the participants at the Munich meeting. Through long argument we were able to avoid it, which led Don Camilo to make a harsh reference to the 'new members of this Cabinet'. Shortly afterwards, I would manage to free my old friend and camp-mate from the militia, Fernando Álvarez de Miranda, who had been deported to Fuerteventura, and successively all the rest. (Fraga, 1980: 41)

This demonstrates the more *aperturista* profile of the new government, that already began to clash with the staunchest sections of the régime, and the desire of the recently-created government team to end the political consequences of the Munich meeting, an event that had been branded as a 'conspiracy' during the smear campaign. This new government proved itself to be more pragmatic politically and more consistent in its pro-European vocation. Its greatest desire was to demonstrate that the Franco régime, with certain small changes, was perfectly worthy of joining Europe, whilst also consolidating the régime's internal legitimacy.

In spite of this moderate reaction brought about by the change of government, counterattacks of another kind continued to be made, such as that represented by the publication issued by Ediciones del Movimiento entitled *Contra la paz de España: Del Pacto de San Sebastián (agosto de 1930) al Pacto de Munich (junio de 1962)*. ('Against Peace in Spain: From the Pact of San Sebastián (August 1930) to the Pact of Munich (June 1962)'). This book, whose title is quite revealing, summarises the official version of the events and a study of it enables us to clarify the repercussions that the Munich meeting had for Francoism.

María Teresa La Porte, in her study on the European policy of Francoism, claims that she is unable to understand the 'excessive reaction' of the régime in view of the conventional explanations that have been provided so far, so she ventures to offer her own version, one that is entirely consistent with the thesis of this investigation, and that is confirmed by the text published by the Movement. La Porte claims, quoting a letter that Gil-Robles sent to Ridruejo in 1962, that:

> for Franco there is no greater danger than the weakening of the memory of the Civil War and, in this sense, the Munich meeting had represented the surmounting of divisions within a significant sector. In fact, it was the actual appearance of the meeting which had been criticised most strongly in the press campaign, and for which the participants from within Spain had been accused of being traitors. Contacts with the opposition in exile revealed the need for former differences to be overcome, when some members of the régime continued to resort to victory in the war as a basis for the legitimacy and worth of the system. (La Porte, 1992: 414–415)

Further on, when dealing with the consequences of the event, she provides the following explanation:

The events at the Munich Congress had touched on two sensitive issues for the régime: reconciliation with the enemy of the Civil War, when the fight against this enemy was what justified the nature of the régime and its political principles, and recourse to Europe in order to force a change towards democracy, which is precisely what the régime was seeking to avoid. (La Porte, 1992: 435)

This interpretation is corroborated by the text published by the Movement, in which the Munich participants were compared to the instigators of the Spanish Civil War and accused of wishing to once again undermine the greatest achievement of Francoism, peace in Spain. In effect, a comparison was established between those who met in San Sebastián in August 1930 to prepare for the arrival of the Second Republic and those who, thirty years later, met in Munich. The text claimed that the political and ideological groupings that came together on both occasions were practically identical and that their aim, both then and now, was destructive: to end the existing legal status quo; the Monarchy in 1930, and Francoism in 1962. If the meeting in San Sebastián had ushered in the Second Republic, and this was responsible for the Civil War, the Munich meeting might also lead to a fratricidal confrontation.

The text went on to ridicule the two most important figures at the meeting, Gil-Robles and De Madariaga. The latter was claimed to be the most ignorant of authorities on Spain and various photocopies of books published by him were enclosed which, in their view, confirmed the author's lack of precision and the contradictions he committed in *Spain: A Modern History*. However, the cruellest insults were reserved for Gil-Robles, who was accused, first of all, of having collaborated with the deposed Republic without being capable of taking control of the situation and avoiding the final confrontation. He was subjected to many other criticisms, but what really irritated them was that a person from the winning side in the Civil War should agree to converse with the defeated, and even contemplate a return to the legal state of affairs which, in keeping with the official version, had caused the war.

According to this book:

Mr. Gil-Robles dares to challenge the Spanish people when he forms a 'pact'...not with Spanish Socialists...but with the Socialists of the Republic of 1936, with those of the Civil War, with those of the revolutionary governments that led Spain towards catastrophe, with those who officially declared themselves to be enemies of the Church, with those who authorised the partition of national territory, with those who handed over the gold of the Bank of Spain to Russia, with those who supported the theft of the 'Vita'...in short, he has formed a pact with those who, in Spain's eyes, appear in burning flames, or bathed in a river of blood...

The Munich Socialists are the ones who have taken up the terrible legacy of Indalecio Prieto. Mr. Gil-Robles cannot form a pact with them without becoming an accomplice to a new disaster, a new conflict among brothers, another civil war, another dispersion of the Spanish people, further bloodshed, mire and tears. This is the enormous responsibility of his act in Munich; in this his guilt resides; in having become reconciled with the 'Popular Front'...

Mr. Gil-Robles does not identify with the Spain that emerged victorious in 1939, he has not made that victory in our war his own, he does not want it, he would like to abolish it; in the same way as Rodolfo Llopis... The difference is that with Llopis this reaction is explained, since he belongs to those groups of Spaniards devoted to making that victory reversible, revocable, to cancelling that victory in order to go back to the starting-point. (Ediciones del Movimiento, 1962: 14)

The aim of this text was to fill society with fear and threaten it with a repetition of the tragedy should it not obey the strict guidelines laid down by the régime. It claimed that, 'the results of the "pact" or "formula" of San Sebastián, a devastated Spain and one million dead, will be child's-play compared to the consequences of the Munich agreement, if the Spanish people allow themselves to be taken by surprise' (Ediciones del Movimiento, 1962: 17).

It was obvious that any attempt to bring about a real reconciliation, to overcome the Civil War, struck at the very foundations of the régime and undermined one of the basic pillars of its legitimacy. A large part of the politics during the Franco period was sustained by this foundational myth and, although it is true that, through time, new and more balanced versions of the Civil War did progressively emerge, the régime never ceased to attempt to legitimise its power based on a victory obtained in a war that it considered to be just and necessary.

In the Francoist Cortes, the Minister for Home Affairs, Camilo Alonso Vega, addressed this episode based on a petition presented by the Conde de Mayalde, a member of the Standing Committee. The Minister took the opportunity to offer an official version of what had taken place and to state that the exiles, in his view driven by resentment and a desire for revenge, had been to be blame for the war and were now intent, through a conspiracy with other powers, on bringing down the régime and replacing it with a state of chaos similar to that represented by the Second Republic. He stated:

One can forgive all ones likes; but there are cases where to forget is to succumb. Forgiving is the Christian tolerance accorded to those who guarantee to rejoin Spanish life as simple citizens; but that indulgence does not extend to the point at which their reintegration enables them to continue pursuing political actions whose characteristics and consequences must never be forgotten on pain of deliberately renouncing the teachings of most painful experience.[119]

Any act carried out, against the régime, or even a declaration made against it, was construed as a long-planned conspiracy, organised from exile and managed by international communism. Any criticism, however slight it was, was received with considerable irritation and interpreted as an assault on Spanish national sovereignty.

Arias Salgado would end up paying the price for an official reaction which, in fact, contributed to preventing the entry of Spain into the European Community. The new government was to take upon itself the task of emphasising the most neutral political issues, as the technocratic politicians had already begun to do, such as the matter of effective economic management and other questions of a technical nature, or the best means of moving towards Europe and gaining recognition. The practices initiated by the members of Opus Dei would thus become established during this period and would contribute, at the expense of avoiding ideological matters – anachronistic and unpopular as they were – to improving Spain's image abroad. Nevertheless, Fraga Iribarne and the rest of the reformists in favour of his policy of *apertura* or openness, did not limit themselves to dealing with economic issues, nor did they adopt a rhetoric that was as rigorously neutral and apolitical as that of the technocrats.

It was at the height of this new approach that the '25 Years of Peace' campaign was carried out. During this new period, the Government not only emphasised the achievements of peace, as we shall see, but also the value of peace as a precious commodity in itself. It is quite possible that the Government's enthusiastic support for the '25 Years of Peace' campaign was simply a way of attenuating the impact of the reconciliatory initiative of Munich and attributing a capacity for integration to itself.

In short, this event made the régime realise that the defeated had a certain voice in Europe and that the arguments that spoke in favour of settling the issue of the Civil War were very well-received abroad. In this sense, the régime came to the conclusion that it was necessary to modify its discourse as far as possible, accompanying this with certain conciliatory gestures – pardons, for example – in order to convince the world that harmony had been re-established in Spain and that at least the peace, if not the victory, belonged to 'all Spaniards'. This is the message that the régime sought to convey through its celebration of the '25 Years of Peace' in 1964. It might be said that this celebration marked the turning-point of official discourse, whilst the Munich Conspiracy marked the turning-point of the collective memory of the war.

119. BOCE No. 743; 14/7/1962; p. 15647–56. At the end of Alonso Vegas' speech, the Bulletin records the following: *'unanimous and prolonged applause and enthusiastic cheers for Spain and for Franco from all of the standing Procuradores'.*

The Execution of Julián Grimau

A year before that huge campaign was implemented, an event of considerable importance and international magnitude took place in which the new government was to demonstrate that it was not as politically aseptic nor anywhere near as conciliatory as its rhetoric attempted to convey. In fact, it was under the mandate of this government, in 1963, that the Communist leader Julián Grimau was executed for alleged criminal activities in the Civil War. The execution provoked massive protests abroad which seriously damaged the image of openness that the régime wished to present. In order to counteract these reactions, various anonymous books appeared which justified the death of Grimau, based on 'information sources' that accused him of the alleged crimes. These were actually drafted, it seems, by the Ministry of Information and Tourism itself, and distributed in a virtually clandestine manner.

One of these books had the significant title of *El caso Grimau o la guerra civil permanente* ('The Grimau Case or The Permanent Civil War') and it stated that the Spanish exiles were 'determined and inexorable enemies of peace in Spain' and that they would do everything in their power to return the country to a state of civil war. It stated that the country was prepared to accept 'noble discrepancies', but it introduced an essential qualification which corroborates our hypothesis regarding origin-based legitimacy:

Of course! We have to start with the fact that the Civil War ended as it did, and no other way; that the victorious weapons were in the hands of those who achieved victory, and no others; that that event is an unchangeable, irreversible fact; that the new organisation of Spain is open to all forms of dignified and just cooperation, free from prior bias, free from prior and forced adhesion to a pre-determined organisation; that there is a place for all Spaniards in Spain, all except the murderers, except those who, during and before the war, stained their hands with blood and burdened their consciences with criminal complicity... As long as these fundamental truths, these principles of conduct are ignored...Spain will have the very real sensation that its enemies have not laid down their arms, and that, consequently, they are pursuing a state of permanent civil war. Communism does not accept its Spanish defeat. It is fighting to redress it... What a bloodbath!... Are we really aware of what a substantial rectification of the outcome of the Spanish Civil War would mean for Red politics? (Ediciones OID, 1963: 18–19)

Another book, entitled *¿Crimen o Castigo? Documentos inéditos de Julián Grimau García* ('Crime or Punishment? Unpublished Documents About Julián Grimau García') argued that:

The Spanish Government has been accused of opening the wounds of the civil war with this execution. On the contrary, the facts have proven that it is communism that has used Grimau...in order to disrupt the peace-making process which is healing those wounds. (SIE, 1963: no numbering)

Later on the book criticises an article published in *Le Monde*, in which Dionisio Ridruejo claimed that the state of war in Spain was on-going. Paradoxically, Ridruejo was described as being 'one of the men who worked hardest to maintain a state of war when peace came to the men of Spain in 1939'. In this case, the régime also found, to its great disgust that, as with Gil-Robles, one of the members of the winning side who had not only held positions of great political responsibility but also fought as a volunteer in the División Azul (Blue Division), had turned against the victors, questioning the legitimacy of their victory. This was something that the Franco régime was quite unable to bear, as it considered such developments as a betrayal of the principles for which it had fought and secured victory.

The resounding voices of condemnation that were heard abroad as a result of Grimau's execution did not fail to point out that twenty-four years had passed since the end of the Civil War and that, to condemn the victim to the death penalty after such a time-lapse based on crimes that he had allegedly committed in the Civil War, was utterly anachronistic, unjust and brutal. The publishing house Ruedo Ibérico produced a book entitled *España hoy* ('Spain Today') which included various commentaries on this event under the heading 'Julián Grimau: el muerto de la paz' ('Julián Grimau: The Casualty of Peace'). In effect, the value of 'Franco's peace', which supposedly began on 1 April 1939, was called into question, given that a quarter of a century after the end of the war this conflict still weighed heavily on judicial decisions and on Spanish life in general, in spite of the pardons that had been issued (Fernández de Castro, 1963: 382–394).

The 25 Years of Peace

The commemoration of what officially came to be known as the '25 Años de Paz' ('25 Years of Peace') involved the staging of the largest propaganda campaign ever carried out under the Franco régime. Very few issues merited such great emphasis or such a huge investment of human and financial capital. Not even the campaigns that were devoted to promoting popular participation in the two referendums which took place were as extensive nor harboured such exhaustive pretensions.

The year was 1964, so twenty-five years had passed since that 1 April 1939 when Franco had read out the military communiqué which was to gain mythical status: 'Today, the Red Army has been captured and disarmed...The war has ended'. The first of April is the date that the victory of the 'Nationalist' side was secured, but it is also the date on which the Civil War ended. Peace, therefore, was officially declared in Spain. However, it was a warlike, tense and fragile peace, in whose name reprisals and purges of various kinds never ceased to be implemented.

We might wonder why 25 years of peace were celebrated and not, for example, 20 years. The truth is that, as of 1964, upon the commemoration of 1 April, references would always be made to 'peace' and the official publications that were produced in order to mark the successive anniversaries were to make this their central theme.[120]

The official commemoration of the '25 Years of Peace' was approved in 1962 by a Decree issued on 26 September of the same year (BOE 16/10/1963). Nevertheless, this decree had various legal and political antecedents that are not usually considered. In 1958, in his capacity as Minister of Information and Tourism, Gabriel Arias Salgado approved a decree by which it was agreed that a 'National Exhibition' was to be staged in 1961 under the slogan '25 Years of Spanish Life (1936–1961)'.[121] A year later, another decree would appear which, in spite of complementing the original decree through the appointment of the Curator of the Exhibition (Lieutenant-General José María López Valencia) and the Committee responsible for carrying out the preliminary plan for it, changed the title of the Exhibition, as well as the period of time it was meant to encompass, without offering any kind of explanation.[122] This decree referred to the commemoration of '25 Years of Spanish Peace (1939–1964)', without even mentioning that a modification had taken place. A third decree extended the make-up of the Committee.[123]

On 20 September 1963 the Cabinet approved a decree by which an Inter-Ministerial Committee would be created in order to carry out the commemoration. By this time, a change of government had taken place and the new head of the Ministry of Information and Tourism was Manuel Fraga Iribarne.[124] This decree, which appeared on 26 September,

---

120. This emphasis on peace was to cause serious suspicion within the staunchest *inmovilista* sections of the régime, although it was not until several years later that those who disagreed with this change of discourse publicly expressed their opinions. Such was the case with Blas Piñar who, at a political rally held at the Calderón Theatre in Valladolid on 22 April 1975, stated the following in reference to 1964:

     'Already then, on the 25th anniversary, we sensed that something serious was happening within the country. The very fact that official propaganda should place the emphasis on 25 years of peace, washing its hands of the Victory which had made it possible and of the sacrifice of one of the most splendid generations which had achieved it, seemed highly suspect' (cited by Rodríguez, 1990).

121. Decree of 28 November 1958 (BOE 19/12/1958).
122. Decree of 11 June 1959 (BOE 22/6/1959).
123. Decree of 22 October 1959 (BOE 30/10/1959).
124. It is curious that Fraga should devote so little space in his *Memoria breve de una vida pública* ('Brief Memoir of a Public Life') to the commemoration of the '25 Years of Peace', which was not only arranged and organised by his Ministry, but achieved an unusually wide impact during the period. In fact, his memoirs include neither the deliberations of the Cabinet that led to the creation of the Inter-Ministerial Committee, nor the appearance of the Decree that was to provide the basis for the organisation of the commemoration.

referred to the preliminary plan prepared by the Committee in 1960 and, after describing it as 'excellent', stated that it was discarded in its day because the economic difficulties of the country at that time had made it unfeasible. By the end of the 1950s the crisis had, indeed, touched rock-bottom, although by 1963 the economic situation had improved considerably. Nevertheless, instead of taking advantage of this 'excellent' preliminary plan, the decision was taken to repeal the previous decrees and create a new team responsible for commemorating, 'an anniversary of such gratifying nature in the sense that it signifies the beginning of an era of peace and work that are decisive in achieving a hitherto unknown level of prosperity in our *Patria*'.[125]

First, however, it appears that the idea of a commemoration was on the verge of being abandoned in 1960, supposedly for budgetary reasons. Nevertheless, it received a further impetus from the new government team that was constituted in 1962. To have celebrated such an event during a period of economic crisis of the kind that was witnessed at the end of the 1950s would not only have been ineffective with regard to the legitimising pretensions of the Franco régime, but even counterproductive, given that the image of unnecessary waste would have harmed its credibility. Only when the macroeconomic figures began to show more promising signs, thanks to the Stabilisation Plan, was the régime able to allow itself such a display.

The impossibility of locating the text of the preliminary plan, which was frozen in 1960 and finally cancelled in 1963, means that we are unable to discover the actual substance of the text. However, we can assume that it was not particularly suitable, since it was produced under a government that was rather less *aperturista* than the one that followed (let us not forget that it was the new government, also upon the initiative of the Ministry of Information and Tourism, which approved the law that loosened control over information in Spain by eliminating prior censorship, and that acknowledged religious freedoms). In addition, the Curator of the preliminary plan was a member of the Army and, although certain members of the Army were also to sit on the Inter-Ministerial Committee that was later appointed, the main positions were to be occupied by civilians, who were supposedly more inclined to consider war and peace from a neutral perspective. Furthermore, it would also be interesting to discover why an event that was initially conceived solely as a 'National Exhibition' encompassing the period 1936–1961 (that is to say, including the Civil War), ended up as a global commemoration which focused, finally, on the period 1939–1964, omitting the war entirely.

It is obvious that this correction aimed to endow the event with a more pacific and conciliatory tone. First of all, it avoided any discussion about the war and, second, it referred to peace as the main event to be

125. BOE of 16/10/1963.

commemorated. Finally, the project was carried out by a more modernising government than that which proposed it.[126]

In addition, the former team at the Ministry of Information and Tourism had been responsible for the campaign organised to discredit the protagonists of the Munich meeting. It is highly probable that the preliminary plan they prepared, like the press campaign that preceded it, was not conciliatory in the slightest. In addition, the new heads of the Ministry would not have wished to continue a preliminary plan drafted by a team of this kind during a period in which it intended to pursue an increasingly open style of government management.

From this time on, we can see how the political discourse tended to refer rather more to peace than to war, more to 1 April than to 18 July. It was also around this time that claims that the construction of the Valley of the Fallen represented a homage to 'all those' who died in the Civil War and that the period of peace that began in 1939 was a peace that belonged 'to all', began to be heard. All of this was no more than an acknowledgement, admittedly limited, of a conciliatory message that had been emanating from a considerable section of society for some time through film and literature.[127]

In order to mark the '25 Years of Peace', a multitude of commemorative activities were carried out for this event. An exhibition of posters toured the country, a special series of stamps came onto the market,[128] a

---

126. No information has been discovered as to who actually proposed in 1959 that the reason for the commemoration should be changed, but the fact that the Valley of the Fallen was inaugurated on 1 April 1959, between the passing of the first decree in November 1958 and the second in June 1959, may have influenced the decision. This inauguration, in spite of its ambiguous meaning, represented the first gesture that led to the beginning of a greater degree of tolerance regarding the memory of the defeated, thus allowing the remains of some victims of the other side to be buried in the gigantic mausoleum.

127. José María García Escudero, Director General of the Press between 1962 and 1969, has stated in an interview that there was no real reconciliation policy in the 1960s, but that:

> socially it did begin...and a series of films were made which were very much in line with the idea of reconciliation... However, of course, the great leap, that is to say, the reconciliation of ideologies rather than the reconciliation of persons, was not yet possible. That is what should have been achieved under the Organic Law and which never took place. (interview carried out by Elisa Chuliá Rodrigo on 8 May 1992)

128. This series consisted of 14 stamps. The first in the series was devoted to the '25 Years of Peace' and the last to 'General Franco'. All of the rest were devoted to praising the achievements of the régime: 'Sport', 'Telecommunications', 'Housing', 'Agriculture', 'Reforestation', 'Economic Development', 'Construction', 'Transport', 'Hydraulic Works', 'Electricity', 'Scientific Research' and 'Tourism'. The first stamp, that commemorated peace presents an open hand holding an olive branch, the symbol of peace. It is extremely enlightening to compare this series of stamps with those that were issued in 1961 in order to mark the commemoration of the '25th Anniversary of the National Uprising', two million copies of which were produced compared to the four million copies of 1964.

special National Lottery draw was held,[129] various medals were produced by the Casa de la Moneda (The Mint) which were awarded to those who made the largest contribution to the celebration of peace (they were not awarded, as one member of the Inter-Ministerial Committee intended, to those who had done the most to promote peace in Spain),[130] numerous official publications were published,[131] competitions were organised for poetry, novels, cinema, journalism, radio and television, and cities, towns and villages were decorated for the celebration of their own fiestas.

The Poster Exhibition that toured the whole of Spain was entitled 'España en Paz' ('Spain at Peace') and a compilation of this exhibition appeared in a book entitled *Viva la Paz* ('Long Live Peace'). This publication brought together all of the posters that featured in the exhibition,

---

War and victory were the themes that were celebrated in 1961. The first stamp, the 'Allegory of Peace', in spite of its name and the doves that flutter about on it, features an angel holding a sword in one hand and a laurel crown, the symbol of victory, in the other. The rest of the stamps include: 'Passage Through the Straits', 'The Alcázar de Toledo', 'The Victory Arch', 'The Battle of the Ebro', 'The Victory Parade', 'The Naval Industry', 'The Spanish Iron and Steel Industry', 'Dams', 'Hydro-Electric Stations', 'Mining' and 'General Franco'. Here we can see how performance-based legitimacy, somewhat timidly, began to be associated with origin-based legitimacy through an exhibition of the great works undertaken by the régime (Dirección General de Correos y Telégrafos, 1989: pp.55 and 64).

129. On 31 March 1964, a draw was held in commemoration of '25 Years of Peace'. The profits obtained were used for the Construction of a Congress and Exhibition Centre, to 'perpetuate and recall such a happy commemoration in future' in the words of the Cortes records. Today, however, hardly anyone recalls that this building was constructed for this purpose. This information can be found in:
    BOCE No. 828; pp.17616–7; 18/2/1964.
    BOCE No. 840; p.17810; 12/5/1964.
    BOCE No. 845; p.18005; 6/6/1964.

130. According to the minutes of the second meeting of the Inter-Ministerial Committee that took place on 13 November 1963, a General from the Air Ministry called Luis Bengoechea Bahamonde proposed the awarding of 'other kinds of medals to those who have contributed to peace in Spain'. The matter was left 'for subsequent deliberation' and in actual fact was abandoned. (General Government Archive (AGA), a Section of the Ministry of Culture, Box 18,724). Deciding upon whom had contributed most to peace in Spain was a sufficiently thorny issue to be discarded by a Committee that did not wish to involve itself in questions of this kind.

131. The following is a representative sample:
    – Temas Españolas No. 417, *XXV Años de Paz.*
    – Robles Piquer, Carlos (dir.) (1964): *El Gobierno Informa: 25 aniversario de paz española.*
    – Servicio Informativo Español (1965): *Informe sobre la comemoración del XXV aniversario de la paz española.*
    – Various Authors (1964): *Panorama Español Contemporáneo. XXV Años de Paz.*
    Suplemento Nacional de la Prensa del Movimiento, *España cumple 25 años de paz.*
    – Instituto de Estudios Africanos (1964): *Los Veintecinco Años de Paz en la España Africana.*
    – Publicaciones Españolas (1964): *25 Years of Peace.*
    – Publicaciones Españolas (1964): *25 Années de Paix.*

accompanied by a series of triumphalist commentaries. The book did not refer explicitly to the Civil War (only one reference to the War of Liberation was made) although the memory of the war was latent within the text. One of the posters, when talking about the new towns of Spain and the reconstruction work that they had carried out, stated: 'The reconciliation of all Spaniards, the first of all our spiritual enterprises, was brought about in many places, thanks to this creative sense of the new State' (Robles, 1964: 2). Poster No. 7 deals with the Magistraturas de Trabajo (Industrial Tribunals) and claims that their creation, 'was the consequence of those turbulent days experienced by our country, whose memory – mixed commissions, arbitration committees – has been eliminated by this plain formula of labour justice' (Robles, 1964: 7). When talking about the Trade Union Congresses, the commentary is very similar: 'Spain was, it is sad to recall, a country of disunity...That was how resentments and conflicts emerged...The collective task of the *Patria* was impossible to carry out in that way' (Robles, 1964: 11). The régime thus attempted to legitimise its management and the creation of new institutions by pointing to the past and stating that these new institutions now played a peace-making role.

When dealing with the regions, special praise was reserved for Navarre, because, 'one day it threw itself entirely and without reservations into the Spanish enterprise' (Robles, 1964: 123). In the section devoted to the Army, it stated that on 1 April:

> the peace arrived which they imposed; a peace for the victors and the defeated, a peace made to promote work, a creative peace. And in that peace, that Army, known as the Nationalist Army, became the Spanish Army. An Army which, like the peace, already existed for all, and in which all were obliged to render service. (Robles, 1964: 134)

Finally, the last poster stated:

> The hazardous times have passed. Arms have been silenced and sieges broken. This was the work of a generation. The long-suffering generation. It inherited the legacy of a divided Spain. The youth of 1936 bore the brunt of the errors of others.

It then referred to the fruits of this peace and stated that:

> [the children] who have never known bloodshed, misery and hate, more than make up for our past suffering and bitterness. That vision of Spain is left behind forever. We have built a better Spain for these children who, with God's help, shall only ever know work and rest, order and peace' (Robles, 1964: 150).

In 1964 a competition of film-scripts on the Civil War was also staged. The first prize was never awarded, but the second prize was presented to

La paz ('Peace') by Feliu and Font-Espina. This film was referred to by García Escudero in his memoirs, which recall his time as Director General. He stated that the script was faithful to the 'instructions which I had set myself: neither rhetoric nor horror; reconciliation. That was also the slogan of the same script-writers in *Tierra de Todos* ('Land of All'), which Isasi directed and entered at the Festival of Mar de Plata in 1962'. He ended with the following prediction: 'There will be those who reproach us for the prize and call us Reds' (García Escudero, 1978: 118). This phrase shows us the limited scope of the reconciliation that was sought. The prize was awarded to a conciliatory script in the certainty that the jury would be accused of being 'Reds' as a result. This is yet another example of how real reconciliation was virtually impossible under the Franco régime.

The texts of various prizes awarded for journalistic articles, as well as radio and television programmes, were compiled in two books: *Veinte españoles hablan... de 25 años de Paz* ('Twenty Spaniards Talk About... 25 Years of Peace') *and 25 años de Paz vistos por 25 escritores españoles* ('25 years of Peace in the Eyes of 25 Spanish Writers'). In 1961 a book had already been published which compiled the newspaper articles that were awarded prizes during the commemoration of the twenty-fifth anniversary of the military uprising: *Artículos premiados en el Concurso periodístico convocado con motivo del XXV aniversario del Alzamiento Nacional*. This book, however, commemorated the 'Uprising' and practically all of the prize-winning articles evoked the 'Crusade'. In 1964, on the other hand, it was a question of commemorating peace and, although many of the articles continued to deal with the war, some already referred to it as the 'Civil War' and addressed the losing side in a somewhat more conciliatory tone.

Another important task is to discover what this grand commemoration was meant to achieve. The text contained in the decree was somewhat vague in this respect. It talked about a hitherto unknown period of peace and prosperity in Spain, but did not explain the objectives of the celebration, or highlight the aspects that were to be emphasised most and whether or not the war should be discussed. It is possible that a general order, more tacit than explicit, may have existed, which recommended placing a certain emphasis on the economic development of the country, the level of prosperity achieved since the postwar period and the achievements of social policy, whilst stressing the fact that all this had been possible thanks to the existing political stability and social peace. In fact, this was the most commonly repeated message during the campaign, although not the only one.

In effect, various sections of society were to conceive of this event in a variety of different ways. It was evidently a question of consolidating the legitimacy of the régime by placing greater emphasis on its management than on its origins, although the latter would continue to emerge during the commemoration. However, the scope of what each element of society was to understand by the term 'peace' was, due to the absence of any explanation in the law, a question that remained open to varying interpretations.

On the one hand, the Army carried out, as they did every year, their Victory Parade, except that on this occasion, it was mostly referred to as the 'Peace Parade'. In successive years, this event would continue to be called the 'Victory Parade', which calls into question the nature of the rhetorical change that was introduced in 1964 and makes it look more like a political marketing stunt rather than a real desire to change people's views on the Civil War. When the emphasis was placed on peace, it was easier to symbolically integrate all Spaniards, the victors and the defeated, under the same umbrella which, supposedly, was meant to encompass both. Nevertheless, by continuing to talk about victory the only interpretation possible was that of the victory of one side over the other, one which, moreover, was considered to be worthy of commemoration by the authorities, thus making it an example of institutionalised memory.

This Peace Parade was one of the most spectacular of all of those that were carried out under the régime.[132] Peace is always something that is celebrated more cheerfully than victory; furthermore, it is much easier to achieve a consensus based on peace than on victory where a civil war is concerned. Franco took advantage of this parade in order to invite Prince Juan Carlos to share the balcony of honour with him for the first time (Princess Sofía was also to attend the military parade, along with Franco's wife, on the balcony located opposite).[133] Curiously enough, the Head of State had stated on various occasions that the future king of Spain should not belong to either of the sides that fought against each other in the war.[134] It is highly probable that Franco sought, on this occasion, to identify the figure of the young Prince with 'peace in Spain', with the period of prosperity and stability that Spain had witnessed in recent years, but also with the war, in order to consolidate his future candidature as a

132. In fact, it was extremely widely covered in the media. The No-Do devoted the three versions of number 1,117 to it (A, B and C).
133. On 26 May the newspaper *ABC* attributed considerable importance to the presence of the Prince and Princess and stated that this was precisely the aspect that had been highlighted most by the foreign press reporting on the parade. As of 1964, the Prince and Princess were to attend all of the parades organised to commemorate victory.
134. The declarations that Franco had made in 1937, 1938 and 1945 appeared repeatedly in the press, especially in the numerous commemorative issues for the '25 Years of Peace'. See the three special issues published by *ABC* under the title 'Pasado, Presente y Futuro. Del gorro frigio, a la hoz y el martillo. Veinticinco años de Paz. De cara al futuro' (31 March and 1 and 2 April 1964). According to the special issue of *ABC* of 1 April, Franco had told the newspaper on 19 July 1937 that 'if the Head of State should ever again be a King, he would have to play a pacifying role and must not be counted among the victors'. He declared the same in 1938 to a Brazilian newspaper. Subsequently, on 17 July 1945, at a meeting of the Consejo Nacional (National Council), he once again stressed this idea.

successor. The Victory Parade, presented now as the Peace Parade, perfectly combined the two forms of legitimacy; it served to commemorate victory (origin-based legitimacy) and peace (performance-based legitimacy). Origin-based legitimacy was to be enjoyed by the successor to Franco, facilitating the backing of the unconditional supporters of the régime, although without performance-based legitimacy it would be impossible to attract the most sceptical, the most apolitical and disaffected young people. It was essential for the young Prince to bring together both forms of legitimacy and thus be able to embody a sense of continuity with regard to the 'spirit of 18 July' and a guarantee of peace and political stability. Later, the newly-enthroned King would be able to embody democratic legitimacy by presenting himself as the focus of reconciliation for the two sides.

One of the most serious concerns of the régime was to guarantee its own continuity, the preservation of its legacy in the future. For this reason, from the very beginning it placed an emphasis on training the youngest members of society by imbuing them with certain values and principles in school, at the camps organised by the Frente de Juventudes (Youth Section of the Falange), through religion, the teaching of history and through books published on the Formación del Espíritu Nacional ('Development of the National Spirit'). The aim was to ensure their allegiance to the régime, based on the fear that the new generations born during this era of peace, stability and relative prosperity would not be able to value the 'sacrifice' made by their elders, let alone identify with a series of principles that they might consider to be unnecessary in times of peace. These new generations might feel that the war had not, in fact, been inevitable, that it had not been essential and that the dramatic memory of it should be erased as soon as possible. This would precisely contradict the official discourse that spoke about an inevitable and necessary war, the ongoing memory of which was compulsory.

This tension can be perfectly observed in the rhetoric surrounding the commemoration. On the one hand, it was a matter of conveying a slightly conciliatory and pacific message to those who had lived through the war and did not need to be reminded of it. The emphasis was placed on a constant comparison between the current situation and the situation that existed before the war, which represented a symbolic invitation for all members of the winning side to participate in the fruits of victory and the success of the régime's administration, given that quite a few might feel marginalised or undervalued, and it is possible that some may have already begun to question the worth of the personal and collective sacrifice they made during the war. On the other hand, however, the aim was to attract those of the younger generations who were far from enthusiastic about the régime. It was not considered to be enough to simply emphasise the existing peace and prosperity, as they had enjoyed both since they were born. This meant that the régime felt an urgent need to remind these generations of a war that they had not actually lived through. It was mainly this section of society to whom the warlike message was addressed. Both heroic and tragic versions of the war were conveyed. The former served the older generations, enabling them to justify their role as combatants and the alleged necessity and inevitability of the war. In order to attract the youngest generations, the heroic version also offered an epic perspective of recent history. The second view, the dramatic version, served to consecrate the dead, to legitimise the survival of the régime in their name, but also, and above all, to convey a menacing message. The aim was to imbue them with a fear of war and, more precisely, of its repetition, which might be brought about should the allegedly peaceful and stabilising legacy of 18 July fail to be observed. This constituted an attempt to convince the youngest members of society, through any means, that the Francoist solution was the only one capable of preventing the Spanish from becoming embroiled in civil war again. In order to do this, the régime employed a number of historical comparisons and claimed that the parliamentary institutions that the oldest members of society had experienced had never worked in Spain and that the party-system was harmful to national harmony. It was possible, they claimed, that other countries might exist, more or less harmoniously, under inorganic democracies, but the Spanish nation, due to the specific nature of its 'national character', would never be able to do so. Any move in this direction would mean a return to divisions, resentment, violence, all of which would lead to a new confrontation.

From the point of view of a régime that had almost entirely removed members of the losing side from public life, it was logical to believe that, should the party system be revived, the defeated would be able to organise themselves politically in an attempt to avenge the repression to which they had been subjected. The Francoists often stated that, if the Republicans had won the war, they would have done exactly the same with members of the opposing side.[135] Nevertheless, those who had chosen such an exclusivist form of coexistence were obliged to mistrust those institutions that they had fought to bring down.

Not all sections of society, viewed either from an individual or a collective perspective, believed that the commemoration should have the limited scope that the state intended to give it. The Spanish Church, for example, through one of the main organs that disseminated its views, the magazine *Ecclesia*, published three successive editorials that made reference to this event. The first, dated 28 March 1964, entitled 'An Historic Date', presented a favourable evaluation of the régime's administration throughout the twenty-five years, although that administration was considered to be insufficient. It did not refer explicitly to the Civil War, although the entire text did highlight the need to overcome this old conflict. The article addressed all Spaniards, 'whatever their affiliations or

---

135. This stance was criticised by Dionisio Ridruejo who stated that 'our conduct should not be determined according to the conjecturable conduct of others' (Ridruejo, 1976: 382).

provenance'. It stated that 'happily...there is now more talk about the years of peace than about victory' and that 'that date tends to be interpreted as the beginning of a Christian embrace which must become stronger each year, if it is not to betray the blood of the dead, reviving an antagonism which they wished to bring with them to the grave'. The article continued with a highly revealing paragraph:

> The very fact that, twenty years after having silenced our arms, we continue to appeal to a sense of brotherhood among Spaniards, reveals that in this house we have not managed to sufficiently fulfil the most urgent legacy of our collective obligations. Peace in Spain will only be guaranteed if we are able to open and purify Spanish hearts more and more each day.

This evaluation, which contained many more subtle nuances than the official version, referred to a peace that was 'not free of tensions' and recommended various norms of behaviour that should be followed in the future. The first, on which all the others were based, consisted of the 'pacification of the spirit'. By this, they claimed:

> we do not understand...the renunciation of ideology itself nor the violent imposition of that ideology on our neighbour, but the acceptance by all of a set of axioms of natural law...which enable us to disagree...within the bounds of our respect for those disagreements.

The editorial then went on to cite the words that the Cardinal Primate addressed to a group of Alféreces Provisionales in 1958:

> The Church has preached and preaches peace and asks for forgiveness, a will to forget, real brotherhood. It knows that it is not enough simply to win, but to convince; that now is not the time to fight with arms, but to work together in order to remedy social injustices.

This editorial, according to Fraga, was received with considerable indignation by the Head of State. Two days later, on 30 March 1964, the Minister of Information and Tourism claims:

> I met Franco... He was displeased by an editorial in the magazine *Ecclesia* on the commemoration of the twenty-five years of peace: peace and order are all very well, but they are not enough. He said to me (referring to the commemorative posters): 'You should stick those posters all over the Primate's palace'. (Fraga, 1980: 106)

Any small nuance that might slightly mar the splendour of the commemoration, any alternative or slightly critical interpretation was very poorly received. It was simply a question of praising, without reservations, the work carried out by the régime, not of each commentator evaluating it according to his own criteria, let alone highlighting what could have been done and was not.

In the following issue of the magazine *Ecclesia*, published on 4 April, the message conveyed was more explicit. One of the sections of the editorial article was entitled 'A Propitious Moment for Forgiveness' and in this respect it stated the following:

> it will have occurred to many Spaniards that, among the auspicious commemorations of this imminent twenty-fifth anniversary of national peace, in addition to the favourable disposition of all towards those who were consciously or unconsciously mistaken...a gesture of grace and legal forgiveness would be perfectly appropriate regarding all prisoners and all the diverse crimes they may have committed...the Church has always supported peace and pleaded for forgiveness, an ability to forget and real reconciliation. This is the best formula, of course, for creating peace among Spaniards.[136]

Given that the commemoration was viewed differently by the various political and social protagonists of the time, it was also used in diverse ways by them in order to legitimise their particular standing. Peace had become a crucial source of legitimacy and all parties assumed their right to use it in their own favour. In this case, the Church claimed that it had 'always' supported peace and had 'pleaded for forgiveness, an ability to forget and real reconciliation'; this is nothing less than a distorted view of its own history. In effect, it suited the Church to 'forget' its warlike and partisan attitude during the Civil War and, although it is true that it was one of the first institutions to have attempted, in a limited way, to enhance reconciliation among all Spaniards, it would take it many years to ask for society's forgiveness.[137]

136. Curiously, on 1 April a pardon had already been passed 'to mark 25 years of Peace in Spain'. It is possible that the editors of *Ecclesia* were unaware of this pardon, as this decree was not published in the BOE until 7 April. Nevertheless, the following issue of the magazine, dated 11 April, made no reference to the appropriateness of the pardon that they had advised.

137. One of the most significant and explicit conciliatory initiatives of the period was carried out by the Spanish Church at a Joint Assembly of Bishops and Clergy, when it asked society for forgiveness for having massively and unconditionally supported one of the two opposing sides in the Civil War. However, as Tusell recalls, it is curious that the most important aspect of this Assembly held in September 1971 should have been, 'a proposal that was not included in the documents prepared for the Assembly and that was not, in short, approved by the majority required: the proposal that the Spanish Church should apologise for not having been an instrument of peace during the Civil War' (Tusell, 1986: 190). Another indication of the desire for reconciliation that existed in at least a significant section of the Church, was the attitude it adopted in 1967 in relation to a series of incidents in Mondragón. A stone tablet, which commemorated the Nationalist fallen in the Civil War, was smashed in the town. Upon the initiative of the Archpriest of Mondragón, according to López Rodó, 'on 7 May a declaration was read out in Spanish and Basque in the churches of Guipúzcoa which, in the opinion of the Governor, incited political agitation'. This declaration called for 'the broken stone tablet not to be replaced or for another "stone of reconciliation" to be put up in its place' (López Rodó, 1991: 173). This earned the Archpriest a fine and elicited a protest from Castiella, the Minister for Relations with the Papal Nuncio, who, nevertheless, openly expressed his support for the Archpriest.

Nevertheless, this second editorial continued to refer to the defeated as those, 'who were consciously or unconsciously *mistaken*', which somewhat limits the scope of this reconciliation (the italics are mine).

In the General Government Archive (AGA), very little documentation exists regarding the '25 Years of Peace'. There is only one box, No. 18,724, that contains material which relates to this event and here we find a compilation of references to the commemoration that appeared in the national and foreign press. It also contains the minutes of the four meetings that the Inter-Ministerial Committee responsible for the celebration held, there are some programmes of the local fiestas that were organised to mark the celebration of 'peace' or 'liberation', and, finally, a series of proposals relating to the candidates for the 'peace medals'.

From the newspaper accounts we can observe that it was still common to refer to 1 April as 'liberation' day. In reality, what many towns celebrated was not so much the arrival of 'peace' on that day, but the victory of the Nationalists and the liberation of their towns. That is how the commemoration seems to have been interpreted in various places. The use of the term 'liberation' implied a lack of development regarding the black-and-white narrative of the war and the continued estrangement of the enemy, who were symbolically deprived of their Spanish identity.[138]

In addition to the programmes of fiestas, in some towns books were published to commemorate the event. Thus, Bechi published *XXV Años de Paz en Bechi* ('25 Years of Peace in Bechi') in July 1963, featuring a print-run of 1,000 copies. This book did not talk about the Civil War, but about the 'Crusade', the 'War of Liberation' and the 'Glorious Uprising'. The text included both praise for Franco, for having 'liberated' the town, as well as criticisms of the 'Reds' for having damaged the religious

---

138.   The town of La Solana celebrated the event in January 1965 and entitled its programme of celebrations: 'Solana: Fiestas of the Liberation'. This programme did not mention economic achievements or peace, but limited itself to presenting an heroic vision of the war through a celebration in which a number of 'ex-combatants' and 'former prisoners' played the leading role. A very different example is provided by the celebrations organised in the name of the patron saint of Chera in 1964, which did in fact talk about peace and development. The celebration was conceived as a homage to Franco, who, according to the programme, the town considered to be the very embodiment of peace and its main artifice. However, this programme is more conciliatory and rather less warlike than that of La Solana, even stating the following: 'we should not live obstinately in the past; let us leave behind our old ways, let us banish...incomprehension and intransigence'. All of this simply proves that no clear and explicit order existed regarding the kind of commemoration that should be carried out. It is as if a certain ambiguity existed regarding the purpose of the commemoration alongside the official instruction that recommended a celebration of the achievements of the period, which enabled the events to lean both towards a heroic recollection of the war and towards a celebration of peace. However, forgetting the war entirely was not feasible at a period in which an obligatory recollection of the war existed. These two programmes can be found in the General Government Archive (AGA), a Section of the Ministry of Culture, Box 18,724.

heritage of the town during the war. It talked about the economic recovery, about the improvements undertaken in the local area and about the reigning climate of peace and tranquillity, contrasting this with the era of bickering and divisions caused by the parties. However, a possible reconciliation with those members of the local area who fought on the other side was not mentioned.[139]

The tone employed in some local areas was much less neutral than that used in the commemorations organised by the Ministry of Information and Tourism which were carried out on a national scale. The message of the anniversary was understood here in a different way, devoid of any subtle differences between peace and victory or any emphasis on the overwhelmingly economic and technical message of the Ministry, and free of its light conciliatory varnish. This direct message of warlike exaltation and the black-and-white reading of the war was the one most prevalent in some towns; perhaps it was also the view that is most commonly recalled. The local political élites appeared to address their remembrance of the war in an emotional way, evoking the 'happy' days of heroism.[140]

The war also appeared in the official commemoration, although only tacitly. In spite of this, certain matters such as the legendary figure of 'one million' dead continued to be frequently used. In this case, the aim was probably to impress, citing a figure that was no doubt exaggerated and that had already been used for propaganda purposes by both sides during the war and after it. This was just another way of magnifying the scope of the tragedy with the aim of enhancing the legitimacy of everything that was done in the name of the dead and of justifying the staunchest views. At an official level, nobody was prepared to contradict this absurd exaggeration because it was useful for the survival of the régime.

The most lavish, extensive and probably the most widely distributed publication at the time was entitled *El Gobierno Informa. 25 Aniversario de la Paz Española*. ('The Government Informs You. The 25th Anniversary of Spanish Peace'). The Editora Nacional published four volumes under the direction of Carlos Robles Piquer, General Curator of the Commemoration. The Minister of Information and Tourism, who was also Chairman of the Inter-Ministerial Committee, wrote the prologue for the

139. The last document of this kind that may be found in the AGA corresponds to the town of Segura de León, which published a pamphlet entitled '25 Years of Peace' in 1964. This publication did not refer to the Civil War either, but to the 'Crusade' and the 'War of Liberation', paying homage to 'our fallen' and not to all the victims of the war. It did not even mention the defeated side. Out of the pamphlet's twenty pages, only one page was devoted to the economic achievements of peace in the town, whilst the other nineteen pages referred to the origin-based legitimacy of the régime, thus turning the official line on its head.
140. It is possible that the Local and Provincial Heads of the Falange, as well as Civil Governors, Military Chiefs and Mayors had something to do with all this, representing as they did authority within the Municipality.

publication. In these introductory pages, Fraga referred to the exceptional nature of such a long period of peace in the history of Spain and the prosperity that peace had brought with it. Here we find, not for the first time, one of the most important constants of the commemoration: the claim that 'peace is the heritage of all'. According to this official version, all those members of the defeated side who wished to rejoin the national endeavour were exhorted to do so, provided that they accepted, quite unconditionally, the existing legal situation. If all Spaniards 'of good will' had been invited to enjoy the peace of the postwar period, even more so were they invited to enjoy the fruits of peace, economic prosperity and economic development.

The logic of this argument was based on the idea that when a country prospered economically, socially and culturally, all of its citizens stood to benefit. This progress belonged to all and all were affected by the improved quality of life, by investments in social policy, public order and financial stability. Social harmony, according to this view, would be consolidated due to the mere existence of a peace that permitted global development to take place, given that those members of the defeated side who had not acknowledged the origin-based legitimacy of the régime would have no other option than to accept its performance-based legitimacy, having participated in it and helped to create it, even though they might have done so unwittingly.

We could say that this explanation is based, at least partially, on a conception of the war as a class struggle. It is not surprising that the leftist whims of Falangist rhetoric focused on the elimination of this struggle through the implementation of egalitarian social policies. According to this version, the war came about as a result of the enormous imbalances that existed between the empowered classes and the most impoverished classes in Spain.[141] The former sinned by being too egotistical and refusing to cooperate in helping to enrich the country as a whole, whilst the latter lived in misery, were uncultured, brutish and lived in a constant state of unease due to the awareness of their own exclusion. The sense of social injustice was overwhelming and the people were not entirely wrong when they made certain economic and social demands. On the other hand, the wealthy classes were logically appalled by the impact that such demands would have on the social and political order. The problem was that the path that was followed by the parliamentary régime of the Second Republic to settle these differences turned out to be

141. Although it is true that the war had been explained in terms of a religious struggle during the first two decades of Francoism, as time passed and the causes that explained the virulence of the conflict were investigated, a different version began to emerge relating to the ancestral confrontation of the classes in Spain, a version that fitted in well with the new performance-related legitimacy of the régime. An attempt was made to demonstrate that, thanks to the prosperity that had been acquired, the causes of the Civil War had been eliminated from the future Spanish panorama forever.

mistaken, given that it was not possible to end social injustice by encouraging a confrontation between the classes, which, according to this interpretation, is exactly what the parties and trade unions did. The only plausible solution would have to come through a harmonisation of diverging interests brought about through joint agencies for the resolution of conflicts (vertical syndicates) and removing all forums that promoted conflict (parties, trade unions, the parliamentary system) on the one hand, and, on the other hand, through investment in social policy (to end the imbalances and injustice) and in public order (to protect private property and the national Catholic cultural patrimony). By entirely eradicating the blemishes of the parliamentary system, it was possible to consolidate national unity on the solid foundations of justice and harmony, at the same time removing the main cause of all civil wars and achieving social reconciliation, not only through justice, but also through a more general access to material prosperity and culture. In this way, the class struggle, that had broken out during the Civil War, would be brought to an end, and the differences between the classes would fade away.[142]

As a result of the reasoning outlined above, it was claimed that the problems of unity had been solved and that reconciliation had been indirectly achieved. According to this version, the defeated would have no other option than to acknowledge the overall effectiveness of the régime's administration, accept the appropriateness of the polices devoted to promoting social welfare, and finally join a régime which, even though it might not be precisely the one that they had fought for, had nevertheless achieved certain material progress and a sufficient degree of legitimacy not to be seriously threatened by alternative political forces.

We shall not enter into a debate here as to whether this development, which was certainly made possible due to the general climate of growth and prosperity that finally reached Spain, was really due to the régime's effective administration. However, we can observe a general level of improvement that effectively took place because the liberalisation of the Spanish economy enabled it to take advantage of the general wave of development that the Western economies were witnessing, a process that required an appropriate infrastructure.

One of the most important objectives of the campaign for the '25 Years of Peace' was to publicise and rally support for the first Development Plan, which began to be implemented that very year. References to this new great macroeconomic plan (the previous one was the Stabilisation Plan of 1959) were constant and were aimed at convincing Spanish society that this was a means of strengthening the effective administration that was being celebrated, and constituted a clear guarantee of rising prosperity.

---

142. Manual workers were referred to rather euphemistically by the régime as 'productores' (producers), a means of lessening the class content of the words 'obrero' (labourer) or 'trabajador' (worker).

In the years after 1964, numerous official publications continued to appear commemorating the successive anniversaries of the uprising, peace and victory. Thus, in the same way as the twentieth anniversary of the victory was commemorated in 1959 (Solís, 1959), and the twenty-fifth anniversary of the uprising was celebrated in 1961 (Seminario Central de Estudios Políticos, 1961; Jefatura Principal del Movimiento, 1961) in subsequent years diverse publications were to appear about these two events.[143]

Freedom of the Press

According to Justino Sinova, censorship of the press[144] was used by the régime in order to humiliate the losing side and constantly remind them of their defeat (Sinova, 1989: 198). In this sense, the liberalisation of the press was to naturally provide a more extensive forum for the defeated. In fact, it is highly significant that the law that liberalised the press was presented as the logical result of 'a quarter of a century of fruitful peace'.[145]

Many of the academic texts that were published during the Franco period were employed in a theoretical and abstract manner to argue in favour of the peaceful reform of the régime and to indirectly promote reconciliation. This was much easier to do with treatises on political science[146] than it was with historical works, the task of which was to deal directly with the delicate issue of the legacy of the war. Because of this, they were monitored more closely by the censors: the Decree of 23 September 1941[147] regarding 'Works That Refer to the War of Liberation or its Preparation' stated that 'since the end of the campaign is so recent, any

143. After 1964, the collection 'Nuevo Horizonte', produced by Ediciones del Movimiento, published the following works on 18 July: *Un tercio de siglo. Resurgimiento español: 18 de julio y Movimiento Nacional*, *'18 de julio'. Franco y la España renacida y '22 de julio'. El Príncipe de España y la Sucesión* and *Horizonte histórico del 18 de Julio, El 18 de Julio como futuro*. Even the annual publications of the Servicio Informativo Español, entitled *España en su prensa*, were not produced by calendar year, but were dated from 18 July of each year. Everything published in this collection on 1 April was to bear the mark of the celebration of 1964, placing an emphasis on peace: in 1966, *Victoria de la paz*; in 1968, *Estrategia social de la paz*; in 1969, *A los treinta años de paz*; in 1973, *Paz y progreso del pueblo español*, and in 1974, *La paz, patrimonio del pueblo español*.
144. The definitive work regarding this matter is the doctoral thesis by Elisa Chuliá, which will shortly be published in non-commercial form by the Instituto Juan March under the title: 'La evolución política de los regímenes no democráticos. Política de prensa y periodismo en el franquismo'.
145. Law 14/1966 of 18 March, regarding the Press and Printed Matter (BOE, No. 67, of 19 March).
146. In the fourth edition of his book, *Los regímenes políticos contemporáneos*, Manuel Jiménez de Parga complained of the limited scope of the new law. He stated that he would have liked to have devoted the bulk of his research to 'expounding upon and evaluating the form of political coexistence established here, thirty years after the end of the Civil War'. However, after explaining that a series of his articles had been cancelled due to their critical tone, he went on to state that he was obliged to resign himself to describing foreign political régimes' (Jiménez de Parga, 1960; 1968: 13–14).
147. BOE of 24–25/9/1941.

passing of judgement might adversely affect the significance of the Movement and historical truth might suffer', which is why it provided for the following:

> Article 1. Civilian and military bodies and persons, authors, publishers or translators of works that address the subject of the campaign for our Crusade, or that in any form or to any extent refer to the military aspects or preparation of same, shall be subject to the prior authorisation of the Ministry for Army Affairs, subject to the provisions that govern all kinds of publications.
>
> Article 2. It is prohibited for publishers, printers or commercial establishments to publish or place on sale works of this kind which, after the publication of this Decree, do not bear the 'visa' granted by the Ministry for Army Affairs.

Such was the importance of controlling, by means of a double censorship – civilian and military – what could or could not be said about the Civil War in the eyes of the régime. It was essential that in relation to an event that was as vital for the legitimacy and survival of the régime as the Civil War, only the officially sanctioned version should be disseminated. Not until 1964 was military censorship of publications relating to the war finally removed. On 23 May of that year, Manuel Fraga Iribarne recorded in his memoirs that he held a meeting with the Minister for Army Affairs in order to, 'remove military censorship of histories produced on the War of Spain'. He continued:

> I sincerely believe that one of the most important services of the liberalisation in those years, both before and after the Press Law, was to break the deadlock on this matter. If it had taken place suddenly, after the death of Franco and without any transitional period, it would have been a disaster' (Fraga, 1980: 112).

The particular zeal with which the Franco régime protected its own reading of the war reveals the extent to which this event, duly manipulated, constituted a basic pillar of its legitimacy.

The New Constitution

These were not the only official uses of the idea of peace in the years between 1964 and 1975. One of the most important examples of the employment of such rhetoric for political purposes took place in 1966, as a result of the referendum on the Organic Law of State, or the New Constitution, as it almost immediately came to be called.[148] This second

148. The most important official publications on this Law included the following:
- Servicio Informativo Español (1966): *Referéndum 1966. Nueva Constitución.*
- Servicio Informativo Español (1967): *Leyes Fundamentales del Estado. La Constitución Española.*
- Servicio Informativo Español (1967): *España en su prensa.*
- Ediciones del Movimiento (1967): *Ley Orgánica, Movimiento y Democracia.*

popular referendum was used in order to create publicity in favour of the régime, once again emphasising the idea that it alone was capable of guaranteeing peace in Spain.

The official campaign which (naturally) supported the 'yes' vote, aimed to convince the public by using the ideas of peace, order and stability. The peace message was used for at least four of the publicity posters. The first featured a housewife in a meditative pose and a slogan that read: 'Think About Your Home. Vote for PEACE.' The second presented a male silhouette holding a small smoking factory in its hand and read: 'Yes to peace and progress'. In the third poster, three children playing with letter blocks were depicted spelling out the message, 'VOTE PEACE'. The last poster showed a hand that was on the verge of blocking the chimney of a factory and a message that read: 'Don't Block the Progress of the Country: Say 'Yes' to the Future' (Servicio Informativo Español, 1966). In this sense, if a 'yes' in the referendum was a vote in favour of peace, 'no' would symbolise war.

The message that was being put out by the Franco régime may be represented by the following equation: Franco régime = development + prosperity = peace + order + stability = guarantee of further development and prosperity. On the other hand, the opposing message was also conveyed: change of régime = chaos + disorder + anarchy = economic slump + social unease = new civil war. This was a vicious circle in which, if the highest priority was to avoid a repetition of the war and the second most important priority was to achieve an adequate level of material prosperity, there was no other option than to renounce the freedoms and party representation of inorganic democracies.

One of the official texts on the Organic Law contains an appendix that brings together various press reports from both Spanish and foreign newspapers, regarding the meaning of this law. The local newspaper, *El Pensamiento Alavés*, published an article on 23 November 1966 entitled 'La Nueva Ley y la Juventud' ('The New Law and Youth') which perfectly reflects the official stance regarding reconciliation. The article states the following:

> what nobody should have expected from the Law was that it would totally disregard what happened between 1936 and 1939, with the ensuing consequences of more than twenty-five years of peace and work...young people today and those of the recent past may not remember the war. They may even wish to know nothing about the Spanish War. What is more, we grant that they might even be against the war of 1936–1939 because they are unable to find any apparent reason for it...But what these young people cannot do under any circumstances is wash their hands of it completely. The war cost the lives of many, and the dead (this is an historical truth) come before all. They cannot wash their hands of it, wipe the slate clean, because all generations (whether they like it or not) are joined and united. And it is through this sense of solidarity that History and nations progress. (Servicio Informativo Español, 1966: 187–188)

The preamble of the Organic Law itself contained a reference to origin-based legitimacy when it mentioned the 'State born on 18th July 1936' (Servicio Informativo Español, 1966: 59). However, through its public discourse the régime attempted to endow this new and important law with a certain conciliatory gloss. In a speech given at the Palacio de las Naciones de Montjuic on this law on 12 December 1966, Laureano López Rodó stated the following:

> The Organic Law of State, which completes our political order and perfects the previous Fundamental Laws, is born now that the passions have been laid to rest and the hatred has been extinguished which once bitterly divided us. The Spain of today is very different from that which collapsed in 1936. Not only because it is wealthier, but also because it is much more educated and united. (López Rodó, 1991: 110)

My aim is not so much to evaluate the real legitimacy of the régime, but to explain the various legitimising attempts made by the Franco government. During the early days of the régime, when greatest emphasis was placed on its origin-based legitimacy, the ferocious repression that was employed seems to indicate that the régime was not as legitimate as some may have claimed, but achieved a good part of society's acquiescence thanks to the use of force and the emigration of a considerable proportion of those who opposed its mandate. Nevertheless, once the Franco régime ceased to be overtly repressive and began to liberalise the economy and relax its stance on some other political issues, the nation began to perceive the benefits of political development and greater freedom of expression and the previous acquiescence took on a different form. We believe that, for a large part of society, the régime acquired a significant degree of legitimacy thanks to its administration, although this legitimacy was somewhat precarious, because its origin was not perceived as being quite so indisputably legitimate.

Another important issue for the régime were the secondary implications of the economic development that was made possible by the Stabilisation Plan. The majority of the commentaries produced under democracy regarding the Franco period have emphasised the negative repercussions that this development had for the régime, that is to say, the undesired consequences of economic liberalisation, such as a degree of cultural and social liberalisation, which made certain aspects of the régime rather obsolete. However, we would prefer to place greater emphasis on a second dimension that we believe was highly favourable for the régime, given that it endowed it with a solid performance-based legitimacy. The overall economic progress that was witnessed in Spain throughout the 1960s, irrespective of whether it made the paralysed rhetoric of the régime more evident, meant that many citizens were prepared to place their trust in it as a result of what they understood to be an effective administration. It was true that a considerable proportion of society was transformed and demanded greater freedom, but it is also true that among certain sections of the population, order, peace and economic development were rated as absolute priorities of political management. This was reflected in the political culture of the Spanish and is revealed in the surveys that were carried out between the latter years of Francoism and the early years of the Transition.

Symbols and Myths Relating to the Civil War

Towards the Convergence of Interpretations

At the end of the Civil War, and even during the course of the war itself, two opposing black-and-white interpretations of it evolved. Both related the history of the events that had been experienced in terms of 'good' and 'evil', always seeking to justify the actions carried out by their own side. Nevertheless, over time, these two interpretations of the war moved progressively closer until they almost converged, in general terms, during the latter years of Francoism and the early years of the Transition. The two sides ended up reaching a kind of agreement regarding their mutual guilt and the inappropriateness of stories relating to rearguard actions.

For the victors, the Civil War was a 'war of liberation', a 'glorious crusade' against the communist, separatist and godless forces that supported the Second Republic which, for many years, had been the cause of Spanish decadence. As highlighted above, at least during the first few decades of the Franco régime, a resentful and distorted discourse regarding the war was elaborated, designed to legitimise the seizure of power by the Nationalist forces and perpetuate the memory of the war in order to avoid, through the exploitation of fear, any attempt to replace the régime. A large part of the symbolic policy of the Franco régime sought to keep its specific version of the war alive, so that it might come to form part of Spanish daily life. In addition to various monuments, commemorative dates of events that had taken place in the war were also established, which in some cases became national holidays: 1 April, Victory Day; 17 April, Unification Day; 18 July, Day of the Uprising (and also the day on which the summer wage bonus was paid, popularly known as the bonus of 18 July, this being one of the many ways that the régime attempted to identify victory in the war with current economic prosperity); 1 October, Day of the Caudillo; 29 October, Day of the Fallen etc.

Political discourse, as well as official historiography, cinema and literature, were full of conceptual dichotomies such as the following: victors and the defeated, good men and bad men, patriots and traitors. The term 'reconciliation' was banished from the political vocabulary, to the extent that even the pastoral letter written by Cardinal Gomá (who had firmly supported the Uprising) of 1 August 1939, entitled 'Lessons of War and

Duties of Peace', was censored for containing the word 'reconciliation' instead of the officially-authorised 'recovery',[149] which signified redemption after due punishment (Preston, 1986: 36). Equally famous was the affair of General Yagüe, who was punished in 1938 for a speech in which he pleaded for forgiveness for the adversary (Tusell, 1992: 292).[150]

Some sections of the defeated forces also entertained a black-and-white view of the war, according to which the revolt of 18 July was an entirely unjustified coup d'état carried out by traitorous forces hostile to the legitimately established Republic. The anarchists, for their part, interpreted the war as a social revolution that failed through the fault of the Communists. These discourses are much more difficult to trace, because a large number of the defeated were forced into exile and those who chose to stay in the country found that they were only able to begin to express their ideas with a certain degree of freedom, albeit with considerable difficulty, during the latter years of Francoism.

In 1945, the defeat of the Axis Powers in the Second World War began to produce a series of modifications in the discourse of the Franco régime, especially regarding the messages that were aimed abroad, although also at home. Spain had been left isolated in Europe and it was no longer a question of emphasising the fascist vestiges of the régime. Just one example of this is provided by the significant alterations made to the script written by Franco for the film *Raza* ('Race'), which was produced after the defeat of fascism in the Second World War (Méndez-Leite, 1975).[151] Nevertheless, what was known as 'cine de cruzada' or the 'Crusade film' continued to be promoted so that the triumphalist and heroic version of the war should not be forgotten.

As of the mid-1950s, a series of events took place that were to progressively change the discourse of both sides regarding the war. Dionisio Ridruejo claims that various exchanges between the most *aperturista* sections of the régime, which presented a mild internal opposition to the régime (monarchists, liberals, some Catholics etc) and the exiles on the other side of the Pyrenees, the historical opposition, began to be take place around 1956. Thus:

> the interpretation that the historical opposition made of the great national trauma became progressively closer, in these matters, to the traditional

149. In relation to this incident, see the book *El franquismo y la Iglesia* (Gómez, 1986: 73).
150. Ridruejo also referred to this incident, stating that Yagüe 're-launched the word reconciliation and even talked clearly about removing discrimination and redressing the persecutions' (Ridruejo, 1976: 151).
151. The film *Raza* was premièred in 1941, and in 1950 it was repeated with a different dubbing 'that played down certain phrases and gestures that recalled the fascist overtones of the early days of the régime too faithfully, and that did not appear to be appropriate for a period in which the Allies had won the Second World War and Franco's Spain was obliged to strive for recognition from the Americans' (Méndez-Leite, 1975: 24).

interpretation of the former adversary as the latter, for its part, began to renounce the convenient simplifications of propaganda. (Ridruejo, 1962: 267)

Conversely, during the Cold War years, international recognition began to be accorded to Franco's Spain, and the Spanish Communist Party (PCE) found it increasingly difficult to maintain its armed struggle. In 1950, the PCE decided to abandon this approach, and in 1956 it proposed at a Congress that the party should implement a 'policy of national reconciliation', which, according to its own members, meant looking beyond revenge and resentment (Ibárruri, 1985: 533–535, 650–653; Carrillo, 1983: 25–30). From that moment on, various left-wing intellectuals, both inside and outside Spain, began to produce films, history books and novels inspired by this conciliatory message, although their scope was necessarily still rather limited.[152]

In response to this, and also as a consequence of the first liberalising attempts of the régime, those inclined towards the most *aperturista* form of Francoism began to favour certain interpretations of the Civil War that were also couched in somewhat conciliatory terms. It is significant that it was during this period that what is known as 'cine de reconciliación' or the 'cinema of reconciliation' emerged (Gubern, 1986), which encompassed films such as *La Fiel Infantería* ('The Loyal Infantry') (1959) by Pedro Lazaga, or *Tierra de Todos* ('Land of All') (1961) by Antonio Isasi Isasmendi. The showing of this kind of film aimed to overcome the divisions that had taken place among Spanish families and emphasise the humanitarian and Christian values of reconciliation. Later on, with the ministerial replacement ordered by Franco in July 1962, by which Fraga became Head of the Ministry of Information and Tourism, the control of information was to become increasingly relaxed, until prior censorship disappeared altogether in 1966. That would facilitate the emergence of the first criticisms of excessively partisan interpretations of the Civil War.

Through the relative convergence of Republican and Nationalist memories it was possible to progress from a state of rancour to the idea of 'never again' and from accusatory charges aimed at others to an acknowledgement of collective blame, avoiding, in both cases, having to address the real historical problem. No genuine consensus existed regarding the substance of that memory, although a consensus did exist regarding the lessons that were to be drawn from it. Neither did any collective reflection exist that explained the brutal behaviour of the Spanish during the war; only an overall and depersonalised repentance existed, which involved a certain degree of amnesia, forgiveness through forgetting, amnesty.

---

152. For example, in 1957 the film *La Venganza* ('Revenge') was produced in Spain by Juan Antonio Bardem (a communist militant). This allegorical film about the Civil War states: 'a friend is one who forgets, and if he has to forgive, he forgives' (Gubern, 1986: 128).

It is obvious that not all of the elements that constituted the official version necessarily convinced all sections of society. However, an undeniable underlying factor did exist in the form of a general acceptance of the political régime that was not for the most part enthusiastic or active, but was tacit and real, once the economic transformation of the country had provided it with the necessary underpinning to guarantee its survival. It is unlikely, otherwise, that the Franco régime would have been able to survive the serious and prolonged economic crisis of the 1960s and 1970s. Repression, along with the origin-based legitimacy that was granted to the régime by a certain section of society, had enabled it to survive during the 1940s and 1950s, combined with a social policy that had helped to alleviate the effects of the crisis. However, as time passed and the founding moment of the régime became more distant, either the régime's performance-based legitimacy had to be consolidated, or it would be threatened with ruin.

Whatever the case may be, the active presence of the Civil War in the collective memory of society basically had two effects. In the first place, it created a general climate of political apathy (which was enhanced by Francoist socialisation) that made people unwilling to take part in acts of mass protest against the régime, one which, in spite of everything, more or less guaranteed them order and stability, irrespective of the means it used to achieve it.[153] Secondly, and directly related to the above, it favoured an essential pragmatism that enabled a large part of society to value material prosperity and social peace above almost any issue of an ideological or political nature. Although no empirical facts exist that confirm this, it seems logical that, after three years of indescribable suffering, the priority of a large majority of Spaniards consisted of ending the war, returning to a state of normality and eliminating the hunger and misery caused by the conflict.

Only a nation traumatised by war could be so devoted to peace, and not only during the postwar period, but throughout the entire Franco era and beyond. This is the only possible explanation for the huge number of books that appeared during the Franco period containing the word 'peace' in their title, the result of a collective reflection on a series of events that must have made a profound impression on social memory. In reference to only some of the best-known examples, we find the novel by Emilio Romero, which was awarded the Premio Planeta in 1957, significantly entitled *La paz empieza nunca* ('Peace Never Begins'), the third volume of the famous trilogy by José María Gironella, *Ha estallado la paz*

153. Both public order and political stability were two of the priorities of official discourse. However, according to surveys, these were also priorities for a large part of society. Nevertheless, it is very difficult to make out whether this coincidence was the result of the effectiveness of the régime's socialisation policy regarding these values or whether this was simply the natural reaction of a society that had suffered a traumatic experience.

(1966) ('Peace Has Broken Out'),[154] or we might mention the silent polemic that existed between the memoirs of José María Gil-Robles, *No fue posible la paz* ('Peace Was Not Possible'), published in 1968, and Joaquín Chapaprieta's, *La paz fue posible* ('Peace Was Possible'), published by his son in 1971. After Franco's death, various apologetic works regarding the régime appeared aimed at pacifying existing passions and criticising democracy, which was considered to be the destroyer of peace and promoter of conflict. The first case is exemplified by the book by Juan Alarcón (1977) entitled *Resumen Político de la Paz de Franco (1 de abril de 1939 – 20 de noviembre de 1975)* ('Political Summary of Franco's Peace (1 April 1939–20 November 1975)'). An example of the second case would be the book by Rafael García Serrano *La paz ha terminado* ('Peace Has Ended'), published in 1980.

Mythical Constructions of Francoism Regarding the Civil War

The mythologisation of the Civil War throughout this period can be understood within the framework of a general process that consisted of the consecration of the founding moments of the régime. This process ties in with the purifying symbols that were used to explain the destruction of what came before.

Official public celebrations of various moments of the past raise ordinary historical memory to a level that is qualitatively different and turns it into a fundamental point of reference with regard to collective identity. This historical landmark does not tend to be a traumatic event that evokes a lack of continuity, such as the American Civil War, for example. In the United States, the American War of Independence was the key point of reference that generated social consensus.[155] After the American

154.   This book came out only two years after the '25 Years of Peace' campaign and, although its stance was biased in favour of the Francoists, it also questioned the meaning of that 'peace'. We could mention numerous sentences in which the injustices committed by the victors during the postwar period were exposed and their warlike attitude was shown up. From the very first paragraph the author writes: 'The war had lasted exactly thirty-two months eleven days. The prospect of Spain was bleak. It is impossible to specify the total number of victims on both sides and in the rearguard. *Neither is it possible to guess at the number of victims of the repression initiated by the victors*' (Gironella, 1966: 15; the italics are mine).

155.   In a similar way, the myths of Spanish national unity during the Franco years included the Spain of the Catholic Monarchs, the War of Independence as well as the Spanish Civil War. It is obvious that these could not be used as unifying symbols during the Transition, which would have to become a unifying myth in itself over time as the definitive transitional process towards peaceful democratic coexistence and as an attempt – for some a relatively unsuccessful attempt – at consolidating national unity. According to Víctor Pérez Díaz (1991a), during the transition towards democracy it was necessary to resort to an invented tradition, given that no adequate historical point of reference existed for the generation entrusted with carrying out this social consensus. This not only entailed references to non-existent traditions, but also required the silencing of those inappropriate historical references that were

Civil War, conciliatory legislation was passed and, since national unity was no longer a burning issue, it was possible to freely cultivate regional diversity.[156] Whilst the subject of commemoration tends to be rooted in the past, the event that underlies its selection and reconstruction always relates to the present.

Throughout the almost forty-year span of the régime, numerous rites were created that established a sense of continuity with a glorious ancestral past and with the spirit of victory relating to the Civil War. However, this process of mythologisation witnessed a number of serious problems given that it evoked a rupture of national unity. It is not possible to construct the founding myth of a nation on a division of this kind, at least not for long.

The war was referred to in the same terms used in end-of-the-world prophecies, exploiting the supposedly purifying effect of destruction, the curative results of expeditious methods applied to an ailing body, in this case, Spain. This, in turn, reinforced the myth that was created by the victors, both during and after the conflict, of the necessity and inevitability of the war. We can observe, then, a multitude of myths that related to the war and which, far from creating contradictions, reinforced and complemented one another.

Underlying the various changes regarding the designation of the Civil War throughout this period was a process that was somewhat more significant than a mere terminological issue. In the majority of cases, these changes reflected developments in the way in which the war was conceived, interpreted and even recalled, given that the mere passing of time was always going to produce modifications with regard to these three aspects.

On the one hand, the narrative regarding the war evolved from an heroic stance to a more shamefaced view. The transition from epic myth to tragic myth was long and complex, but can be traced, even in some official writings. The war ceased to be the main heroic point of reference, the founding myth par excellence, in order to become something which, at best, had been inevitable, but that should never occur again. What is

---

likely to generate conflict rather than consensus. However, as Schwartz points out (1982), there are limits to this ability to use the past: the past cannot be literally built, only selectively exploited, and neither can it be definitively discarded. In fact, as we shall see below, the past emerged time and again during the Transition.

156. In Spain, national integrity, a fundamental source of cleavage in relation to the Civil War, remains an issue that raises problems and controversy, having also been the crucial issue that caused dissent during the Transition. The legislature agreements between the Partido Popular and the moderate Basque and Catalan nationalists could represent a considerable step forward in this respect, since the mere fact that they have agreed to sit round the same negotiating table represents a qualitative leap with respect to the former situation of mutual intransigence.

more, for a large part of society, the Civil War had not only been unnecessary, but could have even been avoided.

On the other hand, the conception of the war as a form of 'collective insanity' prepared the way, as we shall see later on, for the shift from global culpability to collective irresponsibility without needing to distinguish the party who bore the largest share of the blame for the events that occurred.

Official discourse itself also progressively ceased to talk about crusades and wars of liberation in order to adopt a more aseptic term, the War of Spain, without having to use the term Civil War.[157] The form in which references were made to the war was exceptionally important to the Franco régime. The writer Francisco Candel stated in an interview with Antonio Beneyto in 1975:

> I don't know whether you know that when I began to publish, it was not possible to write 'Civil War'. It had to be 'War of Liberation'. Those of us who didn't want to do that, just said 'War' and nothing more... And all those things, with their pros and contras, are still not settled, not settled by half. (Beneyto, 1977: 44)

Conversely, the historian Ricardo de la Cierva, in a personal interview, claimed that one of the aspects that proved his conciliatory and *aperturista* stance at the time was that he was one of the first to publicly refer to the conflict as the 'War of Spain'. In 1966, De la Cierva himself acknowledged that 'strictly speaking, we do not believe that our war should be called a "crusade", although it was in such large part waged for religious reasons' (De la Cierva, 1966: 100). In spite of this, in the same book Gregorio Martín Redondo, a collaborator of Ricardo de la Cierva, found it noteworthy and surprising that Salvador de Madariaga, in his book *España*, should always refer to the war as the 'Civil War' (De la Cierva, 1966: 104). The truth is that the use of this expression would only become practically unanimous with the advent of democracy.

In view of the discomfort entailed by having to face the enormous number of Spanish lives lost on both sides during the war, the decision was taken to expel the enemy from the country, both symbolically and physically. It was for this reason that the régime refused to acknowledge the 'civil' nature of the war that had just been waged and the term was censored. This was demonstrated by García Serrano (1964) in his *Diccionario para un macuto* ('Dictionary for a Backpack') when he stated that

---

157. In one of his writings, Fraga described the war as a 'civil war' and stated that:

> there is nothing wrong with this term'. However, he went on to state that 'it designates the fact that what for many represented a veritable crusade and for others a popular anti-fascist war, was in short, a war among Spaniards...for that reason it has left such a deep impression on the spirits of all... It was a war desired by both sides. (Fraga, 1973: 314–315)

the official term to be used when referring to the war was 'Crusade', which he himself defined as 'A proper name for the Spanish war of 1936–1939. It has no other name, and should not have any other. That war was a crusade through and through... It was defined as a crusade by the Spanish episcopacy' (García Serrano, 1964: 708). Another of the terms used by this author in order to refer to the coup d'état that gave rise to the war was the 'Uprising', which he described as 'the insurrectionary gesture with which Spain reacted to the communist invasion'. He continues:

> Francisco Cossío wrote in war-time that: 'Spanish uprisings have never been civil wars. Civil war implies two diverse or antagonistic conceptions within the historical process, without either of them undermining the essential foundations of national unity. Both sides are Spanish, and the struggle does not affect the roots, but the branches... Uprising is charac-terised by the fact that the enemy is external, because the people rises up to defend itself from a foreign invader, because the struggle does not take place among Spaniards divided into two camps, but between Spaniards and anti-Spaniards... Separatists and Marxists have been understood to be no less than enemies of Spain. They have united in their enmity of Spain, and this union, the logical consequence of hate, is what applies to the current war, dividing the two warring sides into two perfectly-defined bands: Spaniards and foreigners'. (García Serrano, 1964: 389)[158]

As the régime evolved towards a more *aperturista* stance with the passing of time, some historians and journalists progressively ceased to refer to the war as a crusade and a number of ambiguous expressions were cho-sen, that were somewhat milder than the initial black-and-white view. The war began to be called the 'War of Spain' or simply 'our war'. Through this delicate balance, an allusion was once again made to the term 'civil', but now we find the fratricidal substance of a war that was 'ours', per-taining to the Spanish and among the Spanish, and whose sole geographical point of reference was 'Spain'.[159]

---

158. This quote illustrates the reigning official conception of the defeated, especially during the early years of the régime, although this view survived in some of the most recalci-trant sections of the régime until the end. For example, the very fact that García Serrano repeated this interpretation suggested by Francisco Cossío in 1964, in the midst of the commemoration of the '25 Years of Peace' (the purpose of his work was, in fact com-memorative) illustrates that it remained the only valid view in the eyes of many.

159. According to Jervis:

> Because of the dramatic and pervasive nature of war and its consequences, the experiences associated with it...will deeply influence the perceptual pre-dispositions of most citizens. Major wars so dominate the life of a country that in a real sense all those old enough to remember it will have experience firsthand (Jervis, 1976: 266).

If external wars make such a deep impression, civil wars tend to have an even more painful and long-lasting effect.

It is true that, in order to maintain the unity and continuity of a community over time, a series of rites of membership are established that recall particular episodes of the past, and those common ties and characteristics are evoked, and even sometimes invented, and preserved throughout the years. However, it works very differently when we are dealing with memories which, in spite of being of considerable historical importance to the community, evoke tragedies, disasters and ruptures, as is the case with a civil war. This kind of experience is more liable to be brought up, used, forgotten and interpreted according to the needs and purposes of the present, so that it may be transformed, when enough time has passed to permit this, into a warning of what could happen to the society if it does not remain united.

Thus, paying homage to the past depends on the kind of episodes that it encompasses. Some accounts are not conveyed from generation to generation with the pride associated with great deeds, but with shame and fear. A civil war represents a rupture in the history of a country and, for this reason, it is the prototype of the kind of memory that is difficult to face. In this case, the past becomes a dangerous resource when the old squabbles that generated the conflict still remain and when the hatred aroused persists. Nevertheless, at the same time it can play a dissuasive role in relation to internal confrontation by evoking the tragedies of the past that are sought to be avoided in the present. The truth is that the legacy of civil war is always complex. The shared identity of the protagonists is lost in the war when the adversaries seek to exclusively represent the nation and set themselves up as the only true patriots and defenders of the country.

Regarding Reconciliation and the Defeated

In many cases, attitudes towards reconciliation and the defeated were determined by the personal experiences of each party during the war, especially in the early years, during which the governments were made up of members who had actually fought in the war.[160] Some experiences had been especially traumatic and produced radical black-and-white attitudes. Such was the case of Ramón Serrano Suñer, two of whose brothers were shot at Paracuellos. The deep wound of this loss prevented him from regarding the war from a detached and impartial perspective. As Ridruejo pointed out:

the image he held of the two sides in the war was of good and evil. He could not accept any comparisons of behaviour, something that for me was

---

160. In 1959 the first government was set up in which none of the Ministers, except for the members of the Army and the Minister Secretary-General of the Movement, had fought in the war.

unavoidable given that my experience of the events had been contrary to his. This very different image was a topic of discussion between us for many years. (Ridruejo, 1976: 104)

After the first two decades had passed, various authors emerged who, despite stating in the prefaces to their books that their aim was to enhance reconciliation, were ultimately betrayed by their hostile rhetoric and vengeful personal memories. Such was the case, for example, of García Serrano (1964), who wrote in the prologue to his *Diccionario para un macuto* ('Dictionary for a Backpack') that his aim was 'to compile, with piety and understanding, with a sense of love and camaraderie, and with cheerful and generous recollection, the language of my dead friends and my dead enemies' (xiv), also stating that the conflict was a 'harsh and painful war' (xiv). He claims all this only to state, immediately afterwards, that he entirely agreed with a book by Francisco Cavero, 'the account that best reflects the atmosphere of the Crusade', and identifies fully with the author when he states that, contrary to the general trend witnessed in novels about the Civil War, 'I do not condemn war. I recognise that it has its drawbacks, but these are more than compensated for' (xix and xx).

Contradictions of this kind were frequent in writings that at the time claimed to be conciliatory, and which corresponded perfectly to the view held by the Head of State, who never, even at the end of his days, wished to see a real reconciliation brought about with the defeated, refusing, among other things, to accord them equal legal status with regard to the victors.[161]

The Carlist newspaper *18 de Julio. Dios-Patria-Fueros-Rey* perfectly exemplified this openly hostile attitude with regard to reconciliation in

161. Some defenders of the Francoist régime, such as Federico Silva Muñoz, would not entirely agree with this assertion. Silva states in his memoirs: 'I can assure you that behind Franco's passivity lay an extremely strong desire for reconciliation, amnesia and the coexistence of ideas and persons', although he then goes on to acknowledge that Franco knew that that was 'very difficult for him to realize himself, even though he was sure that, having placed Spaniards in the cooler for forty years, he had created the necessary conditions for someone else to achieve it' (Silva, 1993: 228). Subsequently, Franco was unable, during his life and during the existence of the régime that bore his name, to reconcile the Spanish. Silva states that Franco was unable to achieve this but that he laid the foundations for others to do so. These foundations, according to Silva, were none other than what we have called performance-based legitimacy, built:

> upon literacy campaigns for a multitude of Spaniards, the improvement of sanitary and living conditions, reconstruction first and economic development later...upon the elimination of the class struggle and political confrontations, that even though this may have created a 'boring' peace, enabled the country to recover its rhythm. (Silva, 1993: 228)

an editorial of December 1959 entitled 'Neither Victors Nor Defeated'.[162] According to this text, victory was the factor that brought peace and any attempt to revise this war victory would lead directly to a repetition of the conflict. What is more, this victory was conclusive, because the outcome of a civil war is definitive. All of this confirms our thesis that the régime was never capable of bringing about real reconciliation because this would have undermined the foundations of its legitimacy by allowing the population to reach the conclusion that the war had been an unnecessary farce, in the same way as with the subsequent repression that the régime employed in order to maintain its grip on the reins of power. In this sense, the memory of the war, of victory and domination of the defeated was essential in order to avoid a new confrontation among Spaniards and anyone who claimed otherwise, even though he might also claim to agree with the spirit of 18 July, was an impostor and a danger to the *Patria*.

There were other cases in which the author, irrespective of his personal memory, attempted to convey a kind of 'wishful memory' of the war. Thus, Fraga, for example, in various of his writings, based on the lessons of the war, attempted to instil a spirit of harmony, peaceful coexistence and political tolerance, as a means of escaping from a difficult memory that evoked irreconcilable rivalries (Fraga, 1961; 1971; Fraga et al., 1974).

Fraga, however, remained loyal to the origins of the régime. The victory, in his opinion, was merited (Fraga, 1973: 315). The subsequent peace granted the régime more than enough legitimacy:

such a long period of civil peace and effective reconstruction has not existed in many centuries of our history. It is not good enough to complain that this peace, like all periods of peace, has been one that is guaranteed, in

---

162. With the Valley of the Fallen having been recently completed, any possibility of a peaceful understanding among the living was rejected. The following was stated:

Victory ensured Peace among Spaniards. This peace is not possible if the political positions which led to the war are now readopted. Justice and natural law protect all, but not everyone has the right to determine the political direction of Spain, because this issue has been definitively settled on the battlefield. Civil wars have never been reviewed. Turning back means going back to division among Spaniards, stripping the Civil War of political meaning for both sides, making the heroic sacrifice of a people into a stupid massacre. The victors owe it to all. That is to say, they owe it to the Victory which they won on behalf of all. And they must defend their Victory precisely in order to ensure Peace. Those who say that there should be *neither victors nor defeated* simply aim to rekindle the War *in order to see if they can now win it*. That would be a tragedy for Spain. In order to prevent this new tragedy, we must be wary of two grave dangers: One is the danger we have mentioned: that presented by the so-called *advocates of order*, of pacts and reconciliation, who are no more than a Trojan Horse. Everyone understands this and the man in the street fears it. The other danger is presented by those who claim to support the spirit of 18th July and, yet, administer the Victory in such a way that they could give the Reds pretexts which appear valid and reasonable. (Editorial of December 1959 in the newspaper *18 de Julio. Dios-Patria-Fueros-Rey* entitled "Ni vencedores ni vencidos")

part, by the sword, given that in real history, the olive branch is very often shored up by steel. But nobody can deny that the olive trees have grown and prospered in the hard ground of experience, irrigated dramatically by the Spanish blood which has been shed. Precisely for this reason, the moment has also arrived to proclaim that if, when all is said and done, victory has been fruitful for all, now is the time not only to mutually forgive, but also to forget, through that generous and heartfelt will to forget which leaves experience intact. (Fraga, 1973: 315)

Some isolated members of the Army also conveyed messages of reconciliation. As Juan Carlos Losada explains in his study on the Francoist Army, Alfredo Kindelán, starting from the assumption of the completely legitimate nature of the coup d'état of 18 July, was prepared to recognise the Civil War for what it was and stated that:

> in international battles it is sufficient, in general, to win the war, but in civil wars this is not enough; *it is also necessary to win the peace*. It is essential to see that hatred does not become constant and permanent...whoever the victor may be, the loser will always be one and the same, there will always only be one victim: the *Patria*. (Losada, 1990: 115)

Nevertheless, this kind of declaration was to be the exception, the general trend being one of unconditional loyalty to 18 July and criticism of all those who strayed from this view, even though they may have simply raised the possibility of reconciliation.[163] Numerous members of the Army criticised the 'joseantoniano' section of the Falange because of its leftist rhetoric and its tolerant attitude with regard to the defeated.[164]

The most sincere and honest contributions to reconciliation originated from the most orthodox section of the Falangist ranks, from those like Dionisio Ridruejo, who soon began to realise that Francoism was not the

---

163. According to Losada, the Army's criticism of 'intellectuals, the University, the Church and Technocracy...was based on the latter's desire to distance themselves from and betray the spirit of 18th July' (Losada, 1990: 226). The Army, certainly, was one of the main repositories of origin-based legitimacy due to its direct link to this form of legitimacy. What is more, the Army would become the executors of Francoist orthodoxy and, if they had enjoyed greater political power, their criticisms of the régime's liberalising and reformist measures might have had greater repercussions. The Hermandad de Alféreces Provisionales maintained a peculiar struggle with the technocrats, whom it accused of betraying this origin-based legitimacy, stating the following: 'Beware of those who, innocently or deviously, believe themselves to be young technocrats, from whose hands the deceptive doves of peace shall fly, those who are able to ensure the continuity of 18th July' (Cited by Losada, 1990: 254).

164. Once again, according to Losada, 'the Army advocated the maintenance of a victorious and conquering spirit with regard to the defeated. In view of this, the Régime was not to allow itself any indulgent or reconciliatory gesture; the defeated were to be treated with total intransigence and it was not possible to abandon the state of alert regarding the on-going conspiracies of the enemy within' (Losada, 1990: 229).

régime for which they had fought in the war.[165] Stanley Payne, in his study of the Falange, records the testimony of Luis González Vicén, a member of the Consejo Nacional (National Council of the Falange), who stated, in a letter addressed to José Luis de Arrese in 1956, that one of the most important problems which had to be resolved was:

> the failure to liquidate the Civil War, which at the present time still finds itself in almost the same condition as in the year 1939... In this very moment, the difference between being a Red or a non-Red, between having supported the movement or not, in other words between conquerors and conquered, is a reality in national life and in the administrative decisions of the government. The accessibility of power which that is perfectly delimited between conquerors and conquered, the treatment of citizens in which the difference is equally marked, the chance for social influence and many other factors, clearly indicate that this most grave problem still lacks solution. If this is so obvious from our camp, you can easily imagine how it appears from the other side. They not only regard themselves as defeated and politically unsatisfied; they see themselves treated as second-class Spaniards and exaggerate the injustice that they receive, building up hatred against the other half whom they think the cause of the evil. (cited by Payne, 1961: 253)

It is no coincidence, however, that Luis González Vicén had a brother, Felipe, who sympathised with the Republicans and was victimised as a result.[166]

The young generations of the postwar period, part of whom were active in youth organisations that formed part of the Falange and who wrote in their own youth magazines, were portrayed in the book *Pensar bajo el franquismo* ('Thought Under Francoism') by Juan Marsal. For these groups, 'the enemies were never members of the defeated side in the Civil War, the accursed 'Reds' demonised by official propaganda, but the régime and its hierarchies which impeded their development or

---

165. As Ridruejo explained:

> We spent our whole lives telling ourselves that in the war 'we had taken on the valid arguments of the adversary', but in the meantime the military machine progressively crushed that adversary in the most specific way. Who would then represent their legitimate hopes? Us, of course. How innocent we were! Without war, the left-right syncretism that we Falangists believed ourselves to profess was quite fanciful. However, in war-time and in view of the forced alliances of war, that fanciful belief became simply impossible. In short, the syncretism that was fought for in Burgos was already quite different, for any surviving entity to the left of the Falange disappeared completely. Fancy that! (Ridruejo, 1976: 126)

166. Felipe González Vicén, as Ridruejo explained, 'came from the Left and, although his brother's influence spared him from greater harm, this was not enough to prevent the fanatical Enrique Suñer, Head of the State Education Committee, almost a novice in the post and a most implacable inquisitor, from depriving him of his Chair. The slight help that various collaborators of the great Manichean – Valdecasas and even Vegas Latapié – tried to lend him was quite useless' (Ridruejo, 1976: 84).

'betrayed' their ideals' (Marsal, 1979: 43). José Bugueda Sanchís explained the solidarity among young people of different ideologies and their common enmity with regard to the most reactionary institutions of the régime. We have already described the importance of the generational factor. Brugueda himself states the following: 'We never considered ourselves to be the winners of the war. That goes without saying. But I am talking about all young people, not only our group or the young people we had dealings with. It was, in fact, a complete youth consciousness. And those who joined the war victors did so later on. Such was the case with Manuel Fraga, who was of our generation. Fraga now has an awareness of having won the war, but he did not have it before...Those who are older than us did have it...1 April was a dreadful day because it was Victory Day, that meant that for others it was the day of defeat...When we realised that we had an enemy, we found that that enemy was not the defeated side in the war, that enemy was represented by the heads of the Establishment...We were aware that half of Spain had lost the war, but we harboured a utopian hope that we would preserve our generational unity' (Marsal, 1979: 70–71).[167]

However, nobody was as clearly or as explicitly committed to recognising the plight of the defeated as Ridruejo, to the point that he even came to be considered as one of them. His two most important political books, *Escrito en España* ('Written in Spain') and *Casi unas Memorias* ('Almost Memoirs'), were full of conciliatory arguments in which he advocated the immediate rehabilitation of the defeated and the urgent democratisation of the régime. This crucial figure clearly demonstrates the fact that such acts of fraternity and tolerance in the Civil War were quite exceptional and, on occasions, even quite risky. He twice highlighted the generosity of Eugenio Montes in this respect, of whom he wrote: 'without being a hero, he risked his own comfort more than once in order to save, protect and improve the situation of endangered or fallen adversaries' (Ridruejo, 1976: 202; another reference to this matter appears on page 160). In 1940, Ridruejo set up his first conciliatory enterprise, a plural publication that aimed to enhance integration, the magazine *Escorial*. With this publication he attempted:

167. A similar testimony is provided by Carlos París, who stated the following: 'my image of the Civil War underwent a decisive revision. We had a critical view, but one that was entirely experienced from the Nationalist side. Thus, although we believed the war to have been a huge tragedy (José Antonio referred to the war in his testament as an obvious source of anguish) we continued to exalt the Nationalist side and believe that our view had to be based on its perspective, on that of its leftist tendency, so to speak, which is what the Falange originally and purely represented for us. But then I began to see that those who really represented and embodied our ideals were the classic parties of the Left that had fought against Francoism, those whom we had been brainwashed to see in a sinister light. In addition, the horrors of the Nationalist side that had been so carefully concealed, gradually began to come to light' (Marsal, 1979: 208).

to counteract the climate of intellectual intolerance unleashed after the war and create a number of premises for understanding the adversary, furthering the integration of the Spanish etc. In some issues of the magazine the use of the term 'Crusade' when applied to the civil war was brusquely – and not without inconvenient consequences – condemned.' (Ridruejo, 1976: 224)

In 1942 Ridruejo renounced all of his official posts and sent a letter to Franco that openly criticised the course followed by the régime. From that moment on, he was to begin his own unique personal development towards positions that were openly democratic and anti-Francoist, embarking, that very year, on a long journey that was to feature a series of periods of confinement, exile, censorship and imprisonment, a journey that was to continue until the end of his days in June 1975.

On 1 April 1953, he published a controversial article in *Arriba* entitled 'Meditación Para el 1 de Abril' ('Thought for 1 April') essential for studying the development of his interpretation of the war. In this article he stated that 1 April, as it had been celebrated up until that time, did not do justice to such a hard war and that it would have been better if the coup d'état had succeeded on 18 July without any blood being shed at all. In order to acquire 'feeling', 1 April would have to assimilate the valid ideas of the defeated and:

> reveal to the Spanish once again the reasons they have for living together...The attempt to deny this or that part of the Spanish nation their right to be comfortably incorporated into its progress or to be included in it, means not only dismembering Spain – wishing only a part of Spain to go forward – but also progressively leaving gangs of highwaymen by the wayside.' (Ridruejo, 1976: 324–325)[168]

In subsequent years he was to disagree with various figures in the régime regarding these matters. For example, in 1961 he took part in a conflict between José Bergamín and Juan Ignacio Luca de Tena. The latter had refused to sign a reference for the former which would have enabled him to return to Spain and, furthermore, had responded to an article published by Bergamín in exile, accusing him of having carried out criminal activities in the war. Luca de Tena claimed to be prepared to forget, but not to forgive. This attitude provoked a reaction from Ridruejo,

---

168. He continues:

> At heart, all exclusive, partisan, narrowly dogmatic and fervently police-like attitudes that aim to encompass the full meaning of the great opportunity of Victory, are born of a lack of faith and courage, conceal an absence of trust in truth itself, in one's own strength and even in one's own resolution. He who is creatively prepared to engage upon a Spanish enterprise and he who is generously prepared to die for it and, in doing so, 'sacrifice all contingent aspects in order to save what is essential', so that general Spanish harmony and unity may be achieved, does not need to proceed warily. (Ridruejo, 1976: 325)

who sent a couple of letters to Luca de Tena in which he denied the veracity of the criminal charges that had been levelled at Bergamín and reminded him that the history of the war would have to be told by employing the 'humble 'we' form when it comes to recounting the blame' (Ridruejo, 1976: 375).

Ridruejo's obsession in the 1960s and 1970s was to do everything in his power to avoid a repetition of the Civil War and achieve the political amnesty of the defeated and their complete rehabilitation, in order to lay the foundations on which a democratic form of coexistence among Spaniards should be built. These concerns predominated in the majority of his writings on political events of the day, and not only in tacit form, but in an open and honest expression of his beliefs, that brought him further prosecution and censorship. After the Munich episodes, in which he played an important role, he was obliged to reside temporarily in exile. In 1964 he returned to Spain and, after illegally founding the Partido Social de Acción Democrática (Social Democractic Action Party) in 1957, he tried again with the Unión Social-Demócrata Española (Spanish Social Democratic Union) in 1974. The programmes of the two parties he founded were predominantly concerned with achieving a peaceful transition towards social democracy. This objective, according to Ridruejo and many others, would be easier to attain if the Monarchy were to play a mediating and moderating role regarding possible conflicts. Ridruejo, furthermore, was also among those who believed that the social and economic transformation of Spain made any repetition of the war almost impossible.[169] Furthermore, as he stated in an interview given to the newspaper *Ya* in 1975, he believed:

> that reconciliation among the Spanish is more advanced than is generally thought, and it is only denied and disturbed by those who do not wish to see it...in Spanish society the elements of reconciliation are powerful and extremely numerous...I believe that the Spaniard today is horrified by the prospect of a new trauma. Those of us who work in politics in order to

---

169. On 7 June 1979, a few days before he died, he declared the following to the magazine *Blanco y Negro*:

> The exasperating conditions that give rise to violence do not now exist in Spain: there is a sufficiently widespread sense of well-being among the population, and this will tend to preserve the country. The risk resides in the daily humiliation that can, in fact, produce states of repression and a desire for vengeance. (Ridruejo, 1976: 473)

In effect, Ridruejo could see how the performance-based legitimacy achieved by the régime as a result of its economic and social management had removed a large number of the problems that made the outbreak of war possible. Discrimination against the defeated and the repression of freedoms, both contained within the régime's origin-based legitimacy, were, however, much more anachronistic and unpopular. The founding moment, as Robert Fishman (1990) would say, had become obsolete and gave rise to forms of behaviour that were becoming increasingly inadmissible.

further reconciliation, for we have already been reconciled, do so, above all, in order to see that this trauma or tragedy is avoided. (Ridruejo, 1976: 472)

In conclusion, we believe that it is possible to state that one of the clearest means of measuring the degree of dissidence or, conversely, loyalty to the Franco régime, is provided by the evaluation that the person in question made of the war and its outcome, as well as the treatment which, in his opinion, members of the defeated side should receive. Splits within the initial dominant group not only arose in relation to monarchic, fascist and religious issues, but also in relation to the narrative regarding the war and the official attitude towards the defeated. It was the régime's intransigence towards the defeated that provoked dissension at home and distrust abroad, a problem that a section of the Franco régime attempted to attenuate by focusing on its economic management and grasping any opportunity of furthering an apolitical climate.

The defeated, in turn, were 'forgiven' by means of pardons, the exclusive prerogative of the governing party. According to Weber, holding power means possessing a monopoly regarding the legitimate use of violence and, we might add, of clemency. The reasons given by the defeated for having fought in the war were never recognised, nor were their reasons for defending a legitimately established régime ever acknowledged. The errors committed by the winning side were never admitted, no policy of seeking forgiveness was ever considered and no signs of repentance for the purges that were carried out in the postwar period were ever revealed. All this would have meant admitting that the attitude adopted in previous years had been barbaric and vengeful, and that the war, which constituted the very raison d'être of the régime, could have been avoided and peaceful coexistence could have been maintained by other means. Furthermore, it would have meant a return to a parliamentary system, or the admission, at the very least, of a certain degree of pluralism, given that the real reintegration of the defeated would have meant giving them a voice and a vote, committing the Government to listening to their criticisms and granting them equal rights with regard to those enjoyed by the winning side. For the Franco régime all this would have entailed renouncing its origin-based legitimacy and its founding myth, which would have cleared the way for a democratic system, the very form of government that Francoism wished to avoid.

CHAPTER 3

THE MEMORY OF WAR AND THE LESSONS OF PEACE IN THE DEMOCRATIC TRANSITION

At the end of 1975, after the death of General Franco, a gradual process of liberalisation and a movement towards increasing openness commenced within the régime, undertaken by the Francoist institutions themselves. What is known as the Spanish Transition has been the subject of numerous sociological and historical works.[1] Our task, therefore, is not to offer an entire reconstruction of the process, but to try to contribute certain new insights to the existing analysis in order to enrich the general overview of this period and contribute to a better understanding of it.

In spite of all the uncertainties that surrounded the slow transformation of the Franco régime, there were many, both inside Spain and abroad, who appeared to forecast, if not the process which was to be

---

1. Among the historians, we might highlight, in particular, Raymond Carr and Juan Pablo Fusi (1979; 1985): *Spain: Dictatorship to Democracy*, as well as Santos Juliá (in Manuel Tuñón de Lara (dir.) (1992): *Historia de España. Transición y Democracia (1973–1985)*, Volume X**). Studies of the Transition based on the perspective of political science and sociology are much more numerous; we might highlight, among others, those produced by Juan José Linz (1978; 1987), Víctor Pérez Díaz (1987; 1993), José María Maravall (1982; 1985), Julián Santamaría (1981), José Ramón Montero and Leonardo Morlino (1994), Richard Gunther and Roger A. Blough (1980), Donald Share (1986) and many others. The book by José Félix Tezanos, Ramón Cotarelo and Andrés de Blas (1989) features an extensive bibliography of the Transition compiled by José Antonio Gómez Yáñez. The study by Ramón Cotarelo (comp.) (1992) features another bibliographic compilation.

followed, at least its final goal: inorganic, plural democracy, featuring political parties and parliamentary representation. Although this goal was the priority, many of the old institutions and methods for pursuing politics of the Second Republic – the only democratic period in Spanish history up until that time – were not revived. On the contrary, it seemed that the Second Republic could only serve as a contrasting example for the new democracy that, according to all indications, was approaching.

A general sense of collective guilt existed regarding the failure of the Republican experience and every effort was made to ensure that its ill-fated conclusion, the Civil War, was not repeated. There was no better way of avoiding this outcome than changing the means of achieving democracy by attempting to design a process that was different to that which had been used before; a system that benefited from the dissuasive teachings of former experience and, more importantly, sought to obtain maximum advantage from a context that was much more favourable for the establishment of democracy than had previously existed.

The context in which the Second Republic had emerged was very different to that which faced Spanish society in the 1970s. As we have already mentioned, either as a result of Francoist economic management, or in spite of it, the country had become significantly richer. A new, majority middle-class had emerged from the modernising process, endowing the country with a considerable degree of social stability that contributed to the reduction of both the intensity and the radical nature of conflicts compared to those of the Second Republic.[2]

If the context was more liable to favour democratisation than that which had existed before, a serious economic crisis of international scale, which had begun to be felt in 1974, threatened the beginning of this new stage. This crisis could not fail to evoke that which followed the Wall Street Crash of 1929 and had had such serious repercussions, not only for the United States, but also for Western Europe and, therefore, Republican Spain. Furthermore, the last Francoist government had not felt strong enough nor sufficiently qualified to adopt the highly unpopular economic measures (and so face the inevitable social repercussions) which were required in order to face the crisis. This political inhibition had not only worsened the state of the Spanish economy, but also meant that it fell to the first democratically elected government, installed on 15 June 1977, to resolve the crisis, thus forcing the new government to start its administration with a burden that would weaken its position from the

2. The legacy of the economic management of the Franco years was, as José Luis García Delgado and José María Serrano Sanz (1991) have pointed out, somewhat 'ambivalent'. Although, on the one hand, the productive structure which was inherited was fragile and inadequate for the new economic situation, on the other hand, it was impossible to deny the profound and rapid 'process of social modernisation and secularisation' that had taken place in Spain and its repercussions on the political culture of the Spanish (García Delgado and Serrano Sanz, 1991: 190–191).

outset. Under these circumstances it was feared that the corresponding cost might negatively affect the legitimacy of the new régime.

Although the general climate within the country created some favourable prospects for the consolidation of democracy, helping to dissipate, at least in part, the ghosts of the past, the seriousness of the economic crisis and the revival of party politics, as well as the numerous terrorist attacks and social demands of the time, recalled the failures of the past and, for some, led to the fear of a repetition of events. Others were much more fearful of the reaction of the Army, in particular that it might feel provoked into action by terrorism and regional demands for autonomy; this fear of military intervention also evoked the political crisis of the 1930s, and the revolt led by General Franco.

It was precisely these two factors, the memory of historical misfortune and the fear of the dangers of radicalisation, that contributed most to moderating the demands of all the important political and social groups of the time and to legitimising a different means of bringing about political transformations.[3] Negotiation, pact-making, giving ground, tolerance – in short, the famous consensus – were established to the point that they became, at certain crucial moments, an end in themselves rather than a means, irrespective of the substance of the agreement.[4]

Thus, a new form of politics made its debut in Spain, a crucial change that was welcomed by all. Something was brought into play and repeated time and again which is of considerable significance in understanding the importance of historical memory in this process: finally, Spaniards had proved capable of avoiding a kind of historical curse which prevented us from reaching consensus-based solutions that satisfied the majority of the population. Due to the economic, social and administrative transformations of recent years and the harsh lessons of the past, it was possible to break the spell and leave behind, once and for all, a long tradition of intolerance, imposition, subjection of the opponent and '*trágalas*' or 'imposed constitutions'.

3. We agree with the argument that Javier Pradera expressed in his article 'Vísperas Republicanas' (*El País*, 12/4/1990). The author emphasised the importance of 'the historical memory of the Republican defeat' and stated 'that the Republican transition served as a negative model for the protagonists of the post-Francoist transition, to the extent that the course of the events which took place between 1975 and 1982 was conditioned – for better or for worse – by the perception of the errors, of the omissions and of the excesses witnessed during the period between 1931 and 1936'.

4. This argument is intimately related to that espoused by Susana Aguilar Fernández in her degree dissertation, where she stated that the legitimacy that society granted to the democratic system was based more on an acceptance of democracy as a procedure rather than on its substance (Aguilar, 1986). In effect, basic agreement in many cases centred on the means by which the democratic goal was to be achieved, whilst emphasising the importance of these means, given that they had to be different from those employed by the political élite of the Second Republic (Gunther and Blough, 1980).

Economic and Social Characteristics of the Transition

Given that the socioeconomic context of the 1930s and 1970s has already been studied by experts within this field, our intention is not to highlight the real differences and similarities between the Second Republic and the Transition, but to unravel the perceptions of the main actors during these periods. Most of this chapter will be devoted to studying these perceptions through an analysis of the institutional and procedural construction of the new democratic régime. Nevertheless, structural variables are highly important and cannot be isolated completely from political decision-making, given that the social and economic context underpinned such decisions, or from the process of designing the new institutions of the period, as these institutions needed to be flexible enough to adapt to the various determining factors of the time.[5]

The intrinsic importance of the perceptions of the main actors is based on the fact that, although they may not always correspond to reality at any given moment, they can nevertheless lead to the adoption of certain measures which have certain repercussions for that real situation.[6] Below we offer a brief review of the structural conditions in which the new democratic institutions emerged, with a view to highlighting the differences and also some of the similarities between the Republican years and the Transition that began in 1975.

5. Some authors, as explained by Felipe Agüero and Mariano Torcal in their review of recent literature on transitions, have attempted to integrate the two types of explanation, stating that 'the structural context marks the boundaries and, at the same time, the decision-making possibilities of the élite during changes of political régime' (Agüero and Torcal, 1993: 334).
6. We shall never know how the Transition would have turned out if it had not been brought about in accordance with a peaceful and consensus-based process. However, we can state that both this strategy of political change and the excessive caution with which the protagonists guided this change, arose from a perception of the context that was more negative than the context really was, and that this distortion was largely due to the recollection of the failed experience of the Second Republic and its mental association with the present. Furthermore, problems are more visible than advantages in processes of uncertain change. It is no coincidence that during these early years of transition various books were published on the Republican period, some of which explicitly aimed to serve as a lesson for the present through their description and recollection of the past. This was the intention of Santiago Varela, who stated in the final paragraph of the conclusion to his book that, although history does not repeat itself:

    it can be instructive. Today, forty years later, Spain once again stands on the threshold of democracy. And the new democracy will bring with it new institutions and a new system of political forces. It would be worth recalling at such a moment the importance that these aspects had when, in 1931, it was necessary to seek solutions to the old problems of Spanish history, newly brought to light, and reflect upon the scope and opportunities that the *political will* has in order to shape the party system and parliamentary régime that must provide the backbone for democracy and freedom in Spain. At times quite consciously and at others less so, all the pages of this book have been inspired by a concern for the Spain of today and the future. (Varela, 1978: 285)

The social transformations which took place during the Franco period were of considerable importance regarding the peaceful course of the Transition. A good example of this is provided by the new social structure of the rural areas, a factor which facilitated the establishment of the new democracy. Víctor Pérez Díaz reminds us of the mass support which the Uprising received, mainly in the countryside regions of Castile and Navarre. The peasants reacted negatively to the attempts at agrarian reform carried out under the Republic, whose measures 'were interpreted as increasingly urgent threats to the property system in general, and to small and medium-sized property in particular' (Pérez Díaz, 1987: 405–406). In addition, some aspects of the politics of this period were interpreted by rural society as being attacks on religion and on national unity. In view of the traditional beliefs of the agrarian regions of Castile, that is, 'centralism, anti-capitalism and anti-labourism, anti-urbanism in a certain sense, authoritarianism, clericalism and a certain tendency to view conflicts of interest in religious and dramatic terms', their reaction to the Republic and in favour of Francoism was what might have been expected (Pérez Díaz, 1987: 407). The protectionist agrarian policy of the new régime strengthened the basic loyalty of the peasantry, which combined perfectly with agrarian anti-capitalism, supported, at least rhetorically in its early years, by Falangist discourse.[7]

The decade of the 1960s represented a radical transformation of the Spanish agricultural scene. With the incorporation of the technocrats into government, capitalist rhetoric and capitalist practices were imposed and some markets were liberalised, at least partially. The transformations that this and other phenomena, such as emigration, the rural exodus and tourism, brought with them produced 'an increasing secularisation and urbanisation of rural life' which helped to make conflicts within rural areas less ideological. This entire process meant that the agrarian society of the Transition was 'much less easily mobilised by the conservative, dramatic and authoritarian slogans of old'. In addition, in spite of the profound economic crisis witnessed in the 1970s, the peasants no longer tended to blame the same enemies as they had before under the guidance of the Church, not least because 'neither the Church nor the predominant political forces were in any position (nor had any need) to

---

7. One study on the social bases of Francoist support states that 56.1 percent of the mayors appointed and 58.8 percent of the councillors chosen in the municipal elections of 1948 fell within the category of what the author characterises, rather too vaguely, as 'labourers', 'with owners of small and medium-sized agricultural concerns predominating, featuring a significant presence of large-scale landowners', which, according to the same study, 'demonstrates the continuity of social identity with regard to those who had supported the revolt in 1936' (Sevillano Calero, 1991–1992: 59). It is striking that in the table of occupations there should have been such a large difference between the first category of 'labourers' and the next category of 'industrialists' (only 9.1 percent of the mayors and 11.5 percent of the councillors).

propose the traditional depiction of the external enemy as the cause of the crisis, to the peasantry' (Pérez Díaz, 1987: 408–409).

The migratory processes from countryside to city, which represented the progressive replacement of agricultural activity with industrial activity, were especially rapid during the mid-Franco years (between the 1950s and 1960s). What was achieved in Spain in only twenty years, that is, reducing the active agricultural population from 50 percent to 25 per cent, 'in France took almost three-quarters of a century, half a century in Germany [and] a third of a century in Italy' (García Delgado and Serrano Sanz, 1991: 191). Agriculture was mechanised, reducing costs and enhancing production, although it was relegated to third place in order of importance, behind industry and the service sector.

Thus, the logic of the argument that may be applied to the Transition consists of the following:

> at the end of the Franco period, political reformists, unlike the liberals of the nineteenth century or the Republicans of the first third of the twentieth century, did not have among the most urgent measures on their agenda the task of carrying out an agrarian reform which would affect landowning and fulfil the expectations of a substantial section of the Spanish population: nobody expected democracy, as had traditionally been the case in Spain ever since the land seizures of the nineteenth century, to carry out a far-reaching reform of agrarian property and, therefore, nobody was to find that their collective aspirations were frustrated by the fact that pending reform had once again failed to be realised. Political reformists were able to concentrate on the task of democratising Spain without having to simultaneously struggle with discontent and the violent mass protests of landless peasants. (Juliá, 1992: 33–34)

The author concludes: 'Agriculture thus played, unlike in the 1930s, a stabilising role with regard to democracy and did not, as it had then, constitute the main source of social conflict' (Juliá, 1992a: 35). As we can see, one of the constant features of studies on the Transition is to explain its success by appeal to the differences in the socioeconomic context of the 1970s compared to that of the 1930s, although this may not always be made explicit.

The labour movement also witnessed some profound transformations.[8] In order to contrast the situation that existed under the Second Republic with that of the Transition, we must remember that there was no polarised split in the labour movement between anarchists and socialists during the latter period, due to the practical disappearance of the anarchists from political life. It is highly significant that the strongest

---

8. See the various works produced by Pérez Díaz regarding the workers in Spain (Pérez Díaz, 1979; 1980; 1981; 1987; 1993) and the book by Robert Fishman (1990a) regarding the trade unions during the Transition.

and most important trade union in the 1930s, the Confederación Nacional del Trabajo (CNT), progressively dissolved throughout the Franco period until it had lost a large part of its representative power under democracy.[9] Of the possible reasons for this decline (in addition to serious internal problems, which the union was unable to overcome during its clandestine existence) one was the emergence of an international context that was hostile to anarcho-syndicalism. Another was the unpopularity of the movement as a result of the radicalism and violence associated with anarchist commando groups during the Civil War. The ranks of the majority of these groups, which the Republican Government labelled as being 'out of control', and which carried out many of the sadly infamous reprisals of the Republican rearguard, were largely composed of members who called themselves anarchists.[10] This memory of the war was reactivated during the Transition due to the CNT's unwillingness to negotiate with either the Government or the other trade unions.[11]

The anarchist union did not agree with this reformist strategy and, unlike the majority of the parties and left-wing unions, it was not prepared to negotiate with the élite successors of Francoism. Furthermore, the CNT had fared particularly badly in the matter of the trade union assets which were seized during and after the war, and its power was insignificant in

9. Especially the anarchist union that preserved its original acronym, the CNT, which was not in favour of political action within the existing system. The 'pragmatic' splinter group that broke off from this trade union, the Confederación General del Trabajo (CGT), did have a certain degree of representative union power within some sectors of the economy.

10. This does not mean that the anarchists were mainly responsible for the day-to-day executions that took place among the civil population, a highly delicate issue that goes far beyond the bounds of this research. What can be stated is that their actions were fairly visible and were recorded in numerous accounts, to which we must add the demonisation of the anarchist movement by Francoist socialisation, the successor, in part, of the demonised view that the communists had created during the Civil War. This demonised perspective instilled a sense of atrocious and irrational panic, as the anarchists were portrayed in terms of unreal caricature. The image of the communist militant was also deformed to the point of becoming quite grotesque, but never to the same mythological extreme as the anarchists. On the other hand, the anarchist image was also somewhat mythologised, although this time in a positive sense, by various foreign observers and activists who took part in the war, such as George Orwell (1938; 1988) and Burnett Bolloton (1961; 1975). However, other Hispanists such as Gerald Brenan (1960; 1977) would reach the conclusion that certain anarcho-syndicalists had been as murderous as some Falangists.

11. In June 1976 the CNT rejected trade union coordination with CCOO, UGT and USO. Thus, whilst the three latter trade unions would set up the Coordinadora de Organizaciones Sindicales (COS) the following month, the CNT decided not to join this coordinating body. In April 1977, while the COS was attempting to negotiate with the Minister for Trade Union Relations in order to gain authorisation for a demonstration on Labour Day, the CNT refused to even participate in the 1 May event. At the end of 1977, when the main trade unions negotiated the forthcoming staging of trade union elections with the Government, the CNT opposed both the agreement and the staging of elections.

comparison with the stature it had enjoyed in the 1930s. This general attitude, which was perceived as being intransigent in many sectors, led to the resurrection of the old anarchist controversy witnessed under the Second Republic regarding the expediency of intervening actively in politics, and would subsequently provoke the split of the movement.

The main trade unions of the Transition, Comisiones Obreras (CCOO)[12] and the Unión General de Trabajadores (UGT) were very different from those of the Second Republic – CCOO had not even existed then – because they had ceased to be revolutionary and were prepared to create joint platforms in order to present their demands more effectively. Furthermore, the rhetoric and violent practice of before had been abandoned and the trade unions of the 1970s were more prepared to demonstrate their capacity for negotiation and dialogue.[13] Comisiones Obreras, which emerged during the heyday of Francoist Spain and was headed by figures close to the Communist Party, was also intimately connected to progressive Christian groups, something that would have been unthinkable for a communist trade union in the 1930s, in view of the profound anticlericalism which had existed at that time.[14] Anticlericalism was no longer an important factor during the Transition; it did not even exist as a cause of inter- or intraparty conflict, and the Church was not going to intervene openly in electoral campaigns either, as it had in the 1930s. Against all the odds a Christian Democratic Party did not even manage to establish a firm position on the political scene, in spite of the fact that the majority of the Spanish, according to surveys, fell within this ideological sphere.

Furthermore, based on information included in the book by David Ruiz, we have produced an average age for the members of the Secretariat which was elected at the first CCOO Congress, which took place in November 1978 and, discounting two members whose ages do not appear, the average comes to 38 years (Ruiz, 1993: 523). This means that the majority had been born around 1940, in the immediate postwar period, not having had the unique experience of the war, but having suffered its most immediate repercussions.

The UGT, for its part, had moderated its stance considerably with respect to the position it had held before the Civil War and, naturally, its executive had been renewed with younger members, conveying an image

12. See the history of this trade union in the book coordinated by David Ruiz (1993).
13. The trade unions participated in the peaceful demonstrations of 1 May 1977, but as they had not received the government authorisation that they had so earnestly sought to obtain, the reaction of the police was extremely violent and they suppressed all of the most important public events that took place in Spain. After this police repression, the trade unions stated, in order to reassure public opinion, that they would not respond to the provocation of the forces of public order and repay them in the same currency (*El País*, 3/5/1977: p.1).
14. Proof of this is provided by the fact that 'of the seven defendants in the first prosecution of Comisiones Obreras in Biscay, six belonged to the HOAC' (Pérez Díaz, 1993: 188).

of greater tolerance and willingness to negotiate. This trade union was backed by a socialist party, the PSOE, which was destined to play a crucial role in the democratic transition, consolidation and institutionalisation process. The PSOE, after an initial attitude characterised by verbal radicalism, ended up displaying its flexibility and a willingness to negotiate, doing everything in its power to temper the demands of its members and sympathisers, both within the party and within the trade union.[15]

The UGT and the CCOO played the leading role in long periods of strikes and mass demonstrations, both during the final years of Francoism and during the Transition,[16] but they also accepted the economic sacrifices that were imposed on them by the Moncloa Pacts in exchange for concessions of a social and political nature.[17]

This accommodation displays a difference between the policies that were implemented in the 1930s and those of the 1970s to combat economic crisis. The corporate strategy of the second transition process, the result of a general climate of consensus and negotiation, would not have been possible during the Republican period, because of the lack of dialogue among the main protagonists of the time. Neither the Right nor the Left had wished to make concessions, and the Left was not willing to moderate or negotiate its demands, so a strategy of confrontation had prevailed. In 1977, however, all of the parties with parliamentary representation agreed to sign the Moncloa economic agreements.[18] The political agreements were only boycotted by one party, Alianza Popular, which refused to sign them.

The trade union demands that are most important to this study were those relating to the extension of the amnesty to the labour sector, featuring calls for the incorporation of all those dismissed for political reasons, as well as requests for the return of the extensive trade union assets confiscated during the war and the postwar period.[19]

Another factor that had ceased to be a source of conflict was the Catholic Church.[20] The majority of the studies on this matter agree with

15. In general terms, the Left accepted capitalism, although it criticised it, especially at a rhetorical level, and it agreed to sign the Moncloa Pacts, undertaking to convince its allied trade unions and its own members of the importance of limiting their wage demands in order to end the crisis and consolidate democracy.
16. See José María Maravall (1978) and Robert M. Fishman (1990).
17. With regard to the Moncloa Pacts, see Joan Trullen i Thomàs (1993).
18. With regard to the comparison between the two types of economic response to the crisis, see the unpublished study produced by Ana Rico (1990).
19. The return of party assets, an extraordinarily delicate and complex issue, is something that the Prime Minister of the Government, José María Aznar, has publicly committed himself to achieving (*El País*, 6/5/1996).
20. Once again we can turn to the work of Pérez Díaz regarding the development of the Church under Francoism and its role in the Transition. Other authors who have studied this matter from a nonsociological perspective include: Hermet (1985), Fontana (1986), Gómez Pérez (1986), Ibán (1987) and Lannon (1987).

regard to their description of the transformations that the Church witnessed in its internal workings and in its external relations. Within the social and cultural context of the 1960s, the Church was no longer able to maintain the ultramontane position that it had adhered to since the war. Many young clergymen were acquiring a growing awareness of the pressing social problems of the underprivileged classes excluded from the benefits of the economic boom, and revealed an increasing concern for issues of justice and less preoccupation with questions of charity (Pérez Díaz, 1993: 87). At the same time, they maintained close links with Catholic liberal and left-wing intellectuals who were beginning to have a considerable influence on university students (in some cases, training the new generation in the democratic ideals that would play a leading role in the political transition) and on the world of culture.

The Second Vatican Council was crucial when it came to legitimising the changes that had already begun to emerge within the Spanish Church. If the need to define the boundaries between Church and State was becoming increasingly pressing, it was a question of absolute urgency to bring about a reconciliation with the defeated side in the war. A Church that had become progressively independent with regard to the régime and in which the majority of its youngest emissaries directly supported the democratic demands of the workers, could not act as if nothing had happened in the past. On the other hand, the burdensome conscience of its belligerent stance in the war and repressive attitude during the Franco period was becoming increasingly heavy. The year 1975 was officially named the year of 'Reconciliation' by the Church and although no direct references were made to the Civil War, the choice of an issue as closely linked as this to forgiveness, clemency and peace, could be no coincidence.

During the Transition, the Church adopted a largely favourable attitude with regard to democratic change, significantly from the perspective of a detached observer, far removed from its former desire to play a leading role. All of this constitutes yet another objective differentiating factor with regard to the situation under the Second Republic; if the Church at that time had helped to destabilise incipient democracy, now it was to play a radically different and much less visible role. Religion was, nevertheless, one of the most delicate issues of the constitutional debates, if we exclude the debate about the autonomous regions. The PCE, contrary to what might have been expected, did not raise any problem in this respect, doing everything in its power to disassociate its present attitude with the memory of the Second Republic and the Civil War, periods during which the religious conflict had reached its most radical heights. On the Left, the party that aroused the greatest concern in the political centre and on the Right in relation to the religious issue was the PSOE. Eventually, as described in the article by Gunther and Blough (1980), existing differences were to be resolved in the same way as on other occasions during that period, at private meetings featuring the participation of only a few representatives who were authorised to compromise and negotiate for their respective parties. On more than one occasion the negotiators broke the impasse in this way, unlike under the Second Republic, where debates on the most delicate issues became increasingly radical as they were staged at mass public forums that featured the active involvement of a militant press, all of which made calm and moderate dialogue more difficult.

Even though most of the problems that had contributed to destabilising the Republic had been resolved (agrarian, labour and religious issues), one conflict inherited from the Republican era not only survived Francoism, but worsened throughout the Franco period: the issue of the territorial organisation of the State.

During the Second Republic it had been possible to impose the concept of an 'integral state' that enabled certain 'historical' regions to acquire a degree of autonomy from the rest, being governed by their own Statutes (such was the case with Catalonia, the Basque Country and, during the war itself, Galicia). Nevertheless, there were many (especially the Army and the most conservative members of the Right) who considered these autonomous concessions to be a direct attack on the unity of the state.[21]

Peripheral nationalism had lost ground after the victory of the Francoist troops. Franco imposed an absolutely centralised political and administrative structure that repressed many of the cultural manifestations of the regions that set themselves apart by expressing nationalist sentiments. In its attempt to silence these voices, Francoism encouraged a kind of regional folklore that was extremely superficial and innocuous. The regional diversity of the state was exhibited proudly and cited as yet another example of the rich heritage of the nation, being used to support the idea of 'unity through plurality' that was supposedly unique to Spain.

Throughout the last decade of the Franco period, the police and military authorities subjected the Basque Country to an especially brutal hounding. Those were the days when the forces of law and order charged at demonstrators who displayed *ikurriñas* (the Basque flag), when the ETA terrorist attacks on state security forces began and when the régime declared various states of emergency in the region. Nationalist feelings were progressively aggravated through repression, until they reached extremes that would have been unthinkable during the Republican period.

At the beginning of the Transition, radical Basque nationalists carried out some of the bloodiest and most spectacular attacks in its still brief history, some of an indiscriminate nature. This polarisation of the regional and national conflict, combined with the strong mistrust within the security forces of any demand that might conflict with their unitary

21. With regard to this matter see, among others, Chapter 5 of *El problema regional en la Segunda República española*, Santiago Varela (1978) and the article, 'Autonomías regionales y fuerzas políticas en las Cortes constituyentes de 1931', José Luis de la Granja (1981).

conception of the *Patria,* helped to create an atmosphere of increased tension and raised fears of a violent outcome. The victims of the terrorist attacks, which were also carried out by the extreme right, and the deaths at the hands of the police, especially at demonstrations in favour of amnesty, inevitably evoked a period of uncontrolled violence such as that which had been witnessed under the Second Republic. The Republic had been unable to contain its own supporters or exercise any authority with regard to those who sought to destabilise it. In the 1970s there were many who feared that the new democracy was not going to be able to cope authoritatively and sensibly with the various outbursts of violence that were sowing such seeds of uncertainty and fear within the transition process. In spite of this climate, none of the important parties were prepared to push for the passing of anything that even remotely resembled the Law for the Defence of the Republic, in view of the serious limitations on democratic freedoms that this had entailed and the sense of rejection its implementation had aroused in certain sections of society.

Peripheral nationalism was the only example of a serious and unresolved problem inherited from the days of the Republic; one that had, moreover, become increasingly complex over time until it attained a virulence that was difficult to assuage. This was, therefore, the issue that most strongly evoked the errors of the Republic and the horrors of the war. The heavy-handedness and intransigence of the Franco régime had brought about the radicalisation of the regional conflict, but, irrespective of who might have been originally to blame for the situation it was the Transition that was obliged to find a solution. As we shall see later on, the negotiations between the Government and the peripheral nationalist movements were carried out with exquisite care, featuring a persistent attempt not to provoke the sensibilities of either side, although this was not always achieved.

It is quite evident that the international situation of the 1930s was very different from that of the 1970s. The 1970s provided a much more favourable context for the establishment and restoration of democracy for a variety of well-known reasons. The period in which the Second Republic emerged was the heyday of two wide-ranging totalitarian tendencies, Communism and Fascism. European politics was polarised around these two systems and international public opinion was equally radical. The fear of communist revolution such as that which had already taken place in Russia shaped conservative and centrist perceptions, whilst fear of the Fascist advance obsessed the Left. Nobody could have forecast the magnitude of the catastrophe that would lay waste to Europe between 1939 and 1945, but both fears turned out to be more than justified, even though they were manipulated, in many cases, for partisan ends.

Negative reactions to the Republic were motivated, in large part, by the fear that this régime, weak as it showed itself to be, would be unable to halt the advance of the extreme left (communists, anarchists and, within PSOE, the extreme-left followers of Largo Caballero, known as 'largocaballeristas'). The radical reforms that the left-wing governments attempted to implement simply reinforced this perception, and the triumph of the Popular Front in 1936 gave rise to the most pessimistic forecasts that predicted the establishment of Soviet hegemony over Spanish soil. Conversely, the birth of the Falange and other far-right groups, whose aesthetics and rhetoric imitated Italian Fascism and German Nazism, led the Republic to fear for its continuing existence and caused both the Republicans and the Left to prepare themselves to defend it.

In the 1970s the situation was very different. Italian Fascism and German Nazism had been defeated. The long, tense period of the Cold War that followed the Second World War had progressively thawed over recent decades. The United States was prepared to support the restoration of democracy in Spain and the European powers had already demonstrated their willingness to support this process in much more explicit terms.[22] Many of the countries that had initially refused to lend their support to Franco after the Civil War, involving the withdrawal of their embassies and other more drastic measures, had ended up by reestablishing diplomatic and economic relations with the Spanish dictatorship (except for some particularly famous cases, such as Mexico, due to the fact that this country became the destination par excellence for Republican political exiles, and the majority of the communist countries). However, after the death of Franco many countries believed that the moment had come for Greece, Portugal and Spain to swell the ranks of democratic Europe. The democracies had strengthened their position after the traumatic experience of the Second World War and no longer feared a hypothetical communist invasion.

In addition, some European communist parties, in particular those of Spain and Italy, had been distancing themselves from Soviet orthodoxy for a number of years and were formulating a 'Eurocommunist' doctrine that included the full acceptance of democracy and the capitalist system. Communism, at least in Europe, had ceased to be the *bête noire* of democracy. To a varying extent the social democratic policies that many Eurocommunists advocated had already begun to be implemented on the continent some years before and the workers had achieved many of their social, political and economic objectives throughout these years. The Spanish far right continued to claim that, should democracy be restored, Spain would end up in the hands of Soviet agents, making it a satellite of the USSR, but the vast majority of the population did not share this absurd reading. The Eurocommunists and socialists established the boundaries of the political spectrum on the Left and would be the first to lose from any excesses within their own ranks.

As we have been able to observe, in the 1970s both the international context and the domestic situation were much more conducive to the

---

22. We might recall the Munich crisis, described above, and the refusal of the European Community to handle Spain's request for membership until the country met the democratic requirements that had been established.

establishment and consolidation of democracy than had been the case in the 1930s, although these were not sufficient conditions in themselves for it to become a reality. However, memory continued to play its enlightening role with regard to the present, as a number of real similarities regarding the transition of the 1930s did actually exist. The evocative capacity of such crucial periods as the Second Republic and the Civil War had an extremely powerful influence on the transition process, and the strategies of the political élites as well as the behaviour of society in general were conditioned by the memory of the past, the most important lesson of which consisted of the dictum, 'he who avoids the cause, avoids the danger'. In this case, that meant ensuring a different institutional system, one which omitted those aspects that were thought to have contributed most to the radicalisation of political and social life. This explains why, in spite of all the factors described above, which were highly conducive to the establishment of democracy, the main political actors of the Transition proceeded under the assumption that civil war might break out again.

History as *Magistra Vitae*

Some of the questions that almost immediately arise when studying this vivid period are the following: Why did this second transition from an authoritarian to a democratic society not lead to civil war? Why did the processes of the second transition follow such a different course, and witness such different outcomes to those of the first? The answer to the first question is that it would have been highly improbable for the second transition to have ended in civil war. This view is essentially based on two sets of reasons.

The first set of reasons, as we have just explained, concerns a series of circumstances that existed in the 1970s which we might call 'objective advantages' when compared to those of the Second Republic. The economic, social and political context was, in general terms, much more favourable for the consolidation of a democracy. Even the international context was more inclined to welcome and nurture a democratic country as opposed to an authoritarian régime.

The second set of reasons concerns the crucial role that history played throughout the entire process. In reality, it does not seem as if society was interested in analysing in detail whether the existence of a very different series of circumstances compared to those of the Republican period would 'necessarily' have led to a different outcome. This much is quite evident. Surveys have always demonstrated that the vast majority of people are more concerned about their daily problems than about political, economic or social problems of a global nature. Democracies are not exempt from this relative apathy towards public life. Furthermore, it is logical to think that most members of society obtain their bearings based more on their perceptions of what is taking place around them rather than on an exhaustive analysis of the facts that relate to the period in question. None of this should lead us to believe for a moment that people act 'irrationally'. On the contrary, they are guided by their own experience, by intuition and by information filtering through from abroad.[23]

The key aspect in understanding the general attitude of the political and social protagonists requires, then, a study of their subjective perceptions of the similarities and differences between the two situations, irrespective of whether their knowledge of the 'real' facts might have led, to a greater or lesser extent, to optimism.[24] Nevertheless, we should highlight the fact that this idea of historical memory and political learning is complemented by the existence of certain 'objective disadvantages', such as the economic crisis that existed during the period, terrorism and the possibility of military intervention, remembering that disadvantages tend to be more visible than 'objective advantages' in periods of considerable uncertainty such as those witnessed during political transitions. At certain times these serious concerns introduced considerable doses of fear and pessimism. Some voices on the far right even went so far as to blame pluralist democracy for the appearance of these concerns.[25]

As a consequence, due both to historical memory and the existence of a number of real and visible problems, the vast majority of Spaniards acted on the assumption that the Civil War could be reignited at any moment and, therefore, that it was a matter of priority to avoid this outcome at any cost.[26] This circumstance, in addition to the persistence of a

---

23. In effect, the latest transition theories have played down the importance of structural factors and the socioeconomic preconditions designed by functionalists, especially after the 'third wave' of transitions (Huntington, 1991; Chull Shin, 1994). The most recent contributions have highlighted the importance of other variables in relation to the consolidation of democracy (Maravall, 1994a).
24. I refer, once again, to the study by Robert Jervis (1976).
25. Areilza, among others, attempted to refute, in his memoirs, this alleged relationship between cause – democracy – and effect – the crisis. This author, also known as the Count of Motrico, stated that 'the present economic crisis is not due, as some fools or simplistic commentators have claimed, to the fact that Spain is in the process of becoming a democracy' (Areilza, 1983: 176).
26. I believe that remnants of this attitude still survive today. In Spanish political life, especially at critical moments, the protagonists continue to act as though an excessive visibility of certain failings or errors in the workings of the system could lead to an end to peaceful coexistence and once again produce a civil war. The memory of the war continues to be used by various political groups for their own ends. Such was the case with the recent declarations made by Jordi Pujol in *La Vanguardia* (20/11/1994, pages 1 and 17), which were repeated in *El País* (21/11/1994, page 17). The way in which the war is used is nearly always the same. First, the threat is highlighted – although it is not finally realised – of the alleged danger of a repetition of the conflict should certain attitudes fail to change (for example, Pujol stated that Spain ran 'the

---

certain degree of performance-based legitimacy from the previous régime, conditioned the course and the pace of political change. We might point out that, at least up until the passing of the Constitution, a large part of public opinion preferred to maintain economic development and social order (although to an increasingly lesser extent) rather than set up a régime that would ensure them public freedoms; most members of society had become relatively content to limit their expectations to the level of material welfare that the Franco régime had offered. Only when people began to perceive that the new régime would be able to offer them more for less or, at least, the same at a lower cost, did it begin to grant an increasingly significant degree of legitimacy to democracy.[27] If democracy was able to maintain, and even enhance, economic development and social peace and, at the same time, offer a greater degree of freedom and social justice, as well as guaranteeing participation, there was no doubt that, simply from a utilitarian point of view, this was the best possible kind of régime. In this sense, above all, democracy would have to be capable of laying the ghost of the Civil War to rest and avoiding the radicalisation of political life.

As we have stated above, historical memory is essentially activated through an association of ideas. That is to say, if, through the existence of certain real or imagined circumstances or both, society perceives a comparison between the current situation and a past situation, historical memory will begin to act as an enlightening factor with regard to the present, either by favouring the repetition of institutions or forms of behaviour that were successful at some point in the past, or seeking to

---

risk of a very serious civil confrontation', a phrase that appeared in the front-page headlines of *La Vanguardia*). However, following this statement, as if fearing the consequences of his own words, he stated that this conflict would not be possible due to the existing differences between the two historical contexts, claiming that 'fortunately, the situation in Spain is not the same as that which existed in the 1930s', although, he added, 'internal divisions may be serious and important'. This argument is based on the alleged fragility of the democratic system, which depends on conditions beyond its control for it to be maintained: essentially, the economic and social context. Given that these structural variables may alter, the belief persists that, under sufficiently adverse circumstances, the war could be repeated. Whenever a public declaration of this kind appears, it is highly likely that the rest of the political groups will react angrily, reproaching the party in question for having raised the spectre of the Civil War and highlighting the grave danger that such declarations subject us all to. In relation to this kind of reaction, we might refer to that of José María Aznar in *El País* (21/11/1994, page 18), worded in response to the declarations made by Pujol. Aznar accused Pujol of 'mischievously confusing the issues with such nonsense'.

27. We might also interpret this attitude as being mistrust of the political élite rather than one of mistrust with regard to democracy itself. For this reason, society was not prepared to place its trust in the élite until that élite proved itself capable of acting calmly and with tolerance and moderation, quite in contrast to the conduct of the ruling class of the Republic.

avoid certain institutions and forms of behaviour that failed.[28] Memory usually works in both ways simultaneously. Once the democratic transition began, it was natural that all Spaniards, irrespective of whether they had lived through the period of the Second Republic or not, should bear this past episode in mind, given that it was a question of restoring democracy and the free party system, as well as creating a democratic constitution, which would be required to govern political life. In view of the mental association that was established between the two periods, historical memory and the lessons derived from it were activated and became an important factor in the political life of the country, underlying the image of the past and all those aspects that were to be avoided or encouraged, and underpinning all of the key decisions of the period. None of this should surprise us, since, in general, our actions tend to be inspired by other similar actions we have implemented in the past or the past actions of others.

Given that the perception of history and its associations with the present context appear to be more important in explaining the strategies of the protagonists than socioeconomic conditioning factors, even though the latter are still very important, our analysis should focus on the political lessons derived from the failure of the Republic and the trauma of the Civil War. We can trace these by analysing the arguments that were wielded by the most important figures at key moments, not only regarding the institutional design of the Transition, but also at critical stages of its development. The form of political action guided by this perception of the past required the pursuit of three complementary strategies, all aimed at avoiding both the rupture of the régime and the repetition of war.

First, the parties involved sought to create a series of new institutions which might contribute to stabilising the situation. In this respect, a bicameral parliament was conceived (unlike the unicameral parliament of the 1930s) together with a different electoral law and a monarchic form of government instead of a republic.

Second, the means by which the process itself was carried out, inspired, once again, by the undesirable experience of the Republic, was very different. Consensus and negotiation, which were scarcely practised

---

28. In accordance with our analysis of the first chapter, this possibility of political learning based on a past civil confrontation may only be put into effect if that historical episode, however traumatic it may have been, has, in some way, been overcome – either through amnesia, favoured by the passing of time and consequent generational replacement, or through real reconciliation, that is to say, through forgiveness among those who were once bitter enemies. With regard to cases in which, for various reasons, this past of polarisation and violence has not been overcome, and the former causes of the dispute have been preserved over time through the efforts of one side or the other, as was the case with the former Yugoslavia, memory, manipulated by all, only serves to fan the flames of discord once again and annul the possibility of resorting to the past as a means of political learning.

under the Republic, became the typical means of progressing under the Transition. At the same time, the reforms proposed in the 1970s were debated slowly and implemented gradually and moderately, unlike the radical reforms passed under the Republic, which became the source of its most serious problems.[29]

Third, and directly related to the above, as tolerance, moderation and the obsessive search for consensus became institutionalised as the ideal means of achieving any democratic end, the moment was seized upon to promote both reconciliation and the rehabilitation, at least partially, of those Spaniards who had been defeated in the war. This process might be considered both the cause and the consequence of the strategies outlined above. The will to establish equal conditions for the two sides and to compensate the defeated presided, almost unanimously, over the entire transition process. Very few questioned the just nature of the measures that were taken in this respect, although considerable differences remained regarding their interpretation. For example, as we shall see later on, whilst the forces of the Centre and of the Left defended the amnesty as a matter of justice, a large part of the Right considered it to be a question of generosity and clemency.

Institutional Structure

Below, we shall distinguish the characteristics of certain political institutions of the Transition whose design was actively influenced by the dissuasive memory of those of the Republic's institutions that were most heavily blamed for its failure. The absence of a symbolic moderating power such as the Monarchy, an electoral system that more faithfully reflected the ideological make-up of society, a second chamber that might weigh up the measures passed at first instance and of a uniform territorial structure for the entire state were among the most significant deficiencies of the Second Republic. From the opposite perspective, the existence of a virtually powerless President of the Republic, an electoral system that distorted electoral results, a radicalised single chamber and a mixed territorial structure helped to aggravate the multiple problems of the period by adding institutional difficulties to an already problematic international and socioeconomic context. The design of the Republic's institutions might have been quite different, helping to combat, instead of enhance, the centrifugal tendencies of society.

29. The opposition complained of this slow pace throughout the entire process, given that the delay regarding the adoption of certain pressing decisions, far from being the result of a deliberate strategic consideration, was a consequence of the problems of rule which afflicted the Government on various occasions and of the pressures that were exerted on it by the Army and the far right to abandon or, at least, delay the adoption of certain measures. These delays had other undesirable effects, such as the general climate of discontent generated by what was perceived as a vacuum of power, the erosion of the initial enthusiasm with which many welcomed the arrival of democracy and the subsequent partial deterioration of the legitimacy of the system.

When it came to establishing the institutions that would be needed to govern the new political era, an attempt was made to change everything that was not essential to the workings of the system witnessed in the previous democratic experience. It was a matter of changing those aspects which were incidental, such as the design of the institutional system, in order to set up a new system that would avoid the negative repercussions of the previous design. The return of democracy was at the same time both feared and desired. Those who did not desire it, criticised the institutions that were inherent and essential to democracy, such as political parties. Among the democrats, a considerable number feared a repetition of the Republican disaster, and, contrary to what had occurred in the 1930s, proposed the modification of all those aspects of democracy that were optional. In accordance with these priorities, a monarchy was established, along with a bicameral parliament, a proportional electoral system, a territorial system featuring Autonomous Regions and a strong executive.

The Crown

The conduct of King Juan Carlos I throughout the Transition, and even during the waning years of the Franco period, is a key factor in understanding this process. Although it is true that his leading role has been exaggerated on various occasions,[30] one cannot deny the King's considerable skill throughout the entire process and his capacity for negotiation with the country's main political forces. The King was capable of playing the moderating, neutral and stabilising role that was expected of the institution and that the Monarchy had so rarely shown itself to be capable of playing previously in Spanish history.[31] For this reason, the King has proven himself to be worthy of wide-ranging popular support, even among those who do not claim to be monarchists.[32]

In the surveys that have been carried out in Spain over recent years regarding the legitimacy of the various democratic institutions, the Monarchy has systematically obtained a maximum rating at a national level (only in the Basque Country does it fail to gain the highest number of votes among the democratic institutions). In spite of these results, it would be necessary to consider whether this general support exists exclusively (or at least for the most part) for the figurehead who embodies the

30. The title of the book by Charles Powell is highly significant: *El Piloto del Cambio* ('The Pilot of Change'), a name that was given to the King by some monarchists during the Transition itself. More recently, the role of the monarchist supporters of Don Juan, the 'juanistas', under the Franco régime has been exaggerated. One of the many examples of this relative 'invention' of history is the book by Luis María Anson on Don Juan (Anson, 1994).

31. See *La Monarquía Parlamentaria Española*, by Mariano García Canales (1991).

32. Some have even ironically referred to the new régime as a 'Crowned Republic' in reference to the many republicans who offered their support to the Crown during the Transition and the democratising will of the Monarchy as manifested through the person of Juan Carlos I.

Monarchy, or for the monarchic institution itself. If the former is the case, we would be faced with a phenomenon that we might call 'juancarlismo', which would not necessarily ensure the automatic loyalty of the Spanish to the Crown the day its figurehead changes.

When Franco died on 20 November 1975, the mechanisms of succession he had designed for such an eventuality were set into motion. Juan Carlos was one of the great unknown quantities of the new course which was to be undertaken. He had remained by Franco's side since childhood and Franco had taken responsibility for planning his civil and military education. It was known that Juan Carlos was fond of Franco and held him in high esteem; in later years Juan Carlos even presided over the Victory Parades, sitting alongside his mentor on the balcony of honour. On only one occasion, in 1976, was the King to preside over this event on his own.

With the passing of the Law of Succession in 1947, Spain became a kingdom and in 1969 Franco named Prince Juan Carlos as his successor. Juan Carlos was obliged to publicly commit himself to defending the Fundamental Laws and to ensure that what was known as the 'spirit of 18 July' governed his public activity. From this oath it was inferred that that the successor had assumed possession of the régime's origin-based legitimacy, as was also demonstrated by the fact that he accompanied Franco on the day of the Victory Parade. Until the death of Franco, Juan Carlos did not appear to show any political leaning whatsoever towards the democratic transition of the country, although it is true that he had begun, upon his own initiative and almost always in secret, to establish contact with various opposition leaders. As a result of this halo of uncertainty regarding his future intentions, his every word and gesture were studied in minute detail in order to discover any symbolic content.

Once crowned, certain of the King's phrases became famous and were endlessly repeated. Many began to be interpreted by the opposition as encouraging hints of his democratising objectives. At every opportunity he stated that he wished to be 'the King of all Spaniards', meaning by this that he proposed to represent all, both the victors and the defeated, Francoists and democrats, and that he aspired to become an agency for actively promoting reconciliation between the two sides and a moderating influence with regard to conflicts.[33] Among the many trips abroad that were made by the Crown over this three-year period, two were especially revealing. The first of these, which was undertaken at the beginning of June 1976, brought the King to the United States. The King took advantage of this opportunity to openly express what he had never stated so clearly in Spain; the forum he chose was the U.S.

33. The speech that he gave on 22 November 1975, the day of the coronation, is often cited.

Congress and in his speech he undertook to establish a democratic monarchy in Spain.[34]

The second trip, full of symbolic content, which had so often been announced and so often delayed, was to Mexico, the country that had given refuge to so many exiles and was home for a considerable number of years to the Republican Government in exile.

This trip was preceded by various diplomatic feelers. In March 1977 diplomatic relations with Mexico were restored. The following month, the King, who had already invited the President of the Mexican Republic, López Portillo, to visit Spain, repeated his proposal. On 12 October of that same year, the King and Queen of Spain and López Portillo jointly presided over the celebration of the *Día de la Hispanidad* (Day of the Spanish-speaking Countries) in Las Palmas, in an attempt to make amends for Spain's historically clumsy dealings in its relations with Latin America. Rumours surrounding a hypothetical official visit of the King and Queen of Spain to Mexico had begun in August 1977 and were confirmed a month later. A trip that had been planned for the second fortnight of January 1978 did not finally take place until November of the same year.[35] In Mexico, the King did something unexpected and of great importance: he visited the widow of Manuel Azaña, who had been living in Mexico for some considerable time. It was a public act of reconciliation that had the desired effect; another positive gesture aimed at the opposition, especially the republican section.[36]

The other trips that the Monarchy undertook within Spain were equally significant and made its intentions increasingly clear. On 15 February 1976 the King and Queen undertook their first official visit to Catalonia, where, to the surprise of all, the King was to pronounce several phrases in Catalan.[37] Later on, in order not to break the summer tradition established by Franco, they travelled around Galicia in July (at the same

34. The Government of the United States set up a campaign to support the Spanish Monarchy and its democratising initiatives, and *The New York Times* devoted a eulogistic editorial to the King based on his declarations at the US Congress.
35. In reality, the most controversial issue was no longer the programme of activities in Mexico, but the subsequent visit to Argentina that was strongly criticised by the Left, which interpreted it as a symbolic slap on the back for the dictatorship. Events turned out to prove these suspicions more than wrong. When the King travelled to Argentina, not only did he publicly demand support for the respect of human rights, but he also received delegations of the democratic opposition, thereby indicating his support for them.
36. At the homage-exhibition devoted to Azaña between November 1990 and January 1991 at the Palacio de Cristal del Retiro (subsequently extended due to the considerable interest it aroused) photographs of this symbolic gesture, so well received by Azaña's widow, were prominently on display. Details of this exhibition were brought together in a book published by the Ministry of Culture in 1990 entitled *Azaña*.
37. In January 1978 the King and Tarradellas were to have a private audience, after which, in spite of his heartfelt republican convictions, Tarradellas was to have no hesitation in praising the role of the King (*El País*, 19/1/1978).

time confirming their intention to regularly spend the summer in Majorca). Continuing his gestural and conciliatory policy, the King gave a speech in *gallego,* although he also visited Franco's widow in El Ferrol. This ambiguity was one of the keys to his success. Whilst dropping democratic hints and showing himself to be openly in favour of recognising the historical regions of the country, he attempted to contain the civil and military far right, with gestures that were somewhat disconcerting.

For a large section of the opposition, however, the dilemma was not that of monarchy versus republic, but dictatorship versus democracy, especially after the wide approval accorded to the Law for Political Reform in a referendum, which was interpreted by some as a vote in favour of the Monarchy that was established in this law. If the Monarchy were able to coexist with democracy and even, as it seemed, contribute actively to its consolidation, it would be very warmly received, as the leader of the PCE repeated time and again in his memoirs (Carrillo, 1993). In fact, nobody was to seriously question its legitimacy. Only the PSOE, along with a few other minority groups, maintained an essentially half-hearted stance. It insisted on the staging of a referendum regarding the form of the state, denying the Crown the possibility of being established in the Constitution before it had received the corresponding popular backing.

Former examples of this stance may be found in relation to the Munich events, which were described above.[38] The role that this meeting played in the transition to democracy was essential. Up until that time, the opposition had been convinced that the profound differences that existed among its sections would be difficult to overcome. When the opposition forces realised, quite spontaneously, that they had been capable of reaching agreements peacefully and of achieving a consensus in order to produce a final report, the prospects of what might take place in a democratic future became much more promising. Groups that had fought against one another in the Civil War had been brought together and were now united by the common desire to overcome the war and reach a democratic solution. The only aspect that aroused controversy was the monarchy/republic dilemma. However, they were no longer prepared to force a confrontation on an issue that might be considered to be incidental, should it be possible to finally achieve democracy. The advocates of the monarchic solution emphasised the conflictive memory that a republican solution would evoke, as well as the strong capacity of the Crown to

38. At this meeting, for the democratic opposition movements both within Spain and outside the country – disunited in the beginning and happily united at the end – the main point of dissension between the two working-groups that were set up focused precisely on the future form that the state should adopt. Whilst the section of the opposition presided over by José María Gil-Robles took the monarchy for granted, the opposition group led by Salvador de Madariaga contemplated the staging of a referendum in order to clarify the course that should be taken. In the end, a joint text was approved that omitted the issue of the popular referendum.

hold together a society that was divided on the issue of the very territorial make-up of the state. The advocates of a Republic were unable to give ground lightly on an issue that had been their main cause for so many years and which they had fought to defend in the Civil War.

The referendum issue reemerged during the Transition, but it was gradually played down throughout its course. When the Junta Democrática (Democratic Council) was set up in July 1974, a popular referendum appeared among the points on its programme. The Communists ended up by negotiating a bargain with the Government: the party would give way on this point and on several other matters in exchange for legalisation of the PCE. The party was duly legalised on 9 April, and on the 46th anniversary of the proclamation of the Republic, 14 April, the Executive Committee of the PCE accepted the Monarchy and the red and yellow flag, undertaking to prevent the exhibition of the republican standard at its meetings.[39] We might mention a highly significant aspect that serves to highlight the undesirable memory of the Republic and the desire – taken to a rather absurd extreme on this occasion – of the Government to protect the Crown at any cost. The parties that declared themselves to be republican, being few, rather weak and, in many cases, of moderate ideology, were not legalised for the first democratic elections, even though other radical left- and right-wing parties were. The possibility of any of the republican parties gaining considerable political representation was minimal, and yet they were prevented from presenting any candidate at all, maybe as a result of the memory of the last municipal elections that took place during the reign of Alfonso XIII, which were used to proclaim a Republic in Spain. It was a question of preventing the results of some simple elections from being used as a plebiscite on the form that the state should adopt, an eventuality which, as we have emphasised, was extremely unlikely.

The Monarchy was obliged to face another series of problems, whose importance the reformists also sought to play down as far as possible. Given that these consisted of certain highly delicate issues and that the media had decided to actively cooperate in the peaceful process of rebuilding democracy, it was not unusual for these problems to be given no coverage whatsoever. One of the most important questions concerned the dynastic issue. Given that Juan Carlos had always remained by Franco's side, the democratic opposition had begun its contacts with the monarchic semi-opposition within the country, which rallied behind the figure of his father, Don Juan, the legitimate successor to the throne after the abdication of Alfonso XIII. This is not the appropriate place to

---

39. On the same day, the Consejo Superior del Ejército (Higher Army Council) was to distribute a communiqué in which it strongly condemned the legalisation of the PCE, although it expressed its intention to comply with the decision.

describe, let alone judge, the role played by Don Juan during the Franco period. We might simply state that he maintained an ambiguous stance, as he had initially supported Franco during the revolt,[40] and only later, when he began to realise that the Caudillo had no intention of enthroning him, did he undertake to distance himself from the régime, timidly approaching certain sections of the opposition. It was his signing of the Lausanne Manifesto in 1945 that signified his definitive fall from grace in Franco's eyes. Later, other more or less successful (but always tense) contacts between the two were established, until it was agreed that the Prince would be brought up in Spain.

Rumours had always existed regarding the alleged state of enmity between Don Juan and his son, but these intensified considerably when Franco named Juan Carlos as his successor. Don Juan considered himself to be the legitimate heir to the throne, and so he was by birthright, but legitimacy is something that is rarely inherited; it was something that Juan Carlos would have to acquire on his own merit. Juan Carlos began his reign based solely on the legitimacy that derived from the victory of 18 July.[41] He was crowned King only because of a decision taken by Franco at the time, which had obliged Juan Carlos to swear allegiance to the Fundamental Laws and subscribe to the origin-based legitimacy of the previous régime. This legitimacy was, obviously, insufficient. On the one hand, the supporters of Juan Carlos' father, the *juanistas*, were in favour of the restoration of the former monarchy, not of setting up a new one. On the other hand, the democratic opposition was not sure it really wanted a monarchy, although it was better acquainted with Don Juan than with his son. Nevertheless, a section of support that had initially been in favour of Don Juan switched its backing to Juan Carlos as soon as the Prince, recently crowned King, began to reveal a clear desire to democratise the country. Two elements worked in his favour: his youth, which meant he had not lived through the Civil War, and the loyalty that the Army professed to him, which Don Juan would never have been able to obtain.

Thus, at the beginning of the Transition, the King was faced with a claim to legitimacy that worked against him, a dynastic claim, and another that worked in his favour, that of 18 July. He still needed to

40. As we mentioned above, Don Juan twice volunteered to fight on the Nationalist side and was twice turned down by Franco. The mere fact that the pretender to the throne had attempted to enlist in the forces of one of the two sides in the Civil War meant that he was disqualified as a suitable candidate for securing national reconciliation during a period such as that of the Transition. A king with such a past could not aspire, as Juan Carlos could, to be 'the King of all Spaniards'.

41. It appears that the explanation based on the three types of legitimacy that we are propounding here, was used by Juan Ferrando Badía (1980) and subsequently employed by Ramón Cotarelo (1990).

acquire a definitive claim, democracy, which would enable him to discard the latter and acquire the former, with the abdication of his father on 14 May 1977. Thus, an institution that began with a considerable deficit of legitimacy ended up obtaining an extremely high level of popular acceptance thanks to its own performance.[42]

The Electoral System

The establishment of the general guiding principle for the electoral system[43] during the Transition was achieved, first of all, through the passing of the Law for Political Reform. This law provided for the adoption of a proportional criterion for the Chamber of Deputies, although, following the debate that took place on this matter, it was eventually agreed that certain corrective devices would be incorporated into this proportional system, which would facilitate the creation of clear majorities.

The initial draft of this law did not contain the corrective mechanisms that were finally passed by the Cortes and, subsequently, by referendum, although the members of *Ponencia,* the all-party drafting committee, highlighted the need to introduce them. In the final text, the following paragraphs were added to the first Temporary Provision:

(1) corrective mechanisms shall be applied in order to avoid inconvenient fragmentation of the Chamber, in which respect minimum voting percentages shall be established for representatives to gain access to the Chamber of Deputies.

(2) The electoral constituency shall be the province, with an initial minimum number of Deputies being established for each province.[44]

The memory of the Civil War and of the Second Republic was overwhelmingly present throughout the entire discussion on this law. The two topics most hotly debated included, first of all, the advisability of passing a piece of legislation which, according to the most significant enemies of political development, broke the Law on the Principles of the

---

42. The King has even recently been awarded the UNESCO Peace Prize, according to Henry Kissinger, 'for the enormous merit of having avoided a civil war in Spain' (*El País,* 11/1/1995, p.21).

43. In relation to the Republican electoral system see, in particular, Santiago Varela (1978) and Francisco de Carreras Serra (1973). The idea that this electoral system worked as a dissuasive factor during the Transition is reflected, among others, in Gunther (1989) and Montero et al. (1992).

44. The draft of the law that was submitted to discussion may be found in BOCE No. 1532, 21/10/1976. The version produced by the *Ponencia* is in Appendix No. 1 attached to BOCE No. 1538. The text that was finally passed, Law 1/1977, was published in BOE No. 4, 5/1/1977. It may be also be found in the Documentary Appendix produced by María Josefa Rubio Lara, included in Ramón Cotarelo (comp.) (1992).

Movement.[45] According to Blas Piñar and other *procuradores,* the passing of the Law for Political Reform would open the Pandora's box known as democracy that Franco had attempted to seal with so many locks. It would signify the return of street battles and sterile parliamentary debates, in short, civil war. Those *procuradores* in favour of democracy stated that it was quite possible to introduce the new system peacefully and that it was no more than the logical consequence of the economic and social development undertaken during the Franco period. It was, therefore, the very performance-based legitimacy of the régime that had undermined its own foundations and made it an unfeasible system for the new age, an anachronistic form of government within the new context that this form of legitimacy had helped to create. However, those who supported the law did not yet dare state that democracy was the undesired consequence of Francoism. They simply attempted, in vain, to convince the most recalcitrant members of the régime that this outcome was contemplated in the previous Fundamental Laws.[46]

In second place, those who believed in passing the law debated the appropriateness of one electoral system over another.[47] The members of the *Ponencia* attempted, along with other *procuradores,* to promote the virtues of a proportional system, the most commonly employed argument being based on a recollection of the negative experience of the majority system during the Second Republic. Miguel Primo de Rivera, a member of the *Ponencia,* acknowledged that the electoral system was

45. Those in favour of democratising the régime made strenuous dialectical efforts to convince the reactionary clique that the law in question not only did not contradict any of the previous Fundamental Laws, but had emerged from them as their most direct consequence. In fact, the reactionary members were right in arguing that this was not true and that the passing of this law would signify the end of Francoism. It was of utmost importance to maintain the fiction of Francoist legality right up until the passing of the Constitution in order not to provoke greater opposition on the part of the far-Right and the Army. This has led many to describe the early years of the Transition as being 'post-Francoist'.

46. The same thing had occurred previously during the debate on the Law on Political Associations. In this case, many voices had claimed that this law contradicted prior legislative developments given that it permitted the de facto legalisation of political parties. The supporters of the law maintained, to the very end, a conceptual ambiguity regarding what was meant by 'associations' and 'parties'. Once again, this ambivalence enabled the law to be passed without any serious problems and without arousing any considerable opposition either inside or outside the Cortes.

47. Good proof of the importance of this issue can be found in the bundles of papers kept at the Chamber of Deputies Archive, which include all of the documentation regarding the elaboration, discussion and passing of the Law for Political Reform. Among these papers are a number of photocopies underlined by hand and featuring annotations that describe the workings and consequences of the various electoral systems (Archivo del Congreso de los Diputados. Serie General de Expedientes. Legajos No. 1240–1241).

one of the most controversial issues and stated that a proportional system had been adopted because it was the one that adapted best to the Spanish political situation,[48] although 'featuring limitations in order to avoid atomisation',[49] given that it is essential to shun small political parties of slight stature that are the 'ones that destroy the peace and equilibrium of nations'. Finally, in relation to this matter he acknowledged that 'we have taken maximum care with it because we are well aware of what is at stake'.

The most determined advocates of the proportional system were the *procuradores* Carlos Iglesias Selgas,[50] José Meilán Gil[51] and Antonio

48. This aspect refers, indirectly, to the suitability of the proportional system to Spanish regional diversity. An explicit reference was made, in this respect, by the *procurador* Antonio Segovia Moreno, from the Grupo Parlamentario Independiente, when he stated that Spain still had to debate the issue of the autonomous regions and that, 'the adoption of a majority system could wipe out all representation of all the parties of exclusively regional scope from the Chamber of Deputies, with the consequent exacerbation – from my patriotic perspective, undesirable exacerbation – of this issue'.

49. All of the references that relate to the debate on the Law for Political Reform come from the Diario de Sesiones del Pleno, No.29, X Legislatura. 16, 17 and 18 November 1976.

50. This *procurador* stated: 'We understand the strong reasons that have led to the abandonment of the majority system, which, with certain palliatives during the period of the Second Republic – the reserving of seats for minorities – has been traditional in Spain.' Subsequently, he advocated the necessary moderation of the effects of the proportional system, 'in order to avoid an excessive multiplication of the number of parties'.

51. After stating that a civilised and trauma-free transition was being carried out, he went on to praise the proportional system, stating that its defence was based:

> on the desire to prevent the forthcoming elections from being conceived as a dramatic confrontation between only two alternatives and the outcome from reflecting that very confrontation. I sincerely believe that if the elections of 1977 are conceived in such a way, as a simple choice, we would run the risk of provoking what, in some sense, should have been definitively overcome.

That is to say, if the design of the new institutions was not appropriate, history could repeat itself. Many believed that public opinion still rallied around two extreme alternatives and, as a consequence, it was necessary to proceed as if another conflict could ensue. It is common to find contradictions in this kind of argument, since it confuses what it believes to be real with what it would like reality to be. Thus, although his passionate criticism of the majority system was based on the belief that it could reflect social division, Meilán Gil ended by stating the following, 'I cannot believe that Spain, in 1976, is split into two blocks as it was forty years ago.' In effect, he would not wish to believe that is the case, because no country that has an established democracy and moderate public opinion fears the majority system, but he acts, as a precaution, as if it were so. Irrespective of whether this stance should be defended or criticised, if the repercussions of a particular situation are feared that is because that situation is viewed in a particular light. José Meilán Gil finally stated that the proportional system encouraged 'national harmony', negotiation and dialogue.

Segovia Moreno.[52]. Furthermore, as a member of the *Ponencia*, Lorenzo Olarte Cullén defended the First Temporary Provision, admitting that 'the most controversial issue, which has aroused the fiercest passions in this Chamber' was that 'of the election of Deputies by a proportional system'. He emphasised the benefits of this system and denied the disadvantages and dangers highlighted by its adversaries. Olarte stated that, since various currents of opinion would achieve parliamentary representation, it would be easier to involve them in the political game, with the consequent 'effect of tranquillity and stability on the social body'. On the other hand, he criticised the majority system because 'it gives everything to the winner and nothing to the loser' and he added 'but we must recognise, fellow *Procuradores*, that he who loses continues to exist, continues to subsist. Politically he does not perish because he has lost', which aroused a strong rumour of objections, probably due to the fact that the use of the expression 'he who loses' in this context was associated, by some, with the 'defeated' in the Civil War. Olarte once again highlighted the dangers of the two-party system and stated, in obvious reference to the Republic, that 'the split into two blocks was the most typical consequence of the majority system', when the main objective was precisely to eliminate the idea of two Spains.[53]

52.   Along the same lines as the previous *procuradores*, Segovia supported the proportional system, stating that it was necessary to avoid the creation of, 'unstable coalitions destined for subsequent dissolution and whose internal contradictions and divisions would make the composition and measures of the Chambers more unstable than if the real homogeneous groupings were represented there'. Furthermore:

> it is not clearly proven that the majority system creates a tendency towards a reduction in the number of parties, towards a two-party system and stability. If we simply look at our own – and for us most valuable – experience, in Spain from 1876 and up until 1936 – including the liberal Constitution and the Republican electoral system – we witnessed an essentially majority-based system, and we certainly achieved neither a two-party system nor stability.

As we can observe, political learning, in both a dissuasive and persuasive sense, was very much a feature of both the key political decisions of the time and the debate on the Law for Political Reform. Obviously, the use and interpretation that each protagonist sought to make of the same historical period is quite a different matter.

53.   In this respect he stated, 'We do not wish, under any circumstances, to turn these blocks, which have been so widely talked about during these sessions, into two fronts. This is what, above all else, we have the unavoidable obligation to avoid'. He did not need to mention the Republican period in order to make the parallel clear. He also stated that,

> majority representation runs the risk...of favouring and even provoking sharp oscillations in most of the country, featuring a complete renewal of parliament; on the other hand, proportional representation considerably softens such changes, favours gradual renewal and prevents a dramatic fall in representation... through proportional representation it is possible to achieve parliamentary stability...with neither the oscillations nor tumultuous ruptures that have been such a sorry feature of our history.

The detractors of the proportional system included Cruz Martínez Esteruelas, Eugenio Lostau Román[54], Montserrat Tey Planas and Torcuato Luca de Tena.[55] Martínez Esteruelas, the *procurador* who most frequently voiced his criticisms, advocated the majority system because, in his opinion, 'it provides greater stability'. He stated, paradoxically, that Spanish history revealed, 'the failure of the proportional system during the Republic, with the consequent political instability' and he made reference, on various occasions, to the chaos of the Republican period and the level of prosperity achieved under Francoism. He was obsessed by this voting issue because, as he stated, 'a mistake on this point would be the same as leading Spain towards situations of instability and social crisis'. According to Martínez Esteruelas, the proportional system produced division, dissension and splits, in addition to multiparty politics, fragmentation and a consequent 'chronic instability of the political system'. On various occasions he emphasised his belief that Spanish history had shown us 'what multiparty politics has led to in Spain'. If it was a question of carrying out a Transition free of trauma, in accordance with the wishes of the majority, and, 'if at the present time Spanish society reveals a tendency towards division and disintegration, we have the historic duty to combat this political disintegration with the unifying and homogenising mechanisms that the majority system offers us'. Finally, when he saw that the opposing view was gaining ground, although he continued to believe that majority

54. He spoke against proportional representation because he considered it to be the cause of party fragmentation and because 'we have a history that tells us that, in effect, this atomisation has had a harmful effect on the life of the country'.

55. This *procurador* emphasised the 'prudence' that should govern any decision taken. He stated that it was the proportional system that had, 'governed in Spain as of February 1936 – that is to say, under the Popular Front – and that made the extremely painful but essential surgical operation necessary that this country was obliged to undergo'. He then went on to emphasise that the Civil War had been necessary and even attributed responsibility for the war to the electoral system in force in 1936, the system that enabled the Popular Front to rise to power. He stated that he was incapable of understanding how, with a background such as this, the Government dared to offer the country a proportional system. Only a majority system could prevent the Cortes from becoming a 'madhouse'. Luca de Tena stated that he would prefer his ideological adversaries to win 'rather than an ungovernable system, anarchy and chaos'. Finally, he stated that majority voting was, 'the most prudent option in our most imprudent Spain'. Once again, we can see how the advocates of the majority system fell prey to a pessimism based on a negative conception of the real situation in Spain, which originated, in turn, from the historical memory of a recent past of ungovernable circumstances and confrontations. The weight of history was considerably greater among the older *procuradores*, who tended to be the ones who criticised the proportional system, even though the historical example chosen, the Second Republic, was not correct in itself. Those who had been faithful to Francoism were so accustomed to blaming the design of the Republic's institutions for all the country's ailments in the 1930s that, wishing now to defend their points of view regarding the electoral system, they relied once again on their criticisms of the proportional voting system and attributed it, incorrectly, to the Republic.

representation was the most appropriate for the fledgling democracy, Martínez Esteruelas stated the following, 'I have no problem, in the cause of harmony,[56] in saying that the criterion of proportional representation...may be a moralising principle upon being established in a Constitution' although he highlighted the need to find corrective mechanisms that would prevent the fragmentation of the Chamber.

As we can see, the advocates of a majority system had a much more pessimistic view of what might be expected from an unfettered Spanish society than their opponents. They based their view on the assumption that opinion was ideologically polarised, as it previously had been, and that this situation would worsen with the return of party politics if a number of mechanisms were not set up in order to contain this polarisation. They doubted, therefore, the capacity of society to live through the country's democratising process peacefully and consequently proposed a voting system which would be capable of transforming the alleged social radicalisation of the country by drawing together the plural range of options around a few solid political groups.

In this case, the really important factor in understanding the attitude of the political protagonists has nothing to do with the real effects of one electoral system or another, but with their interpretation of the system based on their experience of the Second Republic and their perception of the current situation influenced by their memory of these experiences. In the debate on the Law for Political Reform, an extremely curious phenomenon was witnessed that fully confirms this hypothesis. Both the supporters of proportional representation – the system that was established by the Reform Law – and their opponents used the memory of the Second Republic to promote their arguments. It was a question of attributing the problems of that régime to one system or another, to the extent that each of the groups actually claimed that a different electoral system had existed during the Republican period. The supporters of proportional representation stated that it had been a majority system, whilst their opponents insisted that it had been based on proportional representation. Whatever the case may be, both sides attributed some very similar and perverse effects to the system that they did not wish to see introduced. Those who were in favour of proportional representation claimed that the majority system provoked the polarisation of the party-system, made government more difficult and radicalised political life. The same arguments were employed by the supporters of the majority system in criticising proportional representation. Neither side took the trouble to rectify the version of events adduced by their opponent and they both continued to

---

56. 'Harmony' was the key expression of the debate, especially when it was observed that the discussions were becoming more heated and that it would be necessary to negotiate the final drafting of the text. This word was employed on numerous occasions and by the advocates of opposing arguments.

use the same historical reference-point because they were well aware of the powerful dissuasive effect produced by its evocation.

Studies of an academic nature have not reached unanimous agreement regarding the degree of blame which should be borne by the Republican electoral system. Whilst Santiago Varela (1978) does not consider it to be responsible at all for the perverse effects that are normally attributed to it, most of the sociologists and political experts who have investigated this question do not hesitate to attribute a large portion of the blame to this system for the poor working of Republican political life (Linz, 1979b; Gunther and Blough, 1980; Montero et al., 1992). Varela's research is closest to historical study, although he also employs sociological and political science sources in order to conclude that, 'it does not appear that the electoral régime should be included among the factors which enhanced the polarisation and fragmentation of the party system, rather the opposite' (Varela, 1978: 65). Opposite conclusions are reached by Juan José Linz, José Ramón Montero and others when examining the repercussions of the Republican electoral system. The study produced by Montero states that the negative reference-point of the Republic contributed to the choice of a different voting system in the drafting of the Electoral Law (Decree-Law of 1977), which fits in perfectly with the argument proposed in this chapter. According to Montero's study, by the 1970s there was, 'a certain agreement in attributing [to the electoral system] a decisive influence regarding the difficulties that were witnessed by the Spanish Republic' (Montero *et al.*, 1992: 10).[57] These voting systems, being capable of producing large majorities, majorities that were fictitious if we compare them with popular feeling, 'created the false illusion that the victorious coalition had achieved an overwhelming electoral mandate', which helped to 'reinforce a belief that it was unnecessary to make concessions when it came to adopting fundamental agreements' (Montero et al., 1992: 14). The opposite occurred after the elections of 1977 and 1979, when none of the political groups achieved a majority large enough to govern alone and it was necessary to negotiate with the

---

57. Among the many negative contributions that this study attributes to the Republican majority system are the following: 'it exacerbated the political consequences of the pendulous changes of the Cortes and increased the parliamentary implications that derived from the high degree of fragmentation'; 'it forced the parties to form coalitions which, nevertheless, retained substantial ideological differences'; it attributed a 'disproportionate number of seats to majorities' (Montero et al., 1992: 11). All of these factors were compounded by 'the existence of provincial districts (adopted in order to reduce the influence of tyrannical local bosses', by the restricted electoral roll...and by the high percentage of votes required to achieve parliamentary representation in the first round' (Montero et al., 1992: 12). The article we refer to here clearly and exhaustively explains this whole complex issue, while also providing a summary of the most important pieces of prior research.

rest regarding the course that was to be followed, especially up until the passing of the Constitution.[58]

It is possible that the electoral system of the Republic has been, at least partially, demonised. This may be due to the considerable uncertainty that surrounded the Transition process compared to the promising horizons that the new democracy needed to create. It was a question of identifying historical failure with certain institutions of the past, thus creating the superstitious belief that by removing these institutions it would be possible to eliminate the danger of a civil war. Therefore, the Republican past played an essential role in the process of political construction throughout the Transition by legitimising the adoption of certain mechanisms and not others,[59] and exorcising the ghosts of civil war from the process.

The debate on the creation of parliamentary majorities and the rights of minority groups was to reemerge once again when, both in the Chamber of Deputies and in the Senate, the mechanisms were decided by which the parliamentary groups were to be constituted. The majority parties, especially the PSOE, demanded that the number of members required to set up a group should be very high, whilst the minority groups attempted to lower this figure as much as possible. The majorities pointed to the necessary capacity of the Cortes to be effectively governed, whilst the minorities stated that, if they felt marginalised from the political process, that very governability might well be hindered. In fact, the minority groups were very angry with the scarce representation the electoral system had accorded them and stated that the ideal opportunity to correct the distortions that this system had created was provided, precisely, by the debate on the constitution of parliamentary groups.[60]

The Cortes

The Parliament of the Second Republic had been unicameral. This structure, having been attributed serious blame for the precipitation and lack of reflection that was frequently witnessed when laws were passed, was considered to be harmful for the new democracy that was being set up.

---

58. The proportional electoral system approved in 1977 and ratified in 1985 (Ley Orgánica del Régimen Electoral General / Law on the General Electoral Régime) ended up giving priority to majorities, in the same way as in a majority system. In the current democratic system these majorities are much more representative of the general feeling than in the 1930s. Nevertheless, the corrective mechanisms of proportional representation ensure that the current electoral system allows the existence of overwhelming majorities that may manage to govern alone without the rest of the political groups.

59. A problem may have emerged when two or more political parties employed the same period of the past in order to justify different alternatives. However, the fact is that political life has never required a particularly high degree of rhetorical coherence.

60. This debate in the Chamber of Deputies may be found in DSC No.2, 14/7/1977. In the Senate, it can be found in DSS No.2, 14/7/1977.

Furthermore, the Cortes had been unicameral under Franco. In the Law for Political Reform, a bicameral Parliament was proposed that consisted of a Chamber of Deputies and a Senate, whose members would be chosen by different electoral systems.[61]

Many believed that, although the existence of two Chambers would considerably decelerate the already slow pace of change, this was the most appropriate institutional structure for laws to be sufficiently debated and considered. There was a widespread belief that many of the most controversial issues that had been passed by the Republican Parliament, ignoring the voice of the minorities, would have found it more difficult to pass through two filters than one, although, in this respect, the electoral system at that time was a much more decisive factor, as we explained above.

Under the Second Republic a number of voices had been raised in favour of the creation of a corporativist Senate,[62] thus provoking a long and heated debate whose outcome did not lead to general approval for a possible Constitution.[63] The majority favoured a bicameral system, but it proved impossible to reach agreement regarding the composition of the second Chamber. Finally, the thesis of 'democratic radicalism' was introduced, which held that the mere existence of a second Chamber adulterated the egalitarian idea of democracy. Once again, a constitutional article was passed that went against the thinking of the majority of the Chamber, as a result of the lack of consensus regarding the form that the Senate should adopt. As only one Chamber was created, the Parliament of the Second Republic was deprived of a counterweight, one that would have been essential in the circumstances that it was obliged to operate in. This meant that no second opportunity existed for matters raised in the first instance to be deliberated upon and reconsidered.

Santiago Varela claims that the majority of the studies produced on the effects of the bicameral system as opposed to the unicameral system are based on nothing more than indemonstrable conjecture. Nevertheless, he ventures to offer 'two very general considerations regarding the possible repercussions of the bicameral system'. On the one hand, 'this system would have widened the foundations of acceptance by ensuring the involvement of certain interests in the workings of the régime'; on the other hand, it would have been possible for a more pragmatic approach to decision-making to prevail, as opposed to the ideological issues that played the leading role in all of the debates (Varela, 1978: 97–99). One of

61. With regard to this matter, see Chapter 3 of the book by Francisco González Navarro (1977).
62. The descriptions of the parliamentary system of the Republic are essentially based on Varela (1978: 92 ff.).
63. As soon as the Constitution was passed, proposals were presented in order to reform it. One of the organic aspects that aroused the greatest level of disapproval was the unicameral nature of the Parliament.

the clearest examples of pragmatism, according to Varela, was the case of the Socialist Julián Besteiro, who advocated a bicameral system to the very last in spite of the opposing stance of the majority of his group.[64] It is not surprising that Besteiro was probably one of the Republican politicians most frequently mentioned throughout the Transition by groups of diverse ideological origin.[65]

During the Transition, very few voices were raised in support of the unicameral system and only the former Francoists advocated a corporativist structure for the Senate. These two issues, the number of Chambers and the composition of the second Chamber, emerged during the debate on the Law for Political Reform. Only a very few *procuradores*, almost all of them representing Francoist syndicates, continued to aspire to maintaining the organic structure. They appealed to the need to continue avoiding the class war through an improved understanding, of a corporativist nature, between employers and workers. Nevertheless, these *procuradores* were relatively unconcerned about whether the Parliament should be unicameral or bicameral.

Various *procuradores* stated that Spain should readopt the bicameral constitutional tradition that had only been interrupted in 1812 and 1931.[66] Others, however, believed, for different reasons, that the most appropriate measure would be to reestablish the system that had been dismantled in 1936.[67] Among those who advocated a bicameral system, there were some, such as Jesús Esperabé de Arteaga, who were especially keen to ensure that the Senate would, 'be a call to well-balanced tranquillity, especially in the present circumstances and in view of our congenitally free-flowing Spanish passions'.[68] The same member of the *Ponencia* who first presented the Draft Law, Miguel Primo de Rivera, stated that the

64. In footnote 49 on page 99, Varela mentions a study by Andrés Saborit (no date), entitled *Julián Besterio*, published by Losada in Buenos Aires, which relates how certain opponents of Besteiro's stance, such as Luis Araquistain and Indalecio Prieto, 'acknowledged their error years later' (Varela, 1978: 117). This fact reinforced the perception that existed during the Transition that it was best to set up a bicameral system, as even its Republican detractors had ended up accepting its advantages.

65. In addition to his moderate and pragmatic stance in the Republican assemblies, we must also highlight the part that Besteiro played in the Civil War, in order to explain the positive role which the evocation of this politician was to play subsequently. We might even venture to say that the legacy that the PSOE of today has adopted from the PSOE of the Republic is that of Besteiro, and not that of Francisco Largo Caballero or that of Indalecio Prieto. In fact, the PSOE published a book and a video in homage to this politician in 1990.

66. This was the opinion of the *Ponencia* that had drafted the Law that was being debated.

67. This stance was held by the *procuradores* Carlos Iglesias Selgas and Montserrat Tey Planas.

68. BOCE No. 1538. Appendix 2. Committee on Fundamental Laws and Presidency of the Government. Draft Law: Political Reform. Observations and amendments that may be advocated before a Plenary Assembly at the Cortes.

Senate must fulfil a stabilising and moderating role.[69] This was the very function that it had been unable to exercise during the Republic.

However, the most important factor was not so much whether the bicameral system had the moderating effect that was claimed, but rather the perception that existed regarding the workings of the unicameral system of the Republic and the influence of the many voices, such as that of the President himself, Don Niceto Alcalá-Zamora, that were raised against it, attributing to it a large part of the blame for the poor functioning of the system and for the adoption of radical and rash measures.[70] In addition, the corporativist Senate had become, in general, obsolete. What is more, the Francoist experience had made it unfeasible. What finally happened is that a majority electoral system was established for the Senate in order to avoid the possible fragmentation that could be brought about in the Chamber of Deputies as a result of its proportional basis of representation. This precaution proved to be excessive, as the corrective measures that were passed to complement the proportional system in the Chamber of Deputies meant that its final effects turned out to be similar to those of a majority-based system.

Finally, the strength of the demands for autonomy – perhaps one of the most important aspects of this debate – meant that it became essential to create a second Chamber in which these interests would be more faithfully reflected.[71] The Senate, as we mentioned above, was to be based on a majority representation system, which would cause considerable distortions in regional representation. In the same way as occurred with the Chamber of Deputies, the least populous regions of the interior and, supposedly, the most conservative regions, were considerably over-represented. It is claimed that this was the effect that UCD deliberately sought to produce when designing the electoral system, because the party believed that this would be the structure that would favour it most. Paradoxically, with this very same system, the PSOE was to achieve an absolute majority on more than one occasion, something that UCD never achieved in its entire brief history.

The Territorial Structure of the State

All aspects relating to the territorial structure of the State were intensely debated, and at great length. This was the issue that was to arouse the greatest degree of controversy and became the most significant problem

---

69. Cortes Españolas. Diario de Sesiones del Pleno No. 29. X Legislatura. Session that took place on 16, 17 and 18 November 1976. Draft Law for Political Reform (urgent proceedings). Committee on Fundamental Laws and Presidency of the Government.
70. See the work by Alcalá-Zamora (1936).
71. The politicians at the time did not want the Senate to be a real Chamber of Autonomous Regions, out of the fear that this would arouse strong opposition in certain sectors. The significance of this second Chamber has been strongly questioned and debated ever since.

facing the Transition and (once it had been established) democracy. It became the topic that would most vividly evoke painful memories of the Second Republic, the Civil War and Francoism itself – the régime that the majority blamed for the extreme approach with which territorial issues had come to be handled. Demands for autonomy were regarded by the Right, and especially the Army, as constituting serious attacks on the sacred unity of the *Patria*. From this perspective, it was recalled that the majority of the Catalan and Basque nationalists had fought for the Republic and against the centralist conception of Francoist Spain. The most serious problem witnessed during the Transition, that which enabled anti-autonomy declarations to gain a certain resonance, was the pro-independence terrorism practised by groups such as ETA. If the Transition had not coincided with a growing wave of terrorist incidents demanding the independence of the Basque Country, the debate on the articles relating to the territorial organisation of the state would have been much less intense. The most strained relations, as we shall see below, existed between the left-wing nationalist Deputies and those of Alianza Popular.

In spite of all this, or perhaps because of it, every possible effort was made to ensure that caution and moderation predominated throughout the negotiations concerning pre-autonomous bodies and the debate on Title VIII of the Constitution. This Title governed the territorial organisation of the state, although the overall conception of what the State of Autonomous Regions should be was already established in the much-debated Article 2 of the Constitution. This stated that the Spanish nation encompassed a plurality of 'nationalities and regions', thus enshrining one of the most significant examples of linguistic sidestepping in the Constitution. The inclusion, one might almost say the invention, of the term 'nationalities' was one of the most controversial aspects. Up until that moment, the expression 'nationality' had always referred to a homogenous nation, whilst in the Constitution it is used in order to establish the unique status of the Spanish state as a nation of nations, without needing to confer the status of nation upon certain territorial entities.

However, an attempt was made during the Transition to avoid the model employed under the Second Republic, which consisted of a special territorial structure for the regions of greatest historical consciousness and another uniform structure for the rest of the country.[72] This conception, according to Varela, was a tremendous error that had to be rectified during the Transition. As Varela explains, in relation to the constitutional process that was carried out in the mid-1970s, the creation of the autonomous regions under the Second Republic should have been based on negotiations among the parties of a regional nature and the rest of the

---

72. We might also talk about the dissuasive influence that the memory of the First Republic exercised on the Constitution of 1931, in which it was finally decided that the term 'federal' would be avoided, due to the memory of the explosion of regional demands for independence that occurred at that time.

parties, and not been the result of, 'a "haggling process" between the Central Government and the regions'. No agreement was reached among the various protagonists because they failed to, 'divide the territory into autonomous regions, establishing an equal set of powers for all of them and equal relations with Central Government' (Varela, 1978: 282–283). That is to say, the best means of avoiding conflict or, at least, of reducing its virulent potential, would have been to create a homogenous autonomous territorial structure for the entire country, as occurred in the 1970s, so that resentments would not arise from unequal treatment and differences would not be seen as being so localised.

This was precisely the debate that emerged during the Transition. Whilst the Catalan and Basque nationalist parties advocated autonomy for those regions of distinct historical entity and character, almost all of the parties of state-wide scope advocated the introduction of an autonomous framework for the whole of Spain, based on a need for inter-regional solidarity and a refusal to support any kind of discrimination within the Constitution. The Catalan and Basque nationalists stated that it was absurd to invent historical entities where none had existed before, whilst the nation-wide parties seemed to recall the limitations of the Republican system, which proved unable to involve the rest of the state in the territorial organisation of the country.

It is quite true that the articles that governed this issue in the Republican Constitution and those of the current Constitution present a large number of similarities. However, it also true that the differences between the two texts, which might easily be overlooked in a cursory reading, are quite crucial. First of all, the Constitution of 1978 talks about 'nationalities', a word that is absent in the Republican text. Second, the Republican Constitution:

> permitted the existence of autonomous regions only as a special, or even exceptional, eventuality, by imposing some extremely rigorous conditions concerning the initial proposal and passing of the Statutes, which made it impossible, in the short-term and even in the medium-term, for the majority of the Spanish regions to become autonomous political entities, to the extent that, in practice, the right to autonomy was restricted – as, indeed, actually turned out to be the case – to Catalonia and the Basque Country (Euskadi). (Granja, 1981: 96-97)[73]

73. An example of this rigidity is provided by the fact that the 1931 text demands, as a condition sine qua non for the passing of the Statute, 'that the latter be proposed by a majority of the Local Councils or, at least, by those whose Municipalities encompass two-thirds of the electorate of the region' and 'that it be accepted...by at least two thirds of the electorate that appear on the electoral roll of the region' (Art. 12). The Constitution of 1978, however, limits itself to demanding that, 'the majority of the electorate of each province or island' take the initiative (Art. 143). In addition, the current Constitution features an additional article that reveals a desire to extend the autonomy formula to the entire state, which consists of enabling the state parliament to 'replace the initiative of the local corporations that are referred to in Section 2 of Article 142' (Art. 144).

This had already been detected as a problem by Ortega in 1931 and was sought to be resolved by the institutional structure established in 1978.[74] Third, the distribution of powers was regulated differently in the two constitutional texts: the 1931 text did not list the exclusive tasks that were to be carried out by the regions. Finally, in the 1931 text, when the time came for the Cortes to approve the Statutes, it was provided:

> that Parliament would be able to examine the autonomous powers in detail, whilst remaining faithful to the provisions of the Constitution, which led to a situation in which the Statutes were subject to a veritable haggling process between the Cortes and the regions. (Granja, 1981: 98–99)

All of this slowed down the process by which the Statutes were passed and contributed considerably to the deterioration of a political climate that was already extremely tense.

It is obvious, however, that the climate that existed during the drafting of the two constitutions was quite different. After the death of Franco, the Catalan nationalists did not rush ahead and proclaim their independence within a kind of Iberian Federal State on their own, as they had done in 1931. Unlike the events that unfolded during the creation of the Republican Constitution, the drafting of the current Constitution was not determined by the demands that Catalan nationalists had enshrined in their Draft Statutes, but by Basque nationalism, given the overwhelming presence of radical Basque terrorism during this period. Moreover, it is obvious that Francoism, with its policy of repression, had not only exacerbated the nationalist sentiments of the Basque Country and Catalonia, but also raised the regionalist awareness of many other parts of Spain. Furthermore, because of all this, the struggle for recognition of the unique cultural characteristics of the various regions was inextricably linked, in the minds of many Spaniards, with the struggle for democracy.

Finally, we must take into account the fact that the extension of the autonomy model to the whole of Spain was more satisfactory, despite the lack of enthusiasm that was expressed for it, in the eyes of those who were most resistant to the idea of decentralisation – the Army, mainly – than a structure that only catered for the Basque Country and Catalonia.

---

74. On 4 September 1931, Ortega y Gasset stated the following to the designers of the Constitution:

> The image of our nation that the proposal offers us is a division of the country into two different Spains: one made up of two or three rebellious regions; another, made up of the rest of the regions, more docile with regard to the Central Authority. The proposal establishes autonomy as a special case, since it does not enact it for all the Spanish regions... However, if the Constitution organises Spain into regions, Spain as a whole will not be alone in standing up to two or three disobedient regions, but the regions will be obliged to confront one another, thus enabling the National Authority to reign supreme over their differences, becoming the sole, united and nationwide sovereign. (cited by Granja, 1981: 88–89)

As one of the main unwritten laws of the Transition established that every possible effort should be made to overcome the resistance of those who presented the most serious threat to the democratic cause, it was finally deemed best to adopt an intermediate formula in which the entire country was divided into 'Comunidades Autónomas' or 'Autonomous Regions' (except for Ceuta and Melilla), although not all of the regions would achieve this status by the same means, at the same time, nor have the same powers. Even this asymmetry was denounced by various Deputies who considered it to be discriminatory, which seems to highlight the serious difficulties that would have arisen had the Republican structure been applied to the Spain of today.

Throughout the entire constitutional debate, especially in relation to particularly controversial issues such as the form of the state and its territorial structure, at certain moments the ghost of the Civil War and the failed Republican experience overwhelmed the two Chambers. The constitutional process that was being pursued itself inevitably evoked the former Republican experience. The overarching aim of the Deputies and Senate members was to distance themselves as far as possible from the terrible precedent that the majority of scholars believe to have signified the beginning of the end for the Republic.[75] As in other matters relating to institutional structure under the Transition, the memory of the past was intimately entwined with the debate in the present.

The leader of Alianza Popular, Manuel Fraga Iribarne, at the very beginning of the debate on the Draft Constitution of the Committee for Constitutional Affairs and Public Freedoms, reminded those present that although, 'the most controversial issue of 1931 was the form of Government, today it is the unity of the nation'.[76] Fraga was especially concerned about the unity of the *Patria*, stating that he would even be prepared to die for it if necessary. At the other extreme, some Deputies on the Committee supported the national plurality of Spain, making reference to the Autonomy Statutes of the Second Republic. Antón Canyellas Balcells, of Unió de Centre y Democracia Cristiana de Cataluña, supported federalism. Heribert Barrera Costa, of Esquerra Catalana, warned that the nation was, in his opinion, persisting with the same errors as those committed in 1931 regarding the issue of the autonomous regions, although he highlighted the advantages of the Republican Constitution compared to the present Constitution as far as Catalonia was concerned. The Deputy for Euskadiko-Ezquerra, Francisco Letamendía Belzunce, the spokesman for radical nationalism, supported the independence of the Basque Country and the right to self-determination.

75. With regard to this process, see the following texts: Andrés de Blas (1991); José Luis de la Granja (1981); Justo G. Beramendi and Ramón Máiz (comps.) (1991); and Santiago Varela (1976).
76. DSC No.59, 5/5/1978. Session No.1 of the Committee for Constitutional Affairs and Public Freedoms.

When the Draft Constitution reached the Full Assembly of the Chamber of Deputies, these issues emerged once again, leading to a confrontation between those who considered Spain to be a single nation and those who advocated the idea of a 'nation of nations'. The one-nation advocates accused their opponents of fostering the dismemberment of the *Patria* and of encouraging violent manifestations of radical nationalism. The nationalists, for their part, played on a certain sense of victimisation when it came to making their demands. The new democracy was thus presented with the debts that had been run up under the Franco régime, which had strongly repressed the nationalist sentiments of Catalans, Basques and Galicians and had dismantled all of the bodies of self-government that had been established in their respective Statutes during the Republican period. In the Basque case, the régime's measures had been particularly harsh, especially over the two preceding decades.

These recollections of violence and repression found expression in the nationalists' demands, and the silence, exile, repression and torture they had suffered, and their hatred for everything the former régime had stood for, was clearly revealed. Nationalist claims were, in this respect, directly linked to those of the democratic opposition under Francoism. Both during the Civil War and in exile, advocates of democracy and supporters of autonomy had coexisted on the same side, with the exception of those right-wing nationalists who had either hesitated until the very last moment to decide which side they should support during the Civil War, as was the case with the Partido Nacionalista Vasco (Basque Nationalist Party), or had joined the Francoist side immediately, as was the case with Francesc Cambó and other politicians from the Lliga Catalana. In general, the non-nationalist Right believed that one of the greatest achievements of the previous forty years had been Spanish national unity, and that the Uprising had served, at least in part, to combat the hypothetical dissolution of this unity. All of this clearly hindered the establishment of a common understanding between the participants of the debates during the Transition.

This issue was emotionally charged and required a very delicate handling, something that was put to the test when Article 2 of Title VIII of the Constitution was debated in the Full Assembly of the Chamber of Deputies. This article reflected the idea that Spain was made up of a series of nationalities[77] and regions.[78] The debate was full of historical appeals that supposedly legitimised the various lines of argument, of quotations from the works of scholars on nationalism and, naturally, of allusions to historical politicians of one persuasion or another.

---

77. According to Jordi Pujol, it was his group, Minoría Catalana, that was responsible for the inclusion of the term 'nationalities' within the Constitution. DSC (Plenary Sessions) No.103, 4/7/1978.
78. The debate on this article is contained in DSC (Plenary Sessions) No. 103, 2/7/1978.

Federico Silva Muñoz was the first to present the specific vote of his group, Alianza Popular, requesting the removal of the term 'nationalities'. In doing so he referred, rather curiously, to the Draft Federal Constitution of the First Republic of 1873 and to the Constitution of the Second Republic. In both cases, according to Silva Muñoz, an attempt had been made to hold back separatism, without success, by appealing to Spanish national unity. He even recalled the uprising of the Generalitat against the Republican Government in 1934. Finally, he criticised federalism and called on the authority of José Ortega y Gasset to defend the concept of the unitary State.

The first response came from the Socialist Parliamentary Group, on this occasion represented by Gregorio Peces-Barba. According to Peces-Barba, centralism was the, 'wind which has brought the storms we are now witnessing'. He blamed Francoism for the gravest of problems that now threatened the consolidation of democracy, and he even stated, in reference to the points made by Silva Muñoz, 'that it wasn't exactly that revolt against the legitimate Government of the Republic that prospered and produced the problems we are only now starting to overcome'.[79] For this parliamentary group, Spain was a nation of nations, a reality that presented no danger of encouraging separatism. It is evident that the PSOE had considerably modified its position with respect to the one it had defended in 1931, when it led a number of famous clashes with the Catalan nationalists.

In view of these indirect appeals to the Civil War, the representative of UCD, José María Martín Oviedo, reminded those present that this was precisely the issue that required the greatest degree of calm and dispassionate reflection. On behalf of the Communist Parliamentary Group, Jordi Solé Tura stated that this was, 'the decisive issue which will determine whether this Constitution is workable or unworkable'.[80] Subsequently, he criticised Francoist ultra-centralism and, reiterating the words of Peces-Barba, stressed that no danger of separatism existed. The Left was well aware of the sensitivity of the Army to issues relating to Spanish unity. Furthermore, it knew that the Armed Forces as a whole were resistant to the idea of the State of Autonomous Regions, a reluctance that was strengthened by the constant provocation of terrorist violence. In the eyes of the centrist and left-wing forces, any misunderstanding in this respect could provoke a military intervention in the form of a coup d'état, a reaction that had already been witnessed in 1936 and which it was now a question of avoiding. Therefore, the Centre, the Left and the nationalist groups strove to send reassuring messages to the Army, stating that their greatest concern, the unity of the *Patria*, was ensured, and would be even stronger than before with the establishment of autonomous regions.

79. DSC (Plenary Sessions), No. 103, 2/7/1978.
80. DSC (Plenary Sessions), No. 103, 2/7/1978.

The contributions of Alianza Popular to the debate did not seem to be aimed at reassuring the Army. This party was extremely alarmed by the qualitative leap that the inclusion of the term 'nationalities' entailed with respect to the Constitution of 1931. Fraga even reached the point of saying that, 'it is necessary, on occasions, to speak in anger when it is a question of breaking up the unity of Spain', and he went on to quote both Marcelino Menéndez Pelayo and Manuel Azaña.[81] At the other extreme, Letamendía confirmed, in part, the fears harboured by Fraga and the Army by proposing the abandonment of the circumlocutions of Article 2 in order talk frankly about 'nations', which should be the ones to decide, freely and peacefully, whether they wished to remain united to the rest or not.

In the end, none of the amendments that proposed the elimination of the term 'nationalities' prospered, and the text of the resolution was passed, featuring 278 votes in favour, 20 votes against and 13 abstentions. Despite being the issue that had presented the greatest potential for conflict during the Transition, the final resolution was passed by a comfortable majority, unlike the narrow victories that were witnessed during the Republican constitutional process in relation to the most controversial issues.

The debate on the territorial organisation of the State continued with the discussion of Title VIII. The controversy was reenacted along very similar lines in the Senate, where the solution to this problem was once again associated with memories of the Civil War. As UCD member Antonio Jiménez Blanco stated, 'the problem that we wish to resolve with this Constitution regarding the territorial organisation of Spain, is the problem of peace, of reconciliation, of non-violence, but within Spain'.[82] The tone of the debate was, on occasions, bitter, but this did not mean that extremist attitudes prevailed. On the contrary, in spite of the fact that three members of Alianza Popular abstained and five voted against, eight members voted in favour of the measure in spite of the inclusion of the term 'nationality' and various other matters that the party did not agree with.

The dissuasive memory of the Republican experience was not only reflected in the institutional structure that we have described above. We can also trace this memory by analysing the make-up of other institutions, such as the executive, whose uniquely powerful role is essentially due to the memory of its fragile nature during the 1930s. Both in Spain and Germany, the parliamentary workings of their respective democratic experiences were blamed for their subsequent political instability and weak government. For this reason, in both cases strong executives were created that were difficult to bring down by a vote of no confidence. As Pilar Mellado Prado has explained, 'Spanish law-makers were aware that if all political systems need a strong and stable Government, this need

81. DSC (Plenary Sessions), No. 103, 2/7/1978.
82. DSS No.39, 18/8/1978. Constitutional Committee (First Session).

became quite imperative for the Spanish Governments which were obliged to complete the Transition and consolidate the democratic régime' (Mellado Prado, 1988: 276).[83] Other institutions might be mentioned that reflect the lessons of the Republican period. However, we believe that our analysis of the institutions mentioned above have sufficiently proven this hypothesis.

Reconciliation

The general declarations in favour of the reconciliation of all Spaniards and their integration into political life, free from any form of discrimination, needed to be given shape in various ways during the Transition. A series of policies, both real and symbolic, were to be designed that would require at least the partial rehabilitation of the members of the defeated side.[84] This rehabilitation was never particularly comprehensive, due to the considerable period of time that had passed since the war itself and the abiding desire to simply forget past events. On the one hand, political amnesty, reincorporation into the world of work, the awarding of pensions and historical revision can never entirely compensate for so many years of persecution, exile and imprisonment. On the other hand, many of the individuals whom these measures were aimed at had died along the way. In addition, as this was an issue that could arouse unpredictable reactions, it took some time for other kinds of policies to be adopted that actually sought to provide real compensation for past suffering, given that previous measures had merely acknowledged rights that had been lost for ideological reasons.[85] Below we shall analyse some of the most important policies that sought to bring about a reconciliation among Spaniards.

The Legislation of Rehabilitation: Amnesty and Pensions

Demands for amnesty, especially of a political nature, but also job-related, were frequent throughout the Transition. Numerous demonstrations were organised to achieve this objective, many of which resulted in serious confrontations between the demonstrators and the police. It was claimed that the passing of a wide-ranging amnesty would address the consequences of the Civil War. By the mid-1970s, however, it was practically impossible to find any person still in prison for matters relating to the Civil War. Many had been executed during the early Franco years and the rest had benefited from the successive pardons that had been issued during the Franco period.

83. This is the same idea propounded by Heywood in his study on the Spanish political system (Heywood, 1995: 88 ff.)

84. This distinction is not categorical in the least, given that so-called real policies always have some symbolic dimension and symbolic policies also have real consequences.

85. One of the most important measures in this respect consisted of the possibility of claiming compensation for having undergone imprisonment during the Franco period for political reasons. This measure was not passed, however, until the 1980s.

Both amnesty and pardon, 'are manifestations of the *right of clemency*, that is to say, the right of the State, as the sole possessor of the right to punish, to waive all or part of the fulfillment of a sentence or, if it has already been imposed by the Courts, to ensure its performance'. (Rodríguez Devesa, 1981: 638–639). The qualitative difference between the two is, however, crucial. Amnesty refers to the crime, whilst a pardon applies to the punishment:

> Amnesty is *the total pardon or non-recollection of the crime*. It is as if it had never been committed... If a sentence has been imposed, the punishment and all of its consequences will be considered to have been served...An amnesty automatically entails the annulment of previous convictions. (Rodríguez Devesa, 1981: 641)

This annulment is what Franco had sought to establish with the amnesty of 23 September 1939 for crimes committed during the period between the proclamation of the Republic and the Uprising of 18 July. This was an attempt to gratify all those who had committed offences, even violent crimes, against the Republic. Something very different was intended with the pardons that were issued, given that, 'a pardon *presupposes*, unlike an amnesty, that a punishment imposed by final judgement has lapsed. It consists of the total or partial remission of that punishment' (Rodríguez Devesa, 1981: 641).

The symbolic implications of these differences are extremely important. A pardon is essentially based on clemency, in which respect the offender is forgiven for part or all of the crime, whilst the crime for which he was convicted continues to have effect and the consequent civil responsibility persists. With his pardons, Franco implemented measures based on clemency, which were restricted to specific groups and did not seek to achieve real reconciliation, given that the responsibilities derived from the crime continued to exist. On many occasions, amnesty calls into question the crime itself.[86]. It is recognised that the act for which the offender has been convicted is no longer condemnable and, at least in the case that we are analysing, an attempt was made to compensate for the economic, social and job-related repercussions that the sentence entailed.

Three days after his coronation, the King issued a pardon, 'regarding sentences and punishments involving loss of liberty, financial means and confiscation of driving licenses or which may be imposed for offences and misdemeanours by the Penal Code, Military Code of Justice or Special Penal Laws, in relation to acts committed before 22 November 1975'.[87] The most significant aspect of this pardon was its preamble, a

---

86. In fact, the amnesty passed during the Transition had to be followed up by certain reforms of the Penal Code, given that, for the amnesty to be effective, it was necessary to eliminate certain offences.
87. Decree of 25 November 1975, No. 2940/75, BOE 25 and 26/11/1975.

quite eloquent declaration of intentions regarding the association of the idea of the Monarchy with the reconciliation of the Spanish. The following words were attributed to the King, 'The establishment of the Spanish Monarchy in My person must represent a reaffirmation of the objectives of peace and harmony among all Spaniards.' It was an invitation to attain, 'national harmony in order to consolidate the main objective of the Monarchy: the unwaivable good of peace', which aimed to link up with, 'the Peace that Spain has enjoyed over the last four decades' and pay 'homage to the memory of the eminent figure of Generalísimo Franco'.

On 30 June 1976 the long-awaited Amnesty Law[88] was passed, which, for the first time, was to affect those persons linked with the ideology of the defeated. The purpose of the preamble was very similar, namely, to identify the Crown with reconciliation, except that in this case the allusions to Franco had disappeared (although not those to his legacy) and the wish to overcome the Civil War was made quite explicit.[89] In addition, a clear desire to forget the war was manifested.[90] This amnesty was considered to be insufficient by the majority of the opposition. However, we must bear in mind that it was passed under a government that had not been elected democratically, a fact that imposed strict limitations on the substance of this law.

Demonstrations in favour of amnesty continued to take place throughout the whole country, especially in the Basque Country, the region that featured the largest number of political prisoners per inhabitant in Spain at that time. The demands for amnesty were actively supported by certain sections of the media, such as the newspaper *El País*. This daily newspaper was highly satisfied with the amnesty of 30 July 1976, considering it to be, 'the best of the possible amnesties, although not the most comprehensive of the most desirable amnesties' (*El País*,

88. Royal Decree-Law No.10/76 of 30/7/1976, BOE 3 and 4/8/1976.
89. It stated:

> The Crown symbolises the will of all the peoples and individuals that make up the indissoluble Spanish national community. In this sense, one of its main purposes is to promote the reconciliation of all members of the Nation, thus culminating the various legislative measures that, beginning in the 1940s, have served to overcome differences among Spaniards. Such was the case with the restitution of pension rights for members of the army who were punished after the last war, with the various pardons that were granted and with the prescription, by operation of the law, of all criminal liability for acts committed before the first day of April nineteen hundred and thirty-nine.

90. 'As Spain is now heading towards a fully normal democratic state, the moment has come to complete this process by forgetting any discriminatory legacy of the past in the full fraternal harmony of all Spaniards'. Here we can detect the main qualitative difference with respect to the pardon that was published to mark the coronation of the King. In 1975, Franco's contribution was still favourably acknowledged, consisting mainly of the long period of peace that had been maintained. With the amnesty, the existence of a 'discriminatory legacy', which had to be ended, but also forgotten, was acknowledged.

31/7/1976). It was described as being quite a generous law, in view of the circumstances, and constituted, 'a real indication of having overcome the Civil War'.[91] It obviously did not end all of the consequences of the war, as acknowledged in the editorial. This law would have to be followed up by many other initiatives of the same kind at all levels, such as a measure for controlling the brutality of certain actions carried out by the forces of law and order at demonstrations. However, 'every Spaniard must, thus, heal the inner wounds of the past and help to build a new and democratic Spain based on freedom and justice, the only way of guaranteeing real social order' (*El País*, 31/7/1976).

ABC had a somewhat different perception of this issue. For them it was, 'the most wide-ranging amnesty which might have been expected in bringing about the national reconciliation required' (*ABC*, 31/7/1976). This newspaper did not believe any extension of the amnesty would be desirable, as this would probably include offences relating to the 'shedding of blood'. It addressed the opposition by stating that, 'those who have for so long argued that the granting of an amnesty must be the prior condition for dialogue, must now respond to the amnesty with dialogue on the issue of reconciliation' and it urged them to offer, 'their civilised and unconditional cooperation in the cause of the common good of all Spaniards'. The same editorial article stated that, as those who had been wronged by the offenders covered by the amnesty had found it possible to forgive the offence, the beneficiaries of the amnesty should respond with good-natured moderation. No reference was made at any time to the offences suffered by the defeated or their ideological heirs, as the nature of the offence was not considered to be equal on both sides. In December of that same year, in relation to the kidnapping of Antonio María de Oriol by GRAPO, *ABC* published an editorial in which, having stated that the kidnapping could end in murder, it asked, 'how is it possible to demand, in good faith, a more comprehensive amnesty?' (*ABC*, 16/12/1976).

Nevertheless, the most important Amnesty Law was the one that was passed on 14 October 1977, given that, on this occasion, it was approved by a democratically elected Parliament.[92] The qualitative leap between this and the previous law is quite evident. The 1976 law did not cover any crime that may have 'endangered or harmed the life or integrity of any person'. The most significant aspect of the 1977 law was, however, that it covered, at least up until 15 December 1976 – and until 15 June 1977 in relation to acts concerning the 'reestablishment of public freedoms or demands for autonomy' – 'all acts of a political purpose, *whatever their outcome may have been*' (the italics are mine). A third period, which extended up until 6 October 1977, was also established in relation to acts

91. In fact, as the article itself stated, this is what the Minister of Information, in his comments to the press, claimed the intention of the Law was: to end the Civil War.
92. Law of 15 October 1977, No.46/77, BOE 16 and 17/10/1977.

of this kind 'provided that they did not entail serious harm to the lives or integrity of persons'.[93] The coverage provided by this law was, therefore, quite extensive, in spite of the fact that it provoked protests in the most radical sections of Basque nationalism. For very different reasons, it was not well received by the Right.

The Amnesty Law bill was debated and passed by the Chamber of Deputies on 14 October 1977. It had been jointly formulated by the following parliamentary groups: UCD, the Socialists, the Communists, Minoría Vasca and Minoría Catalana, Grupo Mixto and Socialistas de Cataluña. The main objections came from Alianza Popular, with Antonio Carro Martínez explaining the abstention of his group. It was important in itself that this party did not dare issue a negative vote, as this was a delicate issue that was directly related to the reconciliation of the community and based on a wide-ranging consensus, one which was enhanced by the passions that it generated in the majority of the parliamentary groups.[94] Carro Martínez asked: 'What reason is there for amnesty to continue being the lodestar of our recently-created democracy?'[95] He expressed concern about the desire 'to wipe the slate clean' because, in his opinion, it was 'the most dangerous and destabilising policy among those which could be pursued', given that it created 'a climate of impunity that was entirely negative for peaceful coexistence'. He even appealed to the memory of the Second Republic in order to justify the attitude of his group:

> the notable Socialist Luis Jiménez de Asúa, formerly the Deputy Speaker of this Chamber and Chairman of the Constitutional Committee of the Second Republic...who died in exile within the present decade, wrote that such blind and excessive use was made of the pardon during the advent of the Republic that it provoked disorder and caused the downfall of the Republic itself.[96]

According to Carro Martínez, sufficient disorder already existed in the current situation without fuelling it with this new amnesty.

Francisco Letamendía Belzunce, from the most radical group, Minoría Vasca, explained his own vote of abstention, based on a different understanding of the amnesty. For him, the amnesty should not have been

93. The deadline for the amnesty of blood crimes was, thus, the date of the first democratic elections. It was considered that once the new democratically-based legitimacy had been set up, no further cause for any kind of violent demand existed.
94. The Right wished to distance itself from the image that it had created for itself and that was attributed to it, as a force that obstructed Spain's progress towards democracy, by moderating its stance on certain issues. This meant that it preferred to abstain on various issues rather than clearly vote against.
95. DSC No.24, 14/10/1977, pp.954–974.
96. It is striking that the Right should have blamed the Republic for its own downfall as a result of excessive benevolence, and for having applied an amnesty to persons who would contribute to undermining its own power.

based on 'a shameful pardon' but on an 'acknowledgement of the right of a people to use all of the means at its disposal to defend itself from the aggression of a dictatorship'. In this sense, Letamendía only considered a total and unconditional amnesty to be acceptable. The representative of the Grupo Mixto, Donato Fuejo Lago (from the PSP), also considered the proposal to be insufficient and overdue, in spite of which he stated that he would cast his vote in favour of it.[97] Fuejo stated that the amnesty was the result of a compromise between the various groups that had taken part in drafting the law, a compromise that had been necessary in order not to endanger the existing freedom. Nevertheless, for this reason, it was necessary to accept a series of limitations that were unsatisfactory to his party, because, as justice had not been done with regard to those who had fought for democracy over so many years, a feeling of frustration might build up that would be detrimental, 'for future peace and harmony among citizens'. According to the same testimony, 'it would have been necessary for this proposed bill to have included a form of moral reparation which might bridge the gulf which broke our society in two'. In spite of all this, Fuejo believed that the law was realistic given that it was 'the best possible law' within the existing context.

The rest of the parliamentary groups fervently defended their vote in favour of the law. The Communists, represented by Marcelino Camacho, tried to demonstrate that they had played the most prominent role in producing the Amnesty Law, as it was they who had presented the initial proposal on 14 July 1977, scarcely one month after the general elections. Camacho even went as far back as 1956 in order to argue that the initiative for promoting national reconciliation had originated with the PCE:

> How could those of us who had been killing each other have made the peace if we had not erased the past once and for all? For us, in the same way as with the settlement of the injustices committed over these forty years of dictatorship, amnesty is a national and democratic policy, the sole measure which might close that chapter of civil wars and crusades... We, that is to say, the Communists, who have suffered so many outrages, have buried our dead and our resentments.

Camacho even asked AP to reconsider its position, because the Communists wanted this measure, 'to be an act based on national unanimity'. Another of the uses of the amnesty, and certainly not the least important, was that it facilitated a rapprochement between the Basque Country and the rest of the Spanish community.

---

97. He stated: 'For a year now the Party that I represent has been fighting to politically achieve the amnesty measures from diverse angles'. Through this and many other testimonies we can observe a certain competition to see who was to play the leading role in creating the measures that might lead to reconciliation.

The Socialistas de Cataluña, represented by Josep María Triginer Fernández, stated that they had, 'always supported the amnesty, that they would have liked to have seen a more generous law, but that they were happy to welcome it'. José María Benegas Haddad, representing the Grupo Socialista, was pleased that 'this Chamber, the day after passing its own procedural rules, should begin to forget and overcome forty years of dictatorship, obscurantism, the suppression of all kinds of democratic freedoms and division among Spaniards' and recalled all those who should have enjoyed the amnesty but who perished along the way, 'in the hope that the past that we are just beginning to put behind us today should never occur again in this country'. According to Benegas, the amnesty was delayed by those who had refused to see that it was inevitable:

> I do not wish to recall the number of popular movements, the violence, the deaths that the very achievement of this amnesty has produced...and the circumstances of extreme tension that we have witnessed in some regions, such as the Basque Country, events which, following this turbulent course, have led us to the present moment in which we are finally prepared to put the Civil War behind us.

He also stated that his words did not seek to suggest any 'lingering resentments or a desire for revenge...since, for the Socialist Party, the sole idea of being able to regain freedom for our people appeases us and makes us forget the sufferings undergone by our organisation and our members'. Finally, Benegas called for peace in the Basque Country, stating that nobody was excluded from this amnesty.

Representing the Minoría Vasca, Xabier Arzalluz Antia supported the law and, endorsing the words expressed by Benegas, stated that, 'no Basque will remain in prison or in exile'. According to Arzalluz, the Basque people were the ones who had led the fight for amnesty, although he stated that, 'we are prepared to forget our leading role, because reconciliation should not entail any kind of protagonism'. At the same time as he advised those present to forget the past, Arzalluz reminded them that on that very day in the Chamber of Deputies, 'persons who have been active in many different fields have come together, persons who have even hated and fought against each other'. According to this argument, 'it is not appropriate to cite crimes of blood, because crimes of blood were committed on both sides... Nor should we talk about terrorism, because terrorism was pursued by both sides'. These statements illustrate how difficult it is to forget the past in sections of society that have transmitted a sense of resentment to their children. Nevertheless, according to Arzalluz, forgetting was the only means of consolidating peace.

Finally, Rafael Arias Salgado, representing UCD, defined the amnesty as, 'the ethical-political premise for democracy, which fervently seeks to overcome and go beyond the divisions which divided and set us against each other in the past'. It was, undoubtedly, an indispensable requirement for the construction of our democratic system and its institutions. In the final vote on the bill, 93.3 percent of the members voted in favour, 5.6 percent abstained and only 0.6 percent voted against the measure.

Not all the issues relating to the amnesty were settled on this occasion: on 23 December 1977, the Grupo Comunista was to lodge an appeal in the Chamber of Deputies supporting a 'labour amnesty',[98] and on 19 April 1978, María Izquierdo Rojo, on behalf of the Grupo Socialista, was to present an appeal to the Government in relation to certain teachers from the Republican period who had been purged (those of the teacher-training scheme of 1931 and teacher-trainees of 1936) and whose rights had not been acknowledged in the amnesty law.[99] On 30 November 1978, the Grupo Socialistas de Cataluña presented a motion so that the amnesty arrangements for participants in the Civil War might be accelerated.[100] These initiatives are only a few of the many that were carried out in order to improve the coverage and effectiveness of the amnesty passed in October 1977, based on the same reconciliatory end.

As we have seen, the debate on the amnesty law was intimately linked to the memory of the Civil War. It was a question of rehabilitating those who were serving a sentence, or any other kind of punishment, for having fought against the authoritarian régime that emerged victorious from the war. However, although the amnesty enabled civil servants to recover their posts or their seniority for pension purposes, it did not apply to army officials. Nor was the salary corresponding to the period during which they had been 'separated' from their posts paid to members of either of the two corps.

Another very different issue, although directly related to this, concerned pension rights. Early, and nearly always unsuccessful, attempts to obtain pensions for the defeated originated during the Franco period, as we saw in the previous chapter. Franco's death was the prerequisite for legislation that sought to eliminate repression and remedy its effects to prosper. Various *procuradores*, the majority elected by the *tercio familiar*, had attempted to achieve equal treatment for the Republican war-wounded with regard to the Nationalist war-veterans and had sought to promote the readmission of civil servants who had been purged. In short, they had sought to eliminate the discrimination that the defeated had suffered for decades. After Franco's death, various pleas were presented to this end, such as the petition organised by Montserrat Tey Planas[101] regarding the rights of the widows of Republican veterans, that of Eduardo Tarragona[102] relating to the same issue, and that of Juan Antonio Samaranch[103] concerning the 'implementation of

---

98. DSC No.43, pp.1648–52; 23/12/1977.
99. DSC No.46; pp.1669–79; 18/4/1978. The same Deputy subsequently tabled a motion on the same issue: DSC No. 63; pp.2155–7; 10/5/1978.
100. BOC No.194; pp.4171–2; 30/11/1978.
101. BOCE No. 1497; pp.36271–2; 12/4/1976.
102. BOCE No. 1525; pp.36871–2; 12/8/1976.
103. BOCE No. 1554; pp.37565–7; 8/2/1977.

the pardon granted by His Majesty the King upon his enthronement to the former civil servants of the Generalidad de Cataluña'.[104]

It is obvious that a large number of issues remained pending. For example, whilst the Decree of 5 March 1976[105] granted pensions to the war-wounded of the Republican Army, their widows were unable to benefit from these pensions. This Decree was passed in order to provide a certain coverage to, 'the war-wounded who are unable to join the Cuerpo de Caballeros Mutilados' (Nationalist War Veterans Association), which called into question the reconciliatory intention of the law that, in reality, perpetuated the segregation between the victors and the defeated. On 11 March, the Law on 'War-Wounded for the *Patria*'[106] was passed in order to update certain questions relating to the Benemérito Cuerpo de Caballeros Mutilados por la Patria. As the date approached for the Constitution to be passed, many of the cases of discrimination that were pending were progressively resolved. Royal Decree-Law of 6 March 1978[107] addressed the situation of the professional soldiers of the Republican Army. Royal Decree-Law of 16 November 1978[108] granted pensions to, 'relatives of persons killed as a result of the Civil War'. The preamble of the latter Decree-Law finally made its intentions explicit:

> The need to overcome the differences that divided Spaniards during the last war, whatever army they fought in, has been a constant concern of the Government. In this sense, it is necessary to establish equal treatment for the relatives of those Spaniards who, having died as a result of the 1936–1939 war, have not yet received acknowledgement of any pension rights.

Various reconciliatory measures would have to be passed after the Constitution was passed, such as Royal-Decree No.43/78,[109] which finally granted 'financial benefits to those who were subject to injury and mutilation in the Civil War'.

104. This plea was finally to be met, as reflected by Amnesty Decree No. 1081/78 of 2/5/1978 regarding 'Application to the Civil Servants of the Generalidad de Cataluña' (BOE No.25 of 27/5/1978).
105. BOE No.84, 7/4/1976, p.846 ff. This decree was to be complemented by that which appeared in No. 3025/76 (BOE No. 9, 11/1/1977, p.133 ff.).
106. Law No.5/76, 11/3/1976, (BOE No. 63, p.596 ff.). This Law was complemented by Decree No. 712/77, 1/4/1977 (BOE No. 21 and 22/4/1977, p.1207 ff.).
107. BOE No. 6/78, 7/3/1978, p.507 ff.
108. BOE No. 276, 18/11/1978, p.2751.
109. BOE No. 305, 22/12/1978, p.3032 ff. The preamble of this Decree-Law was equally significant:

> The various Governments of the Monarchy have revealed in numerous provisions their desire to overcome all the differences that may divide Spaniards as a result of circumstances arising from the Civil War. The amnesty laws and other provisions of varying categories have encompassed and resolved the question of civil servants, professional soldiers and the widows of soldiers who have not perceived any pension so far. Those problems that affect the war-wounded of the last war are still pending, given that Royal Decree 670/1976 of 5 March...only partially resolved such matters, it thus being necessary to complement this law.

This issue of the Republican war-wounded constitutes a complex problem that has been subject to excessively detailed and intricate legislation, an analysis of which would require exclusive study, given that this question has still not been entirely resolved today.

Symbolic Reconciliation with the Past: The Bombardment of Guernica

The passing of real political measures, such as those that we have analysed above, was accompanied by another series of measures of extreme symbolic significance. These gestures aimed to compensate for the limitations of the real measures that were adopted in order to achieve the complete rehabilitation of the defeated. Members of the losing side not only needed to see that their rights had been confirmed, but also to receive acknowledgement that their claims were true. They especially needed to be able to defend themselves from the abuse that Francoism had heaped on them. This was partly achieved through a series of measures that were fundamentally symbolic.

The bombardment and consequent destruction of Guernica became a mythical reference-point for the defeated, in the same way as Paracuellos had served, and continued to serve, as a reference-point for the victors. Its appearance in sections of the press that sympathised with the democratic opposition, such as *El País*, was overwhelming.[110] An infinite number of books and articles were published that attempted to clarify exactly where responsibility lay for the events that took place. During the Franco period, the bombardment of Guernica by German aircraft had never been officially acknowledged; it had even been claimed that it was the Republicans themselves who had set fire to the town in order to blame the Nationalists for the outrage. Although many eyewitnesses of the bombardment stated that they had seen German planes drop incendiary bombs on the inhabitants for a period of several hours, the official archives, both Spanish and German, which would have been able to confirm this assertion, remained closed to researchers. To compound the tragedy, the day that had been chosen for the bombardment was a market-day, when the inhabitants of the surrounding towns and villages travelled to Guernica to buy and sell their produce. Bombs had been dropped on the civil population in a town where no military targets of any kind existed.

In this respect, the outraged population – and not only the inhabitants of Guernica – demanded urgent redress for what symbolised the dramatic experiences of a defeated side that had been subject to the reprisals and injustice meted out by the victors. First of all, it was a question of revoking the official and slanderous version of events. Second, it was a matter of clarifying where the responsibility lay. Finally, it was necessary to achieve

---

110.   It is significant to note that, whilst numerous news articles and reports on Paracuellos appeared in *ABC*, hardly any references to Guernica were made. For this reason, this section is fundamentally based on allusions to the event that appeared in *El País*.

some kind of acknowledgement and reparations by the party who turned out to be either directly or indirectly responsible for the bombardment.

In May 1976, Gordon Thomas and Morgan-Witts presented their book *The Day Guernica Died.* They had carried out their research through a series of interviews and using the documentation that existed at that time, and concluded that the bombardment had, in effect, taken place. According to these researchers, the Germans had been given the go-ahead by Juan Vigón, whilst Franco had no prior knowledge of the measure. The fact that the direct perpetrators of the bombardment were German would serve to apportion the blame and delegate, at least partially, the corresponding responsibility for the events that occurred.

As the 40th anniversary of the bombardment approached – it took place on 26 April 1937 – various commemorative acts and ceremonies were organised, which included a roundtable consisting of historians who had begun to study the event. On 21 April 1977, the newspaper *El País* published an editorial entitled 'Germany and Guernica'. It claimed that the destruction of Guernica had been, 'a massive and deliberate attack…against a town that symbolically represented the former *foral* tradition of the Basques within the Spain of olden times' (*El País*, 21/4/1977). According to this editorial, the events were falsified by the authorities in order to avoid negative repercussions at an international level, which meant that 'the survivors were obliged to keep their silence for many years'. All of this had to be acknowledged in order to achieve reconciliation, for, 'if lies are not cleared up, they may become mental traumas from which collective ailments may arise'.

The events organised to commemorate the bombardment began on 23 April 1977. A necessary component of these proceedings was the direct public recounting of the bombardment by various eyewitnesses. It was not possible to present these testimonies in the town itself because of a prohibition imposed by the Governor of Biscay. One of the witnesses acknowledged that he had kept the truth to himself for so many years because, 'we were all frightened to speak out, we lived in constant fear that we would receive a beating' (*El País*, 24/4/1978). The historians played a supporting role during the commemorative events, as they had been entrusted to find out, through objective sources, who bore responsibility for the bombardment. Both the researchers and the survivors of the bombardment issued a communiqué that addressed both the Government and society as a whole, 'in order to request a rectification of the Francoist version of the events in Guernica and the immediate opening of the Spanish war archives' (*El País*, 26/4/1977). A telegram would also be sent to the President of the German Federal Republic requesting his collaboration in the form of the creation of a committee of German researchers to work alongside the Spanish committee that had been set up.

The outcome of these various initiatives was that the Bonn Government agreed to open its military archives to the Spanish–German group of researchers, provided that the Spanish Government undertook to do the same. Rumours began to circulate that the German Government would also be prepared to finance the building of a commemorative monument in Guernica. As it turned out, the Germans were the first to provide access to the relevant documentation and to acknowledge their responsibility for the bombardment, a fact that enormously facilitated the work of the Spanish Government, as the attention increasingly focused on Germany.

It was not until February 1978 that the Spanish Minister of Culture, Pío Cabanillas, authorised a single member of the committee of historians that had been set up to investigate the Guernica bombing to consult the official archives. In this respect, 'only when the investigations of groups of Spanish and German historians demonstrate, in a well-documented and scientific manner, what happened in Guernica in April 1937, will the Spanish Government revise the official version that exists regarding the bombardment' (*El País*, 12/2/1978). One of the most important objectives that was set for the commemoration of the 41st anniversary of the bombardment was to achieve the return of the painting entitled 'Guernica' by Picasso, so that it might be exhibited in the bombed town. Some of the researchers who presided over the commemorative events in 1978, such as Ángel Viñas, in spite of not having been able to consult the Spanish archives, stated that the moral responsibility for the bombardment lay with Franco. As he was the highest-ranking military official, he was obliged to assume both his own responsibilities as well as those of his subordinates (Viñas, 1978). Nobody questioned the fact that the plan had been executed by the German Condor Legion, but it was obvious that Franco had lied in the official version of events that he offered. Both Spain and Germany had maintained a slanderous position for decades, a fact that was serious enough in itself (*El País*, 23/4/1978). Historians such as Tuñón de Lara and García de Cortázar referred explicitly to the cruelty of Franco and defended the committee of researchers from the accusations that were levelled at it by Ricardo de la Cierva. The conclusion reached was that 'General Franco was not, in principle, free from responsibility' (*El País*, 29/4/1978), which was, at least symbolically, very important, as it was a public acknowledgement that Franco had lied (which was to contribute to his demystification), that he had acted cruelly (which meant that he might have acted with equal cruelty on other occasions) and that he was the person ultimately responsible for all of the actions of the Nationalists during the war (even though they may have been carried out by the Germans).

With regard to the return of Picasso's emblematic painting, that was to remain in the United States upon the wishes of the painter himself until democratic freedoms were reestablished in Spain, the Spanish Senate had unanimously given its approval to a motion presented by the Agrupación Independiente on 19 October 1977, which was supported by the Chamber of Deputies on 25 of the same month. Joaquín de Azcárate had tabled the motion in the Senate on behalf of his parliamentary group.[111] He stated that Spain needed the Guernica:

> for what it signifies and symbolises in itself. That series of persons and animals fleeing, yelling, whose horror and fear can almost be heard when we contemplate the painting. All that comes from something that we are painfully aware of; all that comes from the Civil War and that is why we need to have the 'Guernica' there before us in order to remind us that small disagreements can go a very long way. I do not even want to contemplate the repetition of such events, but we must moderate our behaviour in view of the danger of deepening existing rifts without seriously reflecting upon whether it is worth deepening them or it is better to stanch them.

The consensus regarding these considerations was unanimous. What did not produce agreement, however, but, on the contrary, turned out to be a rather controversial issue, was the question of where the painting should be finally exhibited. Martín Fernández Palacio, a Basque Senator belonging to UCD, was the first to request that Picasso's work be exhibited in Guernica. Gregorio J. Monreal, from Senadores Vascos, seconded this request because, 'Guernica was destroyed for representing a symbolic material manifestation of Basque freedoms'. Before a controversy began regarding the final destination of the work, Azcárate took the floor once again to state that, 'we must present an especially united front...in order to ensure that the painting comes, and then we shall decide where it will go'. The unanimous decision of the Senate was conveyed to the Chamber of Deputies, where it also received unanimous approval.

The destruction of Guernica ended up representing all of the defeated during the Transition. This tragedy was to be held up as a national symbol and was seized upon by all to demonstrate the cruelty of the previous régime and its abuses, to counterbalance what had taken place in the Republican zone during the war. Acknowledgement of the bombardment would serve to rehabilitate the defeated population in general and, in turn, reconcile the Basques with the rest of Spain that had lost during the war, with the aim of enhancing their integration into the democratic process. It would not have been good for the Transition if the Basques had appropriated the suffering of the defeated through a monopolisation of a symbol as powerful as the bombardment of Guernica. This consideration helps us to understand why Picasso's painting, against the majority opinion of the Basque Country, ended up in Madrid instead of Guernica. The responsibility for the bombardment of Guernica was finally to be shared, in equal proportion, by the Germans and the Spanish, although to a

---

111.   DSS No. 9; pp.250–5; 19/10/1977.

slightly greater extent by the Germans, since they had been the direct perpetrators of the bombardment.[112]

Transformation of the Victory Parade

One of the decisions of greatest symbolic significance during the Transition was that which annulled the Victory Parade and replaced it with Armed Forces Day. It appeared evident that, in the new era in which the question of reconciliation was beginning to be addressed and a sense of national identity was being strengthened, a parade that commemorated the victory of one side over another in a civil war would constitute an obstacle. It was, however, extremely difficult to cancel a ritual that had been staged, year after year, since 1939. The party that was going to feel especially aggrieved was precisely the one that had to be most carefully and delicately handled: the Armed Forces, the protagonists of the parade. It was, therefore, advisable to maintain the military parade, whilst modifying its meaning and symbolic significance. In this respect, one of the first changes to be made was to move the date on which it took place, since 1 April would always be, in the Spanish historical conscience, Victory Day. At the same time, its name would also change, becoming known as Armed Forces Day, along with its meaning, now signifying the loyalty of all citizens to their Armed Forces.

On 16 May 1975, Jesús Esperabé de Arteaga, along with other *procuradores*, presented the following proposal to the Francoist Cortes, 'that the Victory Parades should be cancelled or be carried out exclusively as a means of paying homage to the Army'.[113] This *procurador* had already stood out for other petitions aimed at bringing about the rehabilitation of the defeated, but on this occasion his proposal must have appeared especially daring – let us not forget that Franco had not yet died – as it received an extremely prompt reply. Esperabé based his argument on the reconciliation that was needed by a society that had been divided by a civil war. Thus, an:

> obstacle to the atmosphere of harmony which is witnessed in all sectors, could be represented by the commemoration of historical events, for although their effect might only be temporary, they do reestablish the former division of the Spanish into victors and the defeated.

For these reasons, in order to mark the fact that the Holy Year of 1975 had been declared the 'Year of Reconciliation', it was essential to cancel the parade, as it was a question of eliminating the rift within society. Finally,

---

112. In fact, Martín Fernández Palacio, the UCD Senator, stated that, 'it is very clear that it was the Condor Legion of the German airforce that destroyed the cradle, the political temple of Euskal Herria on that ill-fated 23 April 1937'. At no time did the Senator enter into the question of Spanish co-responsibility for the event.
113. BOCE No. 1433; 16/5/1975.

Esperabé went on to make a highly significant observation: the historical reference-point of the Civil War did not constitute 'a new Second of May', as the official rhetoric had come to claim. This was obvious, but nobody had dared to raise this point within the Francoist establishment. Although both sides had attempted to usurp the other in claiming this date as their mythical reference-point, the Second of May did not evoke a fratricidal conflict, but the union of the Spanish against the French invader.[114] In this sense, it provided an extremely appropriate mythical historical reference-point for commemorating and strengthening the bonds of national identity, as opposed to the reference-point provided by the Civil War, which only served to disunite and arouse disputes. The Franco régime intended the 18 July, in the same way as 1 April, to be festivities commemorated by the whole community, but no State can turn a civil war into an effective and long-lasting founding myth.

The reaction to the petition presented by Esperabé was entirely unexpected, and came from an entirely unusual source. Another group of *procuradores*, headed by Carlos Iniesta Cano, anticipated the official response of the Government, probably revealing an even greater zeal than that which the Government would have been prepared to exhibit. Iniesta Cano stated that the petition, 'totally lacks sense and provides proof, at the very least, of having little enthusiasm for the glories and heroic achievements of the *Patria*'.[115] These *procuradores* wished to convey to the Head of Government their most 'emphatic condemnation of the attitude that has been adopted by the aforementioned *procuradores*', who 'only constitute a very small minority of the Chamber'. This parade was, in their opinion, immovable, as its purpose was to commemorate and recall, 'the deeds with which Spain, under the supreme leadership of its unconquered leader...was saved from certain ruin, through the patriotism of all the noble hearts who did not hesitate to join the National Movement of 18 July 1936'. This military rite, lacked 'rancour and triumphalism', as 'reconciliation had always existed', given that 'only those who voluntarily preferred exile were discriminated against or alienated, and that is entirely beyond our responsibility'. However, it continued, all countries celebrate their national festivities without any kind of problem, such as the Americans on 4 July.[116]

114. This version has itself been somewhat mythicised, although it is the one that has become most prominent within the collective memory. It was not entirely a battle of Spaniards against the French, because we are faced with the not insignificant participation of the pro-French. Nevertheless, neither can it be claimed that it was a civil war, although it did contribute to clearing the way for subsequent civil wars. The Spanish, in effect, joined together in order to fight the French, but the French were rejected for differing reasons. The liberals rejected the absolutism of the Empire, whilst the absolutists rejected the legacy of the Enlightenment.

115. BOCE No.1437; pp.34948–50; 5/6/1975.

116. This is exactly where the difference lies. The Americans do not celebrate the victory of the North over the South in the Civil War, but the day on which they obtained independence from Great Britain.

The *procurador* Iniesta Cano was a Lieutenant General of the Land Army and Director General of the Guardia Civil. He had fought in the Civil War on the Francoist side, where he had been wounded three times, once seriously wounded, and he had also been held prisoner. For all these exploits he had received a number of medals. This brief biographical profile of the *procurador*, who was 67 years old in 1975, may help us to understand, at least in part, the tone of his reaction to the possibility of cancelling the Victory Parade.

The Government's response was somewhat facilitated by this attitude, as its only reply consisted of subscribing to the statements made by Iniesta Cano. It was stated that the military parades were highly necessary and that the Government was not going to enter into the questions raised by the petition nor the reasons for the commemoration. It was simply emphasised that it was 'a date of authentic patriotic exaltation'.[117]

The following year, after Franco's death, the parade was questioned once again on the eve of the event, which by that time had been staged for some years in the month of May. On 6 May 1976, *El País* published the news article that stated that 'the "Day of the Armed Forces" would replace "Victory Day"', to take place on 30 May. Within two days, the front page of the same daily newspaper was to feature the controversy that had emerged between the Government and the Capitanía General (Military Headquarters) regarding the cancellation of Victory Day. On 11 May it was officially acknowledged that the 'Victory Parade' would be staged on 30 May, until 'Armed Forces Day had been established in official legislation' (*El País*, 11/5/1976). The first round of the controversy was, therefore, won by the Army, because the Government dared not impose its decision in view of the degree of rejection it had aroused. At around the same time, however, various testimonies also appeared from younger members of the military establishment, such as Commander Prudencio García, who openly supported democracy. In an interview with this solider that appeared in *El País*, the memory of the Civil War emerged on various occasions and the headlines of the interview highlighted the following statement made by the Commander: 'The Army should support the political policy that reduces the possibility of civil war' (*El País*, 12/5/1976).

Five days before the parade, the Minister for Army Affairs, Lieutenant-General Álvarez Arenas, made a series of declarations in which he reaffirmed the validity of 'Victory Day'. The Army should recall 'the victory over communism, which has ensured its development, its unity and happy future. The Army shall not tolerate the possibility that that event which caused it such bloodshed and such pain might ever occur again in Spain' (*El País*, 25/5/1976). The King and Queen finally presided, for the first time without Franco, over the commemorative parade that was staged in Madrid to mark the thirty-seventh anniversary of victory, an event that also took

---

117.   BOCE No. 1448; pp.35180–2; 17 July 1975. BOCE No. 1451; p.35242; 28 July 1975.

place in other cities. Juan Carlos I gave a speech that might have given the impression that the apparent victory of the Army over the Government had been rather pyrrhic, stating that on that day, 'the people of Madrid, representing the whole Spanish people, pay homage to the Armed Forces', whilst not making any reference to the victory of the Nationalists in the war, although he did mention his 'especially fond memory of the Generalísimo' (*El País*, 1/6/1976). Once again, the Monarch was obliged to play the game of conciliation, attempting to satisfy the two conflicting sides.

On 6 May 1977, the traditional parade changed its name definitively to Armed Forces Day. This change of name was considered by 'observers...to be part of the set of reconciliatory measures initiated by the Crown' (*El País*, 6/5/1977). In order to mark the new parade, the Presidency of the Government passed a Decree-Law of, 'entire military pardon', which, according to the preamble of the law, 'is set within "the general policy of harmony that is being implemented"' (*El País*, 29/5/1977). The official note that was distributed by Madrid City Council to control traffic on the day of the parade continued to make reference, however, to the 'Victory Parade'. Armed Forces Day in 1977 was surrounded, at least in Barcelona, by riots led by the extreme right. Slogans such as the following were heard: *Queremos otro 18 de julio!* ('We want another 18 July') and *Carrillo, te haremos picadillo* ('Carrillo, we'll make minced meat out of you!'). In the end, the members of the *Alianza Nacional del 18 de Julio* gave voice to the *Cara al Sol* (*El País*, 31/5/1977).

In 1978 the Government established 'Armed Forces Day officially and permanently', to be accompanied by an act of homage that would be staged on the eve of the parade itself. (*El País*, 13/5/1978). Lieutenant-General Gutiérrez Mellado made a series of declarations on Spanish Television in which he explained that the celebration of the flag, traditional in other countries but new to Spain, consisted of paying 'homage to our dead', something that was 'truly desired by all good Spaniards' (*El País*, 27/5/1978). From this it might be deduced that, as of that moment, homage was to be paid to all of Spain's dead, irrespective of the side they had fought on, even though this was not explicitly stated. The parade, for its part, was to feature the leading role of the Armed Forces, which the architects of democracy urgently needed to involve in the construction process.[118] The act of

118. On 28 May *El País* published a highly eloquent editorial on the subject of the Armed Forces. It stated that the political groups, 'appeared determined to avoid an aggressive and tense approach, not only to the "military issue", but also to another series of "issues" that damaged the democratic experience of the Second Republic and created the ideological, psychological and emotional climate for the insurrection of July 1936... Where it is, indeed, essential to recognise that an issue still exists which is capable of turning the Armed Forces against the democratic institutions is in the case of regional demands.' However, 'Armed Forces Day today provides an occasion for acknowledging and paying homage to an Army that has known how to support and assume responsibility for the peaceful transition to democracy' (*El País*, 2875/1978).

homage to the flag, which extreme Rright groups attempted to boycott, was attended by Felipe González and Santiago Carrillo, as this was the first year of the Transition in which Spain had any democratically-elected representatives on the dates that the parade was staged.

As we can observe, the process by which the Victory Parade was finally cancelled was long and tortuous. Any measure that led to the dismantling of the foundations of the origin-based legitimacy of the Franco régime, however out-of-date it might have been, was going to require considerable effort and a large amount of tact, especially in relation to matters affecting the Armed Forces. The King was frequently obliged to intervene in order to pacify the Army and, when necessary, employ his superior military rank in order to impose his will.

The Monument to All the Fallen

On 22 November 1985, in order to mark the tenth anniversary of the King's coronation,[119] a monument was inaugurated in Madrid to all of the Spanish fallen, which constituted a clear attempt to continue linking the Monarchy with reconciliation and with the rehabilitation of the memory of the defeated. It was erected in front of the monolith that already existed in the Plaza de la Lealtad, a site that dated from 1840 and was built in memory of the heroes of 2 May, a date with mythical significance in Spanish history. The King lit a votive flame that burns permanently in front of the inscription 'Honour to all who gave their lives for Spain', after that he addressed 'a group of elderly veterans from the two Armies which fought against each other in the Civil War and who were visibly moved...during the half-hour ceremony... Members of both sides yesterday expressed their satisfaction with the act of "final reconciliation" which the monument to the fallen symbolised for them' (*El País*, 12/11/1985: pp. 1, 13).

This monument of profound symbolic significance represented a clear challenge to the Valley of the Fallen, questioning its alleged reconciliatory intentions. The relatives and friends of the Republican fallen certainly did not identify with the Francoist mausoleum, neither did they consider that this monument paid them appropriate homage. The King, along with various members of the Government and other political figures, carried out a simple, brief and necessary act which, nevertheless, was to make little impression on the popular memory. It is unlikely that the Spanish – or even the inhabitants of Madrid who see it on a daily basis – are aware of the significance of the monolith, which is surrounded by railings that run around the perimeter of the enclosure in order to prevent entry, barely allowing most of the inscriptions to be read. Furthermore, the garden contains a number of trees and high hedges that impede visibility and contribute to the fact that this monument goes quite unnoticed.

---

119. It is highly significant that ten years had to pass after Franco's death for a monument of this kind to be erected.

The War of the Insane

During the Transition, the Spanish Civil War would become known as 'la guerra de los locos' or the 'war of the insane', the period of 'collective insanity' par excellence in the history of Spain. There are numerous references in the 1970s to the war as an event that took place as a result of the mental derangement that affected the Spanish over a period of three years.[120] The implications of this metaphor are not trivial in the slightest.

The conception of the Civil War as a period that reflected a collective ailment enables us to approach the events that took place and their consequences from a very different perspective, especially with regard to the issue of responsibility. According to Spanish criminal law[121] and that of the majority of countries, 'mental derangement' and 'temporary mental disorders'[122] have traditionally provided cause for 'immunity from prose-

---

120. Fernando Díaz-Plaja recalls, in the introduction to one his books, that whilst Antonio Machado addressed his verses to Líster, his brother Manuel praised General Moscardó. 'They were two examples of the madness that had grasped hold of the Spanish. All Spaniards, including the most eminent writers.' He adds in the following paragraph:

> Yes. The whole of Spain lost its head. Passion overcame common sense, reason was defeated by senselessness, the brother of yesterday became the enemy of today; those who drank coffee together or even shared the same family table became mortal enemies whom it was imperative to kill so that the country might be blessed with happiness. A wave of anger crossed the Peninsula, a wave of fury on a scale that none of the enraged could have ever imagined before it was unleashed, a wave of fury that many do not wish to recall after the fact. (Díaz-Plaja, 1979: 11)

Further on, he continues:

> We must take into account the collective insanity of the Spanish at that time when reading each of the works that are brought together here in the convinced realisation that they represent an extreme period, a situation that must be judged in accordance with the corresponding circumstances... Those Spaniards lost their minds, ceased to be themselves, became primitive beings. I would like to emphasise this fact so that the reader can see in these pages an example, at times a horrifying example, of what men can say about other fellow compatriots, and not, I insist, not regard this as a morbid attempt to resurrect old stories, to delve into the background of people who are still alive in some cases... Fortunately, sufficient years have passed for us not to condemn anyone from a political point of view because, as we shall see, both sides were equally guilty of verbal violence and of demanding punishment, and from a human point of view, because in order to understand that time we must picture ourselves in that disturbing atmosphere. (Díaz-Plaja, 1979: 12)

121. No.1 of Article 8 of Chapter 2 ('Regarding circumstances that discharge criminal responsibility') states: 'The mentally deranged person and he who is suffering from a temporary mental disorder' is exempt from criminal responsibility (*Código Penal y Legislación Complementaria*, 1985: 29).

122. A temporary mental disorder may be distinguished from mental derangement because the latter is an extreme form of psychosis or psychopathy (in the widest sense of the term) characterised by the fact that its duration is not limited to the moment in which an act is performed, whilst a patient suffering from a temporary mental disorder is not mentally deranged either before or after the act is committed. (Rodríguez Devesa, 1974: 515)

This is precisely the metaphor that has been applied to Spanish society when stating that the war was an example of 'collective insanity'.

cution' in relation to the matter of guilt.[123] That is to say, if an individual commits a crime in a state of mental derangement, either permanent or temporary, this fact bestows a considerable exemption of responsibility, as it is presumed that the person in question would never have committed the offence if they had not been suffering from the effects of such insanity.

In the case of the Civil War this might be understood as an outbreak of a virus, which spread this madness throughout the entire country, affecting, over a period of three years, the majority of the population. This is the only way of comprehending the actions of the population as a whole throughout this period, maybe because this interpretation helps us to come to terms with a tragedy of such dimensions, one that is otherwise difficult to face from a strictly rational perspective.[124] On the other hand, it frees society as a whole from responsibility because it accepts that everyone was equally subject to this madness. It represents a progression from 'we were all to blame' to 'none of us was entirely to blame', as we were not conscious of our acts and, therefore, not responsible for them.[125]

Consensus

The institutionalisation of consensus was, perhaps, the most outstanding process witnessed during the Transition. It was a question of establishing a new pattern of resolving problems and of inaugurating a new era governed by new principles. It was necessary to break away from an ancestral tradition of civil confrontations that was attributed to the existence of a kind of racial predisposition towards violence and intransigence. For decades, the superstition had been fuelled that the Spanish were incapable of living

---

123. The causes of immunity from prosecution include *'certain personal states that, according to the law, exclude criminal responsibility'* (Rodríguez Devesa, 1974: 501).

124. In the case of the Germans, who were faced with a much greater drama, it was not at all easy to come to terms with past events. As the Mitscherlich have explained (1967; 1973), the Germans were incapable of grieving or feeling pain, as they did not wish to face up to the facts and concentrated their attention on more immediate matters, such as the urgent reconstruction of the country. They remained immersed in a state of ignorance or hostility towards the past, rejecting any introspective analysis of it. This state is described very well in the novel by Walter Abish, *How German Is It - Wie Deutsch Ist Es: A Novel,* and in the film entitled *The Nasty Girl (Das Schreckliche Mädchen)* by Michael Verhoeven (1989).

125. In fact, this is the message that the Spanish film "La guerra de los locos" ("The War of the Insane") attempted to convey. The story it tells is a kind of parable about the Civil War in which a group of lunatics at an asylum suddenly find themselves at liberty as a result of the confusion and disorder resulting from the war. Thus, several of the lunatics form a group and manage to get hold of some weapons and kill anybody prepared to take them on, irrespective of the side to which they belong. This attitude, however, was not especially anomolous within the context of the Civil War, as everyone involved in the conflict seems to have gone insane, although, unlike the protagonists of the film, their insanity may have only been temporary.

together peacefully, of accepting their ideological opponents, of negotiating intermediate stances or of yielding an inch with regard to their advocacy of extreme solutions. This spectre of fratricidal violence had grown over time and the experience of a conflict of the dimensions and significance of the Civil War had only contributed to its importance.

The rhetoric of the political élites during the Transition reflected a practically unanimous desire to break away from this curse, which impelled the Spanish to resolve their differences in a violent manner. In this respect, the phrase that the 'adversary' must replace the 'enemy' became popular, because it is possible to sustain a dialogue and negotiate with a political adversary, whilst the only result of continuing to view the opponent as an enemy would be Civil War.

In this sense, 'consensus' became one of the key terms of the Transition, both in the press and in the manifesto declarations of the parties and, in particular, within Parliament. The design of the institutions themselves represented a good example of the establishment of consensus as a magic formula for resolving conflicts. Even parliamentary members were (and continue to be) surprised, at the recently-discovered capacity for dialogue of the Spanish and the ideologically moderate nature of the majority of the political options available. All observers highlighted the exceptional character of this moment in history and the consequent break with a secular tradition based on an inability to negotiate. The Constitution, with regard to both its elaboration and final drafting, represented the culmination of this process and the best example of the application of consensus. No constitutional text had ever achieved such widespread agreement or been approved by popular referendum.

The Press

The press served as an important source of documentation in this chapter. Nevertheless, it is also essential to analyse its role as a political actor during the Transition. We do not wish to claim that society is simply a passive subject of the information that it receives, as we must assume that the press also serves as a reflection of society, measuring its pulse and sources of motivation. It is interesting to observe in the pages that follow the moderating role which the most important sections of the press played throughout the period. This was in direct contrast with the role they pursued during the Second Republic, when the press bore considerable responsibility for fanning the flames of discord.[126]

---

126. As Javier Pradera explains:

> During the Second Republic, the identification of the large Spanish daily newspapers with the political parties led to fierce controversies and caused deep divisions within the press; the journalism of the Republican period, in addition to reflecting social fragmentation and the lack of political consensus within political life, exacerbated the conflicts between a reactionary Right and a revolutionary Left and contributed to creating a climate of exasperation that led to civil war. (Pradera, 1993: 52)

The methodology that we adopted in order to study the press consisted of the following: two large daily newspapers of national scope were selected, *El País* and *ABC*, due to their mass circulation and subsequent capacity to shape opinion. Having chosen these two newspapers, which represented two extensive and important currents of opinion during the 1970s, a series of dates were chosen based on three criteria. First of all, the five most important dates were selected for their historical evocation of the Civil War. Second, a number of dates were chosen that were considered to be key moments during the Transition itself. The adoption of these two criteria was obviously governed by subjective criteria which, nevertheless, enabled all of the most important dates relating to the war and the crucial moments of the process of political change to be brought together. Because the most interesting articles for this kind of study included editorials, offering the official point of view of each newspaper regarding the event in question, three editorials were chosen for each date: the editorial corresponding to the date in question, that of the day before and that of the following day.[127]

The dates of the editorials selected according to their connection with the memory of the Civil War between 1975 and 1978 included the following: 1 April (end of the war), 14 April (beginning of the Second Republic), 18 July (beginning of the war), 1 October (Day of the Caudillo, which refers to his exclusive acceptance of military and political leadership during the war), and 20 November (anniversary of the deaths of José Antonio, during the war, and Franco).

As may be observed in Table 3.1,[128] in *El País*, 14 of the 37 editorials brought together mentioned the Civil War (nine explicitly and five implicitly) on the dates selected, which represents 37.8 percent of the references that appeared in the editorials as a whole. In *ABC*, however, in spite of the fact that the memory of the war may be detected throughout the newspaper, references to it hardly ever appear in the editorials. This is due to the fact that the newspaper sought to satisfy all those who considered the evocation of the past to be crucial to their lives, and also attempted to adopt a more aseptic tone regarding the Civil War in view of what the future might bring, which meant that the memory of it was finally repressed. The war was only mentioned in five out of a total of 46 editorials, representing only 10.8 percent of the cases. Both this figure, 10.8 percent, as well as the previous figure of 37.8 percent, must be understood based on the calculation made using the three editorials analysed for each date. The

127. In some cases, there were only two editorials, depending on the day of the week on which the news took place. During this period, newspapers did not tend to come out on Mondays. Furthermore, the daily newspaper *El País* was first published in May 1976, thus, there are certain dates that can be analysed in *ABC* but not in *El País*. The dates that were brought together in accordance with our two criteria were also used to create a series of frequency tables, whose results shall be revealed throughout this section.
128. See Tables 3.1 to 3.5 in the Appendix.

most important aspect is to discover whether a mention of some kind was made in one of the three editorials chosen for each key remembrance date, not in all three. As is shown in Table 3.2, the Civil War appeared in *El País*, either connected or unconnected with the date in question, on all five dates selected (100 percent), and only on one of the dates selected for *ABC* (20 percent). In addition, we must point out that not all of these references to the Civil War were connected to the date in question (for example, on 20 November the article may talk about war, but not in connection to the date) and that there were references to the dates in which no direct allusion was made to the war (for example, the article may talk about 18 July without making any mention of the war).

In Table 3.2 we see that the date on which the two newspapers evoked the memory of the Civil War most was 20 November, probably because it was most closely associated with the death of Franco in the memory – José Antonio Primo de Rivera was not mentioned once, despite also having died on a 20 November during the Civil War itself.[129] This date, therefore, is significant both regarding the recollections of war and as a date in itself, as this is when the extreme right stages its mass demonstrations, at which references to the Civil War are constant.[130]

Similarly, on the extreme left there were those who detected similarities between the context of the Transition and that of the pre-Civil War period, as revealed by the fact that, in November 1977, Enrique Líster, one of the most famous generals of the Republican Army, predicted that a coup d'état would take place within a period of four or five years. In the same declarations, the leader of the Partido Comunista Obrero Español (PCOE), a staunch critic of Eurocommunism, stated that his party would do everything possible to:

> prevent a repetition of the tragedy of 1936, since the current political circumstances are very similar to those that gave rise to the civil war. Our politicians, in the same way as the leaders of the Second Republic, do not satisfy the interests of the popular masses, and when the people mistrusts its Parliament, the ideal moment for a military coup will have arrived. (*El País*, 9/11/1977, p.11)

The politicians on both the extreme left and the extreme right detected similarities between the current context and that which gave rise to the Civil War.

129. This is a very important fact if we bear in mind the significance of the figure of José Antonio for Francoism. 20 November never ceased to be commemorated by the Falangists with all kinds of pilgrimages to the tomb of the founding member of their party.
130. *El País*, through its editorial of 21 November 1976, urged the Government to monitor the gunmen and thugs before the democratic elections, supposedly to avoid a repetition of the uncontrolled 'gun happy' climate that pervaded the elections of the Second Republic.

The parties located more towards the centre of the political spectrum tended to emphasise the differences that existed between the two historical periods and only at certain times, including the most delicate moments of the Transition or those at which they perceived a threat to their political maxims, did they tend to draw parallels with the 1930s. However, although it was mainly the extremist political groups that systematically attempted to instil the fear of a repetition of the Civil War in society, the more moderate political groups also contributed, under certain circumstances, to fuelling this fear. Irrespective of the real perception of the political actors, this fear was used, and even magnified, as a political strategy.

In the case of 1 October, very few allusions to the war were found, and these only appeared in *El País*. Nearly all of these references were implicit and none of them were connected to the date in question. In the case of both *El País* and *ABC*, this date lacked any kind of symbolic significance, or at least that is the impression that the newspapers intended to instil in their readers. Either they did not recall the Day of the Caudillo any longer or they did not wish to recall it, due to the difficulty of judging the figure of Franco during those early years of the Transition,[131] a topic that was more problematic than talking about the war.[132]

The remaining dates do not feature any references to the war in *ABC*. Thus, the editorials of this newspaper did not recall the war on 1 April,[133] 14 April or 18 July. This absence of any recollection of the war on a date such as 18 July and in a newspaper such as *ABC* is extremely surprising and highly significant. The eighteenth of July was a date that had been accorded special status under Francoism for commemorating the war, and this newspaper had collaborated, along with so many others, in producing the official evocation. It was as if the editors of the newspaper wished to disassociate themselves from their own history in order to

131. Under democracy, the Hospital '1 October' in Madrid had to change its name to '12 October', the date on which the Day of Spanish-Speaking Countries is celebrated.

132. The figure of Franco, his significance and legacy, are still controversial themes within contemporary Spanish historiography. In 1992, to mark the centenary of the birth of the Caudillo, various biographies were published about him. The work produced by Paul Preston (1993; 1994) focuses on the early years of his life although it continues up to the time of his death, whilst the work by Javier Tusell (1992) analyses the Generalísimo only during the Civil War years. For its part, the National Francisco Franco Foundation, which, at its own convenience, has brought to light documents from the private archive of the Franco family, took advantage of the anniversary to publish an apologetic work entitled *El legado de Franco* ('Franco's Legacy'), that featured the participation of Jesús Fueyo, Gonzalo Fernández de la Mora and Juan Velarde Fuertes, among others.

133. 1 April, best known during the Franco period as Victory Day, was not referred to in either of the two newspapers we analysed and the only reference to the war, in *El País*, was totally unconnected with the date on which it was made. This is a very curious fact, bearing in mind that the Victory Parade still took place the year after Franco's death.

convince society of the sincerity of their democratic intentions. In *El País*, however, two editorials on 18 July talked directly about the Civil War. This newspaper also included a reference to the war around the time of 1 April, although without connecting it to Victory Day,[134] and on three occasions the war emerged around 14 April.

The memory of the war appears much more frequently in the editorials of *El País* than in those of *ABC*. *El País* had a much more clearly defined stance regarding the war than *ABC*. On certain occasions, *El País* also silenced the harshest aspects of that memory in its editorials, accommodating this memory in other sections, in the same way as in the other newspaper. For example, the Máximo jokes, normally placed alongside the editorial, recalled both the war and the Second Republic fairly frequently.[135]

The references to the war in the two newspapers were, as we might imagine, of a quite distinct nature. *ABC*, a monarchist and conservative newspaper, attributed the blame for the Civil War to the excesses committed by the Second Republic and unremittingly praised the peace and development achieved under Francoism, even going so far as to state that 'peace had to be founded on war' (22/11/1978). Therefore, it justified the coup d'état that took place in 1936 and led to the Civil War, claiming that without the war and the subsequent period of prosperity, the democracy that was being established would have been unfeasible. The recollection of the war also emerged, at least on one occasion, in relation to the scourge of terrorism, which was perceived, not only by the Right, as one of the most serious threats to democracy (21/11/1978).

In *El País*, a moderate left-wing daily newspaper, the evocation of the war was of a very different kind. In general terms, the war was depicted as a barbaric and unnecessary tragedy, which had to be recalled in order to prevent its repetition. This newspaper rebelled against the tendency to forget the war, in contrast to the amnesic attitude of *ABC*. The following words appeared in *El País*:

> The aim of eliminating those years from the collective memory and renouncing any analysis of the causes that brought them about would not only be a useless undertaking, but also an involuntary means of facilitating

---

134. The absence of any references to Victory Day in the newspapers may also be partly explained, as we shall see when analysing the transformation of the Victory Parade into Armed Forces Day, by the later date (the end of May) on which that parade was held in 1976.

135. On 18 July 1976, despite being the first anniversary of the beginning of the war since Franco's death, the *El País* editorial omitted any reference to it. Nevertheless, the Máximo drawing did recall the date. The same occurred on 14 April 1978, a date on which no mention was made of the proclamation of the Second Republic in the editorial, but Máximo depicted four persons carrying a garland of flowers towards a broken monolith that bore the inscription 'Second Republic'. Mingote would also devote various sketches to the memory of these historical events alongside the editorials in *ABC*.

the repetition of a series of events that pushed us towards catastrophe. (18/7/1978)

This declaration was made on the occasion of a Euro-fascist rally in Madrid, whose aims included the revindication of 18 July, 'as a symbol of their political enterprises'. On a second occasion, an article by Antonio Tovar, that took the place of the editorial and addressed the future formation of a right-wing coalition whose democratic will was questioned,[136] asked whether Spaniards had forgotten their history and whether they recalled how, 'our country never manages to react in a balanced way, but with the hysterical insanity of civil war' (1/10/1976).

The memory of the Civil War was often used as a weapon for political ends. In some cases, it was a question of delegitimising the adversary by identifying them, explicitly or implicitly, with some aspect relating to the war. On other occasions, this memory was employed in public discourse in order to legitimise the political pretensions of those who made use of it.

The Left complained about the celebration of 18 July and of its sinister symbolic significance. An editorial that appeared in *El País* on 17 July 1977 entitled '18 July', celebrated the decree that cancelled the anniversary commemorating the so-called National Uprising, although it also protested at the slowness with which this measure was to be implemented, as it would not come into effect until 1978.[137] It stated that, 'it is a macabre paradox that the Spanish should celebrate a date that marks the commencement of a bloody Civil War which visited death upon nearly all Spanish families on the two opposing sides'. It also stated that, 'this tragic date, converted into a festivity by the victors, is the pure antithesis of what an historical commemoration should offer in order to serve as a symbol of union...among Spaniards: the defeated and the victors, monarchists and republicans, employers and workers, Catalans, Castilians, Basques, Canary Islanders, Galicians and Andalusians... For it is difficult to create harmony based on the memory of bloodshed among brothers' (17/7/1977). A year later, the editorial read thus:

> THE WILL to cancel the anniversary of the civil war as a national holiday establishes the dividing line between those who wish to base the harmonious existence of all Spaniards on peaceful foundations and those who

136. It is not explicitly stated, but it is very probable that reference was being made to Alianza Popular, a party that was formed some eight days after the appearance of this article.
137. In details such as this we can see to what extent the Transition was 'mortgaged' to the threats of the staunchest section of the Franco régime. The removal of symbolic elements connected to its origins had to be carried out with the greatest delicacy and over an appropriate period of time. Above all, the aim was to avoid giving the impression that a desire for revenge existed within the opposition. This perception may have produced a serious reaction in sections such as the Army and the civil extreme right.

dream of turning the Peninsula once again into a setting for a fratricidal war. (18/7/1978)

According to this view, the cancellation of this celebration was directly related to a strong desire for reconciliation and a desire to avoid the repetition of a civil war.

In *ABC* the anniversaries of 18 July were not used as an opportunity to reflect upon the war openly, neither did it make any references to what was known as the 'régime of 18 July', and the gatherings staged by the extreme right on such dates were not condemned. They were not even highlighted, probably because the newspaper still did not know quite what tone to adopt in this respect, wishing to preserve a large section of its traditional readership.[138] It was as if the newspaper was waiting to see how the process would turn out in the medium-term in order to determine the discourse on the war that it was to convey to society. However, on 18 July 1976, the first year after Franco's death, an editorial was published entitled: 'Goal: National Reconciliation', which supported the amnesty proposed by the Government for political and opinion-based crimes.[139] Amnesty, as we shall see throughout this chapter, was intimately connected to the memory of the war, and it is no coincidence that it was supported in an editorial of 18 July. On 19 July 1977 we find the sole reference to this date in *ABC*, which states, in relation to a failed attempt on the part of GRAPO to jam a radio station, that the day before had been, 'weighed down by dark portents of *revanchism*' (19/7/1977; the italics are mine). This was to be one of the key words that the Right would use when evoking the side defeated in the war. The hypothetical desire for revenge harboured by those defeated in 1939 and who suffered subsequent reprisals, constituted one of the worst nightmares of the Right. The Left, for its part, especially the section that had not experienced the Civil War (which was the majority due to natural generational changes) also feared the opposition forces that had returned from exile, the former war veterans and resistance movement, both because of the uncomfortable memories that their presence evoked, as well as their supposedly diminished capacity for dialogue and negotiation, which resulted from their isolation and the suffering they had borne over a number of decades. For this reason, *El País* and other documents produced by left-wing parties also spoke out against revenge that might be born of resentment, an aspect which could hinder, and perhaps even definitively end, the transition process.

Resentful voices on both sides turned out to be auspiciously absent during the Transition, being effectively marginalised from the political

138. It is evident that the Right was much more concerned about matters such as strikes, left-wing demonstrations and nationalist terrorism than about the right-wing demonstrations that so worried the Left.
139. On 30 July of that same year the Cabinet was to pass a partial political amnesty.

and economic negotiations and gaining practically no parliamentary representation. Society as a whole was firmly against the idea of settling accounts or any exhibitions of bitterness. Those who were resentful, fired up or irreconcilable, both on the right and the left, would end up being excluded from the bounds of parliamentary representation.[140]

The two newspapers also differed substantially with regard to the image they portrayed of the Second Republic and, therefore, of those who continued to defend the republican model. *El País* revealed a benevolent recollection of the Republic and a sympathetic attitude towards the Republicans, whom it considered to be behind the times, yet inoffensive, offering anachronistic solutions that lacked popular support. In the middle of April 1977 a couple of editorials referred to various aspects relating to the Second Republic. One of them criticised a decree-law approved by the Government regarding freedom of expression,[141] which, with the alleged desire to protect the Crown, prohibited 'public discussion of the form of the State'. The editorial stated that Western democratic monarchies 'protect the rights of those who fight against them' and that they feature 'weak underlying republican movements' (13/4/1977).

El País also acknowledged the errors committed by the Republican régime, one of them having been the modification of the Spanish flag. It stated that the Spanish flag did not belong to any political tendency, but symbolised the unity of the state. Therefore, the newspaper believed that the exhibition of the Republican flag at that time, 'was the very best gift which could have been made to the fanatics who wished to appropriate the red and yellow emblem' (15/4/1977). It is clear that the evocations of the Republican period were not entirely pleasant, not only because of the reactions that they could provoke on the civil and military Right, but also because, for a wide-ranging section of society, they did not evoke a very pleasant memory of the past. One year later, in 1978, various incidents (demonstrations, clashes with the police) were witnessed on the 47th anniversary of the Republic. As a consequence of this, *El País* was to publish an editorial in which, despite acknowledging the difficulty of interpreting these events, it reprimanded both the Republicans and those who had attempted to prevent the anniversary commemorations from taking place, for not taking into account everything that the King had

140. Various sections of the radical left remained outside the PCE, for example, the PCOE led by Enrique Líster, who criticised Santiago Carrillo and the Eurocommunists, whom he accused of having abandoned their principles. Furthermore, at least two of the most notable AP Deputies ended up abandoning the party because they considered it too far inclined towards the centre. In this way, the extremists excluded themselves from the transition process.
141. BOE of 12 April 1977, published, curiously, two days before the forty-sixth anniversary of the proclamation of the Republic, when many of the left-wing parties were still advocating, at least to the gallery, the staging of a referendum on the form that the state should adopt.

done so far in favour of democracy, 'without whose decisive support the peaceful and spectacular changes that have marked out the two and a half years following the death of the dictator would not have been possible (15/4/1978)'.[142] We might also say that, for this newspaper, a debate regarding the form that the state should adopt was absolutely nonsensical by that time (this contrasted with its attitude at the same time the previous year). The hypothetical future establishment of a Third Republic, 'is an error or a provocation', being neither possible nor desirable. Alternatively, it was quite possible that the intention of the demonstrators was not to provoke, and anyway, the Republicans had the right to raise their flag (although it may not have been particularly opportune) without this being interpreted as questioning the legitimacy of the Monarchy. What is more, it was the work of the historians, and not of the politicians, to judge the Republican period and interpret the causes of its failure.

The conservative newspaper, as we have mentioned above, had a different view of Spanish history, especially in relation to the Second Republic and what came after it. Nevertheless, its editorial references to this political régime never took place around 14 April, but in relation to other dates and events. Thus, on the first anniversary of the death of Franco, an *ABC* editorial stated that, 'Franco was presented with a Republic that was a constitutional invertebrate: a brawling and Jacobin Parliament, irreconcilable parties, a pre-revolutionary Government and Power in the street; in short, a State in the process of liquidation'. According to this view, Franco took responsibility for restoring order and respect for authority by establishing a legitimate régime. Because of the achievements of his government it was possible to face a democratic future, 'based on determining factors that were very different to those that caused inorganic democracy to fail in the past' (20/11/1976). Be that as it may, and irrespective of the differences between the two historical contexts, for this newspaper the Second Republic was an undesirable reference-point that the new system must not resemble in any way, as, according to this version, the Second Republic had not even been a democracy.

Below we shall attempt to establish the kind of connection that existed between the recollection of the Civil War and certain especially important events that took place during the Transition. As we shall see, the correlation between these dates and the memory of the war was much more pronounced than that between the memory of the Civil War and the crucial dates for its remembrance.[143] This fact is extremely

---

142. The two newspapers we analysed, *ABC* and *El País*, revealed an equal degree of praise regarding the democratising role played by the Monarchy, although the Monarchy was accorded a larger role in *ABC* than in *El País*.

143. The comparison between both sets of dates is summarised in Table 3.5. The percentages obtained for the key dates of the Transition are statistically much more significant because they are based on a larger number of cases: 20 editorials more in the case of *El País*, and 23 in the case of *ABC*.

enlightening since it enables us to observe the importance of the war as a reference-point during the Transition and how discussion on this subject was prudently silenced on the dates that were directly connected to the war. The references to the war turned out to be much more effective and important for the transition process itself and were used as a form of suasive argument (in both senses, persuasive and dissuasive) by advocates of diverse tendencies. The war was destined to be the paradigmatic lesson that had to be avoided. Comparisons between the 1970s and the 1930s were frequent and, in the majority of cases, of peaceful intent.

This correlation is shown in Table 3.3.[144] The first section includes total references to the Civil War on the twenty-four dates selected, although these references may not be connected to the Transition event in question. As we indicated above, for every date, an average of three editorials in each of the two newspapers was selected. In this respect, the percentages in this Table will necessarily be lower than those that appear in the following table (Table 3.4) as the first considers references to the war in all three editorials, whilst the second only considers references to the war in any of the three editorials published on the dates selected, whether or not they were connected to the date in question.

The first aspect that stands out in Table 3.3 is that the Civil War is discussed in 50.8 percent of the editorials in *El País* and in 33.3 percent of the editorials in *ABC*. In *El País*, the references to the war were connected to the key date in question in 33.3 percent of the cases. In *ABC*, references to the war were connected to the key date in 27.5 percent of the cases. These percentages are the result of calculations based on all the editorials published for each date. If we simply take into account references to the war in any of the three editorials, this topic appears in *El País* on 95.5 percent of the dates and in *ABC* on 70.8 percent of the dates. Quantitative figures are probably not entirely appropriate in a study of this kind, but they enable us to demonstrate, in a more tangible (although perhaps more approximate) manner, the importance of the memory of the war during the key moments of the Transition. Even at times which could not be considered to be key moments, the presence of this memory was also very strong.

In more than half of all of the editorials published by the two newspapers, based on a joint calculation,[145] there are only six dates that are

---

144. In this Table, under Total 1 and Total 2, the percentages equal to or above fifty percent appear highlighted. We should recall that *El País* did not begin to be published until May 1976, which means that this newspaper did not encompass the first four dates selected. Its percentages were calculated based on this fact, that is to say, the calculation was made using twenty dates instead of twenty-four, which was the number applied to the newspaper *ABC*.

145. In spite of being considered jointly, the two newspapers did not behave in the same way on these dates, as can be observed in the various tables. Thus, for example, *ABC* did not refer to the Civil War in any of its editorials dated 31 October 1978 (parliamentary approval of the Constitution).

connected to the Civil War: 18 November and 15 December 1976 (which shall be dealt with jointly because they correspond, respectively, to the passing of the Law for Political Reform in the Cortes and to the date that this law was submitted to referendum) 15 June 1977, the date of the first general elections, 1 May 1978, which was when Labour Day was held for the first time, 31 October, the date that the Constitution was approved in Parliament; and, finally, 9 April, the date that the PCE was legalised.[146]

The approval granted by the Francoist Cortes to the Law for Political Reform Law, which took place on 18 November 1976, met with a euphoric response in both newspapers, although it is well known that the left-wing parties welcomed it coolly and with considerable scepticism, to the extent that their advice to society – unheeded as it turned out – was to abstain in the referendum on this law. *El País* welcomed the law with sufficient optimism to state that, for the time being, 'Suárez has won the first battle of what we hope will never become a real war, but a peaceful, sure and complete passage from a dictatorship to a democratic régime' (19/11/1976). Until that time, perhaps, things had not seemed quite so clear, not even the possibility of a 'peaceful passage'. The opposition, who could not have foreseen the self-dissolution of the Francoist Cortes, did not know how to interpret the importance of this gesture for the democratic process. For some time afterwards part of this opposition continued to play down the event which, nevertheless, represented both the end, and the beginning, of an era.

On 18 November, the *El País* editorial proffered its opinion regarding the most controversial aspect of the debate on the Reform Law: the electoral system. The newspaper enthusiastically supported the proportional system and harshly criticised the Right for proposing a system that could lead to 'total rupture'. It stated that:

a majority system would threaten to create a dangerous bipolar trend in Spanish political life: two electoral fronts that would not take long to become the heirs of the régime, on the one hand, and the members of a democratic alliance of all persuasions, on the other. (18/11/1976)

Without actually mentioning the Second Republic, it was cited as an example of what must be avoided. The experience of the two fronts in the elections of 1936 was sufficiently painful for it not to be referred to explicitly, although it was useful for drawing implicit comparisons with the situation at the time. The following day, *El País* expressed its delight at a law that signified the end of Francoism and the beginning of democracy. It

146. This event does not qualify in the same way as the other five to be studied independently. References to this event in connection to the war came to 40 percent, thus falling below the limit of 50 percent. We have, nevertheless, devoted a brief section to it due to the fact that it was, indeed, one of the most significant gestures of the Transition.

advised the Government to ensure that, 'the electoral campaign should not feature any kind of excess, nor cases of revenge or violent incidents' (19/11/1976). This kind of appeal appeared frequently in both newspapers.

On the eve of the referendum on the Law for Political Reform, the *El País* editorial complained about the imprudence of the extreme right in comparing the kidnapping of Antonio María de Oriol, President of the Consejo de Estado (Council of State) with the situation that existed just a few days before the Civil War broke out, specifically, with the murder of José Calvo-Sotelo. It stated that this was the affirmation of an irresponsible and dangerous right-wing, which aspired, 'to destroy the country'. The editorial continued:

> The most important groups are already exploiting the memory of Calvo-Sotelo in an irresponsible manner quite unworthy of their self-professed patriotism, ignoring the fact that the Spanish of today are not in favour of civil war and that it is suicide to weigh down the hearts and spirit of people with acts as unspeakable as those we have mentioned.

All this, it stated, was aimed at persuading people to vote 'no' in the referendum, which would prevent the advent of democracy. The newspaper believed that the situation in Spain was highly unstable and that it was extremely imprudent to play with fire; 'pressuring the conscience with confusing images, harking back to the Civil War... represents an attack on the very life of this nation' (14/12/1976). As we can see, it was easy for fears of destabilisation that could lead to civil war to emerge, if spirits were to be fired up with inopportune historical comparisons. The second editorial of that same day stated that only a 'yes' vote or an abstention was appropriate in the referendum. As the law had a number of defects, the editorial stated that it understood the attitude of the opposition in advising the public not to vote for it, but it also questioned whether such an option was really opportune in the context that presented itself. On the day of the referendum, the newspaper again emphasised that, 'serenity and public spiritedness...must accompany the electoral acts' (15/12/1976). The following day, *El País* praised the overwhelming majority vote in favour and urged the Government to negotiate with the opposition, with whom it had a fundamental aspect in common: a desire to democratise the country, given that the situation was 'not only serious, but dangerous' (16/12/1976).

ABC, for its part, criticised the opposition for asking the public to abstain in the referendum when the democratic objective sought was the same as that of the Government. It stated that this was to be the legal situation for the time being, and this meant that the opposition should not attempt to negotiate the conditions of the referendum with the Government (17/11/1976). This newspaper led its editorial of 19 November 1976 with a sufficiently expressive title: 'The Legalisation of Harmony'.

On this date it evoked the war by stating that 'the Cortes that were founded by a victorious political régime in a bloody civil confrontation (the bloodiest in contemporary European history) have voluntarily held out a hand to those who were once enemies' (19/11/1976). Subsequently, the editorial posed a number of questions regarding the feasibility of the harmony that this gesture sought to bring about and the repercussions it would have.

> What a tremendous responsibility those persons bear who initiated the legalisation of harmony! Will it be possible? Will it be technically feasible? Will it really and truly open up a road towards the reconciliation of all Spaniards or will it be a useless 'hara-kiri', devoid of meaning, unreciprocated by the opposing party and, therefore, ineffective?

It further stated that the origin of this reconciliation resided in the Francoist institutions themselves and that, now, the responsibility for achieving it lay entirely with the opposition. Furthermore, as on so many other occasions, *ABC* attributed all the credit for the entire reconciliatory process to the King, whom it praised for providing the necessary impetus and inspiration. It also commended the role of the Government and of the Cortes. They had voted 'yes', in spite of their 'passions', 'memories' and 'past experiences', 'much more alert to the reconciliation of all Spaniards that the King had requested than to their own particular criteria'.

At around the time of the referendum, *ABC* stated that the campaign led by the opposition in favour of abstention signified 'revenge as opposed to reconciliation' and that even voting 'no' would be more legitimate, although it would also be an error, 'capable of hindering, even making it impossible, for the Spanish people to enter the open country of its own responsibilities' (14/12/1976). It stated that 'Spain has emerged from peace, not from a war', that the personality of Franco was irreplaceable[147] and that voting did not mean wishing to turn the clock back and 'increasing the danger of a coup d'état'. On the day of the referendum itself, the editorial campaigned for the 'yes' vote, basing its decision on the King's wish to be the head of 'all Spaniards', the desire that Spain should cease to be different and a wish that the Transition should be carried out 'based on legality, without any ruptures or battles' (15/12/1976). The following day, the high level of popular participation was highlighted and the editorial claimed that this signified the general acceptance of the

147. After Franco's death, many referred to him as a figure who was 'unrepeatable', 'irreplaceable' or 'exceptional', expressions that frequently meant the commentators were able to avoid involving themselves in any personal judgement of the former Head of State. They were adjectives that indicated the unique nature of Franco's character, from which the usual inference was gained that it was impossible to continue the régime that he had created.

rules of the game. In addition, it stated that, 'perfect law and order, above any other aspect, reigned supreme', as everyone had provided, 'a promising example of peaceful coexistence'. With regard to the referendum it assured its readers, 'We were all winners. Even those who thought they had lost' (16/12/1976).

On 9 April 1977, in a skilful piece of manoeuvring by Adolfo Suárez behind the Army's back, the Spanish Communist Party was to be legalised. The following day, *El País* expressed its considerable satisfaction at this development, although it reminded the PCE that:

> it must bear in mind that it is one of the very few political groups which is entering the elections with leaders and members who played a part in the Civil War and that this will represent an additional obstacle with regard to some sections of the population. (10/4/1977)

In any case, according to the editorial, it was natural for people to mistrust communism, as they, 'do not need to rely on their memory of the Civil War, since they have sufficient experience of the recent conduct of the Portuguese communists'. It seems clear that in relation to the legalisation of the PCE, an almost automatic association of ideas was made with the 1930s, an effect that was strongly enhanced by the fact that this party included figures such as Dolores Ibárruri and Santiago Carrillo among its leaders. The reaction of the Consejo Superior del Ejército (Higher Army Council) was immediate, and on 14 April the Consejo issued a communiqué in which it expressed its strong condemnation of the legalisation of the party, although it also announced its deference to this decision; that very day, the Executive Committee of the PCE was to publicly accept the Monarchy and the flag. The editorials published on this 14 April reflected both the attitude of the Army – the *El País* editorial with some concern, because the Army's protest had been accompanied by some important resignations in its ranks – as well as the dissatisfaction displayed by Alianza Popular and other lesser groups to the right of this party.[148] The Left was obsessively concerned about the possibility of a coup d'état and, consequently, about any

---

148. A good example of this sense of disgust is offered by Fraga in an episode related by Leopoldo Calvo-Sotelo in his memoirs. An account is given of the angry reaction of the leader of AP to the author, who was the Minister of Public Works at that time. Fraga reprimanded the Minister in the following way: 'You have taken on an *extremely grave* responsibility by legalising the Communist Party: you will have to answer before history' (Calvo-Sotelo, 1990: 18). He then added that, 'with a wretched administrative decision...you have turned back the clock forty years, you have ruined the peaceful development of Spain, you have provoked the Army, you have laid the future of our children open to uncertainty' (Calvo-Sotelo, 1990: 19).

possible provocation of the Armed Forces (such as terrorism).[149] *El País* complained about the appeals to the Army made by the Right and stated that, 'only a constitutional and democratic monarchy, like the one that is in the process of being established, which recognises the rights of all Spaniards – Republicans included – can reasonably overcome this transitional stage' (14/4/1977).

ABC did not attempt to hide its disgust the day after the legalisation of the PCE and gave the following title to its editorial: 'The legalisation of the "Communist Party". The reasons for our disagreement'. This editorial expressed its serious concern regarding the legalisation of a party 'headed by the same leaders – Dolores Ibárruri and Santiago Carrillo – as in the terrible years of our civil war' (10/4/1977). It stated, once again, that the Civil War had been the logical and necessary consequence of the chaos that had existed in the mid-1930s and that it was folly to include a party in the political game that would be sure not to respect the rules of democracy. This measure, 'will only serve to rouse passions and spirits in the run up to a series of elections that are rather too close and that we all hope, in spite of this decision, will be peaceful'. In this case, the memory of the Civil War and a veiled warning of its possible repetition were used as a political weapon against a specific party.[150] According to the editorial, this legalisation created 'anxiety and concern' and 'harms the sensibility of a large part of the country, and not precisely the least healthy, the least loyal or the least patriotic section'. When the Consejo

149. The Left's concern about an angry reaction from the Army was such that on occasions it was swept away on a boundless wave of pessimism. It is curious that the second *El País* editorial of 14 April, which addressed the current situation of Spanish agriculture, should have such catastrophic overtones. The editorial started by talking about what was known at the time as 'the asparagus war' and criticised the virulent reaction of the farmers, in spite of the fact that they had good reason for taking action. The editorial stated, in some desperation, that:

> it seems as if we are a people more inclined towards dramatic gestures than reflection and the search for intermediate solutions. Let us only hope that that gesture...is restricted to an isolated incident and does not form a general precedent that leads to other more tragic pyres on which we destroy the achievements we have earned with such great effort as a result of our inability to reach agreements which, whilst not promising a perfect future, seek to bring a better reality within reach!

If this same agricultural crisis had occurred some years later, it is most unlikely that it would have given rise to such an excessive reaction, or one that aimed to bring to light what was happening and provide a warning of the extent to which the political situation could degenerate. In those years, the Left was deeply concerned that the Army, as irritated as it was at that time, would overreact to any case of social disorder or street violence, and on various occasions it was obliged to perform the role of calming down its supporters and attempting to demobilise society, at a rhetorical level at least.

150. As we saw in the previous section, none of this took place on a key date regarding the recollection of the Civil War, but at a crucial moment during the Transition, when *ABC* was to recall the war much less discreetly.

Superior del Ejército issued the communiqué mentioned above, this newspaper unreservedly supported its stance, one in which the Army 'rejected out of conviction, but accepted out of discipline' (14/4/1977) the legalisation of the PCE.

The day before the staging of the first democratic elections, the *El País* editorial advised its readers not to vote for Alianza Popular, stating that:

> the return to power of the leaders who head this party would end all hope of a peaceful change in Spanish politics, would radicalise the various positions and would lead the country towards absolute generational and political rupture, towards a real crisis of State. (14/6/1977)

With regard to the left-wing parties, it argued that the PCE, in spite of the 'moderation' and 'prudence' that it had shown during its campaign, could not avoid the fact that 'the image of its most important leaders continues to be associated with the civil war'. Be that as it may, it advised its readers to vote without fear, as the new democracy, which, 'will entail various problems and tensions, but will avoid the drama of an historic rupture', was considered to be the only system capable of resolving conflicts, 'without the need to resort to violence'. On the day of the elections, the editorial made every possible effort to highlight the differences between the current situation and that of the 1930s, in order to exorcise the ghost of the Civil War. The Spanish people, 'was now ripe for democracy' (15/6/1977), from which we might deduce that, in a paradoxically similar vein to Francoist claims, the country had not been ready for democracy before. The editorial also insisted that there would be no problems at these elections, even acknowledging that Spaniards, unlike before, were now mature enough to live in freedom.

Again, the newspaper highlighted the dangers that might beset democracy: extremist movements of both tendencies and the issue of the autonomous regions. It placed considerable emphasis on the fact that the election results would produce, 'neither winners nor losers' and that it was essential to know how to respect the outcome (unlike during the Second Republic), without 'overbearing triumphalism', 'resentments' or 'retaliation'. 'References to 1936 sound like allusions to a distant past. It is no trick or coincidence that the leaders of the new electoral alternatives who appeared on RTVE on Monday night spoke a very different language to that of the pre-war period'. This kind of formulation of the state of affairs was frequent during the period. A delicate balance existed between what commentators wished to see happen and what they felt the need to say could happen, and this was either extremely hopeful or highly catastrophic. It was either claimed that there was no longer any danger of the war being repeated, in order to instil hope and reduce anxiety during the transition process or, if the situation became tense, it was claimed that this danger did in fact exist, in order to force an approach based on moderation, caution and dialogue. This ambivalent attitude was witnessed time and again throughout the Transition.

The newspaper went on to list the differences between the historical context and the current situation, one of them being the existence of, 'a deep conviction that civil war is the very worst scourge that can befall a nation, and the memory of the horrors of the post-war period'. The country now possessed 'that minimum consensus that has eliminated the spectre of civil war from civilised countries'. The editorial revealed considerable concern about the issue that aroused most controversy: the autonomous regions. The intransigence of the Right and their incomprehension of the sufferings of the Basques and Catalans under Francoism were, in the opinion of *El País*, factors that would contribute to the radicalisation of the nationalist movements, which would signify the beginning of the end. The day after the elections, the newspaper emphasised the 'peaceful nature' of election-day and 'the climate of serenity', 'unanimous calm', 'contained enthusiasm' and 'controlled passion'. Its view was that Spaniards had participated in the event enthusiastically, but with a sense of responsibility, maturity and tolerance.

After the elections, the winners were obliged to govern by respecting the minorities: 'Governing does not mean turning the winners against the losers. Failing to respect the rights of the minorities would be a crime against democracy and constitute a latent form of civil war'. As we can see, the weight of the past continued to be quite overwhelming. During the Second Republic, the rights of the minorities were not respected and they, in turn, tended to become increasingly radical and pursue an extremely damaging struggle against the system. This was, precisely, what had to be avoided.

On 15 June 1977 *ABC* suggested voting for either UCD or AP: 'We must comes to terms with the past...by respecting it...without nostalgia, without revenge and without any desire for retaliation' and it asked society for 'a calm vote' (15/6/1977). The following day it stated that, 'the entire Spanish people was victorious, triumphant. Its triumph was based on order, serenity and on the responsible way in which it fulfilled its duty to vote' (16/7/1977). *ABC* stated that the first aspect that had to be highlighted was, precisely,

> that yesterday, a nation that has seen all kinds of descriptions of incivility and lack of solidarity rained upon it, voted unanimously and in peace...Yesterday, in short, the Spanish people revealed an essential aspect of its understanding of democracy. It voted in peace and in peace it awaits the necessary implementation of its declared will.

As we can see, the two newspapers placed great emphasis on the peaceful nature of the process and on the moderate behaviour of the electorate, which meant that the most optimistic expectations regarding the process had been exceeded. The weight of history and, in this particular case, the recollection of the elections that took place during the Republican period, had led observers to predict more turbulent elections.

On 30 April, the eve of the first authorised celebration of 1 May, *El País* emphasised the 'peaceful' nature of the demonstrations that were planned for the following day: a holiday that is celebrated in democratic societies in a quiet and peaceful manner. Nevertheless, it warned against the presence of agitators. These demonstrations 'are the best proof of just how far our country has travelled in peace'. 'The peaceful purpose and even the holiday spirit of hundreds of thousands of workers is guaranteed'. The social demands included, 'the return of assets to the historical trade unions which were confiscated after the Civil War' by the Franco régime. This return had to be effected without delay, 'if the Government really wants industrial relations befitting an advanced nation to operate in Spain' (30/4/1978). This editorial attempted to reassure society by emphasising the peaceful, normal and even festive nature of the commemoration of Labour Day. The most delicate issue was the question of returning trade union assets, which directly dated back to the confiscation undertaken during the Civil War and the postwar period.

ABC adopted a very similar tone in its editorial on the eve of the holiday. It stated that, 'On no previous occasion...have we ever faced the celebration of a 1 May that is expected to take place... in a more normal, tranquil and peaceful manner'. This was not a question of an officially manipulated date, but a workers' holiday and, thus, was 'accepted by all'.

On 31 October, the newspaper *El País* became the victim of a violent terrorist attack in which two of its employees died. The editorial emphatically condemned the incident, but stated that this should not mar the general delight regarding the Constitution that was to be passed on that day. It recalled how a bloody outrage had accompanied every significant event during the Transition, in spite of which the democratising process was irreversible. 'This country has the right to live in peace' (31/10/1978). The following day, two editorials were published. The first, entitled 'A Lasting Constitution' (1/11/1978), began in the following manner:

> It is worth being wary of historicist approaches...But it is difficult to hide a sense of satisfaction and enthusiasm at finally having a democratic charter of rights and duties to present to the Spanish people in a free referendum, for the first time since 1931 and with a civil war in between... [This Constitution] marks the end of a journey through the desert that this people began, with very few breaks and rests, not back in 1936, but with the disturbances led by Primo de Rivera in Catalonia.

The editorial praised the final outcome:

> a democratic Constitution created, *against all the forecasts*, in the midst of economic crisis and between a series of very serious terrorist incidents.

The annals of history and constitutional law will no doubt record the case of a country that has set aside forty years of autocracy *without breaking apart or suffering deep fissures, without purges or general civil confrontations,* has changed the form of its State and has drawn up a freedom charter. *Who said the Spanish were ungovernable under democracy?* (the italics are mine)

The second editorial commented upon the news that the Nobel Peace prize had been granted to Sadat and Beguin, and brought together rumours regarding the possible candidature of Adolfo Suárez, an eventuality that the newspaper would not have objected to.

On 31 October *ABC* also expressed its disgust at the terrorist attack suffered by *El País*. It criticised, 'the objective of maintaining and enhancing a social climate of terror, insecurity, anxiety', in view of which the Government must find, 'a solution that returns a sense of inner peace to Spain'. The following day, it commented upon the passing of a Constitution that, 'could well be called consensus-based... The various political groups have conceded part of their convictions...in favour of those who, by fair means, are their adversaries, their rivals, their opponents'. Some issues still remained to be resolved, such as the issue of the autonomous regions. It highlighted that:

> for the first time in this ancient and difficult country, a Constitution has been created by the Government and the opposition at the same time, aiming to achieve a balance and not to crush the opponent. They have reached an agreement that will enable them to begin a new future.

Exactly the opposite occurred during the constitutional process of the Second Republic.

We believe that this brief selection of dates provides sufficient evidence both of the overwhelming presence of the memory of the Civil War during the key moments of the Transition and of the conciliatory role played by the press during this period. Although the role of the press cannot be generally applied beyond the scope of the two newspapers we have analysed, we believe that these publications were sufficiently important to enable us to extrapolate their attitudes and consider them to have represented the majority press opinion during the Transition. The attitude of the press in the 1930s was very different and it bore considerable responsibility for the tense atmosphere that so hindered political life and social harmony at the time.

Finally, with regard to the kinds of reports that the press offered about the war, we should highlight the virtual absence of the most dramatic and conflictual accounts of the Civil War, especially those relating to the crimes of the rearguard and the subsequent period of repression, in accordance with the desire for a nonpartisan climate described previously. The Civil War was a topic of research of considerable interest to the reader, especially because of the unreliable nature of the versions received up until that time. However, it was a topic that was approached with considerable caution, in order not to reopen any badly-healed wounds. This desire to tell and listen to stories about the war found freest rein in the cinema and in literature. Historiography was to take a little longer to analyse certain especially sensitive questions regarding the war.

The Parties

Political parties had not only been illegal throughout the Franco period, but they had also been constantly demonised. One of the reasons cited for supporting the Uprising of 1936 had been the desire to end the party politics of the Second Republic. It was stated that the role played by the political groups during the 1930s had been ill-fated, because, being incapable of dialogue, they had developed an intransigent form of conduct that had helped to agitate an already volatile atmosphere. By the end of the Franco period, there were few, even in the ranks of the democratic opposition, who did not recognise the responsibility of the parties in bringing down the Republic.

One of Franco's favourite excuses for not permitting the free expression of ideas through political organisations under his régime, was based on the exaggerated memory of the ill-fated role of the parties in the 1930s. He claimed that the resumption of political competition would lead irremediably back to civil war. Not even the parties on the right, republican or monarchist, escaped from this negative judgement, as it was a question of preventing, at any cost, the reestablishment of an 'inorganic' democracy in which societal representation was channelled through political parties.

The mistrust of political parties had come to be deeply rooted in certain sections of society, and not only as a result of Francoist socialisation, but also because of the personal experiences and messages conveyed by those who had lived through the Second Republic. Surveys carried out during the early years of the Transition revealed the general conviction that liberal democracy was not possible without parties, yet despite this, a certain mistrust existed towards them and many were alarmed at their excessive proliferation. It was necessary to fight against this relatively negative predisposition during the 1970s, with the first important step forward being the passing of the Regulatory Law on the Right of Political Association of 9 June 1976.[151]

The debate itself, which took place in the Francoist Cortes over the two days on which the draft law was discussed, is highly eloquent. It was primarily a question of going beyond the very limited and unpopular Statute of Political Associations of 1974. However, it was also necessary to combat the repugnance that the staunchest section of the régime felt

---

151. All of the quotations from the debate of this Law come from the Diario de Sesiones del Pleno, No. 27; 8 and 9 June 1976, pp.1–145. X Legislatura. Draft Regulatory Law on the Right of Political Association in accordance with urgent proceedings. Committee on Fundamental Laws and the Presidency of the Government.

towards the idea of parties and to overcome the sense of mistrust they aroused even in the most reformist circles, on whose support the passing of both this law and the Law for Political Reform depended. Both laws were debated under urgent proceedings and the alignments in favour and against the two laws were repeated in both. There were many thematic similarities between the two debates, in spite of which, a quite considerable sense of development was witnessed over the six months that separated the two.

In outlining the reasons for the draft law, the *Ponencia* highlighted the, 'analogical or identical nature of political associations and parties' in order to avoid any kind of misunderstanding. In spite of this, however, in order to avoid greater resistance, the title of the law referred to associations. The advocates of the text argued that democracy, and with it the establishment of parties, was nothing but the logical consequence of the economic and social development achieved under Francoism; it was the necessary and inevitable development of the régime of 18 July. Furthermore, precisely because of the Franco years, Spaniards had attained sufficient maturity and material progress to be able to face a democratic experience, this time with moderation and success. The Civil War had, thus, been necessary for the peaceful coexistence that lay ahead. Democracy confirmed both the origin-based and performance-based legitimacy of the Franco régime through a kind of posthumous recognition of its achievements, even though, according to the same argument, the very existence of these two forms of legitimacy was to finally bring the régime to an end.

The most recalcitrant of the *procuradores* revealed a mixture of perplexity and indignation at the explanations offered by the *Ponencia*. The legalisation of parties went against the Fundamental Laws of the régime and against its very foundations; one of the clearest ideas of the 'crusade' had been the root and branch elimination of parties from Spanish politics. It was claimed that the return of parties would lead to a repetition of the Civil War, and that it was wrong to revive institutions that had been removed at the cost of such pain and bloodshed. If one of the justifications of the Uprising and of the subsequent Civil War had been to eliminate what the draft law now aimed to reinstate, then hundreds and thousands of victims had sacrificed their lives in vain. Furthermore, they could not understand how a régime that had been credited with achieving peace within Spanish society and whose favourable economic management had been acknowledged, had become so obsolete. The dismantling of the régime and the return of democracy would bring an end to the peace and development of many years.

The reply formulated by the advocates of the law, in contrast to the objections raised by the opposing group of *procuradores*, was based on a rather ad hoc counterargument. The starting-point, as expressed by José Luis Meilán Gil, a member of the *Ponencia*, was that, 'changes are only made to what is really sought to be preserved'. Based on this idea, much emphasis was placed on the very different context that existed in the 1970s in comparison with the set of circumstances that the Republic had been obliged to face. It was claimed that, thanks to Francoism, a marvellous climate now existed to reintroduce democracy. This was a unique historical opportunity to end the curse that plagued the Spanish, and it was not to be missed. The final conclusion was that, because the context was so different, democracy was now compatible with peace and development, unlike the situation that existed under the Republic.[152]

The long address given on behalf of the Government by the man who was, at that time, the Minister Secretary-General of the Movement, Adolfo Suárez, is famous. This politician was capable of bringing together all of the arguments in favour of passing the law with conviction and coherence. Suárez stated that it was necessary, 'to break, once and for all, all the vicious circles of our History', that it was necessary to remove the drama from Spanish political life, that the nation was no longer beset by the negative conditioning factors of the 1930s and that, in the same way as law and order had been demanded before, freedom was demanded today. He also recalled that 70 percent of Spaniards had only known peace and that both this majority, as well as the 30 percent minority who had experienced the war, wished to avoid any kind of confrontation and develop a peaceful and ordered society. The law was finally passed by a majority of three-quarters of the Chamber.

This was the first significant step towards the resumption of party politics, as the first wave of resistance to the return of parties to political life had been overcome in the Cortes. Now it was up to the parties to demonstrate their will to negotiate and prove their alleged compatibility with social peace and harmony. In order to observe whether this was, in fact, the attitude that the parties finally adopted, a brief review shall be undertaken of some of the most important publications produced by the main political parties, which were based on their programmes and on the decisions reached at their party congresses. In this section we shall analyse the four parties that obtained the greatest levels of representation at a national level in the Cortes: UCD, the PSOE, the PCE and AP.

The book by Carlos Huneeus (1985) on UCD explains how this party contributed to the adoption of a partnership-based strategy (from the perspective of Gerhard Lehmbruch although not in the view of Arend Lijphart) in contrast to the majority strategy that had been adopted during the Second Republic, producing strong centripetal tendencies within the system. According to Huneeus, the heterogeneous nature of the centrist party, which brought together Francoist and opposition sectors,

152. The *procurador* Alberto Cercós Pérez stated that it was a question of achieving 'two objectives that I believe are compatible: consolidating peace and harmony among all Spaniards and ensuring the creation of a democratic system that is comparable to those that exist in Europe'.

forced it to adopt a partnership and negotiation-based formula in order to resolve its internal conflicts. This meant that many tensions were absorbed by the party itself and did not reach the point of spilling over into the political system.[153] The opposite had occurred during the Republican period, where conflicts were addressed in the public sphere, and were characterised by strong confrontation among the parties. This contributed to the radicalisation of political life and aggravated the Government's difficulties in ruling the country.

UCD came to play a role that the centrist alternatives had either not been able, or not known how, to fulfil during the Second Republic, a period in which the establishment and consolidation of democracy did not seem to be the priority of any of the important political groups. In the 1930s, the polarisation of the party system meant that the ideological centre was largely vacant, being absorbed by left and right-wing forces. Centrist parties achieved very poor results during this period, in contrast to those achieved by UCD in 1977 and 1979, although this party never achieved an absolute majority. The mere triumph of a centrist option that brought together various tendencies, both conservative and reformist, introduced an important dose of tranquillity into the political life of the Transition. Spanish society no longer rallied around two opposing ideological poles, but concentrated its representation within the centre and the moderate left and right-wing alternatives. This was something that the group known as the *Tácitos*, whose role was to be essential in creating UCD, managed to perceive.

The *Tácito* group[154] had been the first within Francoism to formulate the need to create a wide and heterogeneous coalition to occupy the centre of the political spectrum in order to endow the process of change that began after Franco's death with sufficient stability. Its overriding objective was to achieve a transition that was neither violent nor *rupturista*, but moved peacefully and cautiously towards democracy. To this end, they advocated the idea that the change towards a new régime should be brought about from within the Francoist system itself, in order not to arouse the anger and possible intervention of the Armed Forces. Many of the *Tácito* group's members had backed Don Juan, but they soon became firm supporters of Juan Carlos, with whom they maintained strong

---

153   This permitted the simplification of the party system, at the same time as it helped to filter social conflicts in advance. If these conflicts had been transmitted directly to the party system they would have unleashed considerable social turmoil. UCD filtered social conflicts – for example, religious and socioeconomic conflicts – and in this respect it made an extremely important contribution to the establishment and consolidation of democracy. (Huneeus, 1985: 25)

Nevertheless, all of this was at a high political cost for the party.

154.   In 1975, the book entitled *Tácito*, by Ibérico Europea de Ediciones, published a compilation of articles by the group's main members. See also the chapter by Charles Powell in Frances Lannon and Paul Preston (eds.) 1990.

personal links and to whose generation the majority of them belonged. The King was born in 1938, in the middle of the Civil War, and those born around this time were known during the Franco period as the 'Prince's generation', emphasising the fact that they had not played any part in the war and had no personal recollections of it.

As highlighted in the study produced by Powell (1990), almost all of the families from which the *Tácitos* came had supported Franco during the Civil War.[155] However, they had neither collaborated actively with the régime nor opposed it. They existed within the 'buffer zone' described by Huneeus (1985: 30ff.) that was populated by individuals who had carried out tasks of a rather more technical nature for the state. This 'buffer zone' was occupied by well-trained economists and lawyers who had managed to gain a thorough knowledge of the workings of the régime. This placed them in an advantageous strategic position during the Transition, enabling them to facilitate change from within. Their presence did not arouse the level of opposition among the staunchest members of the régime that the democratic opposition would have aroused. Furthermore, the kind of transition they seemed prepared to facilitate was more in line with the moderate and prudent desires of the majority of the population, who were not keen on provisional governments or plebiscites on the form of the state. According to Powell, 'at least seven of the twenty ministers in the first Suárez Government were (or had been) active "Tácitos"' (Powell, 1990: 265). For all these reasons, this group was especially well prepared to serve as a bridge between the Francoist élite and the democratic opposition.

Another significant aspect of UCD was that, 'none of the parties which came together in Centro Democrático (CD) and, later on, within UCD, had an ongoing historical link with the Second Republic' (Huneeus, 1985: 140). UCD was created from the Partido Popular (PP) and other political groups by absorbing the ideological stance of Christian democracy, which was destined to fail for this and other reasons.[156] Only 17.5 percent [157] of its parliamentary members were former Francoist *procuradores*, the majority of whom came from the *tercio familiar*, having later been elected by the same provinces as in the Francoist elections. Finally, only 6.7

---

155. The 'Tácitos' included the following members: José L. Álvarez, Marcelino Oreja, Rafael Arias Salgado, Landelino Lavilla, Juan A. Ortega, Alfonso Osorio, Eduardo Carrilles, Fernando Álvarez de Miranda.

156. Cardenal Tarancón, obsessed with avoiding any repetition of history, did not want to back any political acronym that might have religious overtones, so that the Church would not find itself in the midst of political confrontation as it had under the Second Republic.

157. This figure cited by Huneeus (1985: 169–170) does not agree with the figure given in the study by Mariano Baena del Alcázar and José María García Madaria (1979: 18). According to Huneeus, 49 of the UCD parliamentary members had been *procuradores*; according to Baena and Madaria, there were 52 out of 262, which came to 19.84 percent of UCD parliamentary members.

percent of UCD's parliamentary members were aged sixty or over, which meant that the majority had not fought in the Civil War. This was the general tendency among the various parties (Huneeus, 1985: 169–173).

The image that UCD attempted to convey to society was that of moderation. It presented itself as the only party capable of consolidating democracy in a stable and peaceful manner. The ideas of caution, prudence and peace habitually featured in its manifestoes and in declarations made by the party's main leaders. There was also a constant and mostly tacit evocation of the Civil War as an experience that was to be avoided at any cost. José L. Álvarez placed considerable emphasis on the recent history of Spain, stressing that it was essential to learn from past errors. The country, 'has more than its share of confrontations, violence, incomprehension, attempts to reproduce the conflicts of the past, extremist stances on regionalist and political problems' (Álvarez, 1978: 16). This politician also insisted on the need to avoid the possibility of Spain once again being split into two irreconcilable positions, as occurred during the Second Republic, thus, it was important to establish a strong and wide-ranging ideological centre. This was the crucial argument of UCD: the centre was necessary in order to avoid the repetition of our historical errors and, with it, the Civil War. In effect, as explained in the previous pages, one of the most visible problems of the Republican experience was the nonexistence of a solid and feasible centrist option, so the electoral strategy of UCD perfectly matched the process of historical learning that had been pursued by Spanish society.[158] According to Álvarez, civil war was no longer an inevitable outcome, but neither should Spaniards underestimate the danger of its repetition. Fear of this possibility, however remote it might be, was necessary in order to construct this argument. This fear certainly existed in some social sectors and was painstakingly fuelled by all the political groups. The memory of the conflict and fear of its repetition was a powerful card that they all held up their sleeves to be produced at the most appropriate moment. On many occasions, this memory was raised in order to encourage agreement and the consolidation of consensus politics.

Those who ended up forming part of UCD, some of whom had supported the right of political association and the Law for Political Reform as *procuradores* in the Francoist Cortes, grounded their position in the performance-based legitimacy of the previous régime. As was seen in

---

158.   José L. Álvarez stated the following:

> if there is something that it is worth working for in Spain in the organisation of political life, it is to avoid the creation of two fronts. Let none of us forget that the creation of one front invites the creation of the other. And to do this is to create the precise conditions, once again, for a game of winner-takes-all... The only thing I believe we should all agree to do is to discard the idea of two Spains and aim to integrate, with all their differences...all Spaniards within a jointly-accepted political game that does not exclude or destroy any sector. (Álvarez, 1978: 28)

the debate of these laws, they had supported the idea that, due to the effectiveness of Francoist economic management and its undoubted social repercussions, it was now possible to undertake a peaceful transition towards democracy. Formulated in this way, the argument contained a number of fallacies. It seemed to suggest that Franco – consciously or unconsciously – had been preparing the Spanish for democracy. It would probably be more accurate to say that democracy was the unwanted outcome of his political action. However, it was never conceived in this way within centrist ranks, whose members sought to reconcile the Francoist apparatus with the new régime, one that was fully accepted by the opposition. This opposition only needed to be convinced that, under democracy, there was room for everyone and that the various political alternatives would compete on equal terms.

One of the most important manifesto declarations of UCD, entitled *Manuel para 22 millones de electores* ('Handbook for 22 Million Voters'), placed considerable emphasis on the terms 'moderation' and 'reconciliation', and also on the need for consolidating peaceful coexistence. It stated that, thanks to Adolfo Suárez, 'political change was brought about without any serious trauma for our society' (UCD, 1977: 7). The need to learn from history was another of the constant themes of this manifesto:

> History clearly shows us the tendency of the Spanish to split ourselves into two halves: right and left. And this split has nearly always ended in confrontation. Today, however, it is difficult to claim that society only nurtures these two seeds. A greater degree of pluralism now exists. There is a centre-right...and there is a centre-left... This basis, which makes up the extensive grounds of moderation, today represents one of the guarantees...that the Transition will finally come to rest on secure foundations' (UCD, 1977: 7).

UCD presented itself, once again, as the force best prepared to overcome conflict and impose a sense of moderation.

The First National Congress of UCD, which took place in Madrid between 19 and 21 October 1978, confirms everything that has been said concerning the image this party aimed to convey to society.[159] On this occasion it was stated that, for the first time in the history of Spain, a centre movement existed that was capable of imposing peace on the extremist tendencies, of restoring the nation's sense of confidence in itself and of making freedom compatible with a sense of order, security and stability. Only a new party such as UCD, devoid of any historical figures or historical title, was capable, in their view, of carrying out this delicate task. The party emphasised that it was the people who had provided the

---

159. The minutes of this Congress were published by Unión Editorial in 1979 under the title *La Solución a un Reto. Tesis para una Sociedad Democrática Occidental*.

impetus for change, who had conducted themselves in a responsible and moderate manner, dictated by their desire for peace. In this way the party aimed to return Spaniards' belief in their own capacity to democratise the country without trauma or confrontations. In the political publication entitled 'Principios ideológicos y modelo de sociedad UCD' ('Ideological Principles and the UCD Model of Society'), UCD presented itself as the party that had benefited by extracting the most enlightening lessons from history, resulting in their message of moderation.

The role played by Suárez as a source of electoral appeal was extremely important. As President of the Government after July 1976, he had had numerous opportunities to demonstrate his capacity for negotiation and persuasion. He had promoted the passing of the right of political association, the Law for Political Reform, the legalisation of the PCE, and the amnesty, and he also enjoyed the obvious support of the King (who had helped to appoint him as head of government). His charismatic qualities were obvious and his words and delivery were convincing. He made certain ideas famous, which later became the maxims of the Transition, such as the principle that it was necessary to legalise what was normal in the street and that it was essential to remove the drama from Spanish politics. He strove at all times to convince society that the members of his generation, who had not fought in the war, were the only ones capable of steering the Transition towards a safe port and inaugurating a new form of politics based on moderation and tolerance. He never touched upon divisive issues such as exile, repression and other matters relating to the Civil War, but the war featured, implicitly, in every one of his speeches.[160]

UCD was the party that best managed to read Spanish society, whilst also conveying the message of moderation, tranquillity and stability it wished to hear. The image of its leaders and of the groups that made up the coalition did not evoke memories of the Second Republic or the war. The party enjoyed the trust and confidence of the King; it had demonstrated its capacity for dialogue with both the Left and the Right; it possessed a charismatic leader with considerable political talents[161] and it offered a smooth sense of progression with regard to the past. In short, it perfectly suited the role of bridge between the two régimes while democracy was being consolidated.

Unlike UCD, the PSOE was a party with a history, any mention of which evoked its performance during the Second Republic and the Civil War, although none of its most important leaders from that period had

160. See the following compilation: Adolfo Suárez (1978): *Un nuevo horizonte para España. Discursos del Presidente del Gobierno 1976-1978.* Furthermore, Ediciones del Movimiento brought together many of his most important televised speeches and some of his appearances in the Cortes.
161. In early 1995, Adolfo Suárez received at least three awards for his work during the political transition.

survived (Besteiro, Prieto, Largo Caballero, etc.). However, the main reason the PSOE, in spite of its history, appeared to the electorate as a young and different party was because a power change took place in the party leadership as a result of the Congress of Suresnes in 1974. The first serious confrontation between the representatives from exile and those from inside Spain had already taken place before the Congress of Toulouse in August 1972.[162] At Suresnes, the youth section of the party, headed by the recently-elected General Secretary, Felipe González Márquez, had managed to displace the 'histórico' or 'traditional' section, which included many of those who had lived through the war. Although the rhetoric of the émigré section was more moderate than that of the young Socialists within Spain, the latter were capable of presenting a more reassuring image, as they did not bear any historical responsibility for events during the Republican period or the Civil War. González Márquez was born in 1942 and the majority of his Spanish-based colleagues were around the same age.

Furthermore, the anticommunist stance of the exiles was highly visceral, which made them unlikely contenders for the new era of dialogue and negotiation that was approaching, especially in view of the important role that the PCE and CCOO were to play in this process. Some of the youngest Socialists, as had been customary in the democratic opposition to Francoism, had come from families who had supported the Uprising and sympathised with the régime, which meant that they also possessed family ties and personal links within the system. In spite of its break away from the émigré section of the movement, the PSOE retained various emblematic figures among its members, such as José Prat and Ramón Rubial, so that the new direction would be able to maintain links with a past that undoubtedly aroused the sympathies of certain sections of society.

The radical discourse of its early years situated the PSOE to the left of the PCE, in spite of which the PCE was less able to avoid evoking disturbing memories. Felipe González and Alfonso Guerra even stated, in a joint publication in 1977, that if:

> today the Right calls itself the Centre; the Centre, the Left; the Liberals, Social Democrats; the Communists, Socialists; then the Socialists declare themselves to be revolutionaries. Because they are democratic, Socialists do

---

162. Due to a series of problems arising from the confrontation between the émigré and Spain-based members of the party, Llopis had decided to suspend the congress that was to take place in Toulouse in August 1972. This decision was ignored by the representatives from inside Spain, who decided to go ahead with the meeting. Subsequently, the International decided to authorise the section of the party inside Spain and this section, on its own initiative, was to stage a congress in Suresnes (Various Authors, 1986: 364 ff.). The Spanish-based representatives complained about the inflexibility and bureaucratic rigidity of the exiles, of their exacerbated anticommunism (because they had reached agreement with the monarchists of Munich before securing a pact with the PCE) and their ignorance of the state of affairs in Spain.

not believe that real democracy can exist in a capitalist society. (González and Guerra, 1977: 27–28)

The young Socialists would soon realise that, in spite of the asset their youthfulness proved to be and the fact that they had displaced the traditional section of their party, the use of certain expressions would not be of any help to them in winning over an electorate that was much more moderate and conservative than they had envisaged. However, they could not easily abandon certain points of their manifesto, such as republicanism, without suffering significant setbacks among their most radical voters. In reference to this, during the constitutional debate Santiago Carrillo accused them of putting on a show and failing to stand firm with their republican vote, which, according to the Communist leader, they would have withdrawn if they had thought they could win the debate.

The Socialist Party, like almost all of the opposition forces, campaigned for abstention in the referendum on the Law for Political Reform. Although it is true to say that the opposition was not given the same opportunities as the Government to gain access to the electorate, its position had been made sufficiently clear for it to win the votes of those who agreed with it. It is possible that the abstention vote may have achieved somewhat better results if it had been supported with the same number of television, radio slots, and other forms of media coverage as the Government campaign, but the victory of the 'yes' vote would still have been overwhelming. We must also recognise that the left-wing parties felt pressurised by their most radical members to promote a *rupturista* and 'noncollaborationist' strategy[163] and it was natural, up to a point, that being officially illegal, such parties should refuse to support the government campaign. Nevertheless, if the PSOE wished to evolve into a catch-all party, the majority of the electorate had shown the leaders that they would have to advocate reform based on the existing institutional set-up and moderate their rhetoric.

Despite this early failure, the main leaders of the PSOE continued to employ extremist rhetoric for some time, although, on numerous occasions, their flexibility and willingness to negotiate belied their radical pronouncements. At the same time as they talked about socialist revolution and exhibited the victims of Francoist repression among their own rank and file, they emphasised that they were a 'new party'. They made much greater reference to the persecution suffered within Spain, which they were able to confirm with their own experience, than that suffered during the war or in exile, as embodied in the 'histórico' section of the party. In time, the two

---

163. In a PSOE publication coordinated by Francisco Bustelo in 1976 it was stated that, 'after so many years of fighting, it would be absurd for the PSOE to accept collaborationist stances and intermediate positions that...would clearly be detrimental to its public image and prospects, especially among the working class' (Bustelo, 1976: 65–66).

versions of repression would be combined within the same party, as the PSOE finally took up the symbolic legacy of the 'histórico' section.

The resolutions passed at the Congress of Suresnes referred, in a rather anachronistic manner, to the Socialists' intention of facilitating the political and economic seizure of power by the working class and bringing about, 'the radical transformation of capitalist society into socialist society'.[164] Democracy was no more than a means of achieving this goal. The 'right of self-determination of all the Iberian nationalities' was supported and a republican and federal solution was advocated. The language used at the Congress of 1976 was very similar, except for the profuse use of the expression 'peaceful', which was more in line with general social aspirations. Nevertheless, the party continued to advocate Marxism, self-management, social mobilisation as a means of exerting political pressure, the classless society and the disappearance of the state as the final objective. Moreover, they adhered to the statement, 'we do not, naturally, rule out any use of force which may be required'.[165] The party insisted on the return of the assets confiscated by the Franco régime after the war and the necessary liberation of political prisoners. It also proposed that the party should arrange the return of the remains of Largo Caballero to the Cemetery of Madrid, thus 'symbolising through him all of our colleagues who died in exile'.

Throughout 1976 the rhetoric continued in the same vein. One of the publications produced by La Gaya Ciencia entitled *Qué es el Socialismo* ('What is Socialism'), written by Felipe González, was adorned with photos of Lenin, Marx, Engels, Trotsky and Rosa Luxemburg. The failed revolution of 1934 was recounted in heroic terms and the Civil War was interpreted from a class-war perspective. It also referred to the 'history of suffering, imprisonment, exile and death of Spanish Socialists after 1936' (González, 1976b: 44). It was very difficult to relegate all this history to the background, as it constituted one of the PSOE's most important assets in the eyes of a far from negligible section of society. For other sections of society, however, this memory was not especially pleasant. It was this problematic perception of the past that led the PSOE to adopt an ambivalent attitude towards this matter. In another publication produced that year, which brought together the documents of the first PSOE summer school after the war, Felipe González stated that he had taken up the historical legacy of the PSOE out of, 'respect for the struggle, for the considerable effort, for the number of years of imprisonment and exile – and it is not our style to bring it up – for the number of deaths that were witnessed along the way' (González, 1976c: 27). The Socialists denied that their aim was to rub salt into past wounds or exhibit lists of the dead. However, from time to time, they did bring these matters up, because this was the only way of not disappointing those who expected it without

---

164. Resolutions of the XIII PSOE Congress (Suresnes, October 1974).
165. Resolutions of the XXVII PSOE Congress (1976).

causing too much worry to those who feared such references. Nicolás Redondo, from the UGT, also addressed these conferences and stated that his union, 'is not going to sign a social pact' (González, 1976c: 93). These words were to be proven wrong with the acceptance – tacit on the part of the unions and explicit on the part of the party – of the Moncloa Pacts in 1977. As it turned out, in the period between Redondo's declarations and the Moncloa economic and political agreements, a number of tragic incidents took place that were to produce important changes in the rhetoric employed by the Left. These events included the mass murder of labour lawyers in Calle Atocha and the far from negligible number of deaths that occurred in confrontations between demonstrators and the police in the mass marches in favour of amnesty.

In the electoral manifesto of 1977 we can observe a much clearer sense of development. Self-determination was no longer advocated, and neither was self-management nor the nationalisation of the banking system. The PSOE did not wish to be accused of being soft, but it knew that it had to moderate its language in order not to provoke mistrust, fear and rejection. It now stated that it was necessary to establish, 'a system of social relations that enabled conflicts between the various ideological and social groups to be resolved peacefully',[166] and that democracy was, 'necessary in order to preserve civil peace'. It also talked about overcoming the fear of, 'the spectres of the past'. The Socialists did not intend to give way to extreme-right intimidation, but the reforms needed to be introduced without 'any kind of trauma'.[167] With an eye to the forthcoming elections, the party had ended up incorporating the values of peace and moderation preferred by a society traumatised by the memory of war.

When the PSOE leaders were not addressing the electorate directly, but their own members and supporters, they could afford to revive certain forms of verbal radicalism. For instance, in a publication produced in 1977, Bustelo wondered whether a peaceful transition towards democracy would be possible. Naturally, the peaceful path was, he admitted, desirable, but, 'you do not need to be a Marxist to know that the history of Mankind to date has consisted of a succession of violent incidents and conflicts' (Equipo Jaime Vera, 1977: 22). He then went on to support the peaceful course by appealing to two arguments. The first highlighted the socialist ideal of fraternity, which meant that it was only necessary to resort to violence in extreme cases of legitimate self-defence, unlike the actions of the Socialists in 1934.[168] 'In the future,

---

166. PSOE Electoral Manifesto (1977: 4).
167. PSOE Electoral Manifesto (1977: 13).
168. The critical revision of the Socialists' role in the events of 1934 was extremely important, because in other documents the PSOE had vindicated this legacy. In one of these documents it had talked about the victorious revolution in Asturias, 'where the heroic struggle of the Asturian miners resisted the ferocious attacks of the mercenary forces sent by the most reactionary members of government' (PSOE, 1977: 16–17).

Socialists and Communists – and they must state this publicly – will never be the first to resort to violence' (Equipo Jaime Vera, 1977: 24). The second pointed out that, within the Spanish economic and social context of the time, it was possible to resolve the contradictions of capitalism peacefully. It was not necessary to repeat the events of 1936, when the 'peaceful efforts of the Left were cut short with blood and fire by the Right' (Equipo Jaime Vera, 1977: 25). Peace and revolution had to be able to go hand in hand. In the same text, Ignacio Fuejo talked about the need to reform an administration that had been used as a kind of war booty by the victors. 'Eliminating the consequences of the Civil War, an essential requirement for peace and harmony among Spaniards, means removing the consequences in Government as far as possible' (Equipo Jaime Vera, 1977: 91).

In 1977 the publishing company Albia, from Bilbao, carried out an important information-gathering exercise on the political parties, whilst also subjecting the main leaders to a questionnaire. At the time this project was undertaken, UCD had not yet been created, but many other parties had, some of them mere minority concerns, but whose existence was recorded thanks to this collection. Both the renewed PSOE as well as the PSOE-Histórico have their respective volumes; the first, written by González and Guerra, and the second by Manuel Murillo Carrasco. It will be interesting to carry out a brief contrast of their views.

The PSOE-Histórico was much more moderate, prudent and in tune with the times than the renewed party, although the average age of its members and the years of exile it had been forced to endure may have led observers to think otherwise. The only aspect that let it down was the anticommunist stance of its members, a large number of whom had actually experienced the Civil War. The memory of the war led them to reject any kind of understanding with the PCE. All those political actors who refused to enter into dialogue with the rest immediately excluded themselves from the consensus-based transition process that was being carried out. The writings of the PSOE-Histórico featured numerous accounts of personal experiences of suffering during the war, in exile and in French concentration camps. The renewed PSOE also made reference to these sufferings, but always as part of the historical legacy of the party, not as personal experiences of its current leaders. The PSOE-Histórico was, naturally, much more obsessed with the possible repetition of the war, in which respect it did not hesitate to propose carrying out a 'peaceful struggle' from within the current system, in spite of the fact that it would be tainted as a reformist party as a result. 'Let nobody confuse...our revolutionary character, with immature and sometimes violent left-wing tendencies...creating unnecessary tension and even generating reactionary processes' (Murillo Carrasco, 1977: 12). They also appeared to be more conciliatory with regard to the Right, as, according to this party, the Civil War:

was lost by all: those of us who officially lost it and those who say they won it, because, except for the privileged minority who benefited from the fruits of victory in war, we have all suffered the moral and economic misery entailed by civil war. That is to say, it was Spain that lost the war. That is why reconciliation is necessary and why the effort of all is required within a climate of mutual trust so that we might emerge from this stage and make it through the next stage. (Murillo Carrasco, 1977: 54)

None of this, however, could make the electorate forget the intransigence of the PSOE during the Republican period or its responsibility in relation to the war. The average age of the 16 members of the Executive Committee was 53, but if we ignore the four members who were 40 years old or under, 75 percent had an average age of over 60, and so were sufficiently old (between 19 and 22 years of age) to have fought in the Civil War.

The new PSOE talked much about Francoism, but practically never talked about the Civil War, only occasionally mentioning it in passing. The leaders aimed to base society's acceptance of the party on two pillars. The first was the historical character of the party, its secular struggle in defence of the interests of the working-class; the second pillar was a ferocious criticism of Francoism, combined with appeals to the suffering of socialist militants (censorship, imprisonment, trials, exile, persecution). Democracy was not questioned, but the party persisted in its criticisms of capitalism, which it no longer intended to replace, but improve. It believed that it alone was capable of representing the interests of the dispossessed, taking up the legacy of Pablo Iglesias. When looking back over the party's historical past, the leaders moved directly from an account of the Second Republic to the Franco years, avoiding the sensitive issue of the Civil War altogether. Although this presented a magnificent opportunity to dismantle the black-and-white version that the Franco régime had been offering for decades, the occasion was deliberately shunned. They supported the need to reach agreement with other political forces after the elections so that a joint constitutional process could be undertaken featuring the participation of all parties. On the Party Executive, except for Rubial who was born in 1906 and Guillermo Galeote and L. Fajardo (no date of birth is given for either), the average age of the other 14 members was 39, which meant that they had been born, like the King, around 1938, so they had not lived through the Civil War and were not obliged to assume responsibility for the mistakes committed by the PSOE in the 1930s. They claimed, however, to have deep republican convictions and to be in favour of a popular referendum on the kind of State that was to be adopted. The Monarchy, should it come down to it, would have to base its legitimacy on popular sovereignty. However, they were also now prepared to accept another possibility: 'If the monarch, through his decisive intervention, were to assume responsibility for accelerating the democratising process, he could gain a level of popular support that would guarantee his survival' (González and Guerra, 1977: 72). This was nothing less than what Llopis had promised Satrústegui in Munich fifteen years earlier.

The general message of the PSOE-Histórico was, in short, more peaceful, moderate and tolerant, except with regard to the PCE. The radicalism of the renewed PSOE was also, naturally, guided by the youthfulness of its leaders and by a lack of political experience, which favoured the adoption of stances of an extremist nature.

The age of the PSOE parliamentary members was also lower than that of UCD members. In 1977, UCD members featured the following age-group proportions: only 1.2 percent were under 30 years of age, 30.9 percent were between 30 and 39 years of age, 43 percent were between 40 and 49, and 24.9 percent were over 50. With regard to the PSOE parliamentary members, 11.8 percent were under 30 years of age, 44.9 percent were between 30 and 39 years of age, 22.9 percent were between 40 and 49 years old and 20.4 percent were aged over 60.[169]

In order to combat the rhetoric of UCD, the PSOE offered its struggle against the dictatorship and in favour of the freedoms that were beginning to be enjoyed. It also preached distrust of all those who, having collaborated in some way or another with the Franco régime, now presented themselves as democratic candidates. In this way it sought to erode the democratic support of the Centre and the Right by monopolising all the credit for the new era of freedom. The PSOE was unable to play the bridging role required at that time in order to lead a reformist transition, but it was quick enough to offer a moderate image of a party open to negotiation, which was attractive to a very high proportion of society. Instead of being associated with the 1930s, the party had managed to identify itself with the labour and student struggles under Francoism, an identification facilitated by its youthful appeal and the split from the oldest section of the party.

During the Transition, after an early stage in which it called for *ruptura democrática* and the staging of a referendum on the monarchy/republic issue, the PCE – the Communist Party of Spain[170] – did everything in its power not to stir up the old and difficult memories of its role during the Civil War. It presented itself as a new party, having been one of the main architects of the Eurocommunist thesis.[171] A failure to change its attitude would have threatened the legalisation of the party before the elections and, therefore, the party's subsequent electoral results.

The most radical sections of the communist movement had broken away from the PCE in order to form other, lesser, Soviet-style parties, such as the PCOE led by Líster, one of the harshest critics of the direction the

169. These figures come from Huneeus, 1985: 173 (Table 18).
170. Regarding the PCE, see Gregorio Morán (1986) and Eusebio Mujal-León (1983).
171. Various publications produced by Carrillo, which appear in the bibliography, reveal the development of the party: *Nuevos enfoques a problemas de hoy, Demain l'Espagne, ¿Qué es la ruptura democrática?, Partido Comunista de España, 'Eurocomunismo' y Estado*; finally, we might also recommend reading his memoirs, published in 1993.

Communist Party had taken. The leadership of the PCE, however, included members as representative of the Stalinist approach of the 1930s as Dolores Ibárruri and Santiago Carrillo, figures who strongly evoked memories of the Spanish Civil War. Many sinister stories had been circulated by the Franco régime concerning the acts committed by the Communists during the war, particularly regarding the responsibility born by Ibárruri and Carrillo. However, not only had the official historians of the régime condemned the attitude of the PCE during the war, English-speaking Hispanists had been producing documentary evidence for some time regarding their much-disputed conduct. One episode in particular featuring the direct involvement of Carrillo had been highlighted by the Franco régime: the Paracuellos massacre.[172] The Francoist press and historical establishment devoted rivers of ink to an event that had involved the execution of several hundred persons on the Nationalist side between November and December 1936, when Carrillo was the Public Order Adviser of the Defence Council of Madrid. The ultimate responsibility for these events has never been entirely established, and Carrillo has always systematically denied all of the charges levelled against him.[173] The

172. Two of the historians who have attributed responsibility for this massacre to Carrillo are Carlos Fernández (1983) and Ricardo de la Cierva (1994).

173. In the majority of the interviews that Carrillo granted to journalists in those years, the latter ended up asking him about this matter. He always replied by denying any responsibility in the affair, but the irritation that the mere mention of this episode caused him was quite evident. In the book *Demain l'Espagne*, two journalists, Régis Debray and Max Gallo, interviewed him in exile in France in the mid-1970s, and only towards the end did they ask the following question: 'Spanish Television and some articles in the press have presented you as a 'criminal'. 'What effect does this accusation have on you?' He responded as follows:

> Personally it has no effect on me whatsoever. After thirty years listening to the worst fascist slander, I have got used to hearing accusations of this kind. As very often happens in real life, the thief will shout 'there goes the thief' in order to make his own get-away. Those who now seek to open the old wounds of the war in order to stir up hate and prevent reconciliation are playing with fire, because they could find themselves in the dock tomorrow. We have stated that it is essential to overcome the consequences of the Civil War, that it is necessary to regard it as an historical event and draw the necessary conclusions from it for the future. No 'extremist' provocation will force us to abandon this stance. (Carrillo, 1974: 222)

The tone which he adopted in the interview with María Eugenia Yagüe in 1977 was somewhat different. At no time did he suggest placing anyone in the dock, a quite unthinkable possibility during the Transition. He began by stating: 'What I am not, certainly, is a murderer' (Yagüe, 1977: 11). And he devoted several pages to explaining what had happened in Paracuellos, denying any connection with the events that took place there. He also stated:

> They aim to tarnish the PCE now with this tragedy, for which we bear no responsibility whatsoever. I am loathe to enter into a controversy that would lead us away from a sense of reconciliation, something which those who do not wish to see democracy in Spain are attempting to do. I would also like to point out that my alleged responsibility is something that has emerged only very recently, when my political weight in Spain as Secretary General of the Communist Party has begun to be viewed with some concern. Before, nothing was ever mentioned about Paracuellos del Jarama, nor about me. (Yagüe, 1977: 31)

problem arose when Carrillo appeared in the public arena again at the beginning of the Transition, with all of this uncertainty regarding his responsibility during the executions hanging over him. The extreme right daubed numerous walls around Madrid with graffiti relating to this event, such as 'Carrillo, murderer'.[174]

The PCE also carried with it the entire legacy of what communism had represented throughout the world, including the Stalinist purges, the 'Cultural Revolution' in China and many other sinister points of reference. This was the image that it sought to free itself of by supporting Eurocommunist formulae. For a large part of the Right, this conversion to democracy and desire for conciliation was hardly credible, and many claimed that this sheep's clothing simply disguised a revanchist wolf embittered by defeat. The message of national reconciliation that the PCE had sent out from exile in 1956 had been very coolly received on the left, which did not prevent the Communists of the Transition from using this historical reference-point in order to support their moderate and peace-making image. This new message had, nevertheless, entailed a crucial strategic U-turn in PCE policy, which, as of that moment, aimed to erase its past history through the creation of a new history based on the defence of democracy, tolerance and reconciliation.[175]

The formulation of its policy of 'National Reconciliation' in 1956 signified the PCE's renunciation of the use of armed struggle as a means of bringing down the Franco régime. Organised mainly by the PCE, the guerrilla groups, best known as the 'maquis', had represented a pointless loss of life over a number of years. It was necessary to put an end, 'to the painful succession of domestic guerrilla wars and violent incidents that have shaken [*sic*] the last century and half of the history of Spain' (Carrillo and Sánchez Montero, 1977: 18). The cover of the document produced in 1956 is highly significant; it consisted of a map of Spain scattered with expressions such as 'vengeance', 'let's get them', 'one million dead', 'we shall never forget', 'let our guns do the talking', 'revenge', 'crusade', etc., and a hand, which rubbed these expressions out in order to reveal a brilliant and promising sun. It was the twentieth anniversary of 18 July 1936 and the party's Central Committee had decided to issue a document that might take advantage of the divisions they claimed to perceive among the ruling Francoist élite regarding the treatment accorded to the defeated. This document would attempt to establish contact with the new up-and-coming political forces, with those who were dissatisfied with the dictatorship and with the rest of the opposition. The main objective of this new strategy was to establish a common front that would

---

174. Regarding the graffiti that appeared during the Transition, see the book by Pedro Sempere (1977).
175. Declaration by the Spanish Communist Party, June 1956: *Por la Reconciliación Nacional. Por una solución democrática y pacífica del problema español*, 39 pages (PCE Archive).

favour a peaceful transition towards democracy. Time and again, the need to achieve the national reconciliation of all Spaniards and end existing hatreds and desires for revenge was highlighted, in order to reach agreement with former enemies who had become disillusioned with the course the régime had adopted. The document stated that an increasing number of Spaniards wished to overcome the trauma of the Civil War and that Spanish democracy must be founded on amnesty, tolerance and reconciliation. 'Other than national reconciliation, no other course remains except violence' (p.4).

The Communist Party was the first to observe that, since the situation in the mid-1950s was very different to that which had existed two decades earlier, the general understanding it had formerly been impossible to achieve had now become possible. Furthermore, they stressed the idea that the new generations, who had not lived through the war, should not be afflicted by old hatreds and the desire for revenge harboured by their elders. For the PCE, the Civil War had become an enlightening event, albeit one that must never be repeated. It was even explicitly stated that the defeated, in spite of all their sufferings, must never consider promoting the kinds of discrimination that the Francoist régime had subjected them to. The party proposed to establish contact with three political movements that, having initially supported the régime, were now becoming progressively disenchanted with Francoism: the Monarchists, including figures such as Rafael Calvo Serer; the Liberals, including Pedro Laín and Dionisio Ridruejo, and the Christian Democrats. It was necessary to reach agreement with any political force that supported democracy and would be able to contribute to bringing it about peacefully.

The truth is that the PCE had found itself rather isolated in exile, sidelined from the meetings being held by the various opposition groups, and detested by Republicans and Socialists alike. Its attempts to bring down the Franco régime through armed struggle had failed and now it needed to open negotiations with the rest of the opposition forces, paying special attention to those that existed within the country, in order not to be left out of any eventual return to democracy. Its communiqué of 1956 became rather useful during the democratic transition, when, in order to calm the fears the communist movement inspired in certain sections of society, it became necessary to demonstrate that the party had been proposing reconciliation and renouncing vengeance for decades. Carrillo and other leaders stressed that they had proposed the famous policy of 'consensus' and 'reconciliation' of the mid-1970s some twenty years earlier. They were prepared to negotiate on various issues on which they had formerly maintained an intransigent stance. In fact, the greatest difficulties concerning the constitutional handling of certain religious issues and the form of the state were presented by the PSOE, that was able to permit itself a greater degree of inflexibility than the PCE, a party that evoked a series of memories that were considerably less appetising.

Various publications have discussed questions relating to the Atocha murders, and particular attention has focused on the example of moderation the PCE set during the mass demonstration that accompanied the burial of the victims.[176] The same could be said of the process by which the party was legalised and the angry reaction of the political, and especially the military, Right.[177] The Communist Party, for its part, had accepted the red and yellow flag and the Monarchy. It was presented with an opportunity to fulfil the commitment to the Monarchy in the constitutional debates, in which it defended the Crown, citing the constraints and dangers of the situation, and refused to support any of the proposals advocating the staging of a referendum regarding the monarchy/republic dilemma.

In April 1978 the PCE held its first congress in Spain since 1932. Carrillo explained to his party members the difficulties that had been encountered in achieving legal status, mainly due to the fact that, 'in certain sections of the country the idea had become deeply rooted that the war of 1936–1939 had represented the defeat of communism rather than the defeat of democracy. A black legend hung over us that had been created throughout forty years of Francoism' (PCE, 1978: 13–14). Carrillo also emphasised the fact that the moderate, tolerant and serene attitude exhibited by the party since the death of Franco had provided its best democratic credentials, all of which were directly related to an express desire not to repeat the errors of the past.

> We would have preferred to avoid that terrible war which immersed Spain in blood, setting one group of Spaniards against another and leaving deep wounds which have been cauterised very slowly, and our entire policy has, for many years, been inspired by the principle of reconciling all Spaniards and avoiding the repetition of that tragedy at all cost. That has been and continues to be our determined wish. The very experience of those who lived through such events provides the will and the lessons that enable us to work to ensure that it is not repeated. (PCE, 1978: 15)

Nevertheless, Carrillo continued to assert that it was not a question of disowning the heroic struggle the PCE pursued during the Civil War. Rather, it was precisely thanks to this struggle that it had become possible to undertake the peaceful transition to democracy. The party leaders did not renounce the past, as this would provoke rejection by the old party members in exile and at home, but they did stress the importance of creating a new party that looked to the future. It was also pointed out that the form of the state no longer posed a problem, as it had before.

176. Carrillo himself acknowledged that the 'response of the workers, both firm and serene, created a climate that was favourable to the party and helped it to overcome the last pockets of resistance' (PCE, 1978: 14).
177. See the work by Helena Varela (1990).

If the Monarchy continues to play a positive role in the transition, if it respects the people's will and fervently applies the Constitution once it has been passed, the issue of the form of government will lose the dramatic and conflictive significance that it had in other periods of Spanish history, when these premises were not fulfilled. (PCE, 1978: 28–29)

It was in the interests of the PCE to differentiate itself from the PSOE, and it sometimes contrasted the impatience of the PSOE with its own sense of patience. One of the occasions on which it established this comparison was at its Ninth Congress, based on an 'absence of political decision': the postponement of municipal elections until 1979.[178] The historical lesson derived from the negative memory of municipal elections in 1931 lay behind the refusal of the Government to hold these elections at an earlier date. As Carrillo clearly pointed out, after stating that it had been a mistake not to stage these elections before the Constitution was passed:

over these municipal elections hangs the negative memory of certain previous elections, those of 12 April 1931, whose results ushered in the proclamation of the Republic. A certain panic has been witnessed in high circles out of the fear that if the Left were to predominate in urban and industrial centres as it did then, the issue of the form of government would be raised once again. And the PSOE has contributed to this sense of panic by approaching the question of municipal elections as if it entailed a radical inversion of the correlation of political forces... Municipal elections are urgently required. They will decide neither the form of government nor any other political change within the country. (PCE, 1978: 35)

Once again, the experience of the Second Republic emerged as a powerful dissuasive point of reference, which, in this case, helped to delay the staging of a key political event during the Transition.

In spite of this image, the PSOE had a considerable advantage over the PCE: the youthful appeal of its leaders. The PCE had significantly renewed and rejuvenated its ranks, but not to a sufficient extent in the case of its party leaders. Out of a total of 36 members, the average age was 55, which meant they would have been between 14 and 17 years of age during the Civil War. If we do not count the six born after 1936, who accounted for only 16 percent, the average age during the war would have been between 19 and 22 years of age, old enough to have fought in it.[179]

The lesson the PCE had assimilated best was that it must not exercise any kind of pressure regarding those issues that revived memories of the

178. Regarding the importance of silence in politics, see the Stephen Holmes chapter (1988) 'Gag Rules or the Politics of Omission', in Jon Elster and Rune Slagsted (eds.).
179. The age calculations for the leadership of this and other parties were carried out based on the dates of birth that appear in the Albia Collection, in Bilbao, regarding political parties.

Civil War: the form of the state, the flag, the religious issue, municipal elections or street violence. Any allusion to the war in a vengeful sense could be used against it, and it was in the PCE's own interests to free itself of this burden of the past. This approach had a serious electoral cost: it was interpreted by many as being a 'sell-out', a 'reformist' stance. As well as the extreme left, the PSOE also reproached it in this respect. The reconciliation advocated by the PCE meant forgetting the past, but when the Right insisted on recalling the events of Paracuellos, the PCE counterattacked by threatening to stir up memories of Nationalist repression during the war and the postwar period. The PCE's silence on certain matters was in its own interests, but only if it received equal payment in kind.

Alianza Popular was founded by various figures from Spain's reformist right who, in many cases, had held positions of high political responsibility during the Franco period. The percentage of former *procuradores* among its parliamentary members was very high during the first general elections: 81.2 percent (13 out of 16). These two factors helped to arouse the suspicions of a large part of the democratic opposition, who considered this political party to have been formed by undemocratic opportunists who had jumped on the bandwagon of power. Although it was true that some of the most important members of the party had carried out liberalising reforms, such as the Press Law of 1966 introduced by Fraga, the democratic credentials of the party remained rather doubtful.[180] For example, the party's members included Gonzalo Fernández de la Mora, one of the most notorious champions of the former régime.

Alianza Popular displayed a considerable degree of internal dissension, as each group that made up the coalition was headed by a strong and well-known political figure who was reluctant to cede a greater degree of leadership to the rest. Although some of the members were absolutely convinced of the need for democratic reform, others did not take long to reveal their misgivings and ended up leaving the coalition. The most visible leader of the group, Fraga, attempted to convince society of his willingness to engage in dialogue and of his sincere democratising intent. Nevertheless, his rhetoric was sufficiently aggressive and, on occasions, even warlike, for a good part of the country's Right to prefer to place their trust in the younger Unión de Centro Democrático, a party rather less closely associated with the former régime.

The average age of the leaders of Alianza Popular was 54 in 1977, which meant that they were between 13 and 16 years of age during the Civil War. If we exclude Esteruelas, who was born in 1936, the average age during the war would have been between 15 and 18 years of age, which means that the majority experienced the war in the midst of their change from childhood to adolescence, the age at which according to the

---

180. This law was used by the party as one of its main democratic credentials; see Fraga (1977): *Alianza Popular*, Albia, Bilbao.

study by Schuman and Scott (1989), events make the deepest of impressions. What is more, they were old enough for some to have actually fought in the war.

On many occasions, instead of encouraging a sense of trust in the process of change, AP simply emphasised the dangers that it entailed. Its pessimistic predictions, unconditional defence of many Francoist legacies and reluctance to revise past history worked against it in the electoral process. Society needed to know that the party was prepared to place a considerable degree of trust in it, a message the rest of the important parties, especially UCD, were able to convey.

The caution of a large part of the population was justified by certain attitudes that AP displayed once the elections had taken place. The party refused to subscribe to an extended amnesty, an issue that assumed considerable importance during the popular demonstrations of those years. It also reacted angrily to the legalisation of the PCE. It did not wish to sign up to the political section of the Moncloa Pacts that sought to establish certain very basic civil rights and liberties (although it did sign the economic part). In the debate on the Draft Constitution it presented considerable resistance regarding religious issues and refused to accept the inclusion of the term 'nationalities' in the Constitution. In the end, out of a total of 16 AP parliamentary members, three abstained and five voted against the draft, that is to say, 50 percent of the party did not vote in favour of the Constitution, a highly significant percentage.

The AP Programme/Manifesto of 1977 established order, peace and unity of the *Patria* as its main objectives. The party's leaders claimed not to be stuck in the past, however, they talked about the 'Generalísimo' and insisted on preserving the positive legacy of the former régime, and their obsessive anticommunism was self-evident. In the first point of their manifesto they complained about 'excessive concessions to revanchist attitudes that erode peace and order and destroy national unity'.[181] Their stance was highly pessimistic, emphasising the 'risks' of the process, the 'feeling of insecurity' and the threat to 'public order'. They stated that they were not prepared to accept the opinions of those who had made no contribution to the development of Spain over recent decades. They also claimed to reject 'revanchist objectives, the exhibition of resentment, the recourse to physical or verbal violence', whilst announcing that they would oppose 'the legalisation of communist, terrorist or separatist groups', although they offered to enter into talks with all of the democratic groups, 'in the search for peaceful coexistence' (pp.14–17). The Programme concluded with the following, 'we shall serve the Spain of today and tomorrow in a serious and committed desire for reconciliation'

---

181. In the Manifesto/Programme *Qué es Alianza Popular. Federación de ADE, AP, UNE*, Madrid, 1977, p.13 (prior to the elections). The Manifesto came out in October 1976 and the Programme in January 1977.

(p.42). The Right's obsession with what it considered to be 'revanchist', 'resentful' or 'embittered' attitudes was omnipresent in these early years. It feared that the return of the exiles, of the defeated and their ideological heirs, could bring with it a desire for revenge that might lead to political purges. Furthermore, any demand aimed at achieving the rehabilitation of the defeated was viewed with caution and suspicion on the right, as it questioned the ideological assumptions that it had entertained for so many years.

The First National Congress of Alianza Popular took place on 5 and 6 March 1977.[182] The general tone of the speeches made by the leaders of the various groups revealed, first of all, a sense of exaltation of the past, an express acknowledgement of its achievements and a desire for continuation and reform; second, the speeches criticised any break with the past, due to the threat that they claimed it posed, and expressed their rejection of any legalisation of the PCE, a party that was harshly criticised and blamed for the Civil War and the terror of the Republican rearguard. It was stated that the Communist Party had returned from exile with a series of revanchist, destructive and revolutionary attitudes, and the credibility of Euro-communism was scorned. Socialism, they claimed, followed the same path as communism, as did the centre movements, who, through their weakness, had agreed to form a pact with the Marxists. Third, the priorities of AP continued to be peace, stability, order and efficiency. Fourth, the speeches revelled in patriotic feeling, even though they claimed to wish to promote regional differences. Fifth, the memory of the Civil War was employed in black-and-white terms in an attempt to discredit the adversary. According to this line of argument, the failure to maintain the legacy of Francoism entailed a return to that terrible past which must never be forgotten, and represented a renunciation of forty years of glorious history. In spite of the fact that all the speakers claimed to be democrats, not a single criticism was levelled at the former régime. Finally, a rather war-like vocabulary was employed in reference to the party's political adversaries.

In the opening speech at the Congress, Fraga stated the following, 'Whilst others arouse resentment and brandish old grudges, and advocate class wars and regional rivalry, we support the sacred unity of Spain; we propose a strong State, capable of defending order, peace, the law and the national interests of the *Patria*' (p.6). The rhetoric of this speech was rather antiquated at the time, dismissing calls for historical revision on the part of the defeated as a form of revanchism. Several of the speeches that followed were to be even more anachronistic and extremist. Thomas de Carranza described the confrontation between, 'two conceptions of the world that are absolutely and radically incompatible: the humanistic and

---

182.   *I Congreso Nacional de Alianza Popular. Federación de AR, ADE, DS, RD, UDPE, UNE, USP*, Speeches, 5–6 March, Madrid, 1977.

the Christian; the materialistic and the Marxist' (p.9). Laureano López
Rodó stated that

> the Communist Party believes Spaniards can be tricked as if they were chil-
> dren, and it is doing its utmost to brainwash us. But the first thing the
> Communist Party must do is wash its hands, because they are stained with
> blood... Unfortunately, former Communist leaders are once again appear-
> ing before us like characters from a nightmare, with the air – it would be
> ridiculous if it were not sad – of a bunch of resuscitated mummies who still
> have the audacity to pop up again as if Spain were a country inhabited only
> by cowards and the forgetful... We do not wish to see ourselves afflicted by
> a new constitutional epileptic fit in which all things divine and human are
> debated. (pp.27–28)

The final sentence is a clear reference to the founding stage of the Second
Republic. With declarations such as these, it was obvious that any kind of
peaceful understanding between the PCE and AP was going to be
extremely difficult to achieve.

During this First Congress, Fernández de la Mora equated Marxism
with 'terror' and complained that UCD harboured figures who were hid-
ing their past in the most shameful manner. He also highlighted the
importance of the forthcoming elections and recommended that, 'nobody
should view these elections as just a mere procedure; that would be
extremely frivolous, comparable only to the frivolity of certain compatriots in April 1931' (p.37). It was a matter, then, of using the past as a
political weapon and of attempting to influence the electorate by evoking
undesirable memories. Fernández de la Mora offered a somewhat insult-
ing critique of communism and even stated that centrism was a 'fellow
traveller of Marxism' (p.39). Licinio de la Fuente stated that AP had set an
example of moderation compared to, 'those who, whilst flaunting their
desire for agreement are, nevertheless, every day proclaiming all manner
of things that could once again divide and produce confrontation among
Spaniards' (p.53).

Finally, Fraga was the leader entrusted with making the closing speech
at the Congress. In this speech he emphasised that, due to 'historical experience', 'order' and 'ordered coexistence' had assumed priority in Spain. He
praised the past, comparing it to what was being offered by those who
sought, 'a return to 1931, to 1934 or to 1936' (p.64). He placed special
emphasis on the following expressions, that ended up appearing in the
publication in capital letters: 'THE LAMENTABLE PAST of other ages
should teach us prudence in what we do, and remind us that we are also
capable of becoming an anarchic and cruel nation' (pp.64–65). He also
spoke of, 'FRUITFUL PEACE' (p.65), of those who promoted, 'CON-
FRONTATION AMONG MEN AND SOCIAL GROUPS', 'of revenge, of
resentments' (p.66). Finally, he stated that AP represented, 'AN ALTER-
NATIVE FOR ALL SPANIARDS WHO REJECT THE IDEA OF A RED AND

BROKEN SPAIN' (p.66) and he ended with an impassioned patriotic plea in which he referred, on various occasions and in emphatic terms, to 'Spain'.

With the PCE having recently been legalised, the First National Assembly of Nuevas Generaciones de Alianza Popular took place on 17 April 1977.[183] At this meeting the general tone was less pessimistic and anachronistic than at the First National Congress of AP, except when the leaders addressed the meeting. They defended themselves from those who accused them of being nostalgic or fascists and stated that they wished to support reform and moderation. One of the militants of Nuevas Generaciones stated the following: 'we reject the revanchists who obstinately deafen the Spanish people by unnecessarily and groundlessly offending against and humbling our past, forgetting the sentiments of a large proportion of our people, which has nothing to feel ashamed about nor seek absolution for' (p.19). On the other hand, José María Ruiz-Gallardón stated that, 'the slogan of our Federation' is 'focused on change without trauma, without upheavals, ordered change at the lowest possible social cost' (p.26). Towards the end, reference was also made to 'the War of Spain', that sought 'victory over forces such as Marxism and separatism, which represented the break-up of national individuality' (p.82).

In the first public proclamation made by AP after the elections, we can already perceive the adoption of certain modifications regarding both the exposition of the party's principles and objectives, as well as its Programme.[184] The party no longer made reference to the 'Generalísimo', but focused its attention on the King, although it continued to emphasise the need to maintain 'security', 'order', 'peace' and 'tranquillity', contrary to the 'grave danger' threatened at the time by the possibility of 'a swing to the left' (pp.3–4). Towards the end, a series of defensive claims were made that served to distance AP from the extreme right with a view to achieving a greater degree of democratic credibility. The party was aware that its electoral failure was due, in large part at least, to the image of extremism and intransigence it conveyed. It was stated that AP, 'is neither extremist nor reactionary', that, 'its methods are democratic', that it would respect the Constitution that was passed and that it, 'is neither in favour of a coup d'état nor dictatorship', but that it believed that, 'without a strong state, society is set adrift'. The party also advocated the 'reestablishment of a form of coexistence based on mutual tolerance' (p.21). The parties in general tended to be much more cautious when drafting their programmes than in the proclamations they made at their congresses, where they tended to exhibit a more radical and impassioned rhetoric aimed at the militants. Unlike the congresses, none of the AP Programmes of 1977 expressly mentioned the Civil War. The party was aware that this memory

183. *I Asamblea Nacional de Nuevas Generaciones de Alianza Popular, Federación de ADE, UNE y AP*, Speeches and Papers, 17 April, Madrid, 1977.
184. In *Qué es Alianza Popular*, Madrid, 1977 (after the elections of 1977).

was not a pleasant one for society as a whole. In view of the fact that the party had been founded by members of the winning side, a considerable amount of criticism could be aroused that the party felt it would rather not answer in order not to discredit its prodemocracy declarations.

The Second National Congress of Alianza Popular[185] took place on 28 and 29 January 1978. At this congress an attempt was made, in the light of recent experience, to reflect upon the errors that had been committed in 1977 and to decide upon the new strategy to be adopted for the post-constitutional elections. This congress was much more wide-ranging and reflective than the pervious one and the speeches were more carefully prepared. The General Secretary, Manuel Fraga, opened the congress by expressing his great disgust at the criticisms and insults suffered by AP throughout the entire period. He admitted that many mistakes had been made and that many people had condemned the way that the campaign had been carried out. Nevertheless, he blamed the party's failure in the elections on the conspiracy of the left-wing and centre parties against AP and on the effects of the electoral system. He stated that the party's predictions had been accurate, given that public order had deteriorated and the Marxist Left and separatist groups had shown the excesses of which they were capable. The most delicate issue was that of the autonomous regions, given that this question held the key to all the rest. In this respect, the use of the term 'nationalities' was criticised. With regard to the 'revolutionary' and 'Marxist' Left he stated that 'every day we can hear calls from some platform or other for revenge, along with the raking up of everything that has occurred in recent years' (p.7). Fraga also stated that in AP there was no place for resentment, hate or rancour, feelings that he claimed to find in the left-wing and separatist movements.

The political address at this Second Congress made reference to the separatist and federalist tendencies of the history of Spain, against which it was necessary to protect the country.[186] However, a large part of the speech seemed to be directed at the most recalcitrant section of AP, imploring it to understand the need to change the image of the party, thus enabling it to gain democratic legitimacy. In this respect, it was stated that:

> it is necessary to throw out useless nostalgia... We cannot commit the error that on other occasions has led us to a mistaken sense of loyalty...we must act within the bounds of the political game, and respecting its rules... Neither can we accept, naturally, that Spain should return to the violent swings that destroyed and ruined us between 1810 and 1936; neither do we believe that a country can undertake revolutionary breaks with the past in each generation... If our efforts should fail, we will have fulfilled our duty, that of

185. *II Congreso Nacional de Alianza Popular*, 28 and 29 January, Madrid, 1978.
186. Among the criticisms levelled at separatism it was stated that, 'one cannot play with ideas and words that should be forgotten forever, and that led us to the catastrophe of civil war under our two Republics' (p.12).

attempting, by all possible means, to ensure that Spain emerges from the present crisis, without experiencing a new civil confrontation... However, it would be totally irresponsible at the present time to adopt stances that return us to the tragic climate of tension of the 1930s. (pp.10–11)

The address also stated that it understood the 'undoubted patriotism' of the extreme right, whilst recalling the fact that 'any kind of radicalisation is counterproductive' (p.12). The speech made by Félix Pastor Ridruejo, President of the Partido Unido de AP, was even more eloquent in this respect, by taking this self-criticism much further. The past should not be, 'the reference-point for the Spanish Right', and neither does the Right, 'have a monopoly over patriotism'. Alianza Popular should also have a utopian concept of society and believe 'that peace is found on the road to freedom and democracy' (pp.123–124).

Nevertheless, the speech offered by the President of the Federación de Partidos de AP, Silva Muñoz, was not self-critical in the slightest, revealing, in this sense, the internal divisions that existed within the party. Silva Muñoz even complained about the use of the word 'autonomy', due to the grave 'risks' it entailed, and appealed to unity 'so that the revolutionary period may not break out which is welling up on the horizon with all the thunder and lightning of an approaching storm, but...may be diverted' (p.131).

As we can see, over time the rhetoric employed by Alianza Popular became progressively milder, in spite of the fact that the memory of the Second Republic and the Civil War tended to be everpresent in party speeches. As well as placing emphasis on matters such as the Armed Forces, religion and, above all, national unity, peace and order, the party also began to talk about reconciliation, and certain measures were passed that required the partial rehabilitation of the defeated, although not always based on unanimous approval.

The Constitution

The attitude of the four parties, when analysed throughout the course of the constitutional debates was, in general, moderate and based on a willingness to talk. During moments of high tension, of which there were many, a voice of moderation was always heard attempting to reconcile opposing parties, or at least play down the significance of the contested issue.[187] These

187. The highest level of tension I have found during the course of my research was witnessed during a debate on law and order between Carrillo and Fraga, rather than in the constitutional debates [DSC No.43 (Plenary Sessions), pp.1598–1629, 23/12/1977]. This was, possibly, the first occasion on which the dirty linen of the Civil War was explicitly aired. The session in which this debate occurred and in which the past was used as a political weapon, dealt with the possibility of setting up an Inquiry Committee in order to investigate the recent confrontations that had taken place in Málaga and Tenerife between a number of demonstrators and the police and had ended with two deaths. To the considerable disgust of UCD, the debate as to whether such as Committee should be set up or not, turned into a bitter debate on the issue of public order, a matter that had been scheduled for debate a year later (8/11/1978).

conciliatory gestures, supported by the weight of the events whose repetition all the parties wished to avoid, were quite effective and usually ended with a mutual offering of apologies.

The Cortes provided a forum for the debate and approval of the Constitution and it was where the main leaders were given an opportunity to show their promised willingness to negotiate. It is true that the search for consensus presided over most of the process, especially as it proceeded and all the parties began to become impatient at the amount of time being devoted to debating the Constitution. For many, however, this very devotion and the thoroughness with which the Constitution was established provided a guarantee of success, a promising sign in the light of historical memory, which recalled the disastrous Republican constitution that had been passed so precipitately. This was the crucial reference-point the parties sought to avoid, taking precedence over certain specific questions relating to the substance of the Constitution. It was constantly stated that the Constitution should not become a 'trágala' – an imposed constitution – which had so often been the case throughout Spanish constitutional history. Instead, this was to be the Constitution of consensus and agreement. For the first time in Spanish history, after having been accepted by the vast majority of the political groups,[188] the Constitution was submitted to popular verdict and was accepted by 87.8 percent of the voters. Once it had been approved by referendum, there were many who stated that the Civil War had finally ended. This was the Constitution of reconciliation, designed to address all Spaniards in equal manner.[189]

It is worth pausing a moment to consider the term 'trágala', due to its symbolic importance regarding the constitutional design process. Some of those who supported the passing of the Constitution of Cádiz, in 1812, chanted a song known as the 'trágala', (literally 'swallow it'), that symbolised the otherwise ephemeral delight of the supporters of the liberal constitution at having been able to impose it on their adversaries, those whom the song labelled as 'servilones' or 'the servile', as they were in favour of absolute monarchy. The liberals shouted 'trágala' or 'swallow it' in reference to the Constitution, boasting of the considerable displeasure it caused the monarchists. This is precisely what all the parties sought to avoid during the Transition. None of the constitutions witnessed throughout the history of Spain had been established by taking into account all of the most important political trends. On the contrary, many had been the result of conditions forcibly imposed by one section of society on another, with the most obvious and perhaps most flagrant case – given

188. In the Chamber of Deputies there were only 6 votes against and 14 abstentions, whilst in the Senate there were 5 votes against and 8 abstentions.
189. The Constitution of 1978 was to produce a very different feeling in the Cortes to that which the Republican Constitution had produced in its day. In reference to this, a politician as notable as Niceto Alcalá-Zamora had stated: 'it is a Constitution that invites civil war' (quoted by Rubio Cabeza, 1985: 13).

that it referred to a democracy – being that of the Republican Constitution of 1931. The task now was to produce a constitution that would be valid for 'all Spaniards'. This was the goal, repeated time and again, not only of the constitutional process itself, but of the entire Transition. The King wished to be the king of 'all Spaniards' and the Constitution had to be accepted by 'all Spaniards'. The aim was to settle the differences between the victors and the defeated once and for all so that a new régime that was prepared to afford equal treatment to all citizens under the law, might have a chance of succeeding.

It is interesting to observe who the historical characters of constitutional consensus were, which politicians and thinkers were cited throughout the debates and in what context. In many cases, these references entailed the symbolic rehabilitation of figures who had been systematically reviled and abused by Francoism, such as Manuel Azaña,[190] Antonio Machado,[191] Miguel de Unamuno,[192] Julián Besteiro,[193] Niceto

190. Although it is true that Azaña had proved to be quite intransigent at certain crucial moments under the Republic, and that his prewar memoirs reveal a character of considerable arrogance, his attitude changed completely in the face of war. The texts he wrote throughout the three years of war are deeply moving and express the repentance and despair of somebody who believed he may have been able to help prevent the tragedy. Both *La Velada en Benicarló* of 1939, as well as *Los españoles en guerra* and *Causas de la guerra de España* (the last two published by Crítica in 1977 and 1986, respectively), reveal this change of attitude. His writings represent the ultimate expression of the 'three p's': 'Peace, Pity and Pardon'. He also wrote the following: 'it is a profound mystery, in this country of surprises and unexpected reactions, as to what might occur the day that Spaniards, in peace, come to consider what they have done during the war' (Azaña, 1977: 128–129). The speeches that he made in those war years expressed a sense of sadness and impotence at not being able to stop the spiral of violence unleashed in the rearguard.

191. Antonio Machado was a sad symbol of the two Spains, for while he produced propaganda with his writings for the Republican cause, his brother Manuel did the same for the opposing cause. Antonio wrote those famous verses that assured the 'españolito', newly-born to this world, that one of the two Spains would harden his heart and, in the midst of war, those impassioned verses dedicated to Líster that began thus: 'If my pen were your captain's pistol, happily would I die'. Antonio Machado ended up fleeing to France with his mother and died, like Azaña, shortly afterwards.

192. Miguel de Unamuno, like many other intellectuals who began by supporting the Republic, experienced considerable disenchantment with the régime that had led him to sympathise, at a very early stage, with the National Movement. Shortly afterwards, however, the much-related incident took place in which Unamuno, attending an event to support the military uprising in Salamanca, heard the atrocious and violent words expressed by the head of the Legion, Millán Astray. It is said that this outburst of warlike exaltation horrified him to such an extent that he got up and shouted, '¡venceréis, pero no convenceréis!', 'you will win, but you will not convince!'

193. Besteiro, who had been the Speaker of the Constituent Cortes of the Second Republic, symbolised the moderate socialist trend that had been unable to gain control of the PSOE. He was one of the most commonly cited politicians during the constitutional debates, providing a positive reference-point for both sides. It was the legacy of Besteiro, as we have already mentioned, that was finally taken up by the PSOE during the Transition, at the expense of the legacies of Largo Caballero and Indalecio Prieto.

Alcalá-Zamora[194] and others. Regionalist leaders were also cited, especially Catalans such as Francesc Cambó, Lluís Companys, Enric Prat de la Riba, Pedro Rahola, Francisco Pi y Margall and Francesc Maciá. On the other hand, figures who had been harshly criticised by the former régime also came to light whose legacy few were keen to take up at that time as that legacy had not been at all conciliatory, such as Francisco Largo Caballero, Luis Araquistain, José María Gil-Robles, Alejandro Lerroux and others. Neither José Calvo-Sotelo nor José Antonio Primo de Rivera were cited either, although for very different reasons. José Ortega y Gasset was quoted, however, in order to indicate the validity of his arguments with regard to the first third of the century and his current obsolescence. The Spain of today, it was stated, was quite different to the one Ortega described in a tone that, on many occasions, was quite pessimistic. Xavier Arzalluz, for example, stated that an effort should be made to prove Ortega wrong when he wrote that 'Spaniards were condemned to a painful coexistence'.[195] To the same end he also quoted Ortega Heribert Barrera when he said that 'Spain, instead of being an arena of incessant bloody and bloodless conflicts, could become a normal country'.

Few commentators have summarised the conciliatory spirit of the Constitution better than Francisco Rubio Llorente (1984) through his contribution to the *Diccionario del Sistema Político Español* ('Dictionary of the Spanish Political System'). Llorente begins by referring to the recent history of Spain in order to explain both the process and the substance of the Constitution. In fact, he goes as far back as the Civil War in order to explain the traumatic break that was witnessed in Spanish constitutionalism. The text of 1978 represented a negation of both the war and the régime it gave rise to. Based on this perspective, he explains the exceptional historical significance of the Constitution of 1978:

> Throughout our history, except for the relative exception of 1876, the idea of Constitution that has generally prevailed has been decision-based and our Constitutions have, therefore, been founded on the decision taken by the victorious political party. The constitutional arrangements of 1978 were based, on the other hand, on compromise. (Rubio Llorente, 1984: 120)

It was also stated that Spain had chosen the partnership-based route in order to carry out the Transition instead of a majority-based approach adopted by the Second Republic. In the partnership-based route:

194. The moment at which Alcalá-Zamora was forced to stand down as President of the Republic is generally seen as marking the beginning of the end, as the definitive consolidation of radicalism and intransigence. Throughout the Transition it was requested that his ashes be brought back to Spain, along with those of other Heads of State of this century who were compelled to die in exile: Alfonso XIII and Azaña (BOC.S No.24, p.318, 27/10/1977; DSS No.9 (Plenary Sessions), pp.265–268, 19/10/1977).
195. DSC No. 59, 5/5/1978 (Session No. 1 of the Committee for Constitutional Affairs and Public Freedoms).

the binding decision is not simply the decision of the majority, but that which is accepted by all the groups whose peaceful coexistence in peaceful rivalry within a society has, for each of the participants, greater value than any of the specific ends or objectives of their own programmes or ideology. (Rubio Llorente, 1984: 121)

Public Opinion

Francoist attempts at socialisation witnessed varying degrees of success and some of the régime's measures turned out to be complete failures. Nevertheless, Francoism was undoubtedly successful in conveying a fear of disorder in the streets, a mistrust of Spaniards' capacity to deal with problems in a civilised manner, and even a fear of their own freedom and that of others. Furthermore, many came to believe, after the negative propaganda that was produced about political parties, that they were incapable of settling their differences peacefully and that any resumption of party politics would once again create the intransigent attitudes and conflicts that had contributed to undermining the Second Republic.

The success of Francoist socialisation was based on its capacity to create an association between the memory of the war and certain phenomena such as the reestablishment of 'inorganic' democracy and all that it entails. The creation of this sense of distrust, partly inculcated by the régime and partly produced by the negative experience of the Republican period itself, was reflected in the values that, according to surveys at the time, Spaniards considered to be priorities. The surveys carried out on a national scale in 1966,[196] 1975 and 1976 by the Institute of Public Opinion (IOP), have been cited in many publications. In all of them, priority in Spain was given to the political value of 'peace', taking precedence even over 'justice', 'freedom' and 'democracy' (Aguilar, 1986: 78; Juliá, 1992: 48).

Various other studies have emphasised the preeminence of these values, such as the analysis produced by Eduardo López Aranguren and Antonio López Pina (1976). Another famous study regarding the political culture of the Spanish during the later years of Francoism and the Transition was produced by Rafael López Pintor (1982). Pintor was one of the first to underline the relative autonomy of the political sphere, although he acknowledged the conditioning factors of the economic and social context. In this respect, he based most of the evidence for his argument on the surveys that were essentially, although not exclusively, designed by the Institute of Public Opinion (IOP), a body that would later become the Centre for Sociological Research (CIS).[197] Thus, although in 1981 he

196. Institute of Public Opinion: 'Cuestiones de actualidad política', published in the *Revista Española de Opinión Pública*, No. 9, July–September, 1967, pages 185–227. On page 211 it tells us that 49 percent of men and 67 percent of women preferred peace to any other value, including justice and freedom.

197. The author held management posts in both institutions. At the IOP he was the Head of the Technical Department, whilst at the CIS he held the post of Director General.

named one of his best known articles 'Los Condicionamientos Socioe-conómicos de la Acción Política en la Transición Democrática', the conclusions that were based on the results of his surveys made reference to the relative independence of politics with regard to the context in which the Transition took place. The figures revealed quite consistently that society's main concern was to sustain development and peace, ahead of ensuring freedom and democracy, although in time the valuation of freedom and democracy would, progressively catch up with that of development and peace (López Pintor, 1982).[198] No surveys exist for the historical period of the Second Republic, but we might surmise that the scale of values would have been very different as a result of the social polarisation and ideological radicalisation that existed in the 1930s.

The fear that the war would be repeated and the fervent desire that it should never occur again were also clearly reflected in other public opinion studies. The FOESSA Reports, carried out by a private body, and those that were contributed by sociologists such as Juan J. Linz and Amando de Miguel, played a crucial role in the early sociological studies of the time and in the interpretation of many of the key aspects of the Transition. The most important Reports for our study include those of 1966, 1970, 1975 and 1975–1981.[199] The first hardly contains any kind of political analysis, a logical failing at that time and one that the second report sought to remedy. As it turned out, censorship removed Chapter 5 from the 1970 Report, entitled 'Vida Política y Asociativa', this being the first rigorous analysis of Spanish political life within the bounds of the many limitations of the period.[200]

This censored chapter remarked that, 'it is surprising how all the groups have accepted *the preeminence of 'order and peace' as political objectives*...they are explicit within the Spanish context and are placed before any other kind of positive or specific attainment' (Fundación FOESSA, 1970: 72).[201] These values assumed greater importance the older the

---

198. Be that as it may, it is possible to surmise that, had the political transition not taken place in the midst of an economic crisis, the priorities of the Spanish would have focused, at least to a greater extent than they did, on political freedoms rather than on economic and social security. The mere possibility of losing the social and economic stability that had been acquired meant that political issues were pushed into the background for a time. The seriousness of the crisis and the extensive degree of social mobilisation it produced, activated the memory of the Second Republic, during which a grave international crisis also negatively affected social and economic stability.

199. Fundación FOESSA (1966), (1970), (1975) and (1981).

200. Fortunately, this chapter circulated relatively freely in photocopied form and many people had access to it. As an anecdotal note, we might mention that the Contents Page of the 1970 Report actually includes this chapter, although the Report does not, providing yet further proof of the ineffective censorship of the waning years of the Franco period.

201. Whenever I refer to Chapter 5 of this Report, I shall cite the page numbers that correspond to the photocopies that were made available to me at DATA.

respondents were,[202] the lower their professional qualifications, their education level and their level of income. They were especially prominent among women who fell within the category of housewife.[203] For example, 84 percent of unskilled labour gave precedence to the two values of order and peace over the rest. Even among those who preferred other more democratic values, such as the professionals of Madrid, the level of acceptance of order and peace came to 50 percent. With regard to the political objectives of the next few years, peace achieved a prominent position, especially among certain groups (the survey on which this Report was based was not carried out on a national scale, so its results must be interpreted with considerable caution). Here we find a much clearer social division between young respondents, especially university graduates and the most highly-qualified professionals, who preferred justice, freedom and development (democracy still appeared way down the list) and the older and less-qualified majority of the population, who continued to opt for peace, although also for justice (see Tables 5.62, 5.63 and 5.74 of the Report).

Housewives and professionals were also asked 'whether they thought the fact that young people had not lived through the war was beneficial or detrimental'. In this case, the differences between the two groups, very significant in relation to other issues, were reduced, with 82 percent of the housewives and 79 percent of the professionals stating that it was beneficial. The Report reads as follows: 'This is not exactly the "heroic" attitude which, in its day, characterised the "Empire generation". On the contrary, it reveals an attitude of generational disillusionment and disenchantment and even perhaps a kind of bad conscience about what the war meant for all' (Fundación FOESSA, 1970: 74–75). The analysis of this question concluded with the following paragraph: 'Maybe the most positive statement that can be made after a century and a half of civil wars, is that the attitudes of Spaniards seem to indicate a wish to definitively end this collective trauma that has made history among us' (Fundación FOESSA, 1970: 76).

In the 1975 Report, the tendencies outlined above remained: 80 percent of the population claimed to agree with the following statement:

202. This generational break was more abrupt and far-reaching in Spain due to the dividing-line of the Civil War. As this chapter stated, 'historical chance has made the "generational conflict" especially intense in Spain, separating the generations who "waged war" (Civil War of 1936–39) from those who did not and, recently, those who lived through the hard postwar years and those who arrived later on' (Fundación FOESSA, 1970: 74).

203. See Tables 5.47 and 5.48 of Chapter 5 of the Report. We must bear in mind that this question was posed to certain groups. If the Spanish population as a whole had been asked the question, we might expect the average level of acceptance of the values 'order and peace' to have increased. Table 5.48 even exclusively takes account of professionals in Madrid.

'The most important thing in Spain is to maintain order and peace' (Fundación FOESSA, 1975: 1185). Only the option referring to social justice, that stated that it was necessary to reduce the differences between the rich and the poor, achieved a higher level of agreement, although only by one percentage point (81 percent). The maintenance of order and peace, however, was perfectly compatible with more democratic affirmations, although when considered individually they achieved a lower degree of consensus.[204] Thus, only 67 percent agreed that many things in Spain needed to be changed, whilst 60 percent believed that things were not going very well because Spaniards lacked a voice. The defence of peace and order as priority values was, once again, stronger among women, stronger in certain regions (see Table 1.12.B of the Report), in the smallest municipalities, among the lowest income earners, among persons with the lowest levels of education, among the oldest members of society and among those with the lowest professional qualifications.

Finally, the 1975–1981 Report included a series of questions surveyed in 1978 that attempted to evaluate the errors and successes of Francoism. The highest level of agreement, between 76 percent and 79 percent, focused on three criticisms of the Franco régime which referred to social inequality, repression and the lack of freedom. The fourth item in this ranking of agreement indicated a positive rating for Francoism, because 'there was order and peace'. In effect, 68 percent of the population agreed with this statement, although this was also the point that produced the greatest split – of 79 points – between potential extreme-left and extreme-right voters. Only 19 percent of the potential extreme-left voters agreed with this affirmation, whilst 98 percent of the potential extreme-right group subscribed to this view. In relation to other questions concerning the performance-based legitimacy of the régime, 64 percent believed that 'Spain had developed economically' and the same percentage accepted that 'Almost all Spaniards lived better, although some had benefited more than others' (Fundación FOESSA, 1975–1981: 590). In conclusion, although a critical evaluation of Francoism clearly predominated by 1978, in relation to issues such as lack of freedom, repression and inequality, this opinion was perfectly compatible with a benevolent interpretation based, essentially, on what we have called performance-based legitimacy, reflected in aspects such as peace, development and the general rise in the standard of living. Both attitudes existed side by side quite happily during the Transition, and whether the balance was to finally incline towards one side or the other depended, above all, on the capacity of the recently-born democracy to maintain peace and development.

204. The aggregated options of 'reformism/social demands' achieved a higher degree of consent than those of 'conservatism/authoritarianism'. However, on an individual basis, as we stated above, the second most preferred option, with 80 percent approval, was 'order and peace'.

If the values of order, peace and stability were preferred to justice, freedom and democracy – at least during the latter years of Francoism and the early years of the Transition – this was because Spaniards were not prepared to sacrifice the well-being and peace that had been obtained in exchange for opportunities to obtain freedom that had uncertain consequences. If democracy proved to be capable of maintaining the achievements of the former régime, and even building upon them, without disturbing social peace, it would be welcome. However, until it was capable of demonstrating this, the majority of Spaniards were not prepared to trust in it blindly. This explains why it was not until the uncertainties of the Transition were progressively resolved and the population began to realise it was capable of living together peacefully in freedom and that the political parties had a radically different outlook to those that had existed during the Republican period in terms of their willingness to negotiate and their spirit of compromise, that the scale of values began to change around. As Spaniards began to value justice, freedom and democracy more, they conceded less value to peace and order, since they were able to see that these were guaranteed under the new régime which, as we mentioned above, was to prove that it was capable of giving more for less, especially after the passing of the Constitution. It all depended on whether the values 'peace' and 'democracy' were perceived in terms of a dilemma in which the acceptance of one entailed the renunciation of the other. Until the two values were seen to be compatible – a perception that only began to gain general acceptance after 1977 – a cautious and distrustful perception of this dilemma continued to predominate.[205]

After 1978, a clearly democratic culture would help to consolidate institutions and stabilise the process. The legitimacy of the political system would no longer be called into question, not even in the face of the various economic and political vicissitudes the country was to witness.

205. In addition to the studies on political culture cited here there are many others devoted to the same period, which encompass the years from the end of Francoism to 1978. Among others, we find all of the studies produced by the Confederación Española de Cajas de Ahorros, entitled *Estructura Social de España. Comentario Sociológico*; the study by Juan Díez Nicolás (1976) entitled *Los Españoles y la Opinión Pública*; Publication No. 1 produced by the CIS (1977) entitled *La Reforma Política. La Ideología de los Españoles*; the article by Rafael López Pintor (1981) entitled 'El Estado de la Opinión Pública Española y la Transición a la Democracia'; the article by Peter McDonough, Antonio López Pina and Samuel M. Barnes (1980) entitled 'The Spanish Public in Political Transition'; the book by José Enrique Rodríguez Ibañez (1987) entitled *Después de una Dictadura: Cultura Autoritaria y Transición Política en España*. Finally, we might make special mention of the doctoral thesis produced by Mariano Torcal (1995) entitled 'Actitudes políticas y participación política en España. Pautas de cambio y continuidad. Universidad Autónoma de Madrid'.

CONCLUSION

With this book I have attempted to underline the important role that is played by the historical memory of groups, as well as the subsequent lessons that are derived from that memory, in processes of political change. In the first chapter I tried to delimit and define the concept of 'historical memory' and to link it to the concept of 'political learning'. The extraordinarily complex nature of memory, which is subject to constant changes and ongoing fluctuations that may not always be consciously controlled, may have contributed to the lack of clear and concise definitions within academic literature. These unconscious and fluctuating elements of historical memory are the ones that distinguish it most from 'historical consciousness'.

The study of collective memory requires an analysis of those media through which memory is transmitted and preserved, of those moments that activate a certain kind of memory and not others, and of the kinds of lessons that tend to be linked to the activation of this memory. The concepts of 'memory' and 'learning' are inseparable, which obviously does not mean that the appropriate lessons are always derived from past experiences.

According to the view proposed in this research, the past is not immutable, but neither can it be created nor recreated freely from the present. History may be perverted to an extraordinary degree under some régimes, as was the case with the history of the Civil War under the Franco régime, but alternative readings always emerge as authoritarian régimes become more liberal and, in particular, as democracies are instated or reinstated.

It is true that the interests of the present oblige us to focus on one particular reading of the past and not another, but this does not mean that the history of countries can be shaped at will. What does sometimes happen is that the present determines the lessons that must be drawn from the past, as occurred with the history of the Civil War during the Spanish Transition. However, as we can see from the experience of the countries of Central and Eastern Europe, a large part of the effort made by the communist régimes to create a new history for these countries was in vain, given that the societies developed a considerable capacity for resisting any manipulation of their history that went against their existing deeply-rooted traditions and individual memories of the events based on personal experience.

The learning process, whenever it occurs, is based on the existence of a prior experience of a specific event. This experience is normally a personal one, although sometimes it consists of the experience of others. It tends to be more difficult to make use of other countries' experiences than one's own, although this does not mean that some countries are not able to learn from the rest when undergoing similar processes of change by means of what is known in sociology as the 'demonstration effect'.

The memories that are most susceptible to being preserved by the community tend to be both heroic as well as tragic; including those that evoke the founding myths of a country (for example, wars of independence), as well as those moments in which a serious rupture of the national identity occurs (for example, civil wars). Both kinds of events tend to be subjected to mythical elaboration on the part of the state, as well as by the protagonists themselves.

In nondemocratic countries, the historical discourse is either solely created by official authorities or is subject to a more or less exhaustive censorship, or both factors operate at the same time. It is crucial to control the past in order to gain legitimacy in the present, and this is why dictatorships go to such lengths to impose an historical view that is most favourable to them through a variety of sources: the media, text books, monuments, ceremonies, literature, etc.

Francoism, as we have seen, initially attempted to legitimise its government by basing its rule on victory in war. In the beginning, the political authorities refused to acknowledge that it was a civil war they had fought, given that this point of reference established a rather precarious foundation for legitimisation. It was claimed that the war had been fought in order to free the country from a foreign invader and from international communism, establishing a clear historical parallel, which became explicit on many occasions, with the Spanish War of Independence against the French invader at the beginning of the nineteenth century. The initial rhetoric of the régime was packed with references to a warlike struggle replete with heroic and mythical overtones.

When civil war provides the founding basis of a régime, it is very difficult to gain a sufficiently solid sense of legitimacy unless this is reinforced with other complementary elements. The Franco régime maintained its political authority during the early years through a strategy of exhaustive repression and control, which indicates the lack of faith that the régime had in its own legitimacy. The progressive distancing in time from this founding moment happened to coincide, however, with a period of economic liberalisation that would allow the country to benefit from the wave of prosperity that swept through the Western world in the 1960s. This was when the discourse of the régime ceased to focus on the war and began to cede greater importance to what was known at that time as the 'Estado de obras' or 'State of Public Works'.

It is true that, from the very beginning, Francoism had maintained a certain social rhetoric, inherited from the Falangist tradition – a rhetoric that was highly paternalistic and supposedly favourable to the interests of the working class. We should not forget that, among other matters relating to the Welfare State, the Social Security system was created during this period. In the 1970s, economic growth brought about a considerable rise in general standards of living (in spite of the fact that the benefits of this sudden improvement were not fairly distributed), which was experienced at very close hand by the majority of Spaniards. This economic development, along with the progressive international recognition of the Franco government, which had been underway for a number of years, meant that the régime enjoyed a considerable degree of legitimacy derived from its performance. This led the heroic version of the war to be gradually replaced by a tragic reading. The war was no longer considered to have been necessary, but something that, unfortunately, nobody had been able to avoid.

Once the régime considered itself to be more firmly entrenched, it permitted certain movements towards political and religious liberalisation to take place, such as those witnessed during the second half of the 1970s. The Franco régime considerably reduced its initial levels of repression and some of its support groups, especially Opus Dei and its followers, began to advocate a neutral ideological climate that relegated the Civil War to a supporting role, because, by that time, much more solid elements existed to provide the foundations for power.

In this book we maintain, however, that Francoism would never have been able to entirely renounce its original source of legitimacy and, in fact, never did. This was because a considerable part of the population had fought on the Francoist side during the Civil War and was not prepared to forget its victory, nor share the fruits of victory with the enemy, as many continued to consider the defeated side to be. Any renunciation of the founding moment of Francoism or any sincere reconciliation with the adversary would have brought an end to a régime that, for many years, had based its repressive actions on the exaltation of war and hatred of the enemy. Finally, reconciliation would have inevitably meant a return to democracy, as indeed later occurred.

After the death of Franco, although Spaniards might not have achieved a unanimous view regarding what had actually occurred during the Civil

War, they did reach agreement concerning the lessons to be derived from such a traumatic experience. Democracies are able to withstand coexisting heterogeneous memories considerably better than dictatorships, although it is important that a majority consensus be achieved regarding the lessons of history within that society. During the Transition it was concluded that the two sides who had fought against each other in the war had been equally to blame for the barbaric events that ensued. No side was any guiltier than the other, given that unjustifiable atrocities had been committed in both occupation zones. Society was able to come to terms with past brutality through the general sense of blame that was apportioned by interpreting the war as a form of 'collective insanity'. The principal lesson that emerged during the Transition was based on the idea of 'never again'. Never again must such events be allowed to occur, and all political, social and economic movements must contribute to ensuring that they do not. Only in this context can we understand the deep and complex underpinnings of the general consensus that existed during the Transition right up until the passing of the Constitution in December 1978, as well as the national reconciliation policy that was pursued from the very beginning of the Transition.

During this period, a highly intense dramatic memory existed of a series of events that had occurred some forty years earlier. More than seventy percent of the Spanish population had not lived through the Civil War. However, this is exactly the kind of experience that is conveyed from generation to generation, becoming part of a transmitted collective memory, which is still very much alive and influential.

One of the main hypotheses of the first chapter of this book maintains that memories, that are normally latent, are activated by a process of association, and in this sense I have attempted to discover the reasons why the memory of the Civil War emerged so strongly during the Transition. When society perceived, consciously or unconsciously, and more or less correctly, certain similarities between the situation that existed in the 1970s and that of the 1930s, the historical memory of the war reemerged.

After Franco's death Spanish society had existed for nearly forty years without any democratic institutions, as they had been entirely removed from political life. Thus, when parties, trade unions, elections and parliamentary life gradually began to appear, many Spaniards had never experienced such institutions directly.

These institutions were not, however, new in the history of Spain. A minority of Spaniards had experienced them during the Second Republic, having been defeated, along with their institutions, during the Civil War. Francoism condemned and denigrated the Republican experience throughout its entire existence. It blamed it for the break-up of the country, the infiltration of Soviet communism into political power, anticlerical violence and social disorder. These views were not shared by a considerable proportion of the Spanish population. Nevertheless, in spite of this, during the 1970s many Spaniards viewed the Republican period in a critical light, albeit for quite different reasons.

The Republic's weaknesses and excesses were criticised, including the intransigent attitude of the majority with regard to the minority, the imposition of a constitutional text that was not founded on consensus, its military and religious policies and other issues. For many, the failure of the Second Republic, which led to the Civil War, was due, in large measure, to the errors committed by the Republicans and to an institutional structure that magnified these mistakes, combined with an international context that was unfavourable to the consolidation of a weak and incipient democracy. Thus, the memory of the downfall of the Republican régime was associated with the experience of the Civil War. It was logical then, that during the Transition, when the various institutions that had existed during the Republican period were revived (such as parties, trade unions, Parliament, the Constitution), Spaniards should evoke this failed experience as well as its disastrous outcome. This is what we mean when we claim that historical memory is activated by means of association.

As a consequence, Spanish society made every effort to avoid repeating the errors that had led to the downfall of the Second Republic. Any repetition of the institutional design of the Second Republic was almost superstitiously avoided. This is the best explanation for why a monarchic form of government was preferred to a republican model, a proportional electoral system was chosen instead of a majority-based system, why a bicameral rather than a unicameral parliament was established and why a uniform territorial arrangement was introduced for the entire state.

The past defined what was and what was not possible during the political transition, as, at a time so full of uncertainty and caution as this, any clue as to what might occur should certain institutions be established was viewed with considerable trepidation. History, naturally, can also provide a source of legitimacy and stability in democratic régimes. Likewise, every effort was made to ensure that the various political adversaries did not turn the past into a political weapon, an eventuality which, many feared, could have made peaceful dialogue impossible among the heirs of the ideological opponents in the Civil War. It was a question of forgetting the resentments of the past, of 'wiping the slate clean' for all, of retaining the lessons of history without stirring up the past, in order to be able to build a future of democratic peace and harmony together. This logic applied especially to political life, given that at other levels, such as the cultural and academic spheres, the war only became a popular topic after 1978.

The recourse to silence entailed, for many, certain renunciations, which eventually caused some frustration. However, the ultimate objective, which all parties appeared to pursue, was achieved: the peaceful consolidation of democracy in Spain – something which, until that time, had not been possible. The evil curse that some believed the country to be under was finally broken, a curse that had always prevented the harmonious coincidence of peace with a free and democratic society, of tolerance with economic prosperity. All of this enabled the Spanish Transition to become the basic founding myth of democracy and its recollection to constitute a political resource of considerable importance.

BIBLIOGRAPHY

Abish, Walter (1980): *How German Is It - Wie Deutsch Ist Es: A Novel*, W.W. Norton & Company.

Academia de Sargentos (1893; 1943): *Manual para las clases de tropa*, Hernando.

Aguado Bleye, Pedro (1929): *Compendio de historia de España*, Vol. 1, Eléxpuru Hermanos.

Agüero, Felipe and Mariano Torcal (1993): 'Élites, factores estructurales y democratización. (Una discusión de aportes recientes en la literatura)', *Revista de Estudios Políticos*, no.80, pp.329–350.

Aguilar Fernández, Paloma (1995): *La memoria histórica de la Guerra Civil española (1936–1939): un proceso de aprendizaje político*, Instituto Juan March, Madrid.

——, (1996): 'Romanticisme i maniqueisme en la guerra civil: de *Tierra y Libertad* a *Libertarias*', *L'Avenç*, no.204, pp.66–70.

Aguilar Fernández, Susana (1986): 'La legitimidad del sistema democrático en la transición política española', Degree Dissertation, Faculty of Political Sciences and Sociology, Universidad Complutense de Madrid.

Alarcón, Juan (1977): *Resumen político de la paz de Franco (1 de abril 1939 - 20 de noviembre 1975)*, Vassallo de Mumbert, Madrid.

Alcalá-Zamora, Niceto (1936): *Los defectos de la Constitución de 1931*, Imprenta de R. Espinosa, Madrid.

Allardt, Erik (1964): 'Patterns of Class Conflict and Working Class Consciousness in Finnish Politics', in Erik Allardt and Yrjö Littunen: (eds.) *Cleavages, Ideologies and Party Systems*, Westermark Society, Helsinki.

Allardt, Erik and Yrjö Littunen (eds.) (1964): *Cleavages, Ideologies and Party Systems*, Westermark Society, Helsinki.

Álvarez Lastra, Manuel and Eleuterio de Orte Martínez (1955): *Formación del espíritu nacional*, NOS, Madrid.

Álvarez de Miranda, Fernando (1985): *Del «contubernio» al consenso*, Planeta, Barcelona.

Álvarez, José L. (1978): *España desde dentro*, Espasa-Calpe, Madrid.

Álvarez Junco, José (1994): 'España: el peso del estereotipo', *Claves*, no.48, pp.2–10.

Anson, Luis María (1994): *Don Juan*, Plaza & Janés, Barcelona.

AP (1977): *I Asamblea Nacional de Nuevas Generaciones de Alianza Popular. Federación de ADE, UNE y AP*, speeches and papers of 17 April 1977, Madrid.

——, (1977): *I Congreso Nacional de Alianza Popular. Federación de AR, ADE, DS, RD, UDPE, UNE, USP*, speeches and papers of 5–6 March 1977, Madrid.

——, (1977): *¿Qué es Alianza Popular?* (after the elections of 15/6/1977), Madrid.

——, (1977): *¿Qué es Alianza Popular? Federación de ADE, AP, UNE* (before the elections of 15/6/1977), Madrid.

——, (1978): *II Congreso Nacional de Alianza Popular*, 28–29 January 1978, Madrid.

ArósteguI, Julio (coord.) (1988): *Historia y memoria de la Guerra Civil*, 3 vols., Junta de Castilla y León, Valladolid.

Asián Peña, José L. (undated): *Nociones de historia*, Bosch, Barcelona.

Ayuntamiento de Bechi (1963): *XXV Años de paz en Bechi*, Castellón.

Azaña, Manuel (1939; 1981): *La velada en Benicarló*, Río Saja, Madrid.

——, (1939; 1982): *Los españoles en guerra*, Crítica, Barcelona.

——, (1939; 1986): *Causas de la guerra de España*, Crítica, Barcelona.

Baena del Alcázar, Mariano and José María García Madaria (1979): 'Élite franquista y burocracia en las Cortes actuales', *Sistema*, no.28, pp.3–50.

Baldwin, Peter (1990): *Reworking the Past. Hitler, the Holocaust, and the Historian's Debate*, Beacon Press, Boston.

Ballesteros Beretta, Antonio (1942): *Síntesis de historia de España*, Salvat, Barcelona.

Beltrán, Miguel (1985): *Los funcionarios ante la reforma de la administración*, CIS/Siglo XXI, Madrid.

——, (1994): *Política y administración bajo el franquismo: La reforma administrativa y los planes de desarrollo*, Estudio/Working Paper no.53 del Centro de Estudios Avanzados en Ciencias Sociales, Instituto Juan March.

Benet, Juan (1976): *Qué fue la Guerra Civil*, La Gaya Ciencia, Barcelona.

Beneyto, Antonio (1977): *Censura y política en los escritores españoles*, Plaza & Janés, Barcelona.

Beramendi, Justo G. and Ramón Máiz (comps.) (1991): *Los nacionalismos en la España de la Segunda República*, Siglo XXI, Madrid.

Bergson, Henri (1939; 1990): *Matière et mémoire*, Presses Universitaires de France, Paris.

——, (1957; 1987): *Memoria y vida*, Alianza, Madrid.

Bermeo, Nancy (1986): *The Revolution within the Revolution. Workers' Control in Rural Portugal*, Princeton University Press, Princeton.

——, (1987): 'Redemocratization and Transition Elections: A Comparison of Spain and Portugal', *Comparative Politics*, Vol. 19, no.2, pp.213–231.

——, (1992): 'Democracy and the Lessons of Dictatorship', *Comparative Politics*, Vol. 24, no.3, pp.273–291.

Bernecker, Walter L. (1994): 'De la diferencia a la indiferencia. La sociedad española y la Guerra Civil (1936/39–1986/89)', in Francisco López Casero et al.: *El precio de la modernización. Formas y retos del cambio de valores en la España de hoy*, Iberoamericana, Madrid.

Bertrand de Muñoz, Maryse (1982): *La Guerra Civil española en la novela. Bibliografía comentada*, 3 Vols., Porrúa, Madrid.

Blume, Norman (1977): 'Sedes: An Example of Opposition in a Conservative Authoritarian State', *Government and Opposition*, Vol. 12, pp.351–366.

Bolloten, Burnett (1961; 1975): *El gran engaño*, Caralt, Barcelona.

Borrajo, Efrén (1959; 1965): *Política social*, Doncel, Madrid.

Bourdillon, Hilary (ed.) (1992): *History and Social Studies. Methodologies of Textbook Analysis*, Swets and Zeitlinger, Amsterdam.

Boyarin, Jonathan (1994): *Remaking Memory. The Politics of Timespace*, University of Minnesota Press, Minneapolis.

Boyd, Carolyn P. (1989): 'History in the Schools and the Problem of Spanish Identity', in R. Herr and J.H.R. Polt (eds.), *Iberian Identity. Essays on the Nature of Identity in Portugal and Spain*, University of California, Berkeley.

Braga da Cruz, Manuel (1989): 'El modelo político salazarista', in Hipólito De la Torre Gómez (coord.): *Portugal y España en el cambio político (1958–1978)*, Universidad Nacional de Educación a Distancia, Centro Regional de Extremadura, Mérida.

Bravo-Tellado, A. (1976): *Los mutilados del Ejército de la República*, Gráficas Clarcilla, Madrid.

Brenan, Gerald (1960; 1977): *El laberinto español: antecedentes sociales y políticos de la guerra civil*, Ruedo Ibérico, Paris.

Brossat, Alain et al. (1990; 1992): *En el Este, la memoria recuperada*, Edicions Alfons el Magnànim, Valencia.

Brown, Archie and Jack Gray (1977; 1979): *Political Culture and Political Change in Communist States*, MacMillan Press, London.

Bruneau, Thomas C. (1983): 'Popular Support for Democracy in Post-revolutionary Portugal: Results from a Survey', in Lawrence S. Graham and Douglas L. Wheeler: *In Search of Modern Portugal. The Revolution and its Consequences*, University of Wisconsin Press, Madison.

Bruneau, Thomas C. and Alew MacLeod (1986): *Politics in Contemporary Portugal. Parties and the Consolidation of Democracy*, Lynne Rienner Publishers, Boulder.

Bustelo, Francisco et al. (1976): *Partido Socialista Obrero Español*, Avance, Barcelona.

Cabrero, Juan A. (1949): *Historia de la cinematografía española. 1896–1949*, Gráficos Cinema, Madrid.

Calleja Guijarro, Tomás and María Carmen Gutiérrez Ruiz (1971): *España y sus hombres. Sociedad*, Edelvives, Zaragoza.

Calvo, Cándida (1992): 'La fiesta pública durante el franquismo. Instrumento socializador del tradicionalismo en Guipúzcoa, 1936–1951', I Encuentro de Investigadores del Franquismo, Barcelona, (unpublished).

Calvo-Sotelo, Leopoldo (1990): *Memoria viva de la transición*, Plaza & Janés, Barcelona.

Cámara Villar, Gregorio (1984): *Nacional-catolicismo y escuela. La socialización política del franquismo (1936–1951)*, Hesperia, Jaen.

Cambio 16 (1983): 'Encuesta Guerra Civil', September–October, issues 616–619.

Campmany, Jaime (1967; 1971): *Formación político-social y cívica*, Alamena, Madrid.

Campos Matos, Sérgio (1990): *História, mitologia, imaginário nacional. A história no curso dos liceus (1895–1939)*, Livros Horizonte, Lisbon.

Carr, Edward H.(1964; 2nd edition 1987): *What is History?*, Penguin Books, London.

Carr, Raymond and Juan P. Fusi (1979; 1985): *Spain. Dictatorship to Democracy*, Allen & Unwin, London.

Carrero Blanco, Luis (1974): *Discursos y escritos 1943–1973*, Instituto de Estudios Políticos, Madrid.

Carrillo, Santiago (1967): *Nuevos enfoques a problemas de hoy*, Éditions Sociales, Paris.

——, (1974): *Demain L'Espagne*, Seuil, Paris.

——, (1976): *¿Qué es la ruptura democrática?*, La Gaya Ciencia, Barcelona.

——, (1977): *Eurocomunismo y Estado*, Crítica, Barcelona.

——, (1983): *Memoria de la transición*, Grijalbo, Barcelona.

——, (1993): *Memorias*, Planeta, Barcelona.

Carrillo, Santiago and Simón Sánchez Montero (1977): *Partido Comunista de España*, Albia, Bilbao.

Castellet, J.M. (1976): *Literatura, ideología y política*, Anagrama, Barcelona.

Cenarro, Ángela (1992): 'La reina de la hispanidad: fascismo y nacionalcatolicismo en Zaragoza, 1939–1945', I Encuentro de Investigadores del Franquismo, Barcelona, (unpublished).

Centro de Investigaciones sobre la Realidad Social (CIRES), 'Cultura política', June 1991.

Chapaprieta, Joaquín (1971): *La paz fue posible. Memorias de un político*, Ariel, Barcelona.

Chilcote, Ronald H., Stylianos Hadjiyannis, Fred A. López III, Daniel Nataf, Elizabeth Sammis (1990): *Transitions from Dictatorship to Democracy. Comparative Studies of Spain, Portugal and Greece*, Taylor and Francis Group, New York.

Chueca, Ricardo (1983): *El fascismo en los comienzos del régimen de Franco. Un estudio sobre FET-JONS*, CIS, Madrid.

Chull Shin, Doh (1994): 'On the Third Wave of Democratization: A Synthesis and Evaluation of Recent Theory and Research', *World Politics*, Vol. 47, no.1, pp.135–170.

CIS (1977): *La reforma política: la ideología política de los españoles*, Madrid.

Clark, J.C.D. (1990): 'National Identity, State Formation and Patriotism: the Role of History in the Public Mind', *History Workshop*, no.29, pp.95–102.

Código Penal y legislación complementaria, Civitas, Madrid, 1985.

Collicott, Sylvia L. (1990): 'What History Should We Teach in Primary Schools?', *History Workshop*, no.29, pp.107–10.

Colomer, Josep María (1990): *El arte de la manipulación política*, Anagrama, Barcelona.

Conde, Francisco Javier (1941): *Escritos y fragmentos políticos*, Vol. I, Instituto de Estudios Políticos, Madrid.

Confederación Española de Cajas de Ahorros (various years): *Estructura social de España. Comentario sociológico*, Barcelona.

Connerton, Paul (1989): *How Societies Remember*, Cambridge University Press, Cambridge.

Cortes Españolas (1971): *La labor de las Cortes en el año 1969*, Vol. II, Madrid.

Cotarelo, Ramón (1990): 'La Jefatura del Estado en el sistema político español', *Debate Abierto*, no.2, pp.23–39.

Cotarelo, Ramón (comp.) (1992): *Transición política y consolidación democrática. España (1975–1986)*, CIS, Madrid.

Cotterell, Arthur (1988): *Diccionario de mitología universal*, Ariel, Barcelona.

Cuesta, Josefina (1993): *Historia del presente*, Eudema, Madrid.

Cuevas Puente, Antonio (dir.) (1950): *Anuario cinematográfico hispanoamericano. 1939-50*, Servicio de Estadística del Sindicato Nacional del Espectáculo, Madrid.

Davallon, Jean et al. (1993): *Politique de la mémoire*, Presses Universitaires de Lyon, Lyon.

De Areilza, José María (1983): *Cuadernos de la transición*, Planeta, Barcelona.

De Asís, Agustín (1963): *Manual de derecho natural*, Vol. I, Granada.

De Blas, Andrés (1991): 'El debate doctrinal sobre la autonomía en las Constituyentes de la II República', Inaugural Lecture for the 1991/92 Course of the Universidad Nacional de Educación a Distancia, Madrid.

De Bustos, Eugenio (1966): *Vela y ancla*, Doncel, Madrid.

De Carreras Serra, Francisco (1973): 'La legislación electoral de la Segunda República Española'. Doctoral Thesis, Faculty of Law, Universidad Autónoma de Barcelona, 3 Vols.

De Esteban, J. and Luis López Guerra (1977): *La crisis del Estado franquista*, Labor, Barcelona.

De Federico, Jesús (undated): *Historia de España (síntesis completa de la evolución histórica de la península)*, Mariana Pineda, Madrid.

De Guzmán, Eduardo (1982): *Historias de la prensa*, Penthalon, Madrid.

Del Águila, Rafael and Ricardo Montoro (1984): *El discurso político de la transición española*, CIS, Madrid.

De La Cierva, Ricardo (1966): *Cien libros básicos sobre la Guerra Civil*, Publicaciones Españolas, Madrid.

——, (1967): *Los documentos de la primavera trágica*, Secretaría General Técnica, Sección de Estudios sobre la guerra de España, Madrid.

——, (1994): *Carrillo miente*, Fénix, Madridejos.

De La Torre Gómez, Hipólito (coord.) (1989): *Portugal y España en el Cambio Político (1958–1978)*, Universidad Nacional de Educación a Distancia, Centro Regional de Extremadura, Mérida.

Delegación Nacional de Provincias (1961): *Texto de las orientaciones que se consideran son valor permanente*, Secretaría General del Movimiento, Madrid.

Delegación Nacional de la Sección Femenina (1967): *Formación político-social*, Sección Femenina, Madrid.

——, (1970): *Formación político-social y cívica*, Sección Femenina, Madrid.

——, (1971): *Formación político-social y cívica*, Almena, Madrid.

Delfattore, Joan (1992): *What Johnny Shouldn't Read. Textbook Censorship in America*, Yale University Press, London.

De Madariaga, Salvador (1958): *Spain: A Modern History*, Praeger, New York.

De Puelles Benítez, Manuel (1986): *Educación e ideología en la España contemporánea*, Labor, Barcelona.

Diamandouros, Nikiforos (1986): 'Regime Change and the Prospects for Democracy in Greece: 1974–1983', in Guillermo O'Donnell et al. (eds.): *Transitions from Authoritarian Rule. Southern Europe*, Johns Hopkins University Press, Baltimore.

Díaz De Villegas, José (1964): 'Nuestra cruzada no fue, jamás, una guerra civil', *Guión*, Vol. 266, pp.25–29.

Díaz-Plaja, Fernando (1979): *Si mi pluma valiera tu pistola. Los escritores españoles en la Guerra Civil*, Plaza & Janés, Barcelona.

Díez Nicolás, Juan (1976): *Los españoles y la opinión pública*, Editora Nacional, Madrid.

Di Febo, Giuliana (1988): *La santa de la raza. Teresa de Ávila: un culto barroco en la España franquista (1937–1962)*, Icaria, Barcelona.

——, (1992): 'Scoperta e conquista nei manuali di storia nella Spagna franchista (1938–1955)', *Dimensioni e problemi della ricerca storica*, no.2, pp.63–88.

Dirección General de Correos y Telégrafos (1989): *Catálogo oficial de sellos. España*, Madrid.

Durkheim, Emile (1973): *On Morality and Society: Selected Writings*, University of Chicago Press, Chicago.

Ediciones del Movimiento (1962): *Contra la paz de España. Del pacto de San Sebastián (agosto de 1930) al pacto de Múnich (junio de 1962)*, Prensa Gráfica, Madrid.

——, (1966): *Victoria de la paz*, Madrid.

——, (1967): *Ley orgánica, movimiento y democracia*, Madrid.

——, (1968): *Estrategia social de la paz*, Madrid.

——, (1969): *A los treinta años de paz*, Madrid.

——, (1973): *Paz y progreso del pueblo español*, Madrid.

——, (1974): *La paz, patrimonio del pueblo español*, Madrid.

Ellwood, Sheelagh (1987): 'Spanish Newsreels 1945–1975: The Image of the Franco Regime', *Historical Journal of Film, Radio & Television*, Vol. 7, no.3, pp.225–238.

Equipo Jaime Vera (1977): *La alternativa socialista del PSOE (algunas contribuciones)*, EDICUSA, Madrid.

Evans, Richard J. (1989): *In Hitler's Shadow*, Pantheon Books, New York.

Exhibition of posters «España en Paz» (1964): *Viva la paz*, Madrid.

Fanjul, Juan M. (1970): *Dos años de procurador en Cortes por las familias de Madrid*, Artes Gráficas, Madrid.

Fernández, Antonio, Monserrat Llorens and Rosa Ortega (1975): *Historia contemporánea*, Vicens-Vives, Barcelona.

Fernández, Carlos (1983): *Paracuellos del Jarama: ¿Carrillo culpable?*, Argos Vergara, Barcelona.

Fernández-Carvajal, Rodrigo (1969): *La Constitución española*, Editora Nacional, Madrid.

——, (1970): *La sociedad y el Estado*, Doncel, Madrid.

Fernández de Castro, Ignacio and José Martínez (1963): *España hoy*, Ruedo Ibérico, Paris.

Fernández de la Mora, Gonzalo (1965; 1986): *El crepúsculo de las ideologías*, Espasa-Calpe, Madrid.

Fernández Delgado, Javier et al. (1982): *La memoria impuesta. Estudio y catálogo de los monumentos conmemorativos de Madrid (1939–1980)*, Ayuntamiento de Madrid.

Fernández-Miranda, Torcuato (1960): *El hombre y la sociedad*, Doncel, Madrid.

Ferrando Badía, Juan (1980): 'La Monarquía parlamentaria actual española', *Revista de Estudios Políticos*, Vol. 13, pp.7–44.

Ferrero, Guglielmo (1988): *El poder. Los genios invisibles de la ciudad*, Tecnos, Madrid.

Ferro, Marc (1981; 1990): *Cómo se cuenta la historia a los niños en el mundo entero*, Fondo de Cultura Económica, Madrid.

Fishman, Robert (1990 A): *Working-Class Organization and the Return to Democracy in Spain*, Cornell University Press, Ithaca.

——, (1990 B): 'Rethinking State and Regime: Southern Europe's Transition to Democracy', *World Politics*, Vol. XLII, no.3, pp.422–440.

Fitzgerald, Frances (1980): *America Revised. History Schoolbooks in the Twentieth Century*, Vintage Books, New York.

Fontana, Josep (ed.) (1986): *España bajo el franquismo*, Crítica, Barcelona.

Fraga Iribarne, Manuel (1958): 'El articulado de la Ley Fundamental de 17 de mayo de 1958', *Arbor*, no.40, pp.515–522.

——, (1961; 1964): *Estructura política de España. La vida social y política en el siglo XX*, Doncel, Madrid.

——, (1961): *Organización de la convivencia*, Acueducto, Madrid.

——, (1965): *Horizonte español*, Editora Nacional, Madrid.

——, (1971): *El desarrollo político*, Bruguera, Madrid.

——, (1973): *Legitimidad y representación*, Grijalbo, Barcelona.

——, (1976): *España en la encrucijada*, Adra, Madrid.

——, (1977): *Alianza Popular*, Albia, Bilbao.

——, (1980): *Memoria breve de una vida pública*, Planeta, Barcelona.

Fraga Iribarne, Manuel, Juan Velarde Fuertes and Salustiano Del Campo Urbano (dirs.) (1974): *La España de los años 70*, 3 Vols., Moneda y Crédito, Madrid.

Franco Salgado-Araujo, Francisco (1976): *Mis conversaciones privadas con Franco*, Planeta, Barcelona.

Fraser, Ronald (1979): *Recuérdalo tú y recuérdalo a otros*, 2 Vols., Crítica, Barcelona.

Frutos, Eugenio (1959): *Convivencia humana*, Doncel, Madrid.

Fuentes Quintana, Enrique and Juan Velarde Fuertes (1964; 1968): *Política económica*, Doncel, Madrid.

Fueyo, Jesús (1964): 'Desarrollo político y orden constitucional', conference given at the Instituto de Estudios Jurídicos.

Fundación FOESSA (1966): *Informe sociológico sobre la situación social de España*, Euramérica, Madrid.

——, (1970): *Informe sociológico sobre la situación social de España*, Euramérica, Madrid.

——, (1975): *Informe sociológico sobre la situación social de España*, Euramérica, Madrid.

——, (1981): *Informe sociológico sobre el cambio político en España: (1975–1981)*, Euramérica, Madrid.

Gagnon, Serge (1982): *Man and his Past. The Nature and Role of Historiography*, Harvest House, Montreal.

Gallagher, Tom (1983): *Portugal. A Twentieth-Century Interpretation*, Manchester University Press, Manchester.

Gallego-Díaz, Soledad and Bonifacio de la Cuadra (1989): *Crónica secreta de la Constitución*, Tecnos, Madrid.

Garagorri, Paulino (1970): *Introducción a Ortega*, Alianza, Madrid.

García Canales, Mariano (1991): *La monarquía parlamentaria española*, Tecnos, Madrid.

García Crespo, Clementina (1983): *Léxico e ideología en los libros de lectura de la escuela primaria (1940–1975)*, Ediciones Universidad de Salamanca, Salamanca.

——, (1985): 'La ideología del franquismo en los libros de lectura escolares. El componente religioso', *Documentos Didácticos*, no.56, pp.115–26.

García Delgado, José L. and José María Serrano Sanz (1992): 'Economía', in Manuel Tuñón De Lara et al., *Historia de España*, Vol. X**, *Transición y democracia (1973–1985)*, Labor, Barcelona.

García Escudero, José María (1978): *Primera apertura: diario de un director general*, Planeta, Barcelona.

García Martínez, Eladio (1941): *La enseñanza de la historia en la escuela primaria*, Espasa-Calpe, Madrid.

García Serrano, Rafael (1964): *Diccionario para un macuto*, Editora Nacional, Madrid.

——, (1980): *La paz ha terminado. Los «dietarios personales» de 1974 y 1975*, Planeta, Barcelona.

García Venero, Maximiano (1963): *Santiago Alba. Monárquico de razón*, Aguilar, Madrid.

García-Pelayo, Manuel (1970): *Burocracia y tecnocracia*, Alianza, Madrid.

Germani, Gino (1970): 'Political Socialization of Youth in Fascist Regimes: Italy and Spain', in Samuel P. Huntington and Clement H. Moore, *Authoritarian Politics in Modern Society. The Dynamics of Established One-Party Systems*, Basic Books, New York.

Gil Robles, José María (1968): *No fue posible la paz*, Ariel, Barcelona.

Gillis, John R. (ed.) (1994): *Commemorations. The Politics of National Identity*, Princeton University Press, Princeton.

Giménez Caballero, Ernesto (1943): *España nuestra*, Vicesecretaría de Educación Popular, Madrid.

Gironella, José María (1966): *Ha estallado la paz*, Planeta, Barcelona.

Gómez Pérez, Rafael (1986): *El franquismo y la iglesia*, RIALP, Madrid.

Gómez Mardones, Inmaculada (1980): 'No-Do: El mundo entero (menos España) al alcance de todos los españoles', *Tiempo de Historia*, no.66, pp.30–47.

González Cuevas, Pedro C. (1989): 'Gonzalo Fernández de la Mora y la «legitimación» del franquismo', *Sistema*, no.91, pp.83–105.

González, Felipe (1976 A): 'La unidad de los socialistas', *Sistema*, no.15, pp.45–51.

——, (1976 B): *¿Qué es el socialismo?*, La Gaya Ciencia, Barcelona.

González, Felipe et al. (1976 C): *Socialismo es libertad. Escuela de verano del PSOE 1976*, EDICUSA, Madrid.

González, Felipe and Alfonso Guerra (1977): *Partido Socialista Obrero Español*, Albia, Bilbao.

González Navarro, Francisco (1977): *La nueva Ley Fundamental para la Reforma Política*, Servicio Central de Publicaciones de Presidencia del Gobierno, Madrid.

González Seara, Luis (1962): 'En torno a unos textos de formación política de la editorial Doncel', *Revista de Estudios Políticos*, no.121, pp.251–54.

Graham, Lawrence S. and Douglas L. Wheeler (1983): *In Search of Modern Portugal. The Revolution and its Consequences*, University of Wisconsin Press, Madison.

Granja, José Luis de la (1981): 'Autonomías regionales y fuerzas políticas en las Cortes constituyentes de 1931', *Sistema*, no.40, pp.79–100.

Grimá Reig, Juan M. (1959): *Historia. Edades moderna y contemporánea*, López Mezquida, Valencia.

Gubern, Román (1986): *1936–1939: La guerra de España en la pantalla*, Filmoteca Española, Madrid.

Gunther, Richard (1989): 'Leyes electorales, sistemas de partidos y élites: el caso español', *Revista Española de Investigaciones Sociológicas*, no.47, pp.73–106.

Gunther, Richard and Roger A. Blough (1980): 'Conflicto religioso y consenso en España: historia de dos constituciones', *Revista de Estudios Políticos*, no.14, pp.65–109.

Gunther, Richard, Giacomo Sani and Goldie Shabad (1986): *Spain after Franco. The Making of a Competitive Party System*, University of California Press, Berkeley.

Habermas, Jurgen (1989): *The New Conservatism*, Polity Press, Cambridge.

Halbwachs, Maurice (1925; 1975): *Les cadres sociaux de la mémoire*, Presses Universitaires de France, Paris.

——, (1950; 1980): *The Collective Memory*, Harper, New York.

——, (1971): *La topographie légendaire des évangiles en Terre Sainte*, Presses Universitaires de France, Paris.

Hall, Peter (1990): *Policy Paradigms, Social Learning and the State: The Case of Economic Policy-Making in Britain*, Estudio/Working Paper no.4 del Centro de Estudios Avanzados en Ciencias Sociales, Instituto Juan March.

Haro, Juan, José A. Álvarez, Ignacio Cal and Carmen González (1981): 'La guerra civil en los textos de bachillerato (1938–1978).' *Historia 16*, no.63, Vol. 6, pp.107-16.

Hermet, Guy (1985): *Los católicos en la España franquista*, CIS, Madrid.

Hernández, Marta (1976): *El aparato cinematográfico español*, Akal, Madrid.

Herz, John H. (ed.) (1982): *From Dictatorship to Democracy. Coping With the Legacies of Authoritarianism and Totalitarianism*, Greenwood Press, Westport.

Heywood, Paul (1995): *The Government and Politics of Spain*, MacMillan, Houndmills.

Hobsbawm, Eric J. (1972): 'The Social Functions of the Past', *Past and Present*, Vol. 55, May, pp.3-7.

Hobsbawm, Eric J. and Terence Ranger (eds.) (1987): *The Invention of Tradition*, Cambridge University Press, Cambridge.

Holmes, Stephen (1988): 'Gag Rules or the Politics of Omission', in Jon Elster and Rune SLAGSTAD (eds.): *Constitutionalism and Democracy*, Maison des Sciences Press, New York.

Holsti, Ole R. and James N. ROSENAU (1980): 'Does Where you Stand Depend on When You Were Born? The Impact of Generation on Post-Vietnam Foreign Policy Beliefs', *Public Opinion Quarterly*, no.4, pp.1–22.

Huneeus, Carlos (1985): *Unión de Centro Democrático y la transición a la democracia en España*, CIS, Madrid.

Huntington, Samuel P. (1991): *The Third Wave. Democratization in the Late Twentieth Century*, University of Oklahoma Press, London.

Ibán, Iván C. (coord.) (1987): *Iglesia católica y regímenes autoritarios y democráticos (experiencia española e italiana)*, Editoriales de Derecho Reunidas, Madrid.

Ibárruri, Dolores (1985): *Memorias de Dolores Ibárruri*, Planeta, Barcelona.

Instituto de Estudios Africanos (1964): *Los veinticinco años de paz en la España africana*, CSIC, Madrid.

Instituto Nacional de Estadística (1980): *Evolución de la población española en el período 1961–1978*, Madrid.

IOP (1967): 'Cuestiones de actualidad política', *Revista Española de Opinión Pública*, no.9, pp.185–227.

Jefatura Provincial del Movimiento (1961): *Artículos premiados en el concurso periodístico convocado con motivo del XXV aniversario del alzamiento nacional*, Almería.

Jervis, Robert (1976): *Perception and Misperception in International Politics*, Princeton University Press, Princeton.

Jiménez De Parga, Manuel (1960; 1968): *Los regímenes políticos contemporáneos*, Tecnos, Madrid.

Judt, Tony (1992): *Past Imperfect. French Intellectuals, 1944–1956*, University of California Press, Berkeley.

Juliá, Santos (1992 A): 'Sociedad y política', in Manuel Tuñón De Lara et al., *Historia de España*, Vol. X**, *Transición y democracia (1973–1985)*, Labor, Barcelona.

——, (1992 B): 'Franco: la última diferencia española', *Claves*, no.27, Nov., pp.16–21.

Jung, Carl G. (1959; 1980): *The Collected Works of C.G. Jung*, Vol. 9, Part 1, *The Archetypes and the Collective Unconscious*, Routledge, London.

Kammen, Michael (1993): *Mystic Chords of Memory. The Transformation of Tradition in American Culture*, Vintage, New York.

Kurth, John (1977): 'Political Parallelisms in Southern Europe Since 1815', Paper prepared for delivery at the Conference on Southern Europe, Columbia University, New York, 21–23 March.

La Porte, María Teresa (1992): *La política europea del régimen de Franco (1957–1962)*, Ediciones Universidad de Navarra, Pamplona.

Lannon, Frances (1987): *Privilegio, persecución y profecía. La Iglesia católica en España 1875–1975*, Alianza, Madrid.

Licklider, Roy (1993): *Stopping the Killing. How Civil Wars End*, New York University Press, New York.

——, (1995): 'The Consequences of Negotiated Settlements in Civil Wars, 1945–1993', *American Political Science Review*, no.89, pp.681–690.

Lijphart, Arend et al. (1988): 'A Mediterranean Model of Democracy? The Southern European Democracies in Comparative Perspective', *West European Politics*, Vol. 11, no.1, pp.7–25.

Linz, Juan J. (1973): 'Opposition in and Under an Authoritarian Regime: the Case of Spain', in Robert A. Dahl (ed.): *Regimes and Oppositions*, Yale University Press, New Haven.

——, (1974): 'Una teoría de régimen autoritario. El caso de España', in Manuel Fraga Iribarne et al.: *La España de los años 70. El Estado y la política*, Vol. 3, Tomo 1, Moneda y Crédito, Madrid.

——, (1978): *Crisis, Breakdown and Reequilibration*, Johns Hopkins University Press, Baltimore.

——, (1979 A): 'Europe's Southern Frontier: Evolving Trends Toward What?', *Daedalus*, Vol. 108, no.1, pp.175–209.

——, (1979 B): *El sistema de partidos en España*, Narcea, Madrid.

——, (1987): 'Innovative Leadership in the Transition to Democracy and a New Democracy: The Case of Spain', A draft paper prepared for discussion at the Conference on 'Innovative Leadership and International Politics' of the Leonard Davis Institute for International Relations, Hebrew University, Jerusalem, June 8–10.

——, (1991): 'Church and State in Spain from the Civil War to the Return of Democracy', *Daedalus*, Vol. 120, no.3, pp.159–178.

Lipset, Seymour Martin (1959): *Political Man*, Doubleday, New York.

Llamazares, Julio A. (1979): *La lentitud de los bueyes*, Institución Fray Bernardino de Sahagún, León.

Lomax, Bill (1983): 'Ideology and Illusion in the Portuguese Revolution: The Role of the Left', in Lawrence S. Graham and Douglas L. Wheeler: *In Search of Modern Portugal. The Revolution and its Consequences*, University of Wisconsin Press, Madison.

López Pintor, Rafael (1981): 'El Estado de la opinión pública española y la transición a la democracia', *Revista Española de Investigaciones Sociológicas*, no.3, pp.7–47.

——, (1982), *La opinión pública española del franquismo a la democracia*, CIS, Madrid.

López Rodó, Laureano (1991): *Memorias. Años decisivos*, Plaza & Janés/Cambio 16, Barcelona.

López Pina, Antonio and Eduardo L. Aranguren (1976): *La cultura política de la España de Franco*, Taurus, Madrid.

Losada, Juan C. (1990): *Ideología del ejército franquista*, Istmo, Madrid.

Lowenthal, David (1985; 1988): *The Past is a Foreign Country*, Cambridge University Press, Cambridge.

——, (1989): 'The Timeless Past: Some Anglo-American Historical Preconceptions', *Journal of American History*, Vol. 75, pp.1263–1280.

Lühr, Volker (1990): 'Berlín y otros lugares', *Revista de Occidente*, no.112, pp.9–29.

Lummis, Trevor (1987): *Listening to History*, Hutchinson, London.

Madalena Calvo, José I. et al. (1988): 'Los lugares de la memoria de la Guerra Civil en un centro de poder: Salamanca, 1936–39', in Julio Aróstegui (coord.): *Historia y memoria de la Guerra Civil*, 3 Vols., Junta de Castilla y León, Valladolid.

Maier, Charles S. (1988): *The Unmasterable Past*, Harvard University Press, Cambridge.

Mainer, José-Carlos (1992): 'Cultura', in Manuel Tuñón De Lara et al., *Historia de España*, Volume X**, *Transición y democracia (1973–1985)*, Labor, Barcelona.

Malefakis, Edward (1992): *Southern Europe in the 19th & 20th Centuries: An Historical Overview*, Estudio/Working Paper no.35 del Centro de Estudios Avanzados en Ciencias Sociales, Instituto Juan March.

Mannheim, Karl (1952): *Essays on the Sociology of Knowledge*, Routledge, London.

Manzanares Beriain, Alejandro (1957): *Tu patria*, Hernando, Madrid.

Maravall, José María (1975): 'Political Power and Student Radicalism. A Study of Student Radical Politics and Leaders from 1940 to 1970'. Doctoral Thesis, St. Anthony's College, Oxford University.

——, (1978): *Dictadura y disentimiento político*, Alfaguara, Madrid.

——, (1982; 1985): *La política de la transición*, Taurus, Madrid.

——, (1994 A): 'The Myth of the Authoritarian Advantage', *Journal of Democracy*, Vol. 5, no.4, pp.17–31.

——, (1994 B): *Economías y regímenes políticos*, Estudio/Working Paper no.59 del Centro de Estudios Avanzados en Ciencias Sociales, Instituto Juan March.

Maravall, José María and Julián Santamaría (1986): 'Political Change in Spain and the Prospects for Democracy', in Guillermo O'Donnell et al.: *Transitions From Authoritarian Rule. Southern Europe*, Johns Hopkins University, London.

March, James G. and Johan P. Olsen (1989): *Rediscovering Institutions. The Organizational Basis of Politics*, The Free Press, New York.

Marks, Shula (1990): 'History, the Nation and Empire: Sniping from the Periphery' *History Workshop*, no.29, pp.111–120.

Marrero, Juan A. (1972): *Descubriendo España*, S.M., Madrid.

Marsal, Juan F. (1979): *Pensar bajo el franquismo*, Península, Barcelona.

Martínez-Risco Daviña, Luis (1991): 'O ensino da historia no bacharelato franquista (período 1936–1951). A propagacion do ideario franquista a través dos libros de texto'. Doctoral Thesis, Universidad de Santiago.

Maxwell, Kenneth (1982): 'The Emergence of Portuguese Democracy', in John Herz: *From Dictatorship to Democracy. Coping with the Legacies of Authoritarianism and Totalitarianism*, Greenwood Press, Westport.

——, (1986): 'Regime Overthrow and the Prospects for Democratic Transition in Portugal"', in Guillermo O'Donnell et al.: *Transitions From Authoritarian Rule. Southern Europe*, Johns Hopkins University Press, London.

Mayordomo, Alejandro and Juan M. Fernández Soria (1993): *Vencer y convencer. Educación y política. España 1936–1945*, Universitat de València, Valencia.

McDonough, Peter, Antonio López Pina and Samuel M. Barnes (1980): 'The Spanish Public in Political Transition', *British Journal of Political Science*, Vol. 11, pp.49–79.

Mellado Prado, Pilar (1988): *La responsabilidad política del gobierno en el ordenamiento español*, Chamber of Deputies, Monograph no.12 Madrid.

Méndez-Leite, Fernando (1975): *Historia del cine español*, Jupey, Madrid.

Meynaud, Jean (1967): *La democracia en Grecia*, CID, Madrid.

Millas, Hercules (1991): 'History Textbooks in Greece', *History Workshop*, Vol. 31, pp.21–33.

Miller, Judith (1990): *One, by One, by One. Facing the Holocaust*, Weidenfeld, London.

Ministerio de Cultura (1990): *Azaña*, Madrid.

Ministerio de Información y Turismo (1971): *Actividades del No-Do*, Madrid.

Mink, Georges and Jean-Charles Szurek (1995): 'Europe centrale: la revanche des néo-communistes', *Politique International*, Spring, pp.157–168.

Mitscherlich, Alexander and Margarete Mitscherlich (1967; 1973): *Fundamentos del comportamiento colectivo. La incapacidad de sentir duelo*, Alianza Editorial, Madrid.

Montero, José R., Francisco J. Llera and Mariano Torcal (1992): 'Sistemas electorales en España: una recapitulación', *Revista Española de Investigaciones Sociológicas*, no.58, pp.7–56.

Montero, José R. and Leonardo Morlino (1993): 'Legitimidad y democracia en el Sur de Europa', *Revista Española de Investigaciones Sociológicas*, no.64, pp.7–40.

Montes, María José (1970): *La guerra española en la creación literaria (ensayo bibliográfico)*. Appendix no.2 of 'Cuadernos bibliográficos de la guerra de España (1936–1939)', Universidad Complutense de Madrid.

Morán, Gregorio (1986): *Miseria y grandeza del Partido Comunista de España*, Planeta, Barcelona.

——, (1991): *El precio de la transición*, Planeta, Barcelona.

Moreno Luzón, Javier (1989): 'Nacionalismo y escuela en España, 1898–1923. Los textos escolares de historia y los manuales patrióticos', (unpublished).

Moroney, Siobhan (1992): 'Myth and Myth-Making: Civic Education and the Study of American History'. Doctoral Thesis, The State University, New Jersey.

Moya, Carlos (1984): *Señas de Leviatán. Estado nacional y sociedad industrial: España 1936–1980*, Alianza, Madrid.

Mujal-León, Eusebio (1983): *Communism and Political Change in Spain*, Indiana University Press, Bloomington.

Murillo Carrasco, Manuel (1977): *Partido Socialista Obrero Español (Sector Histórico)*, Albia, Bilbao.

Namer, Gerard (1987): *La commémoration en France de 1945 à nos jours*, Harmattan, Paris.

Nelson, Janet L. (1990): 'A Place for Medieval History in the National Curriculum?', *History Workshop*, no.29, pp.103–106.

Nerone, John (1989): 'Professional History and Social Memory', *Communication*, Vol. 11, pp.89–104.

Nietzsche, Friedrich (1990): 'History is the Service and Disservice of Life', in *Unmodern Observations*, Yale University Press, London.

Nora, Pierre (comp.) (1984): *Les lieux de mémoire* (4 Vols.), Gallimard, Paris.

O'Donnell, Guillermo, Philippe Schmitter and Laurence Whitehead (eds.) (1986): *Transitions from Authoritarian Rule. Southern Europe*, Johns Hopkins University Press, London.

Olábarri Gortázar, Ignacio (1985): 'La recuperación en España de la *revolución historiográfica* del siglo XX', in VVAA: *La historiografía en occidente desde 1945. III conversaciones internacionales de historia*, Ediciones Universidad de Navarra, Pamplona.

Oms, Marcel (1982): *La guerre d'Espagne au cinéma. Mythes et realités*, Editions du Cerf, Paris.

Opello, Walter C. (1983): 'The Continuing Impact of the Old Regime on Portuguese Political Culture', in Lawrence S. Graham and Douglas L. Wheeler: *In Search of Modern Portugal. The Revolution and its Consequences*, University of Wisconsin Press, Madison.

Ortega y Gasset, José (1967; 1976): *En torno a Galileo*, Arquero, Madrid.

Orwell, George (1938; 1988): *Homage to Catalonia*, Penguin, London.

Palacio Atard, Vicente (1973): *Cinco historias de la república y de la guerra*, Editora Nacional, Madrid.

Palacio Atard, Vicente, Ricardo De La Cierva and Ramón Salas Larrazábal (1966): *Cuadernos bibliográficos de la guerra de España (1936–1939)*, Leaflets, Series 1, 2 Volumes, Universidad Complutense de Madrid.

——, (1967): *Cuadernos bibliográficos de la guerra de España (1936–1939)*, Periodicals, Series 2, 1 Volume, Universidad Complutense de Madrid.

——, (1967): *Cuadernos bibliográficos de la guerra de España (1936–1939)*, Memoirs, Series 3, 3 Volumes, Universidad Complutense de Madrid.

——, (1970): *Aproximación histórica a la guerra española (1936–1939)*. Appendix n.º1 of 'Cuadernos bibliográficos de la guerra de España (1936–1939)', Universidad Complutense de Madrid.

Pasamar Alzuria, Gonzalo (1991): *Historiografía e ideología en la postguerra española: La ruptura de la tradición liberal*, Prensas Universitarias de Zaragoza, Zaragoza.

Pascual, Javier Maria (1961): 'Criba y comentarios: negación y defensa del 18 de julio como cruzada', *Punta Europa*, Vol. 6, no.62, pp.112–123.

Payne, Stanley (1961): *Falange: A History of Spansh Fascism*, Stanford University Press, Stanford, California.

——, (1987): *The Franco Régime, 1936–1975*, The University of Wisconsin Press, Madison.

——, (1990): *Spain's First Democracy. The Second Republic, 1931–1936*, The University of Wisconsin Press, Madison.

PCE (1956): *Por la reconciliación nacional. Por una solución democrática y pacífica del problema español*, Declaration of the PCE of June 1956, 39 pages.

Pelinka, Anton (1993): 'The Post-1945 Political Functions of Austria's Anti-Nazi Resistance', Congress 'Resistance and Collaboration in Europe, 1939–1945: Experience, Memory, Myth and Appropriation', *Institut Für Die Wissenschaften Von Menschen*, Vienna, 2 to 5 September 1993.

Perelli, Carina (1992): 'Settling Accounts With Blood Memory: The Case of Argentina', *Social Research*, no.59, Vol. 2, pp.415–451.

Pérez Díaz, Víctor M. (1979): *Clase obrera, partidos y sindicatos*, Instituto Nacional de Industria, Madrid.

——, (1980): *Clase obrera, orden social y conciencia de clase*, Instituto Nacional de Industria, Madrid.

——, (1981): 'Los obreros españoles ante la empresa en 1980', *Papeles de Economía Española*, no.7.

——, (1987): *El retorno de la sociedad civil*, Instituto de Estudios Económicos, Madrid.

——, (1991 A): *La emergencia de la España democrática: la «invención» de una tradición y la dudosa institucionalización de una democracia*, Estudio/Working Paper no.18 del Centro de Estudios Avanzados en Ciencias Sociales, Instituto Juan March.

——, (1991 B): *The Church and Religion in Contemporary Spain*, Estudio/Working Paper no.19 del Centro de Estudios Avanzados en Ciencias Sociales, Instituto Juan March.

——, (1993): *La primacía de la sociedad civil*, Alianza, Madrid.

Pion-Berlin, David (1994): 'To Prosecute or to Pardon? Human Rights Decision in the Latin American Southern Cone', *Human Rights Quarterly*, no.16, Vol. 1, pp.105–130.

Plumb, John H. (1969; 1990): *The Death of the Past*, Macmillan, London.

Porto, Manuel (1984): 'Portugal: Twenty Years of Change', in Allan Williams (ed.): *Southern Europe Transformed. Political and Economic Change in Greece, Italy, Portugal and Spain*, Harper and Row, London.

Poveda Ariño, José M. (1966; 1968): *Convivencia social*, Doncel, Madrid.

——, (1966; 1969): *Formación social*, Doncel, Madrid.

Powell, Charles (1990): 'The «Tácito» Group and the Transition to Democracy, 1973–1977', in Frances Lannon and Paul Preston (eds.) (1990): *Elites and Power in Twentieth-Century Spain*, Essays in Honour of Sir Raymond Carr, Clarendon Press, Oxford.

——, (1991): *El piloto del cambio*, Planeta, Barcelona.

Pradera, Javier (1993): 'Jeringas, agendas y silencios', *Claves*, no.32, pp.48–55.

Preston, Paul (1986): *Revenge and Reconciliation: The Spanish Civil War and Historical Memory*, Working Paper Series of the Center for European Studies, Harvard University, Cambridge, Massachussets.

——, (1993; 1994): *Franco «Caudillo de España»*, Grijalbo, Barcelona.

Pridham, Geoffrey (ed.) (1984): 'The New Mediterranean Democracies: Regime Transition in Spain, Greece and Portugal.' *West European Politics*, Vol. 7, pp.1–191.

Priego López, Juan (1963): 'Signo y carácter de nuestra cruzada', *Ejército*, Vol. 282, pp.3–38.

PSOE (1974): *Resoluciones del XIII Congreso del PSOE*, Suresnes.

——, (1976): *Resoluciones del XXVII Congreso del PSOE*, Madrid.

Psomiades, Harry J. (1982): 'Greece: From the Colonel's Rule to Democracy', in John Herz (ed.): *From Dictatorship to Democracy. Coping with the Legacies of Authoritarianism and Totalitarianism*, Greenwood Press, Westport.

Publicaciones Españolas (1964): *25 années de paix*, Madrid.

——, (1964): *25 Years of Peace*, Madrid.

Ramet, Sabrina P. (1992): *Balkan Babel. Politics, Culture and Religion in Yugoslavia*, Westview, Oxford.

Ramírez, Manuel (1978): *España 1939–1975. Régimen político e ideología*, Labor, Barcelona.

Ramiro Rico, Nicolás (1980): *El animal ladino y otros estudios políticos*, Alianza, Madrid.

Rastrilla Pérez, Juan (1974): *Historia universal y de España*, S.M., Madrid.

Rastrilla Pérez, Juan and Antonio Zubia Cincunegui (1973): *Naturaleza y sociedad*, S.M., Madrid.

Rastrilla Pérez, Juan and J.J. Arenaza Lasagabaster (1975): *Geografía e historia*, S.M., Madrid.

Reig Tapia, Alberto (1986): *Ideología e historia: sobre la represión franquista y la Guerra Civil*, Akal, Madrid.

——, (1990): *Violencia y terror*, Akal, Madrid.

Renan, Ernest (1887; 1987): *¿Qué es una nación? Cartas a Strauss*, Alianza, Madrid.

Rico, Ana (1990): 'Different Adaptative Responses to the International Economic Crisis of the 30's and 70's', Instituto Juan March, (unpublished).

Ridruejo, Dionisio (1962): *Escrito en España*, Losada, Buenos Aires.

——, (1976): *Casi unas memorias*, Planeta, Barcelona.

Robles Piquer, Carlos (dir.) (1964): *El gobierno informa. 25 aniversario de la paz española*, 4 vols., Editora Nacional, Madrid.

Rodríguez, Clara Eugenia (coord.) (1986): *Procesos de reconciliación en América Latina*, Instituto de Estudios Liberales, Bogotá.

Rodríguez Devesa, José María (1974; 4 ed.): *Derecho penal español*, Gráficas Carasa, Madrid.

——, (1981; 8th ed.): *Derecho penal español*, Gráficas Carasa, Madrid.

Rodríguez Ibáñez, José Enrique (1987): *Después de una dictadura: cultura autoritaria y transición política en España*, CEC, Madrid.

Rodríguez, José Luis (1990): 'Ideología y léxico político de la extrema derecha española. 1967–1989', in Carlos Clavero (coord.): *Investigaciones políticas III*, AEDEMO, Bilbao.

Roiz, Javier (1992): *El experimento moderno*, Trotta, Madrid.

Romero, Emilio (1957): *La paz empieza nunca*, Planeta, Barcelona.

Rousso, Henry (1991): *The Vichy Syndrome. History and Memory in France since 1944*, Harvard University Press, Cambridge.

Rubio Cabeza, Manuel (1985): *Las voces de la República*, Planeta, Barcelona.

Rubio Llorente, Francisco (1984): 'Constitución', *Diccionario del sistema político español*, Akal, Madrid.

Ruiz, David (dir.) (1993): *Historia de Comisiones Obreras (1958–1988)*, Siglo XXI, Madrid.

Ruiz Carnero, Ricardo (1943): *Historia de España*, Hernando, Madrid.

Ruiz-Giménez, Joaquín (1980): 'El papel del consenso en la construcción del actual Estado democrático español', *Sistema*, no.38–39, pp.159–169.

Rumeu De Armas, A. (1970): *Historia de España contemporánea*, Anaya, Madrid.

Sa'adah, Anne (1992): 'Forgiving without Forgetting: Political Reconciliation and Democratic Citizenship', *French Politics and Society*, Vol. 10, pp.94–113.

Sabine, George H. (1937; 1988): *Historia de la teoría política*, Rialp, Madrid.

Sáez Marín, Juan (1988): *El Frente de Juventudes. Política de juventud en la España de la posguerra (1937–1960)*, Siglo XXI, Madrid.

Sánchez Navarro, Ángel (1990): *La transición política en las Cortes de Franco: hacia la Ley para la Reforma Política (1975–1976)*, Estudio/Working Paper no.11 del Centro de Estudios Avanzados en Ciencias Sociales, Instituto Juan March.

Sánchez-Bravo, Antonio and Antonio Tellado Vázquez (1976): *Los mutilados del ejército de la República*, M.V. Ediciones, Madrid.

Sánchez-Cervelló, José (1989 A): 'El Caetanismo', in Hipólito De La Torre Gómez (coord.): *Portugal y España en el cambio político (1958–1978)*, Universidad Nacional de Educación a Distancia, Centro Regional de Extremadura, Mérida.

——, (1989 B): 'El proceso democrático portugués', in Hipólito De La Torre Gómez (coord.): *Portugal y España en el cambio político (1958–1978)*, Universidad Nacional de Educación a Distancia, Centro Regional de Extremadura, Mérida.

Santamaría, Álvaro (1966; 1968): *Historia universal y de España*, Vicens-Vives, Barcelona.

Santamaría, Julián (1982): *Transición a la democracia en el sur de Europa y América Latina*, CIS, Madrid.

Satrústegui, Joaquín (ed.) (1993): *Cuando la transición se hizo posible. El «contubernio de Múnich»*, Tecnos, Madrid.

Schmitter, Philippe C. (1975): 'Retrospective Thoughts on the Demise of Authoritarian Rule in Portugal', *Armed Forces and Society*, Vol. 2, no.1, pp.5–33.

Schneider, Cathy L. (1995): *Shantytown Protest in Pinochet's Chile*, Temple University Press, Philadelphia.

Schudson, Michael (1989): 'The Present in the Past versus the Past in the Present', *Communication*, Vol. 11, pp.105–113.

——, (1992): *Watergate in American Memory. How we Remember, Forget and Reconstruct the Past*, Basic Books, New York.

Schuman, Howard and Jacqueline Scott (1989): 'Generations and Collective Memories', *American Sociological Review*, Vol. 54, no.3, pp.359–381.

Schwartz, Barry (1982): 'The Social Context of Commemoration: A Study in Collective Memory', *Social Forces*, Vol. 61, pp.374–402.

——, (1991): 'Social Change and Collective Memory: The Democratization of George Washington', *American Sociological Review*, Vol. 56, no.2, pp.221–236.

Scott, James (1990): *Domination and the Arts of Resistance*, Yale University Press, New Haven.

Sección Femenina de FET y de las JONS (1959): *Formación Política*, Sección Femenina, Madrid.

——, (1960): *Formación político-social*, Sección Femenina, Madrid.

——, (1961): *Formación político-social*, Sección Femenina, Madrid.

——, (undated): *Formación política*, Sección Femenina, Madrid.

Secretaría de Formación del PSOE (1990): *Los intelectuales y la política: homenaje a Julián Besteiro*, Fundaciones Sistema y Jaime Vera, Madrid (book and video).

Seminario Central de Estudios Políticos (1961): *25 años de política española*, Delegación de Organizaciones del Movimiento, Madrid.

Sempere, Pedro (1977): *Los muros del posfranquismo*, Castellote, Madrid.

Serrano De Haro, Agustín (1940; 1946): *España es así*, Escuela Española, Madrid.

——, (1961): *Yo soy español*, Escuela Española, Madrid.

Servicio Informativo Español (1963): *¿Crimen o castigo? Documentos inéditos de Julián Grimau García*, Madrid.

——, (1964): *25 años de paz vistos por 25 escritores españoles*, Documentos Informativos no.6, Madrid.

——, (1964): *Veinte escritores españoles hablan de...* 25 años de paz, Documentos Informativos no.5, Madrid.

——, (1965): *Informe sobre la conmemoración del XXV aniversario de la paz española*, Madrid.

——, (1966): *Referéndum 1966. Nueva Constitución*, Documentos Políticos no.7, Madrid.

——, (1967): *España en su prensa*, Documentos Informativos no.14, Madrid.

——, (1967): *Leyes Fundamentales del Estado. La Constitución española*, Documentos Políticos no.8, Madrid.

Sevillano Calero, Francisco (1991–1992): 'Actitudes políticas y opinión de los españoles durante la postguerra (1939–1950)', under Various Authors, monograph from the Annals of the University of Alicante regarding 'España durante el Franquismo', *Historia Contemporánea*, no.8–9.

Share, Donald (1986): *The Making of Spanish Democracy*, Praeger, New York.

Sills, David L. (1968): *International Encyclopedia of the Social Sciences*, Macmillan and Free Press, New York.

Silva Muñoz, Federico (1993): *Memorias políticas*, Planeta, Barcelona.

Solís, José (1959): *Nueva convivencia española*, Servicio de Información y Publicaciones de la Organización Sindical, Madrid.

Suárez, Adolfo (1978): *Un nuevo horizonte para España. Discursos del Presidente de Gobierno 1976–1978*, Servicio Central de Publicaciones de Presidencia del Gobierno, Madrid.

Suárez, Francisco (1612; 1967–68): *Tratado de las leyes y de Dios legislador*, reproduction of the Príncipe de Coimbra edition (1612); Spanish version by J.R. Eguillor Muñozguren, S.I. General intro. by L. Vela Sánchez, S.J. 6 Vols., Madrid.

Suplemento Nacional de la Prensa del Movimiento (1964): *España cumple sus 25 años de paz*.

Sueiro, Daniel (1976): *La verdadera historia del Valle de los Caídos*, Sedmay, Madrid.

Talón, Vicente (1974): *Portugal. ¿Golpe o revolución?*, C.V.S. Ediciones, Madrid.

Tamames, Ramón (1983): *La República. La era de Franco*, Alianza, Madrid.

Temas Españoles no.427, *XXV años de paz*, Publicaciones Españolas, Madrid.

Tezanos, José Félix, Ramón Cotarelo and Andrés de Blas (eds.) (1989): *La transición democrática española*, Sistema, Madrid.

Thomas, Gordon and Max Morgan-Witts (1975): *The Day Guernica Died*, Hodder and Stoughton, London.

Torcal, Mariano (1995): 'Actitudes políticas y participación política en España. Pautas de continuidad y cambio'. Doctoral Thesis, Universidad Autónoma de Madrid.

Torrente Ballester, Gonzalo (1965; 1967): *Aprendiz de hombre*, Doncel, Madrid.

Torres, Federico (1940): *Enciclopedia activa*, Hernando, Madrid.

Trullén I Thomàs, Joan (1993): *Fundamentos económicos de la transición política española. La política económica de los acuerdos de la Moncloa*, Ministerio de Trabajo y Seguridad Social, Madrid.

Tsoucalas, Constantine (1969): *The Greek Tragedy*, Penguin, Middlesex.

Tusell, Javier (1986): *Los hijos de la sangre. La España de 1936 desde 1986*, Espasa-Calpe, Madrid.

——, (1988): *La dictadura de Franco*, Alianza, Madrid.

——, (1992): *Franco en la Guerra Civil. Una biografía política*, Tusquets, Barcelona.

UCD (1977): *Manual para 22 millones de electores. UCD*, Madrid.

——, (1979): *La solución a un reto. Tesis para una sociedad democrática occidental*, Unión Editorial, Madrid.

Umbral, Francisco (1972): *Memorias de un niño de derechas*, Destino, Barcelona.

Unknown (1944): *Manual de historia de España y lecturas históricas*, S.M., Burgos.

Unknown (1963): *El caso Grimau o la guerra civil permanente*, Ediciones OID, Madrid.

Unknown (undated): *Símbolos de España*, Magisterio Español, Madrid.

Unknown: *Santa Cruz del Valle de los Caídos* (1969; 5 ed.), Guía Turística, Patrimonio Nacional, Madrid.

Unknown: *The National Monument of the Santa Cruz del Valle de los Caídos* (1959), Tourist Guide, Patrimonio Nacional, Madrid.

Valls, Rafael (1983): 'La interpretación de la historia de España en el franquismo. Plan de bachillerato 1938–1953', *Estudis d'Historia Contemporania del Pais Valenciá*, no.4, pp.231–55.

——, (1984): *La interpretación de la Historia de España y sus orígenes ideológicos, en el bachillerato franquista (1938–1953)*, Instituto de Ciencias de la Educación, Valencia.

——, (1986): 'Ideología franquista y enseñanza en la historia de España, 1938–1953' in Josep Fontana (ed.), *España bajo el franquismo*, Crítica, Barcelona.

——, (1988): 'La exaltación patriótica como finalidad fundamental de la enseñanza de historia en la educación obligatoria: una aproximación histórica', *Didáctica de las ciencias experimentales y sociales*, no.5, pp.33–47.

——, (1990): 'Fascismo y franquismo: dos manipulaciones diversas de la enseñanza de la historia', in Fernando García Sanz (comp.), *Españoles e italianos en el mundo contemporáneo*, CSIC, Madrid.

——, (1991): 'El bachillerato universitario de 1938: primera aproximación al modelo universitario franquista', Minutes of the Congress *La Universidad Española Bajo el Régimen de Franco*, held in Zaragoza between 8 and 11 November 1989, Instituto Fernando el Católico, Zaragoza.

Varela, Helena (1990): *La legalización del PCE: élites, opinión pública y simbolismos en la transición*, Estudio/Working Paper no.8 del Centro de Estudios Avanzados en Ciencias Sociales, Instituto Juan March.

Varela, Santiago (1976): *El problema regional en la Segunda República española*, Unión Editorial, Madrid.

——, (1978): *Partidos y parlamento en la Segunda República*, Ariel/Fundación Juan March, Madrid.

Various Authors (1984): *Historia de España*, Libro del Profesor, Instituto de Ciencias de la Educación, Salamanca.

Various Authors (1945): *Lecturas*, Edelvives, Zaragoza.

Various Authors (1948): *Historia de España*, Bruño, Madrid.

Various Authors (1949): *Historia de España*, Bruño, Madrid.

Various Authors (1951): *Historia de España*, Luis Vives, Zaragoza.

Various Authors (1962): *Historia de España*, S.M., Madrid.

Various Authors (1964): *Panorama español contemporáneo. XXV años de paz*, Cultura Hispánica, Madrid.

Various Authors (1975): *Tácito*, Ibérico Europea de Ediciones, Madrid.

Various Authors (1977): *Geografía e Historia de España y de los países hispánicos*, Didascalia, Madrid.

Various Authors (1981): 'La República en los textos de bachillerato', *Arbor*, Vol. CIX, no.426–427.

Various Authors (1982): *Geografía e Historia de España y de los países hispánicos*, Vicens-Vives, Barcelona.

Various Authors (1986): *El socialismo en España*, Pablo Iglesias, Madrid.

Various Authors (1987): *Arquitectura en regiones devastadas*, MOPU, Madrid.

Various Authors (1993): *El legado de Franco*, Fundación Nacional Francisco Franco, Madrid.

Various Authors (undated): *Historia de España*, Bruño, Madrid.

Vicens Vives, J. (1942; 1979): *Historia general moderna*, Vol. 2, Montaner y Simón, Barcelona.

Vidarte, Juan-Simeón (1973): *Todos fuimos culpables. Testimonio de un socialista español*, Fondo de Cultura Económica, México.

Viñas, Ángel (1978): 'Guernica: las responsabilidades', *Historia 16*, no.25, Vol. 3, pp.127–143.

Vromen, Suzanne (1986): 'Maurice Halbwachs and the Concept of Nostalgia', *Knowledge and Society: Studies in the Sociology of Culture Past and Present*, Vol. 6, pp.55–66.

Wagner-Pacifici, Robin and Barry Schwartz (1991): 'The Vietnam Memorial: Commemorating a Difficult Past', *American Journal of Sociology*, Vol.97, no.2, pp.376–420.

Weber, Max (1968; 1978): *Economy and Society*, University of California Press, California.

Weschler, Lawrence (1990): *A Miracle, a Universe*, Penguin, London.

Wheeler, Douglas L. (1983): 'The Revolution and Counterrevolution in Modern Portuguese History', in Lawrence S. Graham and Douglas L. Wheeler: *In Search of Modern Portugal. The Revolution and its Consequences*, University of Wisconsin Press, Madison.

Williams, Allan (ed.) (1984): *Southern Europe Transformed. Political and Economic Change in Greece, Italy, Portugal and Spain*, Harper and Row, London.

Winter, Jay (1995): *Sites of Memory, Sites of Mourning. The Great War in European Cultural History*, Cambridge University Press, New York.

Woodward, Susan L. (1995): *Socialist Unemployment. The Political Economy of Yugoslavia*, Princeton University Press, Princeton.

Yagüe, María Eugenia (1977): *Santiago Carrillo. Perfil humano y político*, Editorial Cambio 16, Madrid.

Young, James E. (1993): *The Texture of Memory. Holocaust Memorials and Meaning*, Yale University Press, New Haven.

Zeul, Mechthild and José A. Gimbernat (1990): 'El porvenir de una nación (consideraciones políticas y psicoanalíticas acerca de la unificación alemana)', *Revista de Occidente*, no.112, pp.47–63.

TABLES

Table 2.1 NO-DO Numerical Tables on the Civil War

Year	Newsreels on the war (a)	Total annual newsreels (b)	Total 2 (% a of b)	Total news items on the war (c)	Total 1 Minutes per year on the war	News items on the war: first or last (d)	Total 4 (% d of c)	News items on the Republicans (e)	Total 5 (% e of c)	Total 6 Minutes on Victory Parade
1943	28	85	32.94	33	59	20	60.61	6	18.18	4
1944	12	90	13.33	12	24	10	83.33	3	25	7
1945	13	75	17.33	13	33	10	76.92	1	7.69	7
1950	11	104	10.58	13	31	9	69.23	1	7.69	6
1955	11	104	10.58	12	19	6	50	1	8.33	6
1960	16	117	13.68	18	32	12	66.67	0	0	5
1961	20	156	12.82	23	59	20	86.96	1	4.35	14
1964	34	156	21.79	40	67	24	60	0	0	10
1965	18	156	11.54	18	28	13	72.22	1	5.56	7
1970	9	104	8.65	9	24	7	77.78	0	0	4
1975	5	500	1	5	38	2	40	0	0	6
1976	3	104	2.88	3	7	3	100	0	0	4
1977	4	79	5.06	4	12	4	100	4	100	0
1978	0	0	0	0	0	0	0	0	0	0
1979	3	48	6.25	3	7	2	66.67	3	100	0
1980	1	52	1.92	1	4	1	100	1	100	0
1981	0	0	0	0	0	0	0	0	0	0

Source: own elaboration

Table 2.2 *Category (1)*

Year	Number of news items	Percentage (of a)	Metres	Minutes	Percentage minutes	First or last	Percentage of first or last
1943	5	15.15	356	12.71	21.55	4	80
1944	2	16.67	86	3.07	12.8	2	100
1945	3	23.08	320	11.43	34.63	3	100
1950	0	0	0	0	0	0	0
1955	0	0	0	0	0	0	0
1960	1	5.56	79	2.82	8.82	0	0
1961	4	17.39	263	9.39	15.92	4	100
1964	0	0	0	0	0	0	0
1965	0	0	0	0	0	0	0
1970	1	11.11	60	2.14	8.93	1	100
1975	1	20	735	26.25	69.08	1	100
1976	0	0	0	0	0	0	0
1977	1	25	118	4.21	35.12	1	100
1978	0	0	0	0	0	0	0
1979	3	100	221	7.89	112.76	3	100
1980	1	100	113	4.04	100.89	1	100
1981	0	0	0	0	0	0	0

Table 2.3 *Category (2)*

Year	Number of news items	Percentage (of a)	Metres	Minutes	Percentage minutes	First or last	Percentage of first or last
1943	13	39.39	788	28.14	47.7	10	76.92
1944	5	41.67	299	10.68	44.49	5	100
1945	5	38.46	301	10.75	32.58	4	80
1950	4	30.77	204	7.29	23.5	2	50
1955	7	58.33	257	9.18	48.31	3	42.86
1960	3	16.67	109	3.89	12.17	2	66.67
1961	6	26.09	339	12.11	20.52	5	83.33
1964	7	17.5	297	10.61	15.83	2	28.57
1965	8	44.44	236	8.43	30.1	5	62.5
1970	3	33.33	236	8.43	35.12	3	100
1975	0	0	0	0	0	0	0
1976	0	0	0	0	0	0	0
1977	0	0	0	0	0	0	0
1978	0	0	0	0	0	0	0
1979	0	0	0	0	0	0	0
1980	0	0	0	0	0	0	0
1981	0	0	0	0	0	0	0

Table 2.4 *Category (2^u)*

Year	Number of news items	Percentage (of a)	Metres	Minutes	Percentage minutes	First or last	Percentage of first or last
1943	1	3.03	120	4.29	7.26	1	100
1944	2	16.67	208	7.43	30.95	2	100
1945	2	15.38	209	7.46	22.62	2	100
1950	2	15.38	173	6.18	19.93	2	100
1955	2	16.67	187	6.68	35.15	2	100
1960	2	11.11	162	5.79	18.08	2	100
1961	2	8.7	264	9.43	15.98	2	100
1964	3	7.5	290	10.36	15.46	3	100
1965	3	16.67	207	7.39	26.4	2	66.66
1970	2	22.22	130	4.64	19.35	0	0
1975	2	40	180	6.43	16.92	1	50
1976	1	33.33	125	4.46	63.78	1	100
1977	0	0	0	0	0	0	0
1978	0	0	0	0	0	0	0
1979	0	0	0	0	0	0	0
1980	0	0	0	0	0	0	0
1981	0	0	0	0	0	0	0

Table 2.4 *Category (2ᵇ)*

Year	Number of news items	Percentage (of a)	Metres	Minutes	Percentage minutes	First or last	Percentage of first or last
1943	0	0	0	0	0	0	0
1944	0	0	0	0	0	0	0
1945	0	0	0	0	0	0	0
1950	0	0	0	0	0	0	0
1955	0	0	0	0	0	0	0
1960	0	0	0	0	0	0	0
1961	0	0	0	0	0	0	0
1964	29	72.5	1418	50.64	75.59	19	65.52
1965	1	5.56	33	1.17	4.21	1	100
1970	0	0	0	0	0	0	0
1975	0	0	0	0	0	0	0
1976	0	0	0	0	0	0	0
1977	0	0	0	0	0	0	0
1978	0	0	0	0	0	0	0
1979	0	0	0	0	0	0	0
1980	0	0	0	0	0	0	0
1981	0	0	0	0	0	0	0

Table 2.5 *Category (2T)*

Year	Number of news items	Percentage (of a)	Metres	Minutes	Percentage minutes	First or last	Percentage of first or last
1943	14	42.42	908	32.43	54.96	11	78.57
1944	7	58.33	507	18.11	75.45	7	100
1945	7	53.85	510	18.21	55.19	6	85.71
1950	6	46.15	377	13.46	43.43	4	66.67
1955	9	75	444	15.86	83.46	5	55.56
1960	5	27.78	271	9.68	30.25	4	80
1961	8	34.78	603	21.54	36.5	7	87.5
1964	39	97.5	2005	71.61	106.88	24	61.54
1965	12	66.67	476	17	60.71	8	66.67
1970	5	55.56	366	13.07	54.46	3	60
1975	2	40	180	6.43	16.92	1	50
1976	1	33.33	125	4.46	63.78	1	100
1977	0	0	0	0	0	0	0
1978	0	0	0	0	0	0	0
1979	0	0	0	0	0	0	0
1980	0	0	0	0	0	0	0
1981	0	0	0	0	0	0	0

Table 2.6 *Category (3)*

Year	Number of news items	Percentage (of a)	Metres	Minutes	Percentage minutes	First or last	Percentage of first or last
1943	6	18.18	297	10.61	17.98	4	66.67
1944	2	16.67	74	2.64	11.01	1	50
1945	2	15.38	75	2.68	8.12	0	0
1950	4	30.77	370	13.21	42.63	3	75
1955	2	16.67	57	2.04	10.71	1	50
1960	3	16.67	95	3.39	10.6	2	66.67
1961	5	21.74	322	11.5	19.49	4	80
1964	4	10	134	4.79	7.14	3	75
1965	2	11.11	142	5.07	18.11	2	100
1970	0	0	0	0	0	0	0
1975	0	0	0	0	0	0	0
1976	0	0	0	0	0	0	0
1977	0	0	0	0	0	0	0
1978	0	0	0	0	0	0	0
1979	0	0	0	0	0	0	0
1980	0	0	0	0	0	0	0
1981	0	0	0	0	0	0	0

Table 2.7 *Category (3ᵃ)*

Year	Number of news items	Percentage (of a)	Metres	Minutes	Percentage minutes	First or last	Percentage of first or last
1943	2	6.06	93	3.32	5.63	1	50
1944	0	0	0	0	0	0	0
1945	1	7.69	38	1.36	4.11	1	100
1950	1	7.69	52	1.86	5.99	1	100
1955	1	8.33	39	1.39	7.33	0	0
1960	1	5.56	138	4.93	15.4	1	100
1961	2	8.7	93	3.32	5.63	1	50
1964	0	0	0	0	0	0	0
1965	2	11.11	78	2.79	9.95	1	50
1970	0	0	0	0	0	0	0
1975	0	0	0	0	0	0	0
1976	0	0	0	0	0	0	0
1977	0	0	0	0	0	0	0
1978	0	0	0	0	0	0	0
1979	0	0	0	0	0	0	0
1980	0	0	0	0	0	0	0
1981	0	0	0	0	0	0	0

Table 2.8 *Category (3^b^)*

Year	Number of news items	Percentage (of a)	Metres	Minutes	Percentage minutes	First or last	Percentage of first or last
1943	0	0	0	0	0	0	0
1944	0	0	0	0	0	0	0
1945	0	0	0	0	0	0	0
1950	1	7.69	36	1.29	4.15	1	100
1955	0	0	0	0	0	0	0
1960	7	38.89	345	12.32	38.5	4	57.14
1961	3	13.04	162	5.79	9.81	3	100
1964	3	7.5	124	4.43	6.61	1	33.33
1965	1	5.56	40	1.43	5.1	1	100
1970	1	11.11	51	1.82	7.59	1	100
1975	1	20	42	1.5	3.95	0	0
1976	1	33.33	64	2.29	32.65	1	100
1977	0	0	0	0	0	0	0
1978	0	0	0	0	0	0	0
1979	0	0	0	0	0	0	0
1980	0	0	0	0	0	0	0
1981	0	0	0	0	0	0	0

Table 2.9 *Category (3T)*

Year	Number of news items	Percentage (of a)	Metres	Minutes	Percentage minutes	First or last	Percentage of first or last
1943	8	24.24	390	13.93	23.61	5	62.5
1944	2	16.67	74	2.64	11.01	1	50
1945	3	23.08	113	4.04	12.23	1	33.33
1950	6	46.15	458	16.36	52.76	5	83.33
1955	3	25	96	3.43	18.05	1	33.33
1960	11	61.11	578	20.64	64.51	7	63.64
1961	10	43.48	577	20.61	34.93	8	80
1964	7	17.5	258	9.21	13.75	4	57.14
1965	5	27.78	260	9.29	33.16	4	80
1970	1	11.11	51	1.82	7.59	1	100
1975	1	20	42	1.5	3.95	0	0
1976	1	33.33	64	2.29	32.65	1	100
1977	0	0	0	0	0	0	0
1978	0	0	0	0	0	0	0
1979	0	0	0	0	0	0	0
1980	0	0	0	0	0	0	0
1981	0	0	0	0	0	0	0

Table 2.10 *Category (4)*

Year	Number of news items	Percentage (of a)	Metres	Minutes	Percentage minutes	First or last	Percentage of first or last
1943	1	3.03	71	2.54	4.3	1	100
1944	1	8.33	27	0.96	4.02	0	0
1945	0	0	0	0	0	0	0
1950	1	7.69	50	1.79	5.76	0	0
1955	0	0	0	0	0	0	0
1960	2	11.11	120	4.29	13.39	2	100
1961	1	4.35	135	4.82	8.17	1	100
1964	1	2.5	100	3.57	5.33	1	100
1965	1	5.56	56	2	7.14	1	100
1970	2	22.22	197	7.04	29.32	2	100
1975	1	20	120	4.29	11.28	0	0
1976	1	33.33	31	1.11	15.82	1	100
1977	3	75	232	8.29	69.05	3	100
1978	0	0	0	0	0	0	0
1979	0	0	0	0	0	0	0
1980	0	0	0	0	0	0	0
1981	0	0	0	0	0	0	0

Table 2.11 *General NO-DO Numerical Tables*

Production of Newsreels. January 1943 – May 1981

Year	Numbers	Editions	A	B	C	BW/Colour	Totals	Annual
1943	1 to 19	1	19			B/W	19	
1943	20 to 52	2	33	33		B/W	66	85
1944	53 to 77	2	25	25		B/W	50	
1944	78 to 91	1	7	7		B/W	14	
1944	92 to 104	2	13	13		B/W	26	90
1945	105 to 127	2	23	23		B/W	46	
1945	128 to 156	1	15	15		B/W	29	75
1946	157 to 178	1	11	11		B/W	22	
1946	179 to 182	2	4	4		B/W	8	
1946	183 to 205	1	11	11		B/W	23	
1946	206 to 208	2	3	3		B/W	6	59
1947	209 to 260	2	52	52		B/W	104	104
1948	261 to 312	2	52	52		B/W	104	104
1949	313 to 364	2	52	52		B/W	104	104
1950	365 to 416	2	52	52		B/W	104	104
1951	417 to 468	2	52	52		B/W	104	104
1952	469 to 521	2	53	52		B/W	106	106
1953	522 to 573	2	52	52		B/W	104	104
1954	574 to 625	2	52	52		B/W	104	104
1955	626 to 677	2	52	52		B/W	104	104
1956	678 to 729	2	52	52		B/W	104	104
1957	730 to 782	2	53	52		B/W	106	106
1958	783 to 834	2	52	52		B/W	104	104
1959	835 to 886	2	52	52		B/W	104	104

Table 2.11 *General NO-DO Numerical Tables (continued)*

Production of Newsreels. January 1943 – May 1981

Year	Numbers	Editions	A	B	C	BW/Colour	Totals	Annual
1960	887 to 925	3	39	39	13	B/W	78	117
1960	926 to 938	3	13	13	13	B/W	39	156
1961	939 to 990	3	52	52	52	B/W	156	159
1962	991 to 1043	3	53	53	53	B/W	159	156
1963	1044 to 1095	3	52	52	52	B/W	156	156
1964	1096 to 1147	3	52	52	52	B/W	156	156
1965	1148 to 1199	3	52	52	52	B/W	156	156
1966	1200 to 1251	3	52	52	52	B/W	156	108
1967	1252 to 1255	3	4	4	4	B/W	12	
1967	1256 to 1303	2	48	48		B/W	96	
1968	1304 to 1343	2	40	40		B/W	80	106
1968	1344 to 1356	2	13	13		Mixed	26	
1968	1357 to 1408	2	52	52		Mixed	104	104
1970	1409 to 1460	2	52	52		Mixed	104	104
1971	1461 to 1512	2	52	52		Mixed	104	104
1972	1513 to 1564	2	52	52		Mixed	104	104
1973	1565 to 1616	2	52	52		Mixed	104	104
1974	1617 to 1668	2	52	52		Mixed	104	104
1975	1669 to 1718	2	50	50		Mixed	100	100
1976	1719 to 1770	2	52	52		Mixed	104	104
1977	1771 to 1794	2	24	24		Mixed	48	
1977	1795	2	1	1		Mixed	2	
1977	1796 to 1797	2	2	2		Colour	4	

Table 2.11 *General NO-DO Numerical Tables (continued)*

Production of Newsreels. January 1943 – May 1981

Year	Numbers	Editions	A	B	C	BW/Colour	Totals	Annual
1977	1798 to 1822	1	25			Colour	25	79
1978	1823 to 1874	1	52			Colour	52	52
1979	1875 to 1922	1	48			Colour	48	48
1980	1923 to 1936	1	14			Colour	14	
1980	1937 to 1955	2	19	19		Colour	38	52
1981	1956 to 1966	2	11	11		Colour	22	22

Total = 4,016

Source: No-Do Archive

Table 3.1

Date	References to the Civil War (implicit and explicit)			References to the date			References to the date and the war		
	El País	ABC	Total 1	El País	ABC	Total 2	El País	ABC	Total 3
18th July	2 of 8	0 of 8	2 of 16	2 of 8	1 of 8	3 of 16	2 of 8	0 of 8	2 of 16
1st Oct.	4 of 9	0 of 9	4 of 18	0 of 9	0 of 9	0 of 18	0 of 9	0 of 9	0 of 18
20th Nov.	4 of 8	5 of 11	9 of 19	4 of 8	3 of 11	7 of 19	2 of 8	3 of 11	5 of 19
1st April	1 of 6	0 of 9	1 of 15	0 of 6	0 of 9	0 of 15	0 of 6	0 of 9	0 of 15
14th April	3 of 6	0 of 9	3 of 15	2 of 6	0 of 9	2 of 15	2 of 6	0 of 9	2 of 15
Totals	14 of 37	5 of 46	19 of 83	8 of 37	4 of 46	12 of 83	6 of 37	3 of 46	9 of 83
%	37.8%	10.8%	22.9%	21.6%	8.7%	14.4%	16.2%	6.5%	10.8%

Source: own elaboration

Table 3.2

Date	References to the Civil War (implicit and explicit)			References to the date			References to the date and the war		
	El País	ABC	Total 1	El País	ABC	Total 2	El País	ABC	Total 3
18th July	YES	NO	YES	YES	YES	YES	YES	NO	YES
1st Oct.	YES	NO	YES	NO	NO	NO	NO	NO	NO
20th Nov.	YES	YES	YES	YES	YES	YES	YES	YES	YES
1st April	YES	NO	YES	NO	NO	NO	NO	NO	NO
14th April	YES	NO	YES	YES	NO	YES	YES	NO	YES
%	100%	20%	100%	60%	40%	60%	60%	20%	60%

Source: own elaboration

Table 3.3

	Total references to the Civil War (although they may not relate to the date)			Total references to the Civil War relating to the date			Implicit references to the Civil War relating to the date			Explicit references to the Civil War relating to the date		
	El País	ABC	Total 1	El País	ABC	Total 2	El País	ABC	Total 3	El País	ABC	Total 4
1975												
22nd Nov.		1 of 3	1 of 3 = 33%		1 of 3	1 of 3 = 33%		1 of 1	1 of 1		0 of 1	0 of 1
4th Dec.		0 of 3	0 of 3 = 0%		0 of 3	0 of 3 = 0%						
11th Dec.		1 of 3	1 of 3 = 33%		1 of 3	1 of 3 = 33%		1 of 1	1 of 1		0 of 1	0 of 1
1976												
26th March		0 of 3	0 of 3 = 0%		0 of 3	0 of 3 = 0%						
9th June	2 of 4	2 of 3	4 of 7 = **57%**	1 of 4	2 of 3	3 of 7 = 42%	1 of 1	2 of 2	3 of 3	0 of 1	0 of 2	0 of 3
3rd July	1 of 3	1 of 3	2 of 6 = 33%	1 of 3	1 of 3	2 of 6 = 33%	0 of 1	0 of 1	0 of 2	1 of 1	1 of 1	2 of 2
7th July	1 of 3	1 of 3	2 of 6 = 33%	0 of 3	1 of 3	1 of 6 = 16%		0 of 1	0 of 1		1 of 1	1 of 1
30th July	1 of 3	1 of 3	2 of 6 = 33%	1 of 3	1 of 3	2 of 6 = 33%	0 of 1	1 of 1	1 of 2	0 of 1	1 of 1	1 of 2
23rd Oct.	1 of 3	2 of 3	3 of 6 = **50%**	0 of 3	0 of 3	0 of 6 = 0%						
18th Nov.	2 of 3	1 of 3	3 of 6 = **50%**	2 of 3	1 of 3	3 of 6 = **50%**	2 of 2	0 of 1	2 of 3	0 of 2	1 of 1	1 of 3
15th Dec.	2 of 3	3 of 3	5 of 6 = **83%**	1 of 3	3 of 3	4 of 6 = **66%**	1 of 1	2 of 3	3 of 4	0 of 1	1 of 3	1 of 4
1977												
24th Jan.	1 of 2	0 of 2	1 of 4 = 25%	1 of 2	0 of 2	1 of 4 = 25%	1 of 1		1 of 1	0 of 1		0 of 1
11th March	2 of 3	1 of 3	3 of 6 = **50%**	0 of 3	1 of 3	1 of 6 = 16%		1 of 1	1 of 1		0 of 1	0 of 1
18th March	0 of 3	0 of 3	0 of 6 = 0%	0 of 3	0 of 3	0 of 6 = 0%						
9th April	2 of 2	1 of 3	3 of 5 = **60%**	1 of 2	1 of 3	2 of 5 = 40%	1 of 1	0 of 1	1 of 2	0 of 1	1 of 1	1 of 2
15th June	3 of 3	2 of 3	5 of 6 = **83%**	3 of 3	2 of 3	5 of 6 = **83%**	0 of 3	2 of 2	2 of 5	3 of 3	0 of 2	3 of 5

Table 3.3 *(continued)*

	Total references to the Civil War (although they may not relate to the date)			Total references to the Civil War relating to the date			Implicit references to the Civil War relating to the date			Explicit references to the Civil War relating to the date		
	El País	ABC	Total 1	El País	ABC	Total 2	El País	ABC	Total 3	El País	ABC	Total 4
1977 (continued)												
4th July	1 of 2	0 of 2	1 of 4 = 25%	0 of 2	0 of 2	0 of 4 = 0%						
22nd July	2 of 3	0 of 2	2 of 5 = 40%	2 of 3	0 of 2	2 of 5 = 40%	2 of 2		2 of 2	0 of 2		0 of 2
14th Oct.	2 of 3	1 of 3	3 of 6 = **50%**	1 of 3	1 of 3	2 of 6 = 33%	0 of 1	1 of 1	1 of 2	1 of 1	0 of 1	2 of 2
25th–27th Oct.	1 of 4	1 of 4	2 of 8 = 25%	0 of 4	0 of 4	0 of 8 = 0%						
1978												
2nd Jan.	1 of 3	2 of 4	3 of 7 = 43%	1 of 3	1 of 4	2 of 7 = 28%	1 of 1	0 of 1	1 of 2	0 of 1	1 of 1	1 of 2
1st May	1 of 2	1 of 2	2 of 4 = **50%**	1 of 2	1 of 2	2 of 4 = **50%**	1 of 1	1 of 1	2 of 2	0 of 1	0 of 1	0 of 2
31st Oct.	2 of 2	0 of 2	2 of 4 = **50%**	2 of 2	0 of 2	2 of 4 = **50%**	0 of 2	1 of 1	0 of 2	2 of 2		2 of 2
6th Dec.	1 of 3	1 of 3	2 of 6 = 33%	1 of 3	1 of 3	2 of 6 = 33%	0 of 1		1 of 2	1 of 1	0 of 1	1 of 2
TOTALS	29 of 57	23 of 69	52 of 127	19 of 57	19 of 69	38 of 126	10 of 19	13 of 19	23 of 38	9 of 19	6 of 19	15 of 38
%	**50.8%**	**33.3%**	**41.2%**	**33.3%**	**27.5%**	**30.1%**	**52.6%**	**68.4%**	**60.5%**	**47.3%**	**31.5%**	**39.5%**

The "Total references to the Civil War", although unrelated to the event in question, were calculated based on the number of editorials consulted for each date. The "Total references to the Civil War" that do relate to the date were also calculated based on the total number of editorials. This figure was subsequently broken down into implicit and explicit references to the Civil War, provided that they relate to the date.

Source: own elaboration

Table 3.4

Date	Event	Total references to the Civil War (although they may not relate to the date)			Total references to the Civil War relating to the date		
		El País	ABC	Total 1	El País	ABC	Total 2
1975							
22nd November	Coronation of the King		YES	YES		YES	YES
4th December	Arias President		NO	NO		NO	NO
11th December	First Arias Govt.		YES	YES		YES	YES
1976							
26th March	Unification of Platajunta		NO	NO			
9th June	Law on Political Association	YES	YES	YES	YES	YES	YES
3rd July	Suárez President	YES	YES	YES	YES	YES	YES
7th July	First Suárez Govt.	YES	YES	YES	NO	YES	YES
30th July	Partial Amnesty	YES	YES	YES	YES	YES	YES
23rd October	Platajunta Summit	YES	YES	YES	NO	NO	NO
18th November	Law for Political Reform	YES	YES	YES	YES	YES	YES
15th December	Referendum on Law for Political Reform	YES	YES	YES	YES	YES	YES
1977							
24th January	Atocha Murders	YES	NO	YES	YES	NO	YES
11th March	Extension of Amnesty	YES	YES	YES	NO	YES	YES
18th March	Electoral Law	NO	NO	NO	NO	NO	NO
9th April	Legalisation of PCE	YES	YES	YES	YES	YES	YES

Table 3.4

Date	Event	Total references to the Civil War (although they may not relate to the date)			Total references to the Civil War relating to the date		
		El País	**ABC**	**Total 1**	**El País**	**ABC**	**Total 2**
1977 (continued)							
15th June	First Elections	YES	YES	YES	YES	YES	YES
4th July	Suárez Govt.	YES	NO	YES	NO	NO	NO
22nd July	Opening of Parliament	YES	NO	YES	YES	NO	YES
14th October	Amnesty Law	YES	YES	YES	YES	YES	YES
25th-27th October	Moncloa Pacts	YES	YES	YES	NO	NO	NO
1978							
2nd January	Basque Pre-Autonomy	YES	YES	YES	YES	YES	YES
1st May	Labour Day	YES	YES	YES	YES	YES	YES
31st October	Constitution	YES	NO	YES	YES	NO	YES
6th December	Constitution Referendum	YES	YES	YES	YES	YES	YES
TOTALS		19 of 20	17 of 24	21 of 24	14 of 20	15 of 24	18 of 24
%		**95%**	**70.8%**	**87.5%**	**70%**	**62.5%**	**75%**

In this table, which brings together the most important information from the previous TABLE 3 (in which we considered all of the editorials consulted for each date), we can observe the presence of the memory of the Civil War on the key dates of the Transition rather more clearly. Thus, considering both newspapers at the same time, this memory emerges on 87.5% of the dates. On 75% of the dates this memory is directly linked to the Transition event in question.

Source: own elaboration

Table 3.5

	References to the Civil War (implicit and explicit)		References to the Civil War relating to the date	
	El País	**ABC**	**El País**	**ABC**
Key dates of the Civil War	100%	20%	60%	20%
Key dates of the Transition	95%	70.8%	70%	62.5%

Source: own elaboration

GRAPHS

Graph 2.1 *NO-DO. Time devoted to the remembrance of the Civil War*

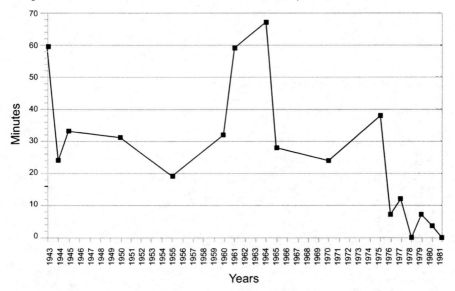

Graph 2.2 *NO-DO. Percentage of newsreels on the war*

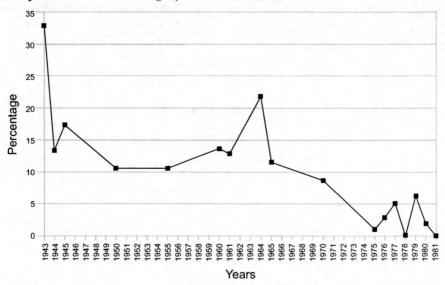

Graph 2.3 *NO-DO. All analytical categories*

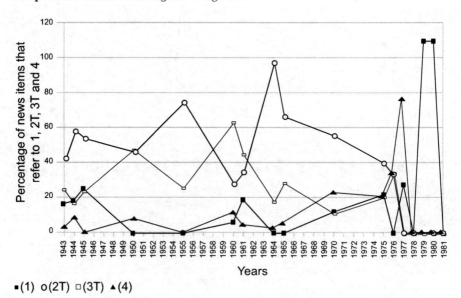

■ (1) o (2T) □ (3T) ▲ (4)

Graph 2.3.1 *NO-DO. Analytical category (1)*

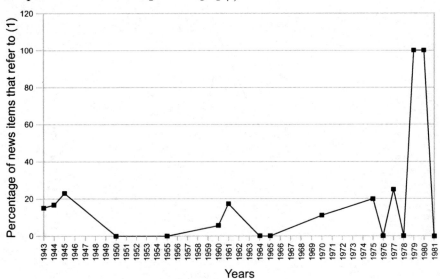

Graph 2.3.2 *NO-DO. Analytical category (2T)*

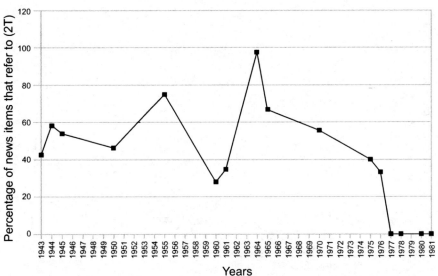

Graph 2.3.3 *NO-DO. Analytical category (3T)*

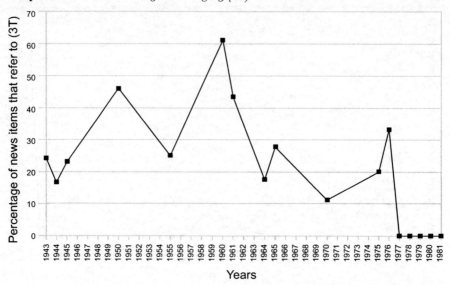

Graph 2.3.4 *NO-DO. Analytical category (4)*

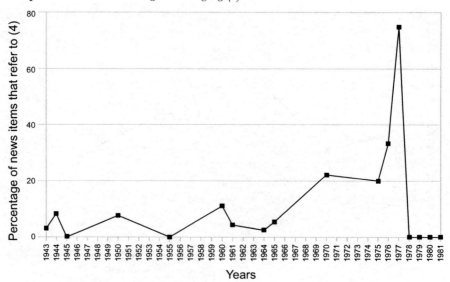

Graph 2.4 *NO-DO. Quality of news items on the war*

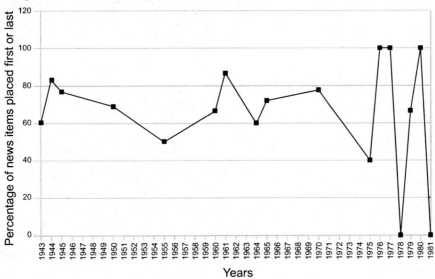

Graph 2.5 *NO-DO. References to the defeated*

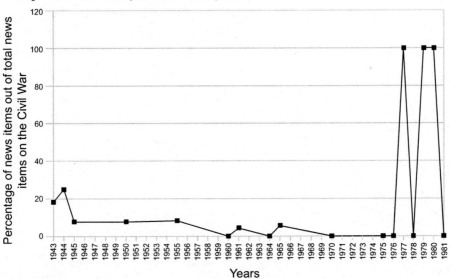

Graph 2.6 *NO-DO. The Victory Parade*

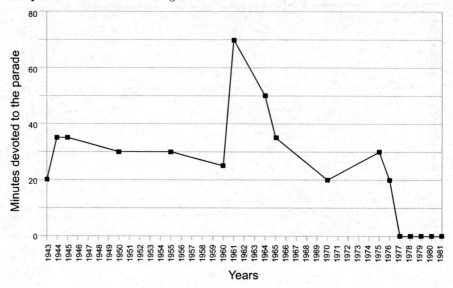

APPENDICES

The Spanish Civil War in the NO–DO Newsreels (1)

4/1/1943	= 1 – INTRODUCTION TO THE FIRST NEWSREEL	
	Shots of fighting and parade	12 metres
5/4	14 – VICTORY PARADE	
	Madrid during the war	21
	The Nationalists enter Madrid	15
31/5	22-A – REPORT ON KATYN	
	Cemetery of Paracuellos del Jarama	15
25/10	43-B – FRANCO SPEECH	
	Ruins of the University City and battle	26
14/2/1944	= 59-A – SPANISH NEUTRALITY	
	Shots of fighting = Madrid during the war	
	= Puerta de Alcalá = War ruins = Queues	
	to buy food = Searching through the	
	rubbish = The Nationalists enter Madrid	28
8/5	71-B – RECONSTRUCTION OF BRUNETE	
	Some shots of Brunete in ruins	5
8/4/1946	= 170-A – RETROSPECTIVE REPORT	
	Madrid = Surrender of arms = The Montaña	
	Barracks = Photo of Stalin = Demonstration	
	= Rally	26
	The Nationalists enter Barcelona	11
	The Nationalists enter Madrid	9
3/11/1952	= 513-B – GENERAL YAGUE REPORT	
	Entering Barcelona	3
1954	= 616-B – BELCHITE RECONSTRUCTED	
	War ruins in Belchite	8

1971	= 1488-B – GENERAL ALONSO VEGA REPORT	
	Northern Campaign = Biscay = Catalonia =	23
1975	= 1714 – DEATH OF FRANCO	
	Battle of the Ebro	8
	The Alcázar in Toledo	5
	The Nationalists enter Barcelona	7
	Entering Madrid	4
	General Varela awards Franco the Laureate	18
	First Victory Parade	8
1979	= 1892 – ANTONIO MACHADO REPORT	
	The Nationalists enter Barcelona	6
	Exodus across the border at Le Perthus	6
	The Nationalists enter Madrid	8

1895 – AIRPLANES OF THE SPANISH CIVIL WAR
Real image   11
PAINTINGS BY JUAN ABELLAN
= The Russian fighter-Plane "Policarpof" =
German "Junkers" = Spanish "Breguet" and
Newport" = Italian "Savoias" = Russian "Natachas"
= Italian "Fiat" = "Hispano" = German "Heinkels"
= Russian "Katiuska" = German "Messerschmidt"   61

1980   = 1955-B – EXHIBITION "THE SPANISH CIVIL WAR"
Exhibition at the Palacio de Cristal in the
Retiro Park in Madrid = Cut-out photographs of
figures relating to the period = Monitors that
project scenes from the war = Machine gun and
small canon at the exhibition = Model ships and
airplanes = Press featuring the dissolution of the
Cortes in 1936 = Elections = Azaña President
= Assassination of Calvo Sotelo = Photo of Franco
in Tenerife = Model of the airplane "Dragón
Rapide" that flew him to Tetuán = Photos:
Exodus = Underground station with refugees =
Rallies featuring Ridruejo and Alberti = Posters
featuring political and social slogans = Weapons
used in the war = Letters from: Franco = Captain
Cortés = Stalin = Largo Caballero = Drawings
that refer to the war = Photos of International
Brigades = Postage stamps = Cigarette packets
from the period = Bank notes = Press
announcing the end of the war   111

THE SPANISH BLUE DIVISION
(See EXTERNAL production catalogue)
Truck with armed militia = Atmosphere in the
streets during the early days = Corpses in the
courtyard of the Montaña Barracks = Corpses
on the road = Militia women with their fists

raised in the air = Destroyed churches =
Revolutionary events in Barcelona = Title
"18th July 1936". Flashes with superimposed
titles: Badajoz, Toledo, Oviedo, Bilbao, Santander,
Teruel, Vinaroz, Battle of the Ebro, Lérida,
Barcelona, Madrid = Final stage of the war =
First Victory Parade = Franco greeting the
crowd with his hand held high, accompanied
by Generals Varela and Saliquet = (1st part)   80

1963   = HAVE YOU SEEN SPAIN?
              (See Documentaries catalogue, page 57)
              Republican soldiers flee to France by crossing
              the River Bidasoa and the international bridge
              = Exodus across the border at Le Perthus =
              Photo of Lenin on the Puerta de Alcalá = Militia
              in the streets = Photo of Stalin = Rallies in the
              towns = Burning of churches = Hermitage of
              San Isidro = Raids in Puerta del Sol and the streets
              of Madrid = Aid from Russia = International
              Brigades = Surrender of arms = Searches for
              weapons = Prison = Corpses in the countryside
              = Photo of Calvo Sotelo = Franco as Head of State
              = The Legion = Falangist parade in Burgos =
              Nationalist army in Seville = Map of Spain
              showing the division of the two zones = Battle
              for the Alcázar in Toledo = Franco at the Alcázar
              = The Nationalists enter Madrid = Exodus
              across the border at Le Perthus = The
              Nationalists reach the border = (1st part)   163

              War ruins: Oviedo and the Montaña Barracks =
              Teruel, Santa María de la Cabeza, Brunete =
              Interspersed shots: Burning fuel dumps =
              Entering Bilbao = Madrid = Plaza de España =
              Uncovering La Cibeles, Ruins of the University
              City = Blown-up bridge = Teruel = Tanks on
              the front = Battle of the Ebro = Factory ruins =
              Corpses = Barbed wire = (2nd part)   44

1974   = DIPUTACION DE BARCELONA 1939
              (See Documentaries catalogue, page 30)
              Shots of fighting = Flashes of the advancing
              Nationalist army = March towards Barcelona
              = Passing through Sitges and Manresa = Entering
              Barcelona = Tanks at La Diagonal = Mounted
              cavalry = Burning and sunken ships in the
              harbour = Crowd in the Plaza de Cataluña =
              General Yagüe and Colonel Barrón = Campaign
              mass = The border route = Republican prisoners   105

1977	= FIFTY YEARS OF CAMPSA	
	(See Colour Documentaries catalogue)	
	Battle of the Ebro	8
	The Nationalists enter Tarragona	6

1978 = UNIVERSAL CATALANS
(Documentary from the series "Pantalla Abierta"
for TVE)
DOCTOR TRUETA SEQUENCE
Bombardment scenes = Airplane shot down =
Trenches in the University City = Tanks at the
Battle of the Ebro = Galloping cavalry = Airplanes
in flight = City bombardment = Republican
advance = Machine-gun fire = Trenches =
Withdrawal of wounded from battle   40

Exodus of the civil population = City
bombardment = Route to exile: civil population
and army = French border = Surrender of arms
to the French authorities   29

INDEX

Lightning Source UK Ltd.
Milton Keynes UK
UKOW021815291211

184504UK00010B/147/P